Soviet state and society between revolutions, 1918–1929

Cambridge Soviet Paperbacks: 8

Cambridge Soviet Paperbacks is a completely new initiative in publishing on the Soviet Union. The series will focus on the economics, international relations, politics, sociology and history of the Soviet and Revolutionary periods.

The idea behind the series is the identification of gaps for upper-level surveys or studies falling between the traditional university press monograph and most student textbooks. The main readership will be students and specialists, but some "overview" studies in the series will have broader appeal.

Publication will in every case be simultaneously in hardcover and paperback.

Cambridge Soviet Paperbacks

1 NICOLA MILLER
Soviet relations with Latin America
0 521 35193 6 (hardback) / 0 521 35979 1 (paperback)

2 GALIA GOLAN
Soviet policies in the Middle East
From World War II to Gorbachev
0 521 35332 7 (hardback) / 0 521 35859 0 (paperback)

3 STEPHEN WHITE
Gorbachev and after
0 521 43374 6 (hardback) / 0 521 43984 1 (paperback)

4 PHILIP R. PRYDE
Environmental management in the Soviet Union
0 521 36079 X (hardback) / 0 521 40905 5 (paperback)

5 PEKKA SUTELA
Economic thought and economic reform in the Soviet Union
0 521 38020 0 (hardback) / 0 521 38902 X (paperback)

6 GAIL LAPIDUS and VICTOR ZASLAVSKY with PHILIP GOLDMAN
(eds.)
From Union to Commonwealth
Nationalism and separatism in the Soviet Republics
0 521 41706 6 (hardback) / 0 521 42716 9 (paperback)

7 RICHARD STITES
Soviet popular culture
Entertainment and society in Russia since 1900
0 521 36214 8 (hardback) / 0 521 36986 X (paperback)

8 LEWIS H. SIEGELBAUM
Soviet state and society between revolutions, 1918–1929
0 521 36215 6 (hardback) / 0 521 36987 8 (paperback)

Soviet state and society between revolutions, 1918–1929

LEWIS H. SIEGELBAUM
Michigan State University

Published by the Press Syndicate of the University of Cambridge
The Pitt Building, Trumpington Street, Cambridge CB2 1RP
40 West 20th Street, New York, NY 10011–4211, USA
10 Stamford Road, Oakleigh, Victoria 3166, Australia

First published 1992

Printed in Great Britain at the University Press, Cambridge

A catalogue record for this book is available from the British Library

Library of Congress cataloguing in publication data

Siegelbaum, Lewis H.
Soviet state and society between revolutions, 1918–1929 /
Lewis H. Siegelbaum.
    p.   cm. – (Cambridge Soviet Paperbacks: 8)
Includes bibliographical references (p.   ) and index.
ISBN-0-521-36215-6 (hardback) – ISBN 0-521-36987-8 (paperback)
1. Soviet Union – History – 1917–1936. I. Title. II. Series.
DK266.S5276 1992
947.084'1–dc20   91–32336 CIP

ISBN 0 521 36215 6 hardback
ISBN 0 521 36987 8 paperback

WD

Contents

Preface and acknowledgments

This book grew out of an essay I wrote in 1987 for a volume on reform in Russian history. That was a heady time to be in Soviet studies, for after years of economic sluggishness, political stagnation and increasing social malaise, big changes were underway in the USSR. Among those changes was what might be called "retrospective glasnost," a peering into the Soviet past to uncover new lessons for the then present. At first tentatively and then with increasing boldness, novelists, film directors, playwrights, editors and eventually professional historians seized upon the ever-expanding opportunities for reinterpreting the past. Much of the reinterpretation was devoted to undermining the credibility of the Stalinist administrative-command system that arose in the course of the 1930s and continued to cast its shadow over daily life. This deconstructive effort sometimes implicitly and sometimes explicitly legitimized an earlier model of statecraft and economic management, that of the New Economic Policy (NEP). In this model, the Communist Party exercised a monopoly of political power but tolerated market forces and a measure of private ownership. It seemed as if I had hit on a "hot" topic.

But even as I began formulating the outlines of this book, extending its chronological dimensions back to civil war and discovering that a great deal more was going on in the 1920s than the elaboration of the NEP model, a strange thing was happening. Under the combined weight of ethnic strife, independence movements in the Baltic and Transcaucasian republics, and economic difficulties everywhere, Soviet public opinion was radically shifting against the Communist Party. Far from rejuvenating the party, Gorbachev's efforts to return it to its pre-Stalinist origins had opened up a Pandora's box of disillusionment. As many party stalwarts had feared, nothing was sacred any longer. The formation of the USSR, the Reds' victory in the Civil War, Lenin, the October Revolution, the ideal of socialism – all were found to be fatally flawed.

However unsettling, this desacralization of the past must be regarded as healthy and is to be applauded. It has meant the end of "official history," an oxymoron long perpetrated on schoolchildren and adults alike. It has given voice to a plethora of perspectives, brought to the surface many painful episodes in the nation's past, and thereby challenged some basic assumptions about national and social identities. All this, I would argue, is a necessary precondition for reconnecting the present with the past or in other words, redoing history.

As of this writing, many of the old stereotypes and myths are being turned upside down: instead of the infallibility of the Communist Party, its fundamentally evil nature; in place of one glorious chapter after another in the building of socialism, uniformly negative images of both the building process and of socialism; rather than the inherent progressiveness of centralized planning, the magic of the free market. It is not yet clear how pervasive this understandable – if regrettable – reaction is and how far it will go. All that can be said with any confidence is that the choices made by the diverse peoples of what has been the Soviet Union about their futures will shape their understanding of their.shared past and *vice versa*.

Meanwhile, I would argue that how Lenin's revolution turned into Stalin's, or more broadly, what happened in the "socialist sixth of the world" between 1918 and 1929 remains an important question for outsiders to consider. If greater exposure to alternative configurations of states and societies helps to generate more informed judgments about the way our own social and political orders have been constructed, then rethinking the Soviet experience of these years should be on our agenda as well. This, in any case, is the premise that has informed this book.

In writing a book of this type, I have become acutely aware of what is meant by a scholarly community. I have accumulated enormous debts which hardly can be repaid in footnote citations or acknowledgments here. It almost goes without saying that I am indebted to the authors whose works are cited. This is especially the case with E. H. Carr whose multi-volume *History of Soviet Russia* has stood the test of time and changing historiographical fashions and which quite literally has been read to shreds.

Beyond that, I would like to thank IREX for making possible research in the Soviet Union; my editor, Michael Holdsworth, and the series editor, Mary McAuley for their encouragement and patience; Diane Koenker who first interested me in this project and gave me the confidence to see it through; the MSG at Ann Arbor and particularly its moving spirit, Ron Suny, for many stimulating discussions which have profoundly shaped my own rethinking; and Bill Chase, John Hatch, and Dan Orlovsky for their generosity with advice and information. Within my local and personal communities, Michigan State University's College of Arts and Letters Research Grants Committee, Gordon Stewart, Gord Morrell, Leslie Moch, Anita Herald, and last but not least, my family deserve my gratitude.

Russian terms and abbreviations

artel	producers' collective formed by artisans or peasants
bedniak	poor peasant
besprizorniki	homeless children
Cheka	All-Russian Extraordinary Commission for the Suppression of Counterrevolution, Sabotage and Speculation
Comintern	Communist International
desiatina	land measure equivalent to 2.7 acres
Evsektsiia	Jewish Section of Communist Party
glavk	main office of administration
GOELRO	State Commission for the Electrification of Russia
GPU	State Political Administration
gubkom	provincial committee (of party, trade union, etc.)
ispolkom	executive committee (of soviet)
khozraschet	commercial cost accounting
kolkhoz	collective farm
kombedy	committees of poor peasants
kommuna	community in which all property is collectivized
komplekt	work unit in textile production
Komsomol	All-Russian Leninist Communist Youth League
korenizatsiia	policy of promoting indigenous peoples and their culture
kulak	a rich peasant exploiting the labor of other peasants
kustari	handicraft or cottage industry workers
lenintsy	workers recruited into the party during the "Lenin levies"
Narkomfin	People's Commissariat of Finance
Narkomprod	People's Commissariat of Food Supply
Narkomtrud	People's Commissariat of Labor
Narkomzem	People's Commissariat of Agriculture
NEP	New Economic Policy

xii

nepreryvka	continuous workweek
nomenklatura	system of selection of personnel by higher organs
NOT	Scientific Organization of Labor
obkom	regional committee (of party, trade union, etc.)
oblast'	administrative region
otkhodniki	migrant laborers
Proletkult	movement for proletarian culture
razverstka	quota assessment of foodstuffs
RKI	Workers' and Peasants' Inspectorate
RSFSR	Russian Soviet Federated Socialist Republic
samogon	illegally distilled spirits, "moonshine"
selsovet	rural soviet
seredniak	middle peasant
Smena vekh	ideological current among *émigrés* advocating reconciliation with Soviet power
smychka	link between town and country
sovkhoz	state farm
sovnarkhoz	regional economic administration
Sovnarkom	Council of People's Commissars
SRs	Socialist Revolutionary Party
stazh	longevity of service
STO	Council of Labor and Defense
subbotniki	Communist saturdays of (nominally) volunteer labor
tovaroobmen	collective commodity exchange
TOZ	association for common cultivation of land
TsKK	Central Control Commission of Communist Party
Uchraspred	Records and Assignment Section of Secretariat
udarnik	shock worker
uezd	county
Vesenkha	Supreme Council of the National Economy
volost	township
VTsIK	All-Russian/Union Central Executive Committee of Soviets
VTsSPS	All-Russian/Union Central Council of Trade Unions
vydvizhentsy	working-class promotees
Zhenotdel	Women's Section of Communist Party

Introduction

This book is about what happened in Soviet Russia (and, from 1924, the USSR) after the October Revolution of 1917 and before the Stalinist Revolution of the late 1920s and early 1930s. It has been conceived as a work of historical synthesis in two senses. First, it seeks to combine social and political history, reflecting my own general belief that political institutions are shaped by the social environment from which they spring and that political behavior in turn effects changes in the social environment, although often in unforeseen ways. The time when Soviet history could be written in terms of pure political voluntarism, of untrammeled state power acting upon a hapless society, thankfully has passed. By the same token, "bringing the state back in" has hardly been necessary, for it has rarely if ever been left out of accounts of this or any other period of Soviet history.

 Secondly, while it draws on my own research, primarily into industrial relations, the book relies most heavily on the work of other scholars, both western and Soviet. Such dependence has its potential pitfalls. Extracting the core of others' arguments inevitably means sacrificing the subtleties and nuances, not to mention much of the substantiating data, on which arguments are based. Squeezing them into my own framework of analysis runs the risk of distorting the original intentions of the authors, though this seemed preferable to merely presenting them in serial form which would have warranted the charge of eclecticism. Finally, in attempting to incorporate the most recent interpretations, it is possible that I have put older no less insightful ones in the shade. Being acutely aware of these problems may help to minimize them, but ultimately that is for the reader to judge.

 As recently as 1982 it was stated that "the period known to Soviet and Western parlance as the NEP . . . has been relatively neglected," the cause of this neglect being attributed to historians' preference for writing about "the epic sweep of revolutions from below and revolutions from above."[1] Much the same could have been written about the

1

civil war years, 1918–20. In the last decade, however, the number of monographs, articles, collections of essays and dissertations devoted to the civil war and NEP years has vastly increased. Part of the reason for this has been Soviet authorities' greater willingness to share their nation's archival treasures with western scholars. Partly, it has had to do with the changing preoccupations of scholars themselves. A generation ago, historians were mainly interested in the early years of Soviet power for what they revealed about the Bolshevik Party as it sought to consolidate its power and then shape the new social order. More recently, a much wider range of issues – and the techniques to deal with them – have come to the fore. Hence, historians of labor and gender, students of popular culture and those concerned with science and technology, demographers and art historians have all weighed in.

The result is a far more complex picture of the formative decade of the Soviet state and society than was previously the case. But it is a picture that resembles an enormous post-modernist collage – disjointed, fragmented, its overall sense remaining elusive. A by-product of the new perspectives has been the loss of consensus about what made these years unique, important, and even recognizable. The displacement of politics – at least as sovietologists used to define that term – from center stage has tended to obscure the traditional historical landmarks. The early oppositions within the party, Lenin's "Testament," Trotsky's struggle against the party Secretariat, the break-up of the triumvirate of Stalin, Zinoviev and Kamenev, the Stalin group's leftward lurch and its condemnation of the so-called Rightist deviation in the party all recede into the penumbra when the spotlight is on time budgets of working-class families, reading habits in the countryside, or the social composition of film audiences. The more historians have borrowed from other learned disciplines and partaken of the new genres and sub-disciplines within history, the more challenging it has become to keep abreast of and even comprehend their work. The need for synthesis therefore seems all the greater, even if, as new work continues to be produced, that synthesis can only be tentative and provisional.

There is yet another reason why a broad overview of these years is in order. Not long after Mikhail Gorbachev became General Secretary of the Communist Party in 1985, the Stalin era and its legacies began to be subjected to intense scrutiny and criticism in the Soviet Union. Simultaneously, NEP began to be reinterpreted both as a positive alternative to the "administrative-command system" that preceded and replaced it, and as a potential model for restructuring Soviet society. As one prominent historian remarked at a roundtable discussion in 1988,

We are turning now to the experience of NEP, seeking and finding in it practical answers to the questions of contemporary life; in and of itself this attests both to the historical significance of NEP and to its incompleteness, because the tasks that NEP was supposed to accomplish remained unresolved, giving rise to very serious difficulties in the further development of Soviet society.[2]

But before one can make an assessment of the usefulness or otherwise of NEP, it is necessary to understand the contexts – social, economic, political, and cultural – within which that policy was introduced, modified and abandoned, and in the light of new research, to reconsider some fundamental questions about its place in Soviet history.

The present book sets out to do this by examining the intervening years between the October and Stalinist revolutions in terms of "state" and "society." The distinction between these two basic building blocks of historical analysis should not be difficult to comprehend. The former can be equated with formally constituted political authority and its exercise by those either elected or appointed to an office or agency constituent of such authority. The latter represents collectivities of individuals interacting in complex and multi-layered ways outside of formal political authority though usually in the context of laws promulgated and enforced by the state. Historically, there have been many stateless societies, but the reverse is not the case. Wherever states have existed, so have there been societies.

How are we to understand the interaction of state and society? This question has been at the heart of western political theory since the dawn of the Enlightenment and has been the source of theoretical refinement and revision ever since. Notions of political and civil societies and "contracts" between them; of the boundaries between public and private spheres; of the maintenance of political sovereignty on the one hand and individual liberties on the other; of the state as regulator or redistributer and society as generator of spiritual and material wealth, of the state as constructed and society as organic, if internally unstable, have all figured prominently in the western liberal political discourse.

The question is whether in addition to these liberal constructs – some predicated on mutual antagonism and others positing a symbiotic relationship – there exist other ways of conceptualizing the relationship between states and societies. I believe there are. In this book, I use "state" and "society" to denote mutually interactive spheres of ideological, political, economic, and cultural life, the boundaries of which are not fixed or hypostatic, but subject to contestation and redefinition. This approach also recognizes the internal composition and institutional frameworks of both states and societies as fluid and contradictory. That is, state and society are conceived not as monolithic blocs or engines, but as force-fields "marked by the complex interplay of attractions and aversions, and thus by dynamic, transmutational structures."[3] Once it is conceded that state and society can assume multiple configurations, it follows that the relationship between them is not necessarily antagonistic. Part(s) of society can be strengthened by state intervention or domination even while others are disadvantaged, weakened, or even obliterated. The reverse is also possible. That is, agencies of the state rise and fall in terms of their command of resources, the urgency of the problems they confront and the degree of their success in accordance with the ability to recruit, motivate, and otherwise depend on elements from society.

In positing such relationships, I do not want to imply that out of the maelstrom of revolution and civil war in Russia emerged a full blown "civil society" with arenas of affective associations nurturing local and particularistic freedoms guaranteed by law. But I do wish to raise the possibility of this line of development. Whether, indeed, one may speak of a Soviet civil society in the period between the two revolutions is one of the major questions examined here.

By focusing on the interpenetration of the Soviet state and society, this study necessarily blots out a good deal of "what happened" in the years 1918–29. Just as it offers very little on Soviet relations with other states, the history of the Third International, and the military dimensions of the civil war, so it almost completely ignores such cultural historical phenomena as child-rearing practices, expressions of love, courtship, and friendship, and, perforce, the richness of popular culture. It is not that Soviet society was unaffected by the stresses and strains of international relations or the uses to which "capitalist encirclement" were put by party leaders. Nor do I believe that affective ties between two people or within a family can be entirely divorced from large matrices. It is rather that in choosing what to include I was guided by two primary considerations: to identify and work through the issues that have figured centrally in the historiography of the period and, where possible, to suggest further lines of research. This is, then, as much a work of historiography as of history. It offers a critical but also friendly reading of the literature produced by colleagues in the field at the same time as it reflects my own proclivities, or, if you will, biases.

It is by paying close attention to what was happening in the force-fields of the Soviet state and society during the interrevolutionary period, by examining the impact of one on the other and indeed, appreciating the extent of their mutual penetration, that, I believe, the synthesis to which I have referred can be achieved. What this period of Soviet history may have lacked in terms of "epic sweep," is more than compensated for by the fascinating interplay of new and old ways of life, utopian dreams and mundane reality, multiple modes of production and social identities – in short, the twin legacies of the previously existing order and the revolution against it, as well as the glimmerings – or shadows – of the revolution that was about to be.

1 Bequeathals of the revolution, 1918–1920

> From capitalism we inherited not only a ruined culture, not only wrecked factories, not only a despairing intelligentsia; we inherited a disunited and backward mass of individual proprietors; we inherited inexperience, an absence of the team spirit and of an understanding that the past must be buried. (V. I. Lenin, speech of 6 November 1920, in *Polnoe sobranie sochinenii*, 5th ed. (Moscow, 1963), vol. 42, p. 5)

> But the question of the *transition period* from capitalism to socialism, i.e., the period of the proletarian dictatorship, is far more difficult. The working class achieves victory, although it is not and cannot be a unified mass. It attains victory while the productive forces are going down and the great masses are materially insecure. There will inevitably result a *tendency* to "degeneration," *i.e.*, the excretion of a leading stratum in the form of a class-germ. (Nikolai Bukharin, *Historical Materialism, A System of Sociology* (Ann Arbor, 1969), pp. 310–11, originally published in 1921)

"At the very pinnacle of power Trotsky, like the protagonist of a classical tragedy, stumbled. He acted against his own principle and in disregard of a most solemn moral commitment." Thus begins the final chapter of Isaac Deutscher's *The Prophet Armed: Trotsky, 1879–1921*, a chapter that he entitled "Defeat in victory." The victory referred to the triumph of the Soviet state over the White armies and interventionist forces in the Russian civil war. The defeat was that of "proletarian democracy," sacrificed on the altar of the dictatorship of the proletariat. Trotsky, as Commissar of War and architect of Soviet military strategy, had done more than any other individual with the possible exception of Lenin to bring about that victory. But, as the proponent of the militarization of labor and a leading opponent of the Workers' Opposition and Decemist (Democratic Centralist) factions within the Communist Party, he also played a vital role in the violation of that "most solemn moral commitment" to which the party supposedly had been dedicated. More than that, he oversaw the final assault in March 1921 against the "strangest of all Russian insurrections," that of the mutinous sailors at the naval fortress of Kronstadt.

This outcome, like classical tragedy, was not without its irony. Having "indefatigably preached for twenty years" the political self-determination of the working class, Trotsky now "initiated courses of action" which were diametrically opposed to that principle. Having celebrated the "Red men of Kronstadt" as the "pride and glory of the revolution," and having in turn been "wildly acclaimed . . . as their friend and leader," Trotsky now condemned their calls for an end to Bolshevik tyranny as counterrevolutionary treason.[1] The implication here, which is taken up in the subsequent volume of Deutscher's trilogy, is that by placing the interests of the dictatorship of the proletariat above those of the proletariat and other toiling masses, Trotsky was sowing the seeds for his own political defeat in the 1920s at the hands of the arch-intriguer Stalin.

Deutscher's theatrical simile unintentionally raises a question which is central to an understanding of the Soviet experience in particular and the historical enterprise in general. It is where to strike the balance between intentionality and inevitability, choice and determinacy, or, as the ancient Greeks conceived of it, ambition and fate. For, what is posited as Trotsky's personal tragedy was in fact endemic to the 1917 revolution and the civil war that erupted in its wake. The tension between proletarian self-determination and the party's vanguard role *vis-à-vis* the industrial working class was woven into the fabric of Russian Social Democracy. It surfaced in Trotsky's denunciation of "substitutionism" in Lenin's *What is to be Done?*, it was the source of the split within the Russian Social Democratic Workers Party between Menshevik and Bolshevik orientations, and it remained a source of controversy both in times of working-class militance and quiescence. After the October Revolution, which catapulted the Bolsheviks into state power, the tension reemerged, as the party redefined its relationship to the working class from that of vanguard to guardian.

But in the complex dynamic of party–class interaction, the party was not alone in defining and redefining its position. Workers, too, took positions *vis-à-vis* the party and more broadly, politics. These positions were contingent not only on how the party represented itself (and represented workers to themselves), but on other forces that impinged on workers' identity and consciousness – general political conditions, working conditions, level of skill and production experience (*stazh*) no less than family situation, sex and nationality or ethnicity. In other words, both the party and the workers made choices and functioned as agents of their own making and destinies in the context of each other's capabilities and limitations.

Extending the scope of Deutscher's inquiry from the biographical and political to the collective and social levels, one immediately encounters other collective subjects. If, by 1920–1, Soviet Russia was essentially a one-party state, it certainly was not a one-class society. Over and above the issue of dictatorship and democracy with respect to workers were the state's and the workers' relations to other social groups – the intelligentsia, technical and cultural; the army of clerical, technical, and military employees within the state apparatus itself; and last but not least, the village-based small property-holding peasantry that comprised the vast majority of Soviet citizens. What it means for the "proletarian dictatorship" to preside over a society in which the proletariat was a tiny and, to use Lenin's term, "unhinged" element – and, indeed, to what extent it did preside – is the fundamental question that is addressed in this chapter. In this way we can examine what the revolution and civil war bequeathed to the Soviet state and society in the 1920s.

The dictatorship of the proletariat – theorization and realization

All modern revolutions worthy of the name are direct assaults against the legitimacy of pre-existing political institutions in the name of some other source of legitimacy. Democratic revolutions, of which that of 1789 is often cited as archetypal, have legitimated themselves in terms of popular sovereignty and the universality of certain inalienable rights; theocratic revolutions, such as the Iranian, obtain their mandate from religious principles as enunciated by religious leaders. The October Revolution of 1917 was the first to derive its legitimacy from the Marxist analysis of society in which the state was seen as an instrument of class rule. The very existence of social classes, which for Marxists implies struggle between them, means that the seizure of political power by the revolutionary forces is only a step in the direction of a more thoroughgoing revolution. This, the social revolution, would inevitably involve further struggle, and, under the new political circumstances, social transformation.

It is well known that in their long careers as revolutionary thinkers and activists, Marx and Engels devoted comparatively little attention to the institutional forms and governing principles of the post-revolutionary political order. Moreover, to the extent that they did discuss this question, their legacy was not without certain ambiguities and contradictions. In the late 1840s and early 1850s when their native Germany was divided among numerous principalities "The utilization and huge extension of the powers of the existing state by the proletariat seem[ed] to encapsulate much of what Marx and Engels had in mind when they recommended the dictatorship of the proletariat."[2] Centralization of credit, of the means of communication and transport, and of the instruments of production were the measures they envisioned in the *Communist Manifesto*. But more than two decades later, when they returned to this question, another model was advanced. Now the aim of the proletariat was expressed not in terms of the capture and utilization of the existing state machinery, but, as Marx asserted in *The Civil War in France*, its destruction. The old state, in this case, the Second Empire of Louis Bonaparte, was not to be replaced by another hierarchical and parasitical state-form, but rather its antithesis, namely, the commune, in which all public functions were to be carried out by the self-organized masses.

In fact, Marxists were presented with not two but three models of the future socialist state. The third, combining the other two, was offered by Engels in his introduction to the 1891 edition of *The Civil War in France*. "Dictatorship of the proletariat," he wrote, "well and good, gentlemen, do you want to know what this dictatorship looks like? Look at the Paris Commune. That was the Dictatorship of the Proletariat."[3]

It was, in fact, this contradictory formulation that Lenin incorporated into his own analysis, worked out in the midst of the revolutionary upheavals of 1917. In *The State and Revolution*, Lenin sought, above all, to give theoretical coherence to the associational forms thrown up by the Russian Revolution. For in the factory and soldiers' committees, the workers' militia units and above all the soviets of workers', soldiers' and peasants' deputies, Lenin discerned the seeds of the future socialist order and the corresponding state formation, which "is *no longer* a state in the proper sense of the term, for . . . these contingents of armed men are *the masses themselves*, the entire people." As for other public functions, the process of centralizing and therefore simplifying administration had proceeded so far under capitalism, that they could be performed by any literate person. Therefore, it would be possible "to cast 'bossing' aside and to confine the whole matter to the organization of the proletarians (as the ruling class), which will hire 'workers, foremen and bookkeepers' in the name of the whole of society."[4]

The main emphasis, then, of *The State and Revolution* and much else

Lenin wrote in 1917 was on the reappropriation by society of the powers hitherto exercised by special state bodies. But, as suggested by the implicit contradiction between "the proletarians" and the "whole of society," such qualifications as "in the proper sense of the word" and the use of inverted commas, this model, which was fully compatible with and indeed revived Marx's vision of the commune, was not without its own ambiguities. As Neil Harding has noted: "There was . . . always lurking in the immediate background, an alternative model which stresses centralisation against initiative from below . . . It was not to be long, a matter of six months to a year, before this background model of the dictatorship of the proletariat emerged to the centre of the stage and drove the commune form into the wings."[5]

The reasons why this was so are many and complex. They have to do not only with "the unresolved dualism in the Marxist theory of the state," but the evident failure of the October Revolution to arrest the catastrophic decline in production, to stem the tide of social disintegration and to ignite the spark of revolution in the more economically developed or "advanced" countries of western Europe to which the Bolsheviks looked for deliverance. Beyond this, one should note the long-standing ambivalence of the revolutionary intelligentsia toward the Russian masses, an ambivalence that Bolshevism inherited. On the one hand, there was a genuine commitment to the liberation of the oppressed, a keen appreciation of their revolutionary potential, and a glorification of their combativeness; on the other, a deep suspicion of their spontaneity and lack of culture. Before 1917, these two attitudes comingled and were constituent elements of the vanguard role which the Bolshevik party assigned itself. In the course of that year and for a brief period after the October Revolution, socialist transformation gained the upper hand over the rhetoric of modernization and Europeanization. Thereafter, the balance shifted in the opposite direction.

Having exhorted the masses to take control over their own lives, to exercise their creative initiative, to learn from their own mistakes, Lenin came to recognize the "necessity" of employing special functionaries who would wield "dictatorial power" over the masses at their places of work, in the factories, offices, and formally constituted regimental units of the Workers' and Peasants' Red Army. Having earlier identified the emerging socialist order with popular control over all aspects of public policy formulation and execution, he came to argue that the form of government through which the proletariat exercised its class power was essentially irrelevant. And, having conceived of the gradual "withering away" of the state as society reappropriated its functions, he now in effect reversed this equation, arguing that the greatest concentration of power in the hands of the state was necessary to radically transform the economic and social base and that the road to a stateless society ran through the temporary strengthening of the dictatorship of the proletariat.

The shift from the ideal of the commune to the idea of the proletarian dictatorship was essentially completed by the latter half of 1919. From this time on, the dictatorship constituted the central principle of Soviet power. It was popularized in *The ABC of Communism*, a party manual composed by the party's chief economic theoreticians, Nikolai Bukharin and Evgenii Preobrazhenskii, and figured centrally in theoretical works composed by Bukharin and Trotsky in 1920.

In formulating their ideas, these party luminaries were responding to two immediate needs. One was to refute charges levelled by Karl Kautsky and other leading Social Democrats in Germany as well as the Mensheviks within Russia that the Bolsheviks had suppressed the democratic potential of the Russian Revolution. Refutation was seen as critical to the survival of the Communist International (the Comintern), the founding congress of which was held in Moscow in March 1919. The other purpose was to provide the theoretical underpinnings for the continuation of domestic mobilization policies initially devised in *ad hoc* fashion to achieve victory over the White and interventionist forces. The extension of mobilization was deemed necessary because if the military struggle was nearing its end, another, that of reconstruction, was only just beginning. The party leaders qualified the exaltation of state power as a temporary expedient. But the instrumentalities designed to sustain, educate and discipline the revolutionary social forces actually swallowed them and in the process came to replace them as active agents of social transformation.

The closest analogy to the theorized dictatorship of the proletariat was ironically what Bukharin had called before the revolution, the Leviathan state – the monopoly capitalist regimes that propped up the bourgeoisie through their active intervention in and control over the production system. This was ironic because it was just this kind of state that Bukharin and others had excoriated as parasitical and oppressive. But in his *Economics of the Transformation Period* (1920), Bukharin argued that

the same method is formally necessary for the working class as for the bourgeoisie at the time of state capitalism. This organizational method exists in the coordination of all proletarian organizations with one all-encompassing organization, i.e. with the state organization of the working class, with the *Soviet state of the proletariat* . . . Thus, the system of state capitalism dialectically transforms itself into its own inversion, into the state form of workers' socialism.[6]

Dialectical or not, the transition to socialism would involve, in Trotsky's words, "the highest possible intensification of the principle of the State . . . Just as a lamp, before going out, shoots up in a brilliant flame, so the State, before disappearing, assumes the form of the dictatorship of the proletariat, i.e., the most ruthless form of State, which embraces the life of the citizen authoritatively in every direction."[7]

While such statements resonate with an ominous "totalitarian" ring, one should also note their philosophical kinship to a model from earlier Russian history. Not for nothing was Trotsky's scheme for the militarization of labor – an essential ingredient of the proletarian dictatorship – attacked as another *Arakcheevshchina*; for, as Richard Stites has pointed out, just as the military colonies overseen by Alexander I's War Minister, Arakcheev, sprang from the "dream of a state power refashioning the land and the people," so the project launched by Trotsky in 1920 was an "administrative utopia." The dream reappeared at this time because of "the reappearance of those things that had given it shape earlier: fear and insecurity, deep anxiety about how to create order and efficiency, the desire to provide the people with justice and food, and the lack of trust in the masses to create their own forms of rule and ways of life consonant with state survival."[8]

The theorization of the proletarian dictatorship thus rested on both a profound sense of the proletariat's historic mission and an acute awareness of the limitations of that class. Rather than admitting their audaciousness, the Bolsheviks sought to compensate for the proletariat's weakness by assiduously building up what in their view all ruling classes required, namely, a powerful state. Almost exactly two years after the October Revolution, as the Red Army was turning the tide against the Whites, Lenin sketched an outline for a never-to-be completed work entitled "The Dictatorship of the Proletariat." In it, he defined the proletariat as "a *special* class" that "alone *continues* to wage its class struggle." and the state of the proletariat as "a weapon . . . [a] special kind of *cudgel, rien de plus!*"[9] Before examining this class in detail, we must first investigate the constituent parts of "its" weapon.

The Soviet state evolved after 1917 not as a monolithic bloc, but as a constellation of four functionally distinct sub-systems or networks – a military and police state, a civilian state focused on the soviets, an economic state revolving around the commissariats and the trade unions, and a political state residing within the Bolshevik (or, as it was renamed in March 1918, the Communist) Party. Relations among these sub-systems, it must be stressed, were not worked out in advance of their creation and indeed provoked considerable debate within the party. Each, though, developed in the same direction, namely towards centralized bureaucratic administration, though the timing, extent and legitimization of that evolution varied.[10]

The constituent organs of these sub-systems differed in their origins. Some were inherited from the tsarist and Provisional Governments along with their staffs who comprised a large bureaucratic stratum. This was the case with the ministries, which became commissariats, with many of the regional and branch institutions governing the economy, and with the Provisional Government's state militia which was renamed the Workers' and Peasants' Militia. Others, such as the soviets, the trade unions and the cooperatives, had constituted non-governmental bodies before the October Revolution but were "statized" after 1917. Still others – the Cheka, for example – had functional equivalents in the tsarist period (the gendarmerie and secret police or Okhrana), but little if any continuity in personnel. Finally, certain institutions, including the court system, much of the educational system and almost the entire party apparatus, were created from whole cloth during the civil war period.

Understandably, the largest of the sub-systems consisted of the coercive organs, specifically, the army and the main security apparatus, the Cheka. From its founding in February 1918, the Red Army was staffed largely by former tsarist officers who were euphemistically referred to as "military specialists." To ensure their loyalty, political commissars, usually communists, exercised supervisory power, and were held jointly responsible for all orders. But the appointment of officers by the Revolutionary Military Council, the allocation to them of special rations and other privileges, rankled with many party members and front-line soldiers. The defense of the appointment principle offered by S. I. Gusev, an important figure in the military apparatus and head of its Political Administration from 1921, richly illustrates the kind of "realism" that had become pervasive at the top:

The issues of voluntarism, of the elective principle and of voluntary discipline all in essence boil down to the question: Is the proletariat disciplined and conscious enough on the day after the "social revolution," after the seizure of power, to show up at the first call in the ranks of the army without any external compulsion and to implicitly obey all commands and to elect not those commanders who will indulge all their weaknesses, but those who will wage an

unrelenting and harsh struggle against those weaknesses which will under-
mine the combat readiness of the army? The answer to this question is clear:
even in countries with a conscious and disciplined proletariat, only a small
minority will satisfy these requirements.[11]

Sociologically speaking, the bulk of the Red Army consisted not of
proletarians, but peasants who were recruited in regular call-ups. By
1920, over three-fourths of the army consisted of peasants, or roughly
the same as their proportion in the entire population. Of every
hundred adult male peasants, eleven served in the Red Army. The
peasant nature of the army presented the party organizations with
a major challenge and opportunity. For beyond transforming often
unreliable recruits into an effective fighting force, the army served as
a "school of the Revolution," one in which soldiers would learn basic
and political literacy, enabling them to become "conscious." Both
during the civil war and throughout the 1920s, the army was the major
Soviet institution through which peasants entered the Communist
Party.[12]

The Cheka (short for All-Russian Extraordinary Commission for
the Suppression of Counterrevolution, Sabotage and Speculation) was
the "sword of the Revolution," explicitly conceived as an organ of
"mass red terror against the bourgeoisie and its agents." Headed by
the Polish-born revolutionary, Feliks Dzerzhinskii, it possessed
unrestrained powers of arrest, interrogation, intimidation and
execution, all of which it applied liberally though probably no more so
than its White counterparts. At the peak of its strength in mid-1921, the
Cheka of the Russian Republic is estimated to have contained 250,000
members including 100,000 Frontier Troops and a civilian staff of
30,000. Data on the social composition of *Chekisty* have never been
published, but it would appear that industrial workers predominated
in its lower ranks. Certainly, the association of toughness with working-
class Bolsheviks, which Sheila Fitzpatrick has noted, would apply to
those who worked in the Cheka. But the predominantly bourgeois and
intelligentsia backgrounds of the Cheka's upper echelon by no means
implies that the leadership of the organization suffered from a tendency
toward softness or "furtive liberalism."[13]

By 1920, as the civil war wound down, the extra-judicial powers
of the Cheka began to create a certain amount of institutional
jealousy. Moreover, the legalization of trade in 1921 narrowed the
definition of speculation and thus limited one of the Cheka's chief
responsibilities. But that some kind of security organ was felt to be
necessary in the uncertain circumstances of the early 1920s is evident in

the replacement of the Cheka by a State Political Administration (GPU) nominally under the authority of the Commissariat of Internal Affairs (NKVD).

To the Bolsheviks, the dictatorship of the proletariat was truly democratic in the sense of representing the class interests of the vast majority of people – the toiling masses – as contrasted with the "formal" democracies that masked the rule of the exploiting minority, the bourgeoisie and landowners, behind the façade of universal rights and liberties. This was a definition of democracy that was based not on legal or juridical principles, but rather on the notion of social dominance, of *vlast'*. Justice was dispensed according to the "revolutionary conscience" of people's courts, consisting of two lay assessors and a full-time judge, and for more serious cases, revolutionary tribunals on which sat six assessors and a judge. In 1920 alone, the people's courts tried 881,933 people, of whom nearly 300,000 were found innocent. Among those convicted, 34 percent were sentenced to confinement, 30 percent were fined and 23 percent had to perform compulsory labor. The revolutionary tribunals handled only 26,738 cases, but the rate of conviction was higher (85 percent, compared to 66 percent) and among those convicted, 16,107 (70.7 percent) were sentenced to confinement and 766 (3.4 percent) were shot.[14]

We do not possess comparable data on the social backgrounds or occupations of those brought before the courts, but we know that these factors were often taken into account in sentencing. For example, the revolutionary tribunal in Lugansk, considering that the two individuals it had convicted of speculation in matches were proletarians, reduced their sentence from five to two years of forced labor. Then again, it was primarily workers who were subjected to another form of revolutionary justice, namely, the comrades disciplinary courts. These courts, administered by the trade unions, had the power to reprimand, dismiss, and sentence to forced labor those guilty of absenteeism and other violations of labor discipline. Archival evidence suggests that this power was used liberally.[15]

In other respects, most notably voting rights, there was no pretence about equality before the law. Certain categories of people – large property owners, clerics, White officers, and many tsarist officials – were deprived of voting rights. To underscore the privileged place of urban workers in the new political order, the Constitution of the Russian Soviet Federated Socialist Republic (RSFSR), which was approved in July 1918 by the Fifth All-Russian Congress of Soviets and subsequently served as a model for the other soviet republics, stipulated that in elections to all-Russian Soviet congresses, one urban voter was to be the equivalent of five rural inhabitants.[16]

If, in Lenin's words, soviet power was "the organizational form of the dictatorship of the proletariat," what was the organizational form assumed by the soviets? The Constitution mandated a federal structure in which local soviets and regional, provincial, county (*uezd*) and district (*volost*) congresses of soviets were obliged to carry out all resolutions of corresponding higher organs of soviet power and otherwise settle questions of purely local significance. Supreme power nominally rested with the periodically convened congresses, and, when they were not in session, with their executive committees. One year after the October Revolution, 6,550 such committees were counted – 6,111 at the volost level, plus 286 uezd, 121 city, 30 provincial and two regional committees. Their number declined thereafter partly because of consolidation and partly because in areas near the front, revolutionary-military committees, with significant Red Army representation, replaced them.[17]

At the summit of the civilian state stood the All-Russian Central Executive Committee (VTsIK). An unwieldy body of several hundred members, VTsIK rarely met in full session and otherwise deferred to its Presidium, which was capably headed by the veteran Bolshevik, Ia. M. Sverdlov, and after his death in March 1919, by M. I. Kalinin. The division of powers between VTsIK and the Council of Peoples' Commissars (Sovnarkom), over which Lenin presided, was left rather vague by the Constitution and caused some acrimony within and outside the Communist Party. Both bodies exercised legislative and executive power and both issued decrees. Increasingly, though, Sovnarkom took advantage of the constitutional loophole to assume sole authority in matters of "extreme urgency," and VTsIK correspondingly rubber-stamped its decisions.

Sovnarkom was, then, "*the* government of the embattled Soviet Republic in fact as well as name." After the withdrawal of the Left SRs in March 1918, its members were drawn entirely from the Communist Party in which they all enjoyed prominence, and with the early exception of A. M. Kollontai who served briefly as People's Commissar for Welfare, were entirely male. In other respects – age, social background, ethnicity, pre-revolutionary occupations, educational levels, and convictions – they were a diverse group, though one dominated by scions of ethnically or assimilated Russian families from the middle and upper echelons of tsarist society, who chose the precarious career of professional revolutionary.[18]

Sovnarkom functioned in many ways as had the Council of Ministers under the tsarist and Provisional Governments, though in the view of its recent "biographer," with more efficiency and attention to detail.[19] The same could be said of its constituent bodies, the People's Commissariats, most of which relied heavily on the talents and experience of former ministerial employees. Still, there was a great deal of fluidity and turnover of personnel within the commissariats and, as the central government assumed ever-growing responsibilities, considerable jurisdictional overlap and friction among them. Whether it was a matter of food supply, labor mobilization, transport allocation, educational policy, or the administration of industry, several bodies inevitably claimed priority and often circumvented decisions taken by Sovnarkom to resolve disputes. Moreover, it was only in December 1920 that the Eighth All-Russian Congress of Soviets defined at length the division of power between central and provincial organs. It did so on the basis of the "dual subordination" of commissariat officials. They were at one and the same time to carry out their tasks in accordance with resolutions of the provincial executive committees to which they were assigned and the commissariats from which they received instructions – no easy task. But, as E. H. Carr has remarked, "If the system of 'dual subordination' worked, it was because central Soviet organs and local executive committees both ultimately recognized an authority outside the Soviet system," namely, the Communist Party.[20]

This was no less the case with respect to relations between the RSFSR and its constituent organs of government on the one hand and their equivalents in the nominally independent republics of Ukraine, Belorussia and Transcaucasia on the other. It should be recalled that throughout the civil war, Ukraine and Belorussia were only intermittently under Soviet rule, and, with the exception of the short-lived Baku Commune of 1918, soviets were virtually absent as governing institutions in Transcaucasia. Sovietization was achieved in these areas essentially by extra-territorial means, that is, by Red Army conquest and the efforts of the Commissariat of Nationalities and various party commissions and bureaus dispatched from Moscow to supervise the process. Behind the façade of government-to-government treaty relations between the RSFSR and these republics lay the reality of military-political dependence of the latter on the former and the dependence of both on the army and the party.

The pattern of relations among the republics was delineated in a VTsIK resolution of 1 June 1919 which called for the unification of the military, transport, finance, labor, and economic administrations. But even before this resolution was discussed by VTsIK, the Central Committee of the Russian Communist Party had passed a directive toward this end.[21] What then of the vaunted principle of national self-determination which Lenin defended against "proletarian inter-nationalist" opposition within the party? Contrary to what many western historians have argued, this was neither a dead letter nor merely a cynical ploy. Indeed, how much national/ethnic sensibilities were to be accommodated as unification proceeded, was an issue that would divide not only local communists from those sent by Moscow, but also Lenin from his erstwhile protégé, Stalin who, as Peoples' Commissar of Nationalities, spearheaded the drive for unification.

It is no simple matter to separate immediate military and security considerations from longer-term desiderata. Obviously, it made sense from an administrative point of view to unify under one command the army and various support structures in the struggle against the Whites and various "bourgeois-nationalist" forces. But as the military struggle gave way to that for economic reconstruction, it was almost impossible to avoid looking at the question of center–periphery relations and the entire federal structure through "economic eyes."[22] Those eyes saw the wheat of Ukraine, the oil of Baku and the cotton of Turkestan as vital to the survival of Soviet power in Russia. In this sense, the Bolsheviks were operating within the framework of the economic geography inherited from the tsarist empire. Their mental framework, however, differed radically from their "military–feudal" predecessors. Their aim was not merely to deny to the imperialists the possibility of exploiting these peripheral areas, but to integrate them into a dynamic industrial economy in which all citizens were to be workers employed in one gigantic metaphorical factory operating, as Lenin put it on several occasions in 1918, "like clockwork."[23]

This vision combined the worship of up-to-date technology and its emphasis on standardization, precision, and punctuality with the classical Marxist notion of communism as the popular administration over things rather than people and the corresponding "withering away" of the state. In Trotsky's rendition of 1920, "the whole popu-lation of the country will be drawn into the general Soviet system of economic arrangement and self-government. The Soviets themselves, at present the organs of government, will gradually melt into purely economic organizations."[24]

But, until then, the highest degree of political centralization, "systematically applied universal labor service, and a centralized organization of distribution" had to be achieved. In asserting these priorities, Trotsky was only repeating party orthodoxy. That orthodoxy is usually associated with "War Communism," a term coined by Lenin to refer retrospectively to the party's civil war induced economic policies. But, as several neo-Marxist commentators have argued, these priorities were always latent in the Bolshevik project and became manifest even before the onset of full-scale civil war. As early as December 1917, VTsIK established a Supreme Council of the National Economy (Vesenkha) to organize a general economic plan and financial administration for the state. Initially headed by V. Osinskii and from April 1918 by A. Rykov, Vesenkha took its place in Sovnarkom and developed an elaborate infrastructure of sections and departments to handle its enormous but none too clearly defined responsibilities.[25]

However, Vesenkha's pretentions to establishing itself as the core of the economic state were stymied by a variety of countervailing forces. From the start, its attempts to control the pace of the nationalization of industry were sabotaged by factory committees, soviets and other local bodies that confiscated or "nationalized" from below hundreds of enterprises. Among the multitude of other problems that bedevilled Vesenkha during the civil war, two stand out as particularly vexing. One was competition from other economic organs, particularly the Commissariat of Food Supply (Narkomprod) and the Council of Workers' and Peasants' Defense, which made Vesenkha's attempts to formulate an economic plan and supervise the system of collective commodity exchange between town and country virtually impossible. The other had to do with tensions between central control of individual products or branches of industry and territorial economic administration of nationalized enterprises.

In institutional terms, branch administration was exercised by *tsentry* (centers) and *glavki* (main administrations), many of which were holdovers from attempts by the tsarist and Provisional governments to regulate the market; territorial jurisdiction was in the hands of regional, provincial and uezd economic councils (*sovnarkhozy*) which, confusingly, were overseen by corresponding soviets and Vesenkha – another instance of dual subordination. The dry recitation of Vesenkha's institutional structure can hardly convey the constant state of emergency, the crush of conflicting demands, the intensity of internecine battles, and the violent swings between abject despair and romantic euphoria to which the economic apparatus was subjected. The simple fact that some glavki did not even know the exact number of enterprises they were supposed to supervise gives some idea of the organizational mayhem that was endemic to the period. In such circumstances, Vesenkha's standing fell. When, in March 1920, the Ninth Party Congress acknowledged the need for an all-embracing plan for economic reconstruction, it looked not to Vesenkha, but to the Council of Workers' and Peasants' Defense – soon to be renamed the Council of Labor and Defense (STO) – to generate one.[26]

Within the arena of the economic state there was yet another major player, the trade unions. Initially eclipsed as workers' organizations by the soviets and factory committees, the trade unions were themselves arenas of struggle between the Bolshevik and Menshevik parties. This was, however, an unequal struggle, owing to the Bolsheviks' near monopolization of state power. Only in a few cases, most notably the printers' and bakers' unions, did the Mensheviks retain a strong presence throughout the civil war and into the 1920s.

The organizational structure of the unions, which remained virtually unchanged until recent times, bore close similarities to that of the soviets. Supreme authority rested with annually convened all-Russian congresses consisting of delegates elected by their territorially based equivalents. An All-Russian (later All-Union) Central Council (VTsSPS) was elected at each congress and charged with carrying out its decisions. Toward that end, it could issue instructions and resolutions that were binding upon all territorial councils as well as the central and regional committees of individual unions. From the spring of 1918, the unions began to be reconstituted according to the production principle, which is to say by industrial branch rather than craft. The amalgamation of smaller craft unions into national industry-wide bodies chiefly accounts for the decline in the number of unions, from approximately seventy at the time of the October Revolution to twenty-five by early 1919.[27] Finally, at the local or enterprise level, unions were represented by (previously autonomous) committees, which, being closest to rank-and-file workers, often faced the unpleasant task of mediating between the grievances of their constituents and directives from higher bodies.

What then was the relationship between the unions and the fledgling Soviet state? There was no question of the Bolsheviks accepting the Menshevik position of trade union neutrality and independence. But the Bolsheviks' own formulations were fraught with ambiguity. The first All-Russian Congress of Trade Unions, which met in January 1918, stipulated that unions should become "organs of state power." But the party's new program, passed at its eighth congress in March 1919, appeared to sanction a more syndicalist conceptualization of the state, in effect, making it an organ of the unions. The relevant section of the program declared that the unions should "proceed to the practical concentration into their own hands of the work of administration in the whole economic life of the country."[28]

In the heat of the civil war, the disparity between the two positions could be ignored. Labor power, after all, had become a service to render, not a commodity to be sold. The differences between labor service and military service were as blurred as the distinction between the unions and state organs, such as the Commissariat of Labor and Vesenkha, to which the unions sent their nominees. Both, side by side and sometimes together performed disciplinary, administrative and mobilizational functions. The unions organized the wage-tariff system, distributed (and as a punitive measure, could withdraw) ration coupons, presided over health insurance and occupational safety, endeavored to raise productivity through labor disciplinary courts, moral suasion and the application of bonuses, and recruited members for service in state organs ranging from individual commissariats and Vesenkha to food supply detachments.

It was in 1920 that the issue of the unions' proper relation to the state was once again joined. The *ABC of Communism* foresaw "the day when the whole of economic life, from top to bottom, shall constitute a unity which is effectively controlled by the industrial (productive) unions." But, in the shorter term, the unions "must develop in such a way that they will be transformed into economic departments and instruments of state authority; they must be 'statified.'" This position in favor of "statization" was amplified by Trotsky as part of his scheme for the militarization of labor. More than that, it was applied in connection with Trotsky's efforts to rehabilitate the transport system and coal mining in the Donets Basin. This involved, among other things, using Glavpoliput, the party's organizational and propaganda organ within the Commissariat of Transport, to deregister the recalcitrant railway workers' union and replace it by a "statized" union, the Central Transport Commission (Tsektran); the establishment of a Political Department for Donbass Coal which effectively superseded the provincial party committee; and the organization of shock troops (*udarniki*) of labor, that is, workers who were enlisted for especially urgent tasks on the "labor front." These measures, which had the full backing of the party leadership, did enjoy success. But the harsh rhetoric that Trotsky used to justify them and the prospect that they would become standard policy aroused intense hostility among workers, trade union activists, and many high-ranking party members, including Lenin. Indeed, to the extent that the Workers' Opposition faction was able to achieve rank-and-file support within the party, it had Trotsky partly to thank. In any case, the issue continued to boil until the Tenth Party Congress in March 1921.[29]

We can now turn to the last of the sub-systems within the proletarian dictatorship, that is, the political state. By 1920–1 this effectively meant the Communist Party. From what already has been discussed, it should be apparent that the party exerted direct influence over the other three sub-systems. It did so mainly in two ways, by "nominating" its members to key positions in the military, soviet, and economic apparatuses, and by making it encumbent upon members to form party fractions "strictly subject," in the words of a resolution of the Eighth Party Congress, "to party discipline."[30] But what of the party itself? What was its organizational framework and what kind of politics took place within it?

Data on party membership are notoriously unreliable for the civil war period, reflecting not only the ebbs and flows in the fortunes of the Reds, but the primitive state of record keeping. We know that in 1918, after rising sharply, the number of members fell just as precipitously. An upward trend in membership in the last months of 1918 was reversed thereafter. What proved to be the low point for the entire post-October Revolution period was probably reached in August 1919, when the party's Secretariat estimated total membership at no more than 150,000.[31] Many factors were involved in limiting the growth of the party's rank and file: political disenchantment, especially in the spring of 1918, the elementary struggle for survival which left little time for sustaining active membership, fear of White reprisals, death at the front, and a purge (that is, removal) of passive members, deserters from the Red Army and other undesirable elements which was carried out in the spring of 1919.

Recruitment to the party was conducted in earnest during the autumn of 1919, that is, at the height of the military struggle against the Whites. As a result of the "party weeks," an estimated 200,000 people entered the party, swelling its ranks to some 430,000 by January 1920 and perhaps as many as 600,000 by March. But despite special efforts to recruit workers, their proportion within the party fell steadily throughout these years, from 57 percent at the beginning of 1918, to 48 percent in early 1919 and 44 percent a year later. The proportion of peasants, particularly lads who had entered the Red Army, and what the sources refer to as "employees" (sluzhashchie, or in western parlance, "white-collar workers") correspondingly rose. By January 1921, the party consisted of 240,000 workers (41 percent of all members), 165,300 (28.2 percent) who were classified as peasants, 138,800 (23.7 percent) "employees," and 41,500 (7.1 percent), whose social origins were unknown.[32]

Put another way, by the spring of 1921 approximately 90 percent of the membership had joined the party after the October Revolution. Most had had some experience in the military or security organs and brought into the party "a military, if not a militaristic, political culture" which "persisted, in different forms, for decades."[33] Many, having recognized that the regime would survive for the foreseeable future, had joined for careerist reasons. They were the main targets of a massive purge in 1921 that reduced the size of the party by as much as one-third. Still, the question of whether the enormous number of new members, whose experience and culture differed so markedly from the "old guard," could be reeducated or on the contrary would themselves determine the nature of the party was a very real one.

According to its statutes, the party was supposed to function on the basis of committees elected periodically at conferences and congresses. Such committees were established at all levels, from the Central Committee elected by the All-Russian Congress to republic and regional committees, provincial committees and so forth down to the volost level. Relations within this hierarchy were to be governed by the principle of "democratic centralism" whereby authority flowed upward from the smallest cells to the Central Committee and discipline flowed in the opposite direction. In reality, centralism always had the upper hand, as it almost inevitably does in large organizations, and the gap between principle and practice widened in the course of the civil war. This was so not only because the leadership was predisposed or found it expedient to preempt discussion, deliberation and elections at lower levels or because it lacked faith in the ability of rank-and-file members – most of whom had little formal education – to act in a manner consistent with its definition of the party's best interests. Ironically, the process of centralization was aided by local committees, many of which experienced an acute shortage of competent personnel and pleaded with higher bodies for information, cadres, and guidance.[34]

"Centralisation," as Robert Service has noted, "is a word covering a multitude of organisational possibilities," and the party manifested several of them during its first years in power. Provincial committees experienced an "astounding rise in stature" at the expense of both supervening regional (*oblast'*) committees and lower bodies. Within local committees, there was a "persistent drift" toward individual secretaries assuming responsibility for day-to-day affairs. There was also increasing reliance on "appointmentism" via the cooptation of new members by depleted committees, the nomination by higher bodies of individual officials to run lower committees, and the assignment of plenipotentiaries and their staffs by the Central Committee to take charge of certain operations in the provinces. These involved food delivery and military conscription, but also intervention in disputes within local committees and attempts to otherwise put their affairs in order. All these measures could be (and were) justified by civil war conditions, which, as a resolution of the Eight Congress (March 1919) put it, placed the party "in a position where the strictest centralism and severest discipline are an absolute necessity."[35]

The congress also took the momentous step of formally reconstituting the Political Bureau (Politburo) and creating two new organs, an Organizational Bureau (Orgburo) to deal with party appointments and a Secretariat with (as of then) undefined responsibilities. The aim here was to facilitate the work of the Central Committee, a body of nineteen full and eight candidate members, several of whom often could not make it to Moscow for plenary sessions. But the effect, felt almost immediately in the case of the Politburo, was that these organs appropriated the decision-making and administrative roles previously monopolized by the Central Committee itself.[36]

Several points can be made about this drift toward centralism. First, it did not go unchallenged. *Gubkom* defiance of central directives and other manifestations of "localism" were not infrequent. "They don't want to accept emissaries from other provinces," was how V. M. Molotov explained his ouster from the Nizhni-Novgorod gubkom to A. I. Mikoian, his successor as senior Moscow-appointed official.[37] In the army, a Military Opposition objected to the replacement of elective party committees by political departments that took instructions from political commissars. Charges that democratic centralism had been replaced by bureaucratic centralism within the civilian party structure were voiced at the eighth and ninth congresses by the Democratic Centralists, a Moscow-based faction. The accusation also figured in the indictment drawn up by the Workers' Opposition.

The second point is that just as centralism did not necessarily preclude the airing of different points of view, so local autonomy did not always mean respect for democratic procedures. On the contrary, district party chairmen, invoking the war-time emergency, often assumed dictatorial authority, while even those who denounced "bureaucratism" at higher levels, were not above stacking conferences to ensure their reelection. And as illustrated by struggles within the unions, appointees charged with executing central party policy sometimes far exceeded in manipulativeness and coercion what the center sanctioned.[38]

Finally, the degree of efficiency within the party imparted by centralization should not be exaggerated. The vision of a "sleek hierarchy of uniformly organized committees" articulated by L. M. Kaganovich (then a budding *apparatchik* in the Nizhni-Novgorod provincial committee) was just that, a vision. If the Moscow provincial party organization of mid-1919 could be described as "ramshackle," those at the same and lower levels elsewhere were and remained in a more disorganized state still.[39] But then, we must be careful not to impose a latter-day standard of efficiency. What needs to be considered is how efficient the party needed to be. And the answer is that so long as it was able to mobilize popular support for and participation in the civil war effort, so long as it could penetrate existing social institutions, deny other political organizations a secure existence and otherwise oversee the absorption of civil society by the proletarian dictatorship – in short, so long as it could plausibly represent itself as the vanguard party of a class that previously was defined by its exploitation but was now (oxymoronically) ruling – it was efficient enough.

However, once military victory had been achieved, a crisis erupted within the party. The crisis only partially concerned organizational questions. More explosive was the question of whether the policies that had seen the infant Soviet state through its baptism of fire should be continued in the face of the disintegration of the social class that had given birth to that state.

The "ruling" proletariat

Writing in July 1919, on the eve of the most decisive campaigns of the civil war, Lenin defined the proletariat's mission in the following terms:

In order to achieve victory, in order to build and consolidate socialism, the proletariat must fulfill a twofold or dual task: first, it must, by its supreme heroism in the revolutionary struggle against capital, win over the entire mass of the working and exploited people; it must win them over, organise them and lead them in the struggle to overthrow the bourgeoisie and utterly suppress their resistance. Secondly, it must lead the whole mass of the working and exploited people, as well as all the petty-bourgeois groups, on the road of new economic development, towards the creation of a new social bond, a new labor discipline, a new organization of labor, which will combine the last word in science and capitalist technology with the mass association of class-conscious workers creating large-scale socialist industry.

Of the two, he argued that the second was the more difficult and essential "because, in the last analysis, the deepest source of strength for victories over the bourgeoisie . . . can only be a new and higher mode of social production, the substitution of large-scale socialist production for capitalist and petty-bourgeois production."[40]

This was a tall order for a class that already had experienced five years of mobilization and social upheaval associated with war and revolution, and, in any case, never constituted more than a minute proportion of the entire population. It was, in fact, just this gap between what was being demanded of the proletariat and its capacities that had propelled the Bolsheviks to construct their dictatorship of the proletariat and to defend it by what subsequently became known as "War Communism." But what happened to the proletariat, putatively the ruling class in the new social order? Did the proletarian dictatorship, by demanding so much of and drawing so deeply on the social resource after which it was named, actually – and ironically – contribute to its disintegration?

In considering the fate of the proletariat, we must first define it. The term, as employed in Bolshevik discourse, was alternately broader and more narrow than the aggregation of industrial or "blue collar" workers. As of the beginning of 1917, the core of the proletariat consisted of about 3.5 million industrial workers, a mere 2.5 percent of the empire's total population though a considerably higher proportion of all urban inhabitants. Leaving aside landless peasants whom Lenin occasionally referred to as a "rural proletariat" or alternatively, a "semi-proletariat," there were also approximately a million railroad workers, and several hundred thousand involved in construction and other forms of transport.[41]

While proletarian status was conferred on these millions in certain contexts, in others the criterion of occupation was insufficient. Even factory workers were said to be infected with petty bourgeois attitudes, some, so it was asserted, because of their lack of production experience (stazh) and skills, others because of their ties to the village, and still others because of their proximity to urban elites. In other words, proletarian status implied a certain cast of mind (oblik) or consciousness, one that not surprisingly correlated with support for Bolshevik positions or better still, membership in the party. This definition therefore was more of an ideological than a sociological map. Irrespective of objective criteria, workers who failed to recognize the necessity for "a new social bond, a new labor discipline, a new organization of labor" were at best part of the "working masses" who had to be won over to the proletariat.

There are thus two problems that need to be addressed, one quantitative and the other qualitative. The first, how many and what kind of workers remained in industry by 1920–1, has received much more attention from scholars, particularly Soviet scholars, than the latter. This might be formulated in terms of how workers adjusted to deteriorating urban conditions and what effect conditions had on their consciousness, or *mentalité*. Statistics on the industrial work force and its internal composition vary depending on the territory encompassed and the efficiency of data collection. But generally, they tell the same story of diminution. From a high point of 3.5 million, the number of workers in "census" industry (i.e., industrial enterprises employing more than 16 workers) dropped to slightly over 2 million in 1918, between 1.3 and 1.5 million in 1919, and roughly 1.5 million in the latter half of 1920. The latter figure, incidentally, was slightly less than that for handicraft or cottage industry workers (*kustari*).[42]

Losses were greatest in the most populous industrial centers, that is, in Petrograd, Moscow, the Donbass, and the Urals. The number of industrial workers in Petrograd plummeted from 406,000 in January 1917 to 123,000 by mid-1920. They also declined as a proportion of the city's population – from 45.9 percent of able-bodied adults, in 1917, to 34 percent by the autumn of 1920. Between 1918 and 1920, Moscow experienced a net loss of about 100,000 workers, and over the same period, the number of factory and mine workers in the Urals dropped from 340,000 to 155,000. Among the major branches of industry, textiles experienced the greatest contraction, declining in terms of its work force by nearly 72 percent between 1917 and 1920. The number employed in machine and metalworks factories fell by 57 percent, from 537,508 to 231,159, while the fuel industry registered a more modest decline of 25 percent and printing a small gain of 7 percent. Large enterprises, where the Bolsheviks had concentrated their agitational and recruitment efforts, suffered disproportionately, partly owing to the shutting down of entire shops (*tsekhy*) and partly due to heavy mobilization for the Red Army and food procurement detachments. Whereas in 1913 enterprises employing over 500 workers accounted for 55.2 percent of the industrial work force, by the end of 1920 their proportion had dropped to 48.3 percent. By contrast, the proportion in enterprises with from 21 to 100 workers doubled.[43]

The decline in the numerical strength of the proletariat was part and parcel of the depopulation of the major cities during the civil war. Petrograd, whose population had swelled to 2.5 million by 1917, had only 722,000 inhabitants by 1920, or approximately the same number as in 1870. Moscow's population, which had stood at slightly more than 2 million in February 1917, shrank to just over 1 million by late 1920, or less than the number recorded in the 1897 census. Kiev lost more than a quarter of its population during these years. Only in smaller provincial towns on the periphery of European Russia and indeed outside of Soviet territory for much of the civil war was there any increase in population. Urban contraction was essentially the result of the catastrophic decline in supplies of food and fuel. This decline was itself the product of a combination of factors – the breakdown of the rail transport system owing to war-time overstrain and the inadequacy of repairs; foreign and/or White occupation of some of the former Empire's richest food and fuel producing regions; peasants' reduction of sown area and resistance to grain requisitions; priority given to the Red Army in the field.[44]

Lacking adequate nourishment, shelter, warmth and medicines, many urban residents found themselves engaged in what Isaac Deutscher called "an almost zoological struggle for survival." In this struggle, the microorganisms often triumphed. Epidemics of typhus, cholera, influenza and diphtheria carried off tens of thousands of urban residents, many already weakened by deficiency diseases. In Moscow, the death rate soared from 23.7 (per thousand) in 1917 to 45.4 in 1919 and was 36.3 in 1920. Meanwhile, the birth rate, which had declined every year since 1913, reached its nadir in 1918 (14.8 per thousand inhabitants) before rising again to 21.4 in 1920.[45]

But urban depopulation was not simply or even mainly a function of an excess of deaths over births. Reversing the centuries-old dynamic of urban growth, out-migration from the cities accounted for the greatest loss of people, among them many workers. Two broad avenues out of the city were available to workers: flight to the countryside and mobilization by the Red Army or food detachments. It would appear that relatively recent migrants to the cities comprised the majority of those who took the first route. Their departure began already in 1917 and continued into the following year in connection with peasant seizures of landlords' property and its redistribution. Subsequently, many others left – how many cannot be determined with any accuracy – to reconnect themselves with relatives or *zemliaki* (people hailing from the same village or district) as a means of surviving.

Almost continuous mobilizations by the Red Army removed about 600,000 workers between 1918 and 1920, while another 75,000 served in food army detachments under the People's Commissariat of Food Supply (Narkomprod). In contrast to those who fled to the countryside, they included the most "conscious" elements of the proletariat, those who were members of the Komsomol (the party's youth organization created in 1919) or were already communists, had voted for the Bolsheviks in the Constituent Assembly elections of November 1917, and formed the backbone of the factory committees and soviets. Their rate of attrition was high. Of the 500,000 Communists who served in the Red Army in the civil war (not all of whom were workers), it has been estimated that at least 200,000 lost their lives.[46] Among the survivors, many were lost to industry (though not to the cities) either because of physical disabilities, or assignment to the burgeoning soviet, party and trade union administrations.

The departure of so many workers from the shop floor provokes one to ask whether there remained a proletariat in any meaningful sense of that term. Soviet historians generally concede that as a result of the civil war, the working class lost its best elements and had become adulterated with those previously engaged in cottage industry, former employees and other interstertial groups. From these quantitative and qualitative changes, they conclude, much as Lenin and other leading Bolsheviks did at the time, that industrial workers had become atomized, dispersed, and declassed. But they add reassuringly that the proletariat was able to maintain its leading role in the struggle to defeat the exploiting classes because its vanguard, the Communist Party, succeeded in rallying the class to political activism and organizational unity.[47]

Western scholars have been at one with their Soviet counterparts in stressing the impoverishment and dispersal of the proletariat, but draw very different conclusions about the consequences of these catastrophic developments. Focusing on Moscow, William Chase has described the proletariat of 1920–1 as "a bifurcated class" consisting of a "small core of experienced and skilled workers, a majority of whom were males over thirty years old," and a majority of "inexperienced and reluctant workers." This class had now become "estranged" from the state. Its "revolutionary agenda" of higher wages, better working conditions, improved housing and diets, greater respect and workers' control as a means of achieving these aims had been "crushed and deformed," and its institutions, the soviets and factory committees, had been transformed by a "frustrated government" into "executors of unsuccessful and increasingly unpopular policies."[48]

Diane Koenker has offered an alternative perspective. In an article that also draws heavily on demographic data from Moscow, Koenker rejects both the traditional western emphasis on the "withering away of the proletariat" and the Soviet view that equates true proletarian consciousness with the Communist Party. She interprets class consciousness as a function of workers' urban experience, which entailed not only the workplace but kinship, neighborhood, and cultural facilities. For her, the departure of so many Bolshevik supporters and agitators did not result in the disintegration of the working class but a transformation of its consciousness. While the skill levels and work experience of workers may have become more differentiated, this did not necessarily produce a bifurcated class. For one thing, workers were bound together by family ties. It is striking that of the 100,000 workers who left Moscow between 1918 and 1920, less than 10,000 were female. Indeed, throughout Soviet Russia the proportion of women in the industrial work force rose from 37.5 percent in 1913 to 44.4 percent by mid-1920. Many may have been "inexperienced and reluctant workers," but among them were the wives, sisters and mothers of army recruits. Second, the flight to the countryside of the least urbanized strata meant that the remaining proletariat – predominantly older men and women of all ages – shared a greater degree of urban culture than previously. As for the urban environment itself, the record is mixed. On the one hand, shortages of all kinds meant that workers were compelled to spend an inordinate amount of time scrounging for the basic necessities of life. On the other, municipal services and facilities such as transport, electricity, accommodation, and public baths bore no cost to users, cultural life in the form of the theater and the Proletkult movement remained vibrant, while schools and libraries proliferated.[49]

Koenker's approach has the advantage of underscoring the contingent nature of workers' support for Bolshevism, one based on their identification of the party with peace, class separateness, and economic improvement. But her association of working-class culture with urbanism raises certain problems. For if, historically, working-class culture had been spawned within an urban environment, its perpetuation was itself contingent on other factors. Clearly, kinship, neighborhood and employment patterns continued to matter, but the evidence adduced by Koenker for their positive influence remains open to question. While the sharp rise in the number of civil marriages from 1918 does suggest a preference for a secular culture which was not shared by most peasants, it can only be interpreted as evidence of "a consolidation of urban *working-class* society" if the partners were themselves working class, rather than from, say, petty trader, shopkeeper or professional groups. The "tendency toward more interclass mingling," a function of the housing crisis and working-class resettlement in domiciles of the bourgeoisie, may indeed have spurred more interclass nuptials. Finally, while class should not be reduced to production relations, the fact that workers spent less time in production and more on *"personal* trips to forage in the countryside" implies a resort to individual rather than collective solutions to the problems of daily existence and a corresponding weakening of class as opposed to other kinds of identity.[50]

An even more radical departure from both Soviet and western historiography is offered by Sheila Fitzpatrick. She notes that class categories were ubiquitous during the civil war, figuring prominently in Bolshevik rhetoric and Soviet legislation, but as guides to social reality they are misleading. So great was the social flux, so frequently did individuals change occupations and social positions, that both as analytical categories and clues to social behavior, "class" is not very useful. Even less so is the concept of "proletarian consciousness" which is inevitably tainted with "Marxist assumptions" to which many western historians, consciously or unconsciously, have succumbed. Better to study the variety of trajectories and "pluralism of *mentalités*" (Fitzpatrick mentions acquisitiveness, materialism, competitiveness, individual ambition, inclination towards brutality and violence, anti-semitism, xenophobia and anti-intellectualism) exhibited during the civil war, without prejudging or even being concerned about what was true and what was false consciousness.[51]

Notwithstanding her animus against Marxist class categories, Fitzpatrick is compelled to employ them in analyzing social mobility and *mentalités*; and rightly so. For, to strip "class" of certain hypostatized encrustations is not to deny its usefulness in social analysis but to increase it. Class, like ethnicity or gender, becomes a relational term referring to processes of social interaction and the subjective appreciation of those processes. It is at once the product of the ever-changing (or to use Anthony Giddens' term, "structurated") social division of labor and the representations of that division in political and cultural discourse.[52] What is so fascinating but also confusing about the first years of the Soviet republic is the extraordinary degree of indeterminacy in the social division of labor simultaneous with a powerful impetus from the ruling Communist Party to impose its own representation on that fluid reality. That representation itself was at one and the same time retrospective, referring to the pre-revolutionary class structure that was now in ruins (at least in the urban areas), and anticipatory (Lenin's "new social bond"). And one of the secrets of both its strength and its weakness was that, more than usually, most people were too involved in the struggle to survive in the present to openly or collectively challenge its applicability or legitimacy.

To better appreciate the fluidity of social relations, we need to examine the division of labor in the factories and the ways workers responded to the challenge of forging a new organization of production. As we have seen earlier, the October Revolution left the factories in the hands of factory committees that exercised workers' control over production. But these organs of workers' democracy were no more capable of arresting the revolutionary disintegration of industry than the management they had replaced. Competing among themselves for scarce resources and often under attack from their disgruntled constituents, the committees were in effect rescued by the trade unions and converted into local arms of those bodies. The unions in turn reorganized themselves to conform to the emerging administrative structure of Vesenkha and Narkomtrud. These three apparatuses, and to a lesser extent, the executive committees of the corresponding soviets, exercised appointive power in staffing the glavki, sovnarkhozy and factory management boards. Incomplete statistics exist for the proportion of production workers, specialists and clerical workers appointed to these boards as of 1920. They show a preponderance of production workers at the factory and shop level, but in the glavki, they were outnumbered by both specialists and clerical workers.[53]

The essential function of these bodies was to restore some semblance of order to the production process. As far as the party leadership was concerned, the key to restoring order was the imposition of "labor discipline," a concept aptly defined by Chase as "[a] wide variety of production traits and attitudes [such as] punctually arriving at work; conscientiously performing one's job; respecting machinery, materials, and products; obeying the instructions of foremen, and other responsible personnel; and minimizing absence from work."[54]

Why was there so little labor discipline during the civil war? To some extent it had to do with the late and only partial imposition of an industrial capitalist factory regime in tsarist Russia. Russian factory workers of the early twentieth century were notorious for the number of religious holidays they observed, their maintenance of village ties which kept them away from the factory for extended periods of time, and a typically pre-industrial pace of work characterized by bursts of activity interspersed with periods of lethargy. Second, the 1917 Revolution had won workers a measure of control over production that many were loathe to sacrifice. While much still remains to be learned about the internal arrangements within factories in the years following the 1917 Revolution, scattered evidence indicates that managers and technical personnel experienced great difficulty in asserting their authority. Whether this was a function of the influx of new elements into the factories and their manipulation by Mensheviks and SRs – as claimed by party leaders at the time and Soviet historians since – is doubtful. Indeed, it is more likely to have been older workers who were most adamant about not giving up what they thought they had won from the Revolution.[55]

Overwhelmingly, though, the lack of labor discipline can be correlated with the critical shortage of food and the manner in which the shortages were handled by the authorities. From the declaration of the "food dictatorship" in May 1918, the state sought to replace trade with the distribution of foodstuffs at fixed prices on the basis of rationing. From the autumn of 1918, the level of rations was tied to the "class principle" according to which manual workers (and among them, those engaged in the most physically demanding work) were accorded more than administrative and clerical personnel who in turn received a higher ration than those classified as belonging to the bourgeoisie. The system proved cumbersome and, as Carr notes, led to "widespread anomalies, jealousies and discontents."[56] But aside from administrative difficulties, the system was deficient in two major respects. First, by linking rations to occupation rather than individual performance, it provided little or no incentive for higher productivity. Second, the inability of the state to accumulate sufficient quantities of food meant that even for workers in the highest category, the amount of rations remained well below the caloric minimum.

In such circumstances, workers and most other urban inhabitants had to resort to other sources, either the illegal but nonetheless flourishing private markets that sprang up in and around the towns, or nearby villages. According to one estimate, such illegal channels accounted for 60 percent of the urban consumption of bread grain in 1918–19 and 70–80 percent of all food products consumed in provincial capitals in the latter year. But as the state increasingly resorted to raising funds by printing more paper money, the value of currency plummeted and peasants and the notorious "bagmen" who sold food were increasingly reluctant to accept money at all. Indeed, monetary wages became almost meaningless and the state gradually acceded to the demands of trade unions for payment in kind, that is, in "natural" goods. These rose as a proportion of the average Moscow worker's wage from 48 percent in late 1918, to 93 percent two years later.[57] "In effect," as William Rosenberg notes, "virtually all enterprises, large and small, were manufacturing 'currency' . . . since almost any item could be used for wages or as a medium of exchange."[58]

The resort to natural wages, however, did little to stimulate productivity or reduce workers' dependence on the accursed market. On the contrary, receiving their wages in the form of whatever goods the factory could supply, even the most "class conscious" workers headed for the Sukharevka, the Okhotnyi Riad or other markets where they bartered their nails, matches, bolts of cloth or food stocks with what other workers and peasants had to offer. The rate of absenteeism soared, reflecting not only the demoralizing search for food, but the deterioration of workers' health. According to the calculations of the Soviet economist Strumilin, the number of absences measured in days per worker per year jumped from 12.6 in 1913 to 22.7 in 1917, 29.0 in 1918, and 68.4 in 1919.[59]

These figures by no means represent the total days lost to production, as an additional 51.2 days per worker were lost in 1919 as a result of stoppages due to lack of fuel, lack of raw materials and breakdowns. Moreover, even when workers were at the job, many used available equipment to fashion articles they could barter, or simply pilfered tools and spare parts. Productivity consequently plummeted. If in 1917 each worker produced only 66 percent of what was produced in 1913, then in 1918 the figure was 36 percent and in 1919, 33 percent. According to Lev Kritsman, the most ardent post-hoc defender of "War Communism," Soviet society had achieved "consumer communism" in the sense that whatever was being produced was immediately consumed. Accumulation of stocks simply did not occur.[60]

The state, including its political apparatus, the party, fought back on "the labor front" – almost everything had become a front in the course of the civil war – in three ways: by imposing military discipline on the work force, by offering what material incentives it could to increase productivity, and by encouraging workers to emulate the most "class conscious" elements who donated their labor. The militarization of labor evolved from the notion of labor as a service (povinnost') to society, from the conscription of members of the bourgeoisie to perform labor as required by the state, from the decree of 31 October 1918 outlining the "general principles of compulsory labor," and from numerous measures, adopted in 1919, to raise labor discipline. Among these were the following: the "freezing" of mineworkers to their jobs; the introduction of labor books to workers and Red Army soldiers which amounted to a general registration of the urban population and a mechanism for controlling the distribution of food ration cards; the establishment of forced labor camps; and the setting up of comrades disciplinary courts which were attached to the trade unions and vested with the authority to impose penalties up to and including assignment to hard labor and confinement in labor camps.

But in and of themselves, these measures did not necessarily lead to what was in effect, and was explicitly defended as, the militarization of the labor force. After all, the same weapons were employed in one form or another during the First Five-Year Plan without recourse to militarization. That militarization came about in 1920 was a function of the progressive disintegration of the economy (that is, the failure of all previous measures to arrest the decline in productivity), the persistence of Soviet Russia's economic and political isolation, and the recent successes enjoyed by the Red Army on the military front. It was the combination of these factors that stimulated interest in the military model of organizing labor and catapulted Trotsky, as Commissar of War, to the forefront of those advocating its implementation.

As already indicated, the project encountered stiff opposition from a variety of quarters. Menshevik trade unionists denounced it as "a monstrous perversion of Marxism," analogous to the "methods which the Egyptian Pharaohs used in building the pyramids."[61] Some leading communists objected to the extension of military authority at the expense of the trade unions, the soviets and the party; others doubted that compulsory labor could be productive; while still others feared rebellion among rank-and-file workers. Still, none of the alternatives to militarization appeared as compelling, and the party's Ninth Congress endorsed it with Lenin's backing.

Militarization did not only affect industrial workers. What amounted to the reverse process, that is, converting units from the Red Army released from combat into Labor Armies, commenced in January 1920. Each Army was overseen by a Revolutionary Council composed of representatives of various commissariats and headed by an appointee of the Council of Labor and Defense. For the most part, they performed unskilled labor such as cutting timber, loading and unloading freight, and clearing roads and rail lines. Similar tasks were performed by peasants under the authority of the Commissariat of Internal Affairs and a special agency, the Central Extraordinary Commission on Firewood and Cartage Duty.

But the most ambitious and controversial scheme associated with militarization involved organizing industry on a new basis, so that, as Trotsky described it, "every worker feels himself a soldier of labor who cannot dispose of himself freely. If an order is given to transfer him, he must carry it out. If he does not carry it out, he will be a deserter who is punished."[62] In the course of 1920, more than twenty "mobilizations" of industrial workers were issued, some fixing workers to particular enterprises, others ordering their transfer to areas of labor deficit. The mobilizations covered a variety of occupations, ranging from metal and shipbuilding workers to those engaged in the woolens and fishing industries and even "tailors and shoemakers who worked in Great Britain and the United States."[63] The entire operation was placed under a Main Committee for Compulsory Labor (Glavkomtrud) which was chaired by Dzerzhinskii and which established a network of regional and local commissions.

Simultaneously, the party moved to streamline the administration of industry by replacing managerial councils and boards with one-man management (*edinolichie*) at the factory level. Promoted in the name of personal responsibility and efficiency, one-man management inevitably became linked with what the resolution carried by the Ninth Party Congress described as the "irreconcilable struggle against that obnoxious form of ignorance and conceit which deems the working class capable of solving all problems without utilizing, in the most responsible positions, the services of specialists of the bourgeois school."[64] For Lenin, who spoke at length in favor of the resolution, collegial management was associated with that period when "chaos and enthusiasm reigned" and the party "swam with the current because it was impossible to distinguish the correct from the incorrect." But, he added, "we must not sit in preparatory school for ever! ... We are now adults." It was time to "struggle against the remnants of [this] notorious democratism" and all these cries about appointees, all this old harmful rubbish." Or, as he put it when addressing the Eighth Congress of Soviets in December 1920, "Industry is indispensable. Democracy is a category proper to the political sphere."[65] Thus, more than two years after Lenin had argued for the necessity of *unquestioning subordination* to a single will" in all the nationalized enterprises, the party went on record as favoring this approach and the trade unions somewhat grudgingly acquiesced. By late 1920, more than 80 percent of large-scale industrial plants had converted to one-man management.[66]

These measures marked the apotheosis of "War Communist" labor policy. That such a policy was instituted *after* the military threat to the survival of the Soviet state had subsided does not necessarily invalidate the argument that it was essentially induced by the civil war. For, while the war had ended, the economic breakdown continued apace. But by the same token, party leaders' claims that these policies were leading society toward the framework of a single economic plan and thus were part of the transition to socialism should not be dismissed as mere ideological window dressing. For "statism," the association of proletarian power with the military–bureaucratic organization of the social order, reached its post-1917 height just when the military threat to the state's survival was receding. Not until the party was confronted with a major revolt within its ranks as well as among the "broad masses" was the leadership persuaded that this was not the way to proceed. What retrospectively was ascribed to flights of rhetorical fancy nonetheless remained an important component of the revolutionary-heroic tradition of Bolshevism, or, as Robert Tucker has argued, its civil war ramified political culture.[67]

Whatever the impetus, militarization did not substantially increase the state's control over social resources or reverse the decline in labor productivity. On the contrary, it only enmeshed the state and society more deeply in the vicious circle of coercion, evasion, and more coercion. Despite an elaborate apparatus to detect and punish "deserters," available statistics suggest that nearly as many workers avoided mobilizations as were recruited. One of the reasons for this was the inability of many economic units to pay recruits; another was that the demand for labor, particularly skilled labor, exceeded the supply by such a wide margin, that local authorities were loathe to release workers for service elsewhere or turn over absentees to the punitive authorities. One estimate for October 1920 put the shortage of skilled workers in industry and transport at 160,000.[68]

Attempts to provide high-priority factories with necessary resources by designating them with "shock" (*udarnyi*) status and guaranteeing their workers an "iron-clad" food ration above what other workers received, enjoyed short-lived success. For, as each factory administration pleaded its special case, the status became devalued, and efforts to undo one bottleneck reproduced shortages elsewhere.[69] Similarly, the resort to in-kind bonus payments to workers who overfulfilled their monthly work program – an elaboration of the piece-rate system of wages that the trade unions applied to a steadily increasing number of workers – foundered because much of the special fund of goods set aside for rewarding such workers found its way into the regular pay of workers irrespective of output.

Was it then the case that the deep reservoir of support that the Bolsheviks had received from workers in 1917 was drained by 1920–1? Had the Soviet regime, in winning the civil war, lost the proletariat? It would seem so. Yet, the mobilization and even militarization of labor was not necessarily experienced as oppression by all those who were conscripted. *Trudovaia povinnost'* may have meant compulsory labor for some, but the alternative translation, labor duty or service, may be closer to the way it was understood by others. And then there was the phenomenon of the *subbotniki*, specially designated days during which urban residents performed labor-intensive tasks such as loading and unloading, repairing buildings and roads, and removing rubbish without direct compensation. What indeed impelled hundreds of thousands of people to donate their labor to the republic? As argued by William Chase, there was no single factor, but rather a combination of "voluntarism, mobilisation and coercion," the balance of which depended on whether participants were party members, Red Army soldiers or non-party civilians, whether subbotniki coincided with military campaigns against the Whites and the Polish Army, and whether the tasks performed had a direct bearing on the well-being and even survival of participants. The requirement that party members participate twice a month and the assignment of garrisoned soldiers suggest at the very least that the authorities were unwilling to count on voluntaristic impulses and that for many participants subbotniki were hardly festivals of labor. Then again, at least in Moscow, participation of party members was far from universal and there is no evidence that direct coercion was exercised against non-party civilians.[70]

It is thus possible that for many urban residents the subbotniki did represent a way of expressing their support for the revolution. But what support for the revolution meant is open to question. Did it mean an identification with the Bolshevism of 1917 or the proletarian dictatorship of 1920–1? Did it mean opposition to the enemy armies besieging the Soviet republic or the other enemies – hunger and cold – that were even closer and more threatening? These questions are not merely of retrospective academic interest. For the disposition of the working masses – that is, both what was left of the proletariat in the cities and the peasants in the villages – played a not inconsiderable role in the rethinking that was taking place at the highest levels of power.

The awkward peasants

The relationship between the urban-based "proletarian" revolution of 1917 and the simultaneously unfolding agrarian revolution was complex and contradictory. On the one hand, each clearly fueled the other. As urban society polarized along class lines, central political authority was weakened, thereby opening up unprecedented opportunities for peasants to avoid fulfilling their tax and military recruitment responsibilities and to lay siege to the property of large landowners and the state. Correspondingly, the progressive disappearance of external authority in the villages and the breakdown of exchange relations between town and country exacerbated shortages of food and other basic necessities in the towns, sharpening the urban class struggle and the hostility of the lower social orders towards the Provisional Government. On the other hand, the revolutionary agendas of peasants and workers only coincided temporarily and in the years after 1917 the differences would become ever sharper.

This was because the revolutionary clocks in the cities and the villages ran according to different schedules. If, as Trotsky had asserted, the "law of combined and uneven development" made revolutionary upheaval in Russia inevitable, the characters of the urban and rural revolutions were fundamentally different. Despite the inroads that capitalism had made in the countryside, despite the social engineering that the tsarist government had undertaken in the form of the Stolypin reforms, and despite the educational and cultural work promoted by the zemstvos, the agrarian revolution was essentially animated by grievances left over from 1861, that is, from the emancipation of the serfs. Class differentiation in the countryside had proceeded in the decades after 1861 (although not nearly to the extent or even in the manner assumed by Lenin and other Russian Marxists); the repartitional commune of Central Russia did show signs of withering; and one can even discern mounting tensions within the traditional patriarchal peasant household. Yet, none of these trends had reached the stage where it could displace or supersede the peasants' aspirations for more land and the freedom (*volia*) to reap its fruits.

From a Marxist perspective, these aspirations were progressive insofar as they helped to rid Russia of large noble estates and other "feudal" remnants. But this was only the first stage after which, it was assumed, class antagonisms among the peasantry would come to the fore. A little over six months after the October Revolution, even as the clouds of civil war between Reds and Whites were darkening the horizon, the Bolsheviks were urging the poor and "working peasants" to launch a second revolution, this time against the kulaks.[71]

But we are getting ahead of ourselves. The initial policy of the Soviet state was to legitimize the seizure of landlords' property and promote the equal distribution of land among those who worked on it. This policy, announced in the Decree on Land of 26 October/8 November

1917, was elaborated in the law "On the Socialization of the Land" of 19 February 1918.[72] Both acts were loosely based on the agrarian program of the Socialist Revolutionary Party and the "Socialization" was jointly conceived by the Bolsheviks and their coalition partners, the Left SRs. Although providing for the retention of some state land and the best-run estates for the establishment of communes and model state farms, there was no getting around the fact that the Socialization Law was a surrender to the peasants, who were largely left to implement it as they saw fit. As Rosa Luxemburg noted from abroad, it was not, therefore, a socialist measure. "It even cuts off the way to such measures; it piles up insurmountable obstacles to the socialist transformation of agrarian relations . . . creat[ing] a new powerful layer of popular enemies of socialism in the countryside, enemies whose resistance will be much more dangerous and stubborn than that of noble large landowners."[73]

Lenin did not necessarily disagree, but ever since the summer of 1917 he had become convinced that to defy the peasants on this question would be tantamount to political suicide. Speaking in favor of the law, he asserted that "As a democratic government, we cannot circumvent the decisions of the masses, even if we disagree with them . . . Let the peasants themselves solve all the problems; let them themselves arrange their life." And so they did, largely via assemblies (skhody) of the village communes and volost' soviets. In some places, particularly the non-Black Soil region in the north, land was distributed on the basis of "toilers"; in others according to the number of "eaters" in each family; in most places, only confiscated lands were partitioned; but there were also instances of all land being pooled and redivided, a method known in rural Russia as a "black repartition." This was especially the case where villages were inundated with returning *otkhodniki* (seasonal laborers), more permanent urban residents who nonetheless still retained ties with the village, and peasant soldiers all claiming their share of the land. Finally, "in virtually all areas of the country those peasants who had separated from the community before 1917 lost some or all of their land," this being the price they paid for the relative security of rejoining the commune.[74]

The agrarian revolution, which added some 150 million desiatina to the pool of peasant land, thus had several consequences of immense significance for peasant–state relations as well as for relations among peasants. First, it eliminated large landed property from the Russian countryside, even if in isolated places some former landlords managed to hold onto portions of their former estates and/or were included in the redistributions. This was a major gain to the peasants – more so in the Black Soil region where renting and share-cropping on estate land were more prominent than in the north where estates were few and far between – and was to prove decisive in how peasants interpreted and responded to the struggle between Reds and Whites.

Second, the revolution caused a leveling-down among peasants. As a result of the redivision of land, the number of landless peasant households (which for statistical purposes often included schoolteachers, artisans and other non-cultivators) dropped from 15.9 percent of all households in 1917 to 8.1 percent by 1920. But, at the same time, peasant households that had separated from the commune thanks to the Stolypin reforms or had supplemented their allotments by purchasing additional land engaged in a high rate of partitioning (partly to escape confiscations) and thus experienced a significant reduction in their holdings of both land and livestock. This, coupled with the absorption of part of the urban population and the return of ex-servicemen, led to a substantial increase in the total number of households and an aggregate shift downwards in average sown area and number of horses per household. In short, the peasantry became more homogeneous in socio-economic circumstances if not outlook as a result of the revolution.[75]

Finally, the agrarian revolution strengthened the village commune and in many areas revived its repartitional functions. This was an ironic if understandable outcome. It signified that a process of "traditionalization" had occurred in peasant life, a process that was integral to what Moshe Lewin has called the "'archaization' of the socio-economic system." Reverting to a form of self-government (*samoupravlenie*) that was as old as serfdom and relying on methods of production that were likewise centuries old, the peasantry retreated from urban society and its twentieth-century ways and thereby was able to survive the depredations of the civil war better than any other social class. Indeed, it survived not merely as a class but as "a social system with its own specific culture . . . a world in its own right . . . a dense social environment, reacting to every external influence like a sieve or a filter."[76] It was this very denseness that made the peasantry so awkward, so impenetrable to the designs of "intruders," and for most peasants, both Reds and Whites were intruders.

Rural autarchy posed a great threat to the towns. Lenin may have assumed that in return for land the peasants would hand over their grain, but that is not how the peasants necessarily viewed the matter. "I am reluctant to speak of the crude taunting, the vengeful mockery with which the village greeted the hungry people of the town," wrote Maxim Gorky in a bitter diatribe against the "semi-savage people" of the countryside. Exercising a monopoly over food production and having little incentive to market their surpluses, the peasants found themselves in the relatively advantageous position of needing the towns far less than the towns needed them. What the peasants couldn't procure from the towns in the form of mass-produced goods they often could obtain from cottage industry. This form of production, which has yet to receive the attention it deserves from historians, assumed increasing import-ance during the civil war thanks to the near collapse of large-scale industry and the return of workers to the countryside where they applied their skills. The towns, on the other hand, had no other recourse to obtaining food, foreign imports being almost non-existent and market gardens (*ogorodniki*) supplying only a small fraction of what was needed.[77]

What then was to be done to feed the cities and staunch the hemorrhaging or the urban population that already was in evidence in 1917. A variety of methods were tried. Trainloads of industrial goods were amassed (thereby depriving the cities of these items) for shipment to grain-producing areas; a progressive food-supply tax was decreed with the aim of soaking up surpluses; arrests of speculators and so-called "bagmen" (individuals who brought sacks of grain to towns for barter or monetary exchange) occurred on the railways, and armed detachments were dispatched to the villages to conduct searches of storehouses. But all these measures failed. The goods trains rarely reached their intended destinations; the food tax remained a dead letter partly because of the opposition of Left SRs and partly because there was no way of assessing what was owed; punitive actions encountered resistance and circumvention. Over and above these difficulties, state agencies ranging from Narkomprod to regional soviets and even indi-vidual factors were competing with each other in trying to obtain food supplies and thus willy nilly driving up prices. The loss of sizeable grain-growing areas as a result of the Brest–Litovsk Treaty made the situation even worse.

At this juncture, in May 1918, the regime declared its "food supply dictatorship," often considered the foundation of "War Communist" agricultural policy. According to the VTsIK decree announcing this dictatorship, Narkomprod was vested with extraordinary powers to extract surplus stocks from the rich peasants and kulaks, if possible via obligatory exchanges at fixed prices, and if not, then by force. Narkomprod was to carry out its mandate through two mutually reinforcing agencies – food supply detachments and the committees of poor peasants (*kombedy*). The former, said by Lenin to consist of *"iron detachments* of the conscious proletariat" would "go to the 'people'" as mentors "in making the revolution the real antechamber of socialism." The latter were to serve as the "alert eyes" (in the phrase of A. D. Tsiurupa, Commissar of Agriculture) of the food supply apparatus, replacing the unreliable local soviets in food detection and collection. Together, the two organs would catalyze a second "October," a social-ist revolution in the countryside.[78]

The food supply dictatorship was intended to make the state the sole distributor of grain. To what extent this quintessentially "War Communist" policy was dictated by circumstances or was ideologically driven is difficult to unravel. As Lars Lih has pointed out, Imperial Germany adopted a grain monopoly during the First World War and one of the first actions of the Provisional Government in Russia was to decree a state monopoly in grain. In this sense, he argues, the Bolsheviks' food-supply dictatorship was entirely compatible with Lenin's notion of state capitalism, merely extending or giving "teeth" to a policy previously based on voluntary compliance. On the other hand, the village-splitting tactics inherent in the resort to the kombedy, the class-struggle motif in which they were characterized, and the under-lying assumption that the proletarianized cities knew what was best for the predominantly "petty bourgeois" countryside originated in the ideological arsenal of Bolshevism.[79]

Whatever the inspiration, the consensus among western scholars is that the kombedy were miserable failures and that no second revol-ution occurred in the countryside. There are many reasons why this was so. Of the 122,000 kombedy said to exist by November 1918, most were in the consuming (primarily northern) provinces where local surpluses were scarce.[80] As for peasants in the producing provinces, however sharp the grievances felt by poor peasants toward their wealthier neighbors – and they had been partially mitigated by the redistribution of the land – this was a family affair (in some cases quite literally so), a matter to be sorted out among fellow villagers. Where surpluses were extracted, it was often the middle peasants who suffered. For, as Lenin himself admitted, it was no easy task for agitators to distinguish between middle and rich peasants, or rich peasants and kulaks. Nor did the agitators from the food detachments always behave in a manner consistent with their high calling as communists. Ostensibly performing a state service, many recruits simply took what they felt they were entitled to, repeating the old

Muscovite practice of feeding off the land (*kormlenie*). Worst of all, perhaps, rather than risk expropriation, many peasant households sub-divided, left in the ground what they didn't need for their own subsistence and illicit distilling and prepared to cut back on sowing.[81]

As the peasantry retreated further into its village shell, the central authorities gave up on the kombedy (except in Ukraine where they were only introduced in 1919 and persisted into the 1920s), though not the poor peasants. They were now encouraged to form agricultural associations (*artels*), communes (*kommuny*, not to be confused with the traditional village commune or *mir*) and other forms of collectivized agriculture. As for food procurement, the state opted for the policy of *razverstka* ("quota assessment"), a method that had been pioneered by the last tsarist minister of agriculture, A. A. Rittikh, as an alternative to state monopolization. Less "socialist" than the preceding policy, razverstka was also less administratively demanding. Instead of attempting to determine the peasants' needs and claiming the rest for the state, razverstka merely required the state to calculate its needs, exchanging industrial goods for grain to achieve the required amount and leaving the residual to the peasants.[82]

Concomitantly, the Bolsheviks sought to establish an alliance with rather than "neutralize" the "middle peasants." The justification for this shift comprised most of Lenin's remarks on the agrarian question to the party's Eighth Congress. The earlier policies, including the kombedy, had been dictated by circumstances ("We had to hurry . . . to make the most desperate efforts"). But their time had passed. "You cannot create anything here by coercion. *Coercion applied to the middle peasants would cause untold harm.*" And again, "Nothing is more stupid than the very idea of applying coercion in economic relations with the middle peasant."[83]

This policy of moderation, coming in the midst of the civil war, inevitably raises the question of whether it anticipated the New Economic Policy. Carr dismisses this notion as "misleading," but in the same paragraph acknowledges that the "compromise . . . was a fore-taste of the far wider operation undertaken in March 1921." In any case, the distinction between a War Communist Lenin and a NEP Lenin, posited by Robert Tucker among others, would seem to be an over-simplification, at least as far as his thinking about the peasants was concerned.[84]

But then, Lenin was not in the countryside helping to identify middle peasants and trying to convince them that in the absence of sufficient industrial goods to exchange for grain, they should part with the latter as a "loan." For their part, the peasants preferred to reduce sowings, rely on local exchanges or sell their surpluses on the black market. It was this basic contradiction that transformed razverstka into forced requisitioning and explains why razverstka was popularly identified with state coercion and retrospectively considered as a prime example of War Communist extremism.

Like much else, accurate statistics were a casualty of the time. But it is safe to conclude that the cumulative effects of the war for grain were catastrophic for agriculture. Between 1917 and 1920, the amount of sown area for food grains dropped by some 20 percent. Yields were off as well, particularly in the grain surplus areas, though by exactly how much is difficult to say, since it is believed that in 1920, the peasants concealed from state authorities as much as one-third of their grain harvest. Counting on grain deliveries of 260 million puds for 1918–19, the state managed to collect a mere 108 million, or 41.5 percent of its target. The following year collections increased substantially to 212 million puds (66 percent of the target), but was of poorer quality. Moreover, this was over a larger area (including Siberia), and, as the ratio of exchange between grain and manufactured goods was even less favorable to the peasants than previously, inevitably involved more force.[85]

By 1920, what Deutscher refers to as the "vicious circle of war communism" reached its fullest extent. Unable to supply enough goods to the peasants or food to the cities, the state had to tolerate, if not itself rely on, private trade. But private trade only siphoned off goods that otherwise would have gone toward collective commodity exchange and from the communist point of view represented the ultimate capitulation to petty bourgeois anarchy and proletarian demoralization. One possible solution, forwarded by Trotsky to the party's Central Committee in February 1920, was to replace razverstka with a tax in kind and permit peasants to consume or sell to the state what remained. The proposal was rejected, however, on the grounds that the problem lay not so much with the principle of razverstka as with its irresolute application. The solution, strongly defended at the Second Food Conference in June, was to beef up the food supply apparatus and crack down on the illegal market.[86] But the more this solution was applied, the more enemies the state made. This was particularly the case in the countryside, where few could have been deceived by Kalinin's characterization of razverstka as "an educational measure" that was preparing the peasants for participation in running the government. Peasant–state relations had indeed "turned full circle."[87]

Once the Whites and Polish invaders had been cleared from Soviet territory, the major confrontation in the civil war shifted to that between the Reds and the "Greens." Usually characterized in Soviet historiography as "bandits," or kulak- and SR-led counterrevolution-aries, the Greens were irregular bands of peasant insurgents, most of whom had seen service in the tsarist army and/or deserted from the Red or White camps.[88] The Greens' primary aim was to rid their districts of all officials, both *zolotopogonniki* (gold-epaulettes, meaning White officers), and "commissars" (a generic term for representatives of soviet power that included local communists, food collectors, and Chekists), as well as city influences, which frequently meant the Jews. Their characteristic military action was raiding railway depots, local military training units, and state farms, though occasionally they seized and briefly held uezd towns. Their punishment of captives took such ancient and brutal forms as live burial and disembowelment.

The size of the Green armies and the degree of local support fluctuated from one region to another and over time. They were few and far between in the northern "consuming" provinces where visits by food detachments were a rarity, but more numerous in the south and east. In 1919, their greatest strength was in Ukraine, homeland of the most notorious of Green leaders, ataman Grigor'ev, and the most inter-esting, Nestor Makhno. A year later, it was in the central Black Earth region, along the Volga and in western Siberia, that is, the traditional grain surplus areas. But after the requisitions of the previous year, and a particularly poor harvest, there was little or no surplus to be had. In the late summer, full-scale insurrection erupted in Tambov province where as many as 50,000 insurgents were led by a former left-SR peasant, A. S. Antonov. By January 1921, much of Omsk province in western Siberia was in the hands of peasant insurrectionaries. These and many other widely scattered rebellions lasted well into 1921. They are particularly graphic evidence that the peasant had ceased to be merely awkward for the state and instead, as was to be the case again during forced collectivization, had become its main antagonist.[89] In between, during the NEP period, "these two profoundly different forces faced each other nationally in an uneasy truce."[90]

This analysis, which has focused on the burning issues of land and bread, needs to be supplemented with a consideration of other levels of peasant–state relations. It is by dealing with these other levels that we can begin to appreciate the role that generational, gender, and religious divisions among the peasants played in modifying or intensifying their suspiciousness of state "intruders." Reference has already been made to the predominantly peasant nature of the Red Army and the opportunities it offered for consolidating the worker–peasant alliance. But recruiting and relying on peasant soldiers also had its difficulties and dangers. Desertion, or more commonly, failure to turn up at the recruiting station, was a serious problem. Official army statistics record over 1.7 million "deserters" for 1919 alone. No less importantly, the preponderance of peasants in the ranks weighed on the High Command, affecting its decisions about organizational structure, the content of political education, and even operational strategy. Peasant soldiers simply could not be trusted. Fighting the Whites and the Poles was one thing; but when it came to combatting peasant insurgency in 1920–1, recourse was had to units consisting exclusively of party members or the Cheka. Indeed, as late as 1925, Mikhail Frunze, Trotsky's successor as Commissar of War, considered the army "not suitable for fighting a war" because "our soldier is not quite the one we want to have."[91]

But there was one crucial respect in which the army did have a major influence on the peasants who served in it as well as their fellow villagers. This was to break or at least strain the patriarchal hold that the household elders exercised over their sons. Returning from military service, most peasant youths were better educated, more technically skilled and world-wise than their fathers. This, of course, was likely to have been the case under the Tsars. But advances in rural schooling during the last decade of imperial Russia, exposure to the revolutionary vocabulary and culture of Bolshevism and lack of employment opportunities in the towns all exacerbated tensions within the peasant family.

While the elders undoubtedly still held sway in communal assemblies, there was now a new institution, namely the soviet, where younger peasants could make their mark. Of course, not all demobilized soldiers were inclined toward soviet power. But among them were literally tens of thousands who had been recruited into the party or its youth organization, the Komsomol, during their military service and who represented a cohort of potential cadres for the regime. Writing on the rural soviet elections of 1919 in the Middle Volga region, Orlando Figes has observed that "The correlation between Bolshevism and youth was far stronger than the correlation between any social factor and the age structure of the soviets," and concluded that it was peasants aged between 25 and 35, and especially those "who had been taken outside the village by military service, who took over the reins of Soviet power in the countryside after 1919." That power increasingly resided in the volost executive committees (*volispolkomy*) rather than the volost congresses or the village soviets and their executive committees. And it was in the volispolkomy, often elected with Red Army and party agitator "assistance," that the proportion of Bolsheviks and youths was highest.[92]

Thus, to the extent that Bolshevism was able to penetrate the countryside, it did so via peasant (male) youths for whom the party represented a means to reverse the patriarchal order. That they were not averse to throwing their weight around should not be surprising. For these ex-soldiers, described by Lenin as "jaded people accustomed to war as to a trade," the revolution meant a kind of social dominance (vlast') that further discredited soviet power in the eyes of their elders.[93]

Another attempted reversal of the old order in the villages was the Bolsheviks' efforts to organize and empower landless laborers and poor peasants. Indeed, to the extent that poor peasants were encouraged to stand in soviet elections after the phasing out of the kombedy, the village soviets seem to have lost what legitimacy they previously had among their more well-to-do neighbors. The same could be said for large-scale collective farms which relied heavily for recruits on the village poor. Having only just become masters (khoziaine) of their property, household elders were usually not keen to amalgamate it with other families in the name of an experiment fostered by an urban-based government.

As daunting as was the task of overcoming rural isolation and backwardness, as suspicious as were most peasants of outside initiatives, the commitment of the Bolsheviks to extend their secular world view to the villages can hardly be exaggerated. Even as they recognized that a vast gulf of experience separated the peasantry from the urbanized proletariat (and still more, the intelligentsia), the party devoted no little effort to bridge the gap via the written word. Hence, the establishment of primary schools for village youth, a mass adult literacy campaign organized around literacy schools (likpunkty), libraries, village reading rooms (izby-chital'ni) and where the means were lacking for the latter, Red Corners.

In strictly numerical terms, the results of these efforts were impressive. By 1921, the villages of European Russia contained some 70,000 primary schools, 30,000 likpunkty, 13,532 libraries, and nearly 20,000 reading rooms. But what impact they had on village life is not so clear. Again, it would seem that youths were less resistant than their elders. Certainly the majority of rural teachers and izbachi (directors of the reading rooms) were young. We also know from a 1920 survey that the vast majority of literate peasants did not avail themselves of the libraries or reading rooms. In the twenty-seven provinces of European

Russia, an average of only 12 percent subscribed to libraries, while the highest percentage of subscribers to the reading rooms was 16.6 percent in Kaluga. Part of the problem was a shortage of competent personnel and means to pay them, but the dearth of reading matter that would appeal to peasant tastes was perhaps even more serious. As late as the mid-1920s, it was reported that the most popular activities associated with the reading rooms did not revolve around reading but rather singing, acting and sewing.[94]

In this context one wonders about peasant women, those "hired laborers within their own households." Did they take to the newly imported culture? Much more work needs to be done on the impact of the revolution on gender relations in the countryside before any definitive answer can be given. But it would appear that with some exceptions, Bolshevism represented more of a threat than an attraction for peasant women. The reasons for this are not hard to fathom. Generally less familiar with urban ways than their husbands, brothers, or sons, peasant women remained more firmly rooted in the domestic rather than the public sphere. And, although their lot was not a happy one, they had developed strategies for coping, especially folk wisdom and, of course, religious observance. Both were frowned upon by the intrepid Bolshevik agitators who, at considerable personal risk, sought to bring enlightenment to the villages. Alternative living arrangements such as the kommuny do not seem to have appreciably reduced women's burdens and, like their Owenite predecessors, inspired all sorts of fearful rumors.[95]

Nevertheless, some women did venture across the formidable cultural chasm. Defying male mockery and prohibitions, they attended literacy classes, voted in soviet elections, served in rural soviet administration, and participated in meetings and excursions to the towns sponsored by Zhenotdel, the Women's Section of the Party. Who these women were is not entirely clear, but Red Army wives and widows, often single householders, appear to have been the most venturesome.

Finally, religion was a powerful force in the villages, although the extent to which it was successfully invoked by the Whites against the atheistic or "New Communists" can easily be exaggerated. The fact is that very few in either the Red or White camp understood how religion, as distinct from the institution of the Orthodox Church, worked among the Russian peasantry, and scholars are only now beginning to improve upon them. Suffice it to say here that popular religion was intricately bound up with the peasants' material existence and far from being a bedrock of unchanging "tradition," was sufficiently porous to absorb outside influences. The dualistic quality of the peasants' religion – semi-Christian, semi-pagan – has been noted by many commentators. But even this notion can be misleading, for while in some respects the two faiths existed side-by-side (or in physical terms, in opposite corners of the peasant hut), in others they intermingled to produce a syncretic blend.[96]

In time, some of the rituals and symbols of communism would be added to this blend. Indeed, already during the civil war, several religious sectarian movements (Dukhobors, New Israelites, Free Christians, Spiritual Christians) declared themselves "communist," and on the basis of strict egalitarian principles and abstention from alcohol, organized collectives and communes that exhibited high rates of productivity. In subsequent years, as religious sectarianism flourished, the upholders of militant atheism would come to regard it as the most pernicious current, and a Soviet *Kulturkampf* ensued. But in the desperate circumstances of 1920–1, party officials, including Lenin, viewed with a kind of bemused gratitude the willingness of these communities to recognize Soviet power.[97] For their own part, the peasants in such communities did not have much difficulty in apprehending the revolutionary upheavals in familiar idioms.

The intelligentsia and significant "others"

The "intelligentsia" is a notoriously slippery term. In Russian history alone, it has lent itself to numerous definitions, some more narrowly conceived and chronologically specific than others, some couched in political terms, others denoting a cultural orientation, and still others expressing sociological relationships. What Gramsci called "'traditional' intellectuals," that is, ecclesiastics, scholars, administrators, and other literates long existed as special castes or in the interstices of the social order. The intelligentsia, by contrast, is a nineteenth-century phenomenon that was carried over into the twentieth. It was the product of "a parting of ways" among the educated elite, in fact a dual parting – the detachment of a segment of the educated elite from the state, and that segment's anomalous position *vis-à-vis* the estate (*soslovie*) system.[98]

The importance of the radical intelligentsia was out of all proportion to its numbers, which were always small. By articulating alternative visions of the social and political order, it cast itself in the role of vanguard of society or the people (*narod*). But lacking an organic connection to any particular social group, it was a vanguard without a following. The peasantry, the object of the Populists' attention, proved none too receptive, while the urban social classes were only weakly formed. Gradually, however, space was opened up within both the political system and urban society for the intelligentsia, which correspondingly became "organicized" and professionalized. The zemstvos attracted a "third element" consisting of teachers, agronomists, statisticians, and medical personnel, the modernized court system was a boon to the legal profession, the arts flourished under the patronage of railway magnates and merchants, and, with the beginning of industrialization in the 1890s, polytechnics trained an incipient technical intelligentsia.

All this may be viewed as part of the growth of civil society in late tsarist Russia. But, constantly hemmed in by the autocracy and lacking a strong private entrepreneurial class, it was a civil society that remained stunted and insecure. Neither the Duma nor other concessions wrested from the Tsar in 1905 provided the means for overcoming this insecurity, as the state set about (and partially succeeded in) reclaiming some of the ground it had lost. When tsarism was overthrown in 1917, the previously established civil institutions proved inadequate to the task of either restoring order or creating a new one. That opportunity fell to the Bolsheviks, whose leading cadres had trained themselves as professional revolutionaries – yet another, if deviant, example of the professionalization of the intelligentsia.

What, then, did the revolution bequeath to the intelligentsia? To answer this question, we need to successively consider the three spheres of intellectual activity – political, cultural, and scientific-technical – in which the pre-revolutionary intelligentsia distinguished itself. While by no means comprehensive, this survey may be taken as representative of what was generally a complex, often tortured relationship.

The fate of the non-Bolshevik political intelligentsia was intricately bound up with that of the political parties. The Kadets (Constitutional Democrats), who enjoyed the largest intelligentsia following, constituted the thin political infrastructure of the White governments. As such, P. N. Miliukov and other leading Kadet politicians hoped to enhance the international respectability of the anti-Bolshevik counter-revolution. However, neither the Germans in 1918 nor the Allied powers thereafter were willing to commit themselves to full-scale armed intervention. Beset by internal wrangling as well as conflict with the White generals, the Kadet politicians eventually removed themselves from Russian soil and took up residence in Paris and other

European centers of Russian emigration. Meeting in cafes where they occupied "the still warm seats vacated by the Bolsheviks," they tried to make sense of the catastrophe that had befallen them. Such a reckoning inevitably involved recriminatory accusations, but also some astute analysis of why the intelligentsia had failed the narod, or alternatively, why the narod had failed the intelligentsia. For better or for worse, this community of *émigrés* laid the intellectual foundations for western scholarship on Russian history and served as mentors for the first generation of sovietologists.[99]

The Right SRs followed a similar trajectory. The regional governments in which they participated in 1918 depended for military support on legions of Czech prisoners-of-war, contingents of Allied forces that had landed at Arkhangelsk, an insurgent peasant and worker army based in Izhevsk, and Admiral Kolchak's White Army. The problem was that the agenda of these forces differed from that of the civilian politicians as well as from each other. In November 1918, the SR-dominated Directory based at Omsk was overthrown by Kolchak and for all intents and purposes, the Right SRs were finished as a political movement. Forced into emigration, such leading SR politicians as N. D. Avksentiev and V. Zenzinov urged the Allies to step up the interventionary campaign, but to no avail.[100]

The fate of the non-Bolshevik left (primarily the Mensheviks and Left SRs) was more complex if only because they claimed the same constituency as the Bolsheviks, that is, the "toiling masses." Not long after withdrawing from the government coalition over the signing of the Brest Litovsk Treaty, the Left SRs reverted to conspiratorial activity, carrying out a number of assassinations and organizing coups in several provincial capitals. The Soviet Government responded in kind. It ruthlessly suppressed the provincial insurrections, arrested most of the Left SR delegates to the Fifth All-Russian Congress of Soviets, executed those who had used their positions in the Cheka to arrange the assassination of the German Ambassador and the head of the Cheka in Petrograd, and closed down several SR newspapers.

The Mensheviks meanwhile fractured over how to respond to what all generally considered Bolshevik authoritarianism. The splits more or less followed the pattern of divisions during the world war: "defensists" such as A. N. Potresov were most adamant in denouncing the Soviet regime and calling on workers to rise up and overthrow it; Iulii Martov and other "internationalists" on the Central Committee temporized their criticisms of the Bolsheviks in lieu of what they perceived as the common enemy.[101]

The easing of Bolshevik repression in early 1919 appeared to vindicate Martov's position as well as the more conciliatory faction within the Left SR camp. After VTsIK revoked its decree of the previous June that effectively had outlawed both parties, their newspapers were briefly permitted to appear, and their delegates were able to take part in the soviets, albeit under rather severe constraints. It has been suggested that this brief "political thaw" was the product of the ascendance of Bolshevik "moderates" such as Kamenev and Osinskii who simultaneously launched a campaign to limit the arbitrary power of the Cheka and strengthen the soviets.[102] When, however, the Mensheviks took advantage of the situation to call for free trade, the right to strike, and an end to the civil war, the "policemen" within the party reasserted their power.

Such an explanation is at least plausible but needs to be placed within the broader context of revolutionary politics. Referring to the Reign of Terror during the French Revolution, Robert Darnton has written that "[a]fter the religious schism of 1791 and the war of 1792, any opposition could be made to look like treason, and no consensus could be reached on the principles of politics."[103] Like the Jacobins of those years, the Bolsheviks were sailing in uncharted waters. In such circumstances, those who argued that a firm hand was needed on the rudder usually held sway. But how the crew and passengers were to be treated was the source of constant debate and adjustment.

As material conditions worsened, it became all too easy to construe opposition as treason and to make Menshevism a convenient scapegoat for unrest among workers. From worker protests to petty bourgeois infiltration of the working class to SR and Menshevik agitation – such was the syllogistic chain constructed by Lenin and other Bolshevik leaders. From Menshevik cavilling to SR audacity to "Kolchakia" – this was another chain by which the non-Bolshevik socialist intelligentsia was linked to counterrevolution and foreign intervention. "The experience of Kolchakia is a most valuable experience for us," Lenin wrote in July 1919.

It shows us on a small scale what is going on all over the world . . . We have become infinitely strong because millions of people have realized what Kolchak is . . . They called for the Socialist-Revolutionaries and put them in power but from their having placed the Socialist-Revolutionaries and Mensheviks in power they got the old Russian monarchy, the old Russian policeman, who introduced incredible lawlessness into the country together with the "democracy."[104]

Either the proletarian dictatorship or the restoration of capitalism in Russia; either the spread of the proletarian revolution to Europe or imperialist barbarism. There was no third way.

"Back to bourgeois democracy and nothing more," was the way Lenin characterized Martov's declaration to the Seventh Congress of Soviets in December 1919. Since bourgeois democracy had been shown to lead to Kolchak and foreign intervention, it was an illusion and a dangerous one at that. Thus, "when we hear such declarations, coming from people who profess sympathy with us, we say to ourselves, 'Yes, the terror and the Cheka are absolutely indispensable.'"[105]

This was no mere idle threat. Yet, both Mensheviks and Left SRs continued to participate in the soviets, had a tenacious following in the trade unions and sent delegates to the next all-Russian soviet congress. The end of these parties' existence in Soviet Russia came in early 1921 not because of anything that they did, but rather because of Bolshevik fears of what they could do if given the opportunity. Widely spread strikes among workers, peasant insurrections and the Kronstadt rebellion provided ample evidence of popular disenchantment with the Bolshevik dictatorship and the dictatorship of food supply. Moreover, the party itself was riven by dissent from within in the form of the Workers' Opposition. With the banning of factions at the Tenth Party Congress, "the toleration of dissentient minorities outside the party became all the more anomalous."[106] Just as the party was embarking on a policy designed to loosen the reins of economic control, it was tightening the political reins.

Without any formal decree, the Soviet government rounded up the leading figures of the opposition parties and imprisoned them. Some, including leading Socialist Revolutionaries, were eventually put on trial and convicted of "terroristic" acts for which they received (commuted) death sentences and long terms of imprisonment. Some were permitted to emigrate, others were released after promising to abandon all political activities, while still others were sent into internal exile. In this fashion, a political intelligentsia outside the Communist Party ceased to exist in Soviet Russia. As E. H. Carr has noted, "the party had drawn into itself the whole political life of the country. Its internal affairs were henceforth the political history of the nation."[107]

The annihilation of the non-Bolshevik political intelligentsia three years after the October Revolution was in striking contrast to the fate of intellectuals whose public activity was primarily outside the political sphere. Of course, the arts and sciences were not exempt from politics, but this was politics of a different sort, not war which Lenin (parroting

Clausewitz) defined as "the continuation of the politics of revolution
... the epitome of politics," but the politics of negotiation, compromise
and alliance-building.[108] While most intellectuals were openly hostile to
the Bolsheviks' seizure of power, viewing it in apocalyptic terms, some
within the literary and artistic communities took a broader and more
favorable view. They reveled in the excitement of a new world being
born amidst the destruction of the old, in the potential energy of the
masses becoming kinetic, in Asiatic Russia turning its back on Europe
and in proletarian culture supplanting that of the bourgeoisie. The
revolution thus breathed new life into a variety of artistic and literary
movements, from the Scythians to the Futurists, and inspired the belief
that the boundary between art and life could at last be transcended.

The subsequent relationship between the cultural intelligentsia and
the new regime has been well documented. It is a story of fierce
competition among different movements for the right to officially
represent the new revolutionary culture (and perhaps more importantly, to be subsidized by the state); of the Commissariat of Enlightenment (Narkompros) seeking to channel the enthusiasm of writers and
artists into practical work (teaching, the preservation of historical
artifacts, the administration of cultural activities, participation in
festivals, etc.) and avoid squandering its meager budget; and of the
party leadership becoming increasingly impatient with Narkompros'
failure to exercise effective control over the revolution's erstwhile
supporters – to say nothing of its detractors – among the cultural
intelligentsia.

The main competitors for the state's support were the Futurists,
whose most voluble spokesman was the self-proclaimed "soldier poet
of the Revolution," Vladimir Maiakovskii, and the Proletkultists,
advocates of the dictatorship of the proletariat in the cultural sphere.
While both movements stood for a decisive break with the past, and
while several prominent Futurists participated in Proletkult activities,
the two movements diverged in a number of important respects.
Futurism was essentially an avant-garde movement confined to the
intelligentsia. Not unlike their Italian counterparts, the Russian
Futurists presupposed the existence of an audience of refined tastes
even as they railed against effeteness and taste.[109] Proletkult, by contrast, was dedicated to actualizing the masses' creativity and invoking
proletarian consciousness to evaluate all works of art. It thus became a
magnet for people from many walks of life, but particularly factory
workers. By 1920 when it was at the peak of its numerical strength,
the movement claimed half a million followers and 84,000 members

organized in 300 local chapters. Yet, with its origins in "the science fiction and Tectology of Bogdanov, the Godbuilding of Gorky and Lunacharsky, and the machine-worship of Gastev," Proletkult was from first to last a movement guided by intellectuals. The fact that attempts to limit non-proletarian influence and promote workers to leadership positions were only marginally successful is strongly suggestive of "the practical and ideological limits to the rapid redistribution of cultural skills and authority during the early Soviet years."[110]

While evoking varying degrees of sympathy and financial support from Narkompros officials, both movements were far too radical and undisciplined for the likes of the party leadership. Lenin's utilitarian attitude towards culture is well known. For him, Soviet Russia needed less revolutionary play-acting, rhetorical bombast and avant-gardism and more attention to mass literacy and material culture. This was what he meant by "cultural revolution," bringing the fruits of "bourgeois culture" to the workers and peasants who were steeped in precapitalist traditions.[111] In the event, on 1 December 1920, the Central Committee issued a statement, apparently drafted by Zinoviev, which strongly condemned Futurism and called for Proletkult to be subordinated to the organs of Narkompros. Shortly thereafter, a Politburo commission under E. A. Litkens drafted a plan for the radical reorganization of Narkompros. Despite receiving Lenin's support, the plan was watered down by bureaucratic trench warfare.[112]

Among the arts, the cinema probably suffered more than any other. This was ironic, given Lenin's well-known assessment of it being the most important art form. None of the 143 theaters operating in Moscow before the world war showed films by the fall of 1921. Literature suffered too, if only because of the acute shortage of paper and the appropriation of much stock by the party press. In 1913, 392,000 tons of paper and cardboard were produced within the Empire; by 1920, Soviet Russia produced only 34,700. Compared to 1913, when 20,000 book titles were published, only 3,260 appeared in 1920. Figures for the following year show that of 4,130 titles, over half were in the social sciences (compared to less than a third in 1912), while *belles-lettres* comprised a mere 308 titles (compared to 7,137 in 1912).[113]

But other art forms flourished, most notably poster art and the theater, both of which pulsed with the life of the revolution. Westerners visiting the new revolutionary meccas of Moscow and Petrograd reported with amazement that workers and soldiers, cold and hungry as they were, filled the theaters, providing an appreciative audience for all manner of dramatic works. Indeed, translating the revolution onto the stage appears to have become something of a popular pastime, with everyone from Proletkult collectives to the Commissar of Enlightenment, A. V. Lunacharskii, trying their hand. Pageants, that most participatory of dramatic forms, took the stage out into the streets, combining elements of buffoonery and solemnity, carnival and high rhetoric to celebrate the "utopia of release and reversal."[114]

Still, we should not underestimate the difficulties of sheer physical survival among the cultural intelligentsia. Rarely has the romantic tradition of the starving artist or writer had so many exemplars, though it was seldom a matter of choice. Rather than facing the vagaries of life in Soviet Russia, many cultural figures with already established international reputations emigrated. Others put their talents at the disposal of one or another Soviet agency, for example, ROSTA – the Russian Telegraphic Agency – under whose auspices D. Moor, V. Deni, Maiakovskii and other graphic artists and writers composed thousands of posters; Glavpolitput', the Commissariat of Transport's political-administration department, which ran the "agittrains"; and the Red Army's Political Administration (PUR), considered to have been "the most successful propaganda agency during the years of fighting." Still others temporarily abandoned their literary or artistic careers to take up other professions, both adventurous and mundane. Few, if any, were able or wished to carry on as before.[115]

Those with academic connections were generally less adaptable. Like other professionals, academics were almost universally hostile to the Bolshevik seizure of power. Many had been associated with the Kadet Party and not a few served in the Provisional Government. But neither their political views, nor their self-professed commitment to pure science (nauka) and the value of education in its own right adequately explain their antipathy to Bolshevism. The fact is that academics had struggled long and hard to establish a measure of autonomy from the petty control of tsarist officials, and were extremely reluctant to sacrifice it in the name of the proletarian dictatorship.[116] In the iconoclastic rhetoric of Proletkult and the programmatic statements of many soviet officials, the professoriate saw its worst fears being realized.

At the same time, the institutions to which they were attached – the Academy of Sciences, universities, polytechnics and other institutes – gave academics considerable collective bargaining power vis-à-vis Soviet authorities. For their part, Bolshevik leaders had no intention of abolishing the "bourgeois" universities and the Academy – though such sentiment existed among rank-and-file members – but rather sought to open them up to the proletarian masses. Towards this end, they attached to the universities "workers' facilities" (*rabfaky*), where students delegated by the trade unions and local soviet and party organizations would spend three or four years before entering the university proper. They also decreed the establishment of Sverdlovsk Communist University which opened in late 1919 as a training school for party and soviet officials, and a Main Committee for Vocational-Technical Education (Glavprofobr) to organize the production of "trained human specialists."[117]

Throughout this period, pitched battles were waged between Narkompros and the governing bodies of institutions of higher learning, the academic councils. The main issue was the extent of the former's jurisdictional power over such institutions. Formally, the autonomy of universities and their faculties were severely circumscribed; in actuality, decrees setting forth such restrictions were routinely ignored. Part of the reason for this was that Narkompros itself was divided between "hard-liners" such as the deputy commissar (and former history professor) M. N. Pokrovskii and relative moderates such as Lunacharskii. Partly it was because Narkompros had no muscle, Pokrovskii's threat to "militarize" the universities notwithstanding.[118] But certainly a major factor then and for some time to come was the Bolsheviks' lack of cadres to replace the "bourgeois" professors. The consensus among the party's leaders appears to have been that it was better to have bourgeois professors (who in time, it was hoped, would become more cooperative) than no professors at all.

In the meantime, a *modus vivendi* was reached between the Scientific-Technical Section (NTO) of Vesenkha and scientists engaged in applied research. Headed by N. P. Gorbunov, a chemical engineer who served as Lenin's personal secretary, NTO financed and supervised the work of hundreds of researchers who were able to "realize a number of projects that they had only dreamed about before 1917."[119] A similar relationship was established between the Commissariat of Health under N. Semashko and the medical profession.

After experiencing acute material hardship in 1918–19, the scientific community became eligible for a special ration, the so-called academic ration. According to S. F. Oldenberg, an Indologist of aristocratic background who served as secretary of the Academy of Sciences, it was only thanks to "the limitless authority of Lenin and the enormous popularity of [Maksim] Gorky" that such a privilege was introduced. By 1921, over 6,000 daily rations were being distributed to scholars and their families in Petrograd. Certainly, it could not have been popular with the hungry

masses. There was also a special relief commission set up at the behest
of Gorky. The commission administered a number of Houses for
Scholars and Scientists (*Doma uchenykh*) which provided working,
eating, and living facilities. Gorky immodestly considered the commission "one of the most successful creations of Soviet power." Still,
James McClelland is undoubtedly correct in asserting that most
academics "suffered severe material deprivation" during the civil
war.[120]

If most academics felt threatened by the Bolshevik take-over of
educational administration, engineers and other specialists employed
in industry were no less alarmed about what the revolution had in store
for them. Active Bolsheviks and even those who had personal ties with
party members were a tiny minority within the technical intelligentsia.
A larger group whose political sympathies lay with the Constitutional
Democrats (Kadets) and the Provisional Government were openly
hostile and many of them fled to White-held territory or emigrated.
Among those who remained, and they were the majority, the view that
Russian science and industry needed to be defended against assault by
the "one-class dictatorship" was strongly represented. Thus, the All-
Russian Union of Engineers (VSI), which according to Bailes, expressed
"an important segment of opinion among politically-conscious representatives of the technical intelligentsia," initially denounced
workers' control and called on its members to boycott any institution in
which workers' organs usurped engineers' functions. But this position,
which paralleled that of the doctors', teachers' and civil servants'
unions, eventually gave way to a more accommodationist line. Part of
the reason for the change had to do with the regime's own attempts to
curb "excesses" by workers against technical personnel and the
dwindling of workers' control as it had been practiced in 1917–18. It
was the more conservatively oriented scientists, such as the renowned
chemist V. N. Ipatieff, who viewed the Bolsheviks as a force of order
amidst the enveloping chaos and who were most willing to work with
them.[121]

The solicitude shown by the Bolshevik leadership and particularly
Lenin toward the technical intelligentsia was largely pragmatic, being
based on the belief that specialists could render valuable assistance in
arresting the disintegration of industry. Beyond this immediate and
immensely important task, Lenin saw science and technology as help-
mates in harnessing Russia's vast, largely untapped natural resources,
educating and disciplining its labor force in the new work culture, and
thereby transforming a backward, "semi-Asiatic" society into one that

was more modern and European. Political indifference and even hostility on the part of the representatives of science and technology were therefore to be tolerated so long as such attitudes did not lead to active collaboration with counterrevolutionary forces. As he reportedly told Lunacharskii "One must spare a great scientist or major specialist in whatever sphere, even if he is reactionary to the nth degree."[122]

The groundwork for cooperation between the regime and the "technostructure" was laid in August 1918 with the creation of Vesenkha's Scientific–Technical Section and the subsequent formation of Scientific Councils within different industries. While the government refused to recognize the right of VSI to represent engineers before the state, space was provided for engineering-technical sections (ITS) within the industrial trade unions. In 1921 these sections amalgamated to form a *de facto* engineers' union, the Inter-Bureau of Engineering Sections (VMBIT). In the meantime, the most highly qualified engineers organized a professional society, the All-Russian Association of Engineers (VAI), to represent their own special interests.

Even not-so-great specialists could potentially contribute to the restoration of production, a fact that was not lost on the trade unions. In 1920 and 1921, the unions of mineworkers and metalworkers besieged the Cheka with requests to release specialists and even foremen so that they could be thrown into the effort to put the mines and factories in working order. At the same time, however, dissident voices were raised within the party against "pandering to the specialists" and there were instances of specialist-baiting – up to and including the murder of engineers – in the Donbass and Urals mines.[123]

Defining itself as a proletarian dictatorship, the Soviet state nonetheless depended heavily on intellectual "cadres" to administer the dictatorship. This paradox, or contradiction, produced much tension within the Communist Party, as one after another oppositional faction, each employing the sobriquet of "Workers'," arose to articulate the frustrations, suspicions and resentments of rank-and-file members and wider circles of proletarians. While by 1920, no more than 10 percent of the party membership consisted of *intelligenty*, they occupied the most critical (*boevoi*) positions within the party apparatus.[124] This, of course, had been the case since 1917 (and, for that matter, since 1903), but the increasingly large role which the apparatus played in party affairs made their presence more strongly felt.

Within the armed forces, as mentioned earlier, carry-overs from the tsarist and Provisional governments were particularly numerous and prominent. This was also the case in economic administration. Many of those who had served in the tsarist government's Special Councils, in leading positions within the War Industries Committees and other public organizations, and in private enterprise found their way onto tsentry and glavki boards. Thus, by 1920, 39 percent of all board members consisted of "bourgeois specialists," and in the factories, where one-man management was rapidly being introduced, over one-third of directors were so classified.[125]

Might we conclude, therefore, that out of the crucible of revolution a new coalition had been forged, one linking the Bolshevik to the technical (and to a lesser extent, the scientific and cultural) intelligentsia? Did the revolutionary dictatorship identified with workers actually amount to "the social paramountcy of the experts, the administrators and the policemen"?[126] This indeed was the case, though with one very important qualification. In Bolshevik Russia, the paramountcy of the experts could not be ramified ideologically. So long as specialists continued to be identified as "bourgeois," their prestige and power, to say nothing of their individual security, rested on weak foundations. It was not only that the party leadership was ambivalent about its coalition partners, but also that rank-and-file elements begrudged being bossed around. As we shall see, the Red–expert alliance remained a strained marriage throughout the 1920s. While Reds openly worried about being deceived about technical matters and about the political loyalty of the experts, the latter, frustrated by political interference from above and harassment from below, flirted with technocratic solutions to their and industry's ills. There thus were ample grounds for divorce or at least trial separation, which was effectuated by the Cultural Revolution of the late 1920s and early 1930s.

If specialists made awkward partners with the Bolshevik intelligentsia, there was another social group whose participation in the revolutionary state was far more obscure but no less important. This was Russia's "lower middle strata," or petty bourgeoisie, a heterogeneous group of "white-collar workers, employees, technical personnel, proto-professionals, and professionals, of the public, private and state sectors." The fact that their contribution to soviet state-building has remained obscure is not only a function of the reluctance of the party and official historians to acknowledge it, but also of the ability of these strata to engage in what one Bolshevik despairingly called "social mimicry," their "penetrat[ion of] the institutions created by the working class."[127]

As Daniel Orlovsky has pointed out, such penetration began before the October Revolution and was not limited to working-class institutions. Aside from comprising a substantial proportion of trade union membership, white-collar employees figured prominently in the zemstvos, the public organizations formed during the war, and the cooperative movement. This "third element," a substantial proportion of which was of peasant background, was imbued with populist anti-capitalist sentiment. As Russia's capitalist infrastructure and Provisional Government administration crumbled under the weight of war and social polarization, they were both well placed and favorably disposed to become the new infrastructure of the emerging soviet state after October 1917.

There thus occurred "revolutionary state building from below." "Zemstvos and town dumas . . . did not disappear when abolished by decree: rather, they became soviet departments staffed by Third Element functionaries." The same thing happened to Provisional Government food supply and land committees. Consumer and credit cooperatives did not even have to change names. Transformed into state institutions by a Sovnarkom decree of 20 March 1919, they remained vital organs of mass distribution throughout the civil war.[128]

While not formally state institutions, unions combining professionals and proto-professionals made possible the "statization" of their services. We have seen how this happened among industrial engineers and technicians. Similar, if more stormy, developments occurred in education and medicine. In both cases, the elites of the professions stubbornly resisted the subordination of their associations to respective commissariats. But they were eventually outflanked by state-sponsored unions whose identification with soviet power and the proletariat appealed to many rank-and-file members of the professions.[129]

It was noted earlier that by 1921 nearly one quarter of Communist Party membership consisted of those who declared their social origin as white-collar workers. By function, though, the proportion is likely to have been higher, as many claiming peasant origin served as employees of soviet organs. Within soviet administration, 57.1 percent of the members of provincial executive committees, and 46.4 percent of uezd executive committees were of white-collar background by 1920.[130] Here again, the actual proportion of white-collar workers was probably higher, since many teachers, feldshers and cooperative workers rose from peasant backgrounds to occupy positions in provincial and uezd administration.

The lower middle strata thus successfully grafted themselves onto the workers' and peasants' revolution. The result was that the social composition of the revolutionary state was more heterogeneous and less proletarian than generally has been acknowledged. What impact these "alien elements" had on the day-to-day functioning of the state, whether they possessed a specific psychology that was itself alien to the original revolutionary project, is not entirely clear. But a starting point for determining their role must be the recognition that there were a variety of hopes invested in the revolution, that is, a multiplicity of revolutionary projects. Providing badly needed skills and experience, the lower middle strata were important contributors to the state-building process that proceeded far in the course of the civil war. As such, they came to identify strongly with the state that provided them with a degree of security in a strife-torn situation. With the end of the civil war, as the political authorities found themselves in strife with workers and peasants, their dependence on these strata in turn was strengthened. These, then, were the authentic origins of the process of bureaucratization that prominent (and not so prominent) party members decried but were powerless to reverse during the 1920s.

Conclusion: deconstructing "War Communism"

The attentive reader will have noticed that references to War Communism have been accompanied by inverted commas or qualifications such as "normally understood" and "subsequently defined as." It is time to make explicit the reason why this was done.

"War Communism" was invented by Lenin in 1921 as a rhetorical device, one of many he employed in seeking to persuade the party that what previously was anathema – the legitimization of domestic trade – had to be tolerated.[131] It has since come to signify many things: the Draconian measures adopted by the Soviet state during the civil war, the period during which such measures were adopted, a mentality which survived throughout the NEP period, and a "model" of economic organization to which the state returned under Stalin. With reference to the economic policies themselves, some historians emphasize their "communist" component, others stress the force of circumstances. According to the former view, War Communism was "an attempt which proved premature, to realize the party's stated ideological goals."[132] These goals were "implicit in the doctrine of revolutionary Marxism and were largely the expression of the doctrinaire zeal of Russia's new rulers."[133] On the other side are those who, while not denying the "flights of leftist fancy" to which leading Bolsheviks were prone, see War Communism as an "empirical creation," a series of improvisations shaped by military urgency and economic scarcity. Typically, they argue that "the Bolsheviks had no well-defined economic policies upon coming to office (sic) in October 1917" and that the initially "state capitalist" program articulated by Lenin in the spring of 1918 was no less authentically "Bolshevik" than War Communism.[134]

Both of these interpretations can be supported by quotations from Lenin. If in the spring of 1921 Lenin argued that "[i]t was the war and the ruin that forced us into War Communism," then by the autumn of that year, he spoke of "the mistake of deciding to go over directly to communist production and distribution," labelling defenders of such a "mistake" as "dreamers" who considered it "possible in three years to transform the whole economic foundation." Of course, it is not inconceivable (and indeed has been argued) that both necessity and ideological extremism were involved, that once having been forced to abandon its supposedly more "moderate" policy of "state capitalism," the party came to interpret (mistakenly, as it turned out) the situation as presenting an opportunity to push on directly to communism. For this, there is an appropriate quotation from Lenin too, namely, that being "[c]arried away by a wave of enthusiasm, . . . we thought that by direct orders of the proletarian state, we could organize state production and distribution of products communistically in a land of petty peasants."[135]

But as Lars Lih has argued with respect to the critical issue of food supply, "the actual relation between military necessity and ideological radicalism is the reverse of this supposed chain: the outbreak of civil war caused a conscious retreat from ideological ambitiousness." This strikes me as a brilliant insight. There is, after all, no *a priori* reason why state capitalism has to be identified with moderation. As already noted, the creation of the poor peasant committees, infused by a class war understanding of relations among peasants, dates from the supposedly moderate pre-civil war period. By contrast, the strategy of winning over the middle peasant was adopted in 1919, that is, during the period universally identified with War Communism. Similarly, razverstka, subsequently regarded as the most egregious of "war communist" excesses, was introduced in late 1918 as a retreat from the policy of determining peasants' individual needs and appropriating the surplus, that is, the food supply dictatorship. "Thus," writes Lih, "the term war communism seems particularly inappropriate: the war part of the food-supply policy was not communist and the communist part was not appropriate for war."[136]

The same might be said of fiscal policy. It is true that *The ABC of*

Communism boldly proclaimed that "Communist society will know nothing of money," and that Preobrazhenskii dedicated his book on *Paper Money in the Epoch of the Proletarian Dictatorship* to the printing press, "that machine gun of the Commissariat of Finance" which would destroy the bourgeois system.[137] It was also the case that by 1920, state accounting was calculated on the basis of clearing balances and that a commission was hard at work to develop a new (non-monetary) labor unit of account. But few, including Preobrazhenskii, were under the illusion that the money economy could or should be abolished so long as the state sector remained dependent on small-scale peasant agriculture and cottage industry. As Silvana Malle has concluded:

money issue was not aimed at reaching the point when the annihilation of the purchasing power of the rubles hoarded by the "wealthy" would automatically ensure full control of the economy, but the other way round: the issue was needed to purchase goods and services which still remained outside government control in spite of its efforts. It was simply used to finance government expenditure, *just as in so many other countries.*[138]

The same hard-headed realism is evident in policy discussions (as opposed to public statements at the time and subsequent accounts) about the naturalization of wages and the policy of free public services – both of which proceeded very far in the latter half of 1920. Both were driven by expediency. The former was a direct outgrowth of rationing (by no means an exclusively "communist" policy) while the latter relieved the state of the burden of collecting negligible revenues.[139] In short, once these policies are stripped of the obfuscating rhetoric that accompanied their implementation, they appear no more indicative of a "War Communist" inspired attempt to drive money out of the economy, than the introduction of a tax-in-kind, the founding charter of NEP. As for the militarization of labor, notwithstanding Trotsky's dialectical pyrotechnics, it bore more resemblance to imperial German wartime practice than anything found in the corpus of Marx's or Engels' writings. In sum, the progressive "statization" of economic life, considered to be "the most characteristic feature of the 1918–21 period," was hardly unique to the civil war – or to Russia.[140] It actually began during the world war and was supported at one time or another in Russia by tsarist and Provisional Government officials, by liberals such as Petr Struve, and, at least until the October Revolution, by leading Mensheviks. What was new to the period of Bolshevik rule was the association of state power with the dictatorship of the proletariat and the extension of ("proletarian") state power with the construction of socialism. Although NEP temporarily reversed the trend, the aggrandizement of state power at the expense of the market and other autonomous forces remained on the revolutionary agenda.

Finally, in the realm of foreign affairs, it can be asked whether the Bolsheviks were less "communist" in the winter of 1918 when Trotsky led the Soviet delegation at the Brest Litovsk negotiations than, say, in the early months of 1920 when the All-Russian Union of Consumer Cooperatives (Tsentrosoiuz) established direct trading relations with western firms, a peace treaty was signed with Estonia, and a Soviet trade delegation was dispatched to Sweden. What, indeed, was "War Communism" about the agreement to exchange Soviet gold and short-term bills for Swedish agricultural implements, and railway and telephone equipment?[141]

None of this is to discount the role of ideology or deny that it contained a strong utopian component. Utopianism is discernable at all levels of the party throughout the civil war. But, then, so it was before the middle of 1918, if not before the October Revolution. Recognizing this to have been the case, Lars Lih has asked provocatively:

[w]hich interpretation is *a priori* more plausible: that a group of extremist revolutionaries took power in a year of tumult, preached moderation and then grew radical – or that they came in breathing fire and learned moderation as they shed their inexperience and took on responsibility for complex national problems?[142]

Used by Lenin both apologetically ("war and ruin . . . forced us") and to discredit the "dreamers" who persisted in their opposition to NEP, "War Communism" became an integral component of Soviet historical rhetoric. Its pervasiveness among western scholars is more difficult to explain. It may be that, like feudalism, the industrial revolution, and other retrospective historical categories, "War Communism" has satisfied a felt need for coligation. But a close inspection of the policies with which it is normally associated and a comparison between those policies and what preceded them reveals a lack of analytical specificity.[143]

At heart, "War Communism" is a contradiction in terms, a conceptual trap that has hindered more than it has helped to make sense of Bolshevik attitudes and behavior before 1921. The only reality assumed by War Communism was retrospective, that is, as a foil against which could be highlighted more "realistic," or even "human" policies.[144] Other than to interpolate later Communist Party discourse, it should be dropped from our vocabulary.

2   The crisis of 1920–1921

All is sold, all is lost, all is plundered,
Death's wing has flashed black on our sight,
All's gnawed bare with sore want and sick longing –
Then how are we graced with this light?
(Anna Akhmatova, *Anno Domini MCMXII*, quoted in Jurgen Ruhle,
Literature and Revolution [London, 1969], p. 98)

"The state swelled up; the people grew lean." Such was the verdict of
the great nineteenth-century Russian historian, Vasilii Kliuchevskii, on
the frenzied years of Peter the Great's reign. Such might also serve as a
depiction of Soviet Russia after six years of war, revolution, and civil
war. By 1921, the Soviet state had swelled up in three respects. First,
after being reduced in 1919 to an area roughly the same as sixteenth-
century Muscovy, Soviet power was extended to the borders of the
Baltic states and Poland in the west, the Arctic Ocean in the north, the
Black Sea in the south and the Transbaikal region in the east. Second,
having appropriated economic, social and cultural transactions
formerly performed by non- or semi-governmental institutions and
individuals, the state had expanded its administrative apparatus.
Third, the number of state officials and employees correspondingly
grew, overwhelming the party that was supposed to be guiding
them.

The leanness of "the people" was the direct consequence of the afore-
mentioned cataclysms. But was it just that, or did it also stem from the
swelling of the state and particularly, the amalgam of policies that subsequently became known as "War Communism?" The question might
seem perverse, for it is difficult to imagine how any revolutionary
regime could have survived the onslaught of counterrevolutionary and
interventionist armies without privileging its own military forces and
militarizing much of civilian life. Yet, the dismantling of the political
and food dictatorships did not follow upon military victory. The result

was a continuation or transformation or the civil war, with the military-bureaucratic apparatus now ranged against rebellious workers and peasants.

The last of the battles pitting the Red Army against the Whites were fought in the Crimean peninsula in the middle of November 1920. What remained of Wrangel's Armed Forces of South Russia was thereafter evacuated by ship across the Black Sea to Constantinople. The civil war, as it is conventionally understood, was over. All of European Russia and much of Siberia was at least nominally under Soviet power.

In the course of that three-year struggle, the nature of Soviet power had been fundamentally transformed. The state's coercive organs and the militarized revolutionary political culture that sustained and was perpetuated by its functionaries had swelled up. The democratic components of the state – the trade unions, factory committees and soviets – had atrophied. Industry and transport had been ravaged and, consequently, the proletarian base of the regime had dwindled. At the same time, the writ of centralized state power did not extend much beyond the cities and the (partially destroyed) rail lines connecting them. In the broad expanses of the countryside, peasants, who comprised upwards of 80 percent of the total population, hunkered down in their communes, having both economically and psychologically withdrawn from the state and its military and food detachments.

Thus, by the end of the civil war, an appalling isolation confronted Soviet authorities. Not only had the revolution failed to spread beyond Russia's borders, but even within them the vast majority of people were out of reach – weary, destitute, and estranged. Much heroism and sacrifice had been displayed in meeting the challenge of counterrevolution and intervention. But now that the threat of the Whites had receded, there was little left to sacrifice and a lot less willingness to do so.

As had been the case so often in the past, much depended on the annual harvest of grain. Reports reaching Moscow in the summer of 1920 had not been encouraging in this respect. Although the previous year's (1919–20) procurement campaign in European Russia had netted only 55 percent of the targeted amount of grain (180 million of a targeted 327 million puds), it had cut into peasants' food and seed stocks. The result was reduced sowings which, combined with severe frost then drought in the central agricultural and Volga provinces, foretold disaster.[1] In August, the grain levy had been set at 224.5 million puds, but as one procurement official from the Volga region reported in September, "It is already abundantly clear that any measures to collect the levy will be doomed to failure from the start ... there is simply no grain left to take." Anticipating charges of "localism," he added: "I have lived through more than one year of hunger in Moscow, and I am just as eager as they are to take as much surplus grain as possible for the starving proletariat in the north; but I repeat, whatever measures are taken, IT WILL BE IMPOSSIBLE to achieve any positive results!"[2]

The proletariat was starving, but peasants were smarting under the lash of razverstka. District and provincial assemblies of soviets passed "dozens of resolutions against the continuation of requisitionings," and in Tambov province, a major rebellion was gathering pace. When, in October, Lenin told chairmen of Moscow volost and uezd executive committees that the peasantry could expect little relief until Wrangel was defeated and industrial production was restored, he was upbraided and accused of "evading the issue." The issue, of course, was the continuation of razverstka levies which Lenin himself admitted were excessive.[3]

Why then, asks Orlando Figes in his recent study of the Volga countryside, "was the food requisitioning allowed to continue during the autumn of 1920 and the spring of 1921, when the civil war had already been won and the famine crisis was already widespread?"[4] Several lines of inquiry suggest themselves. One would be to look at the local level where, as discussed previously, the food detachments and the Red Army pursued requisitions with a ferocity that bespoke both loyalty to the revolution (or at least their conception of it) and the perquisites of their own power. Charged with the task of procuring so much grain and livestock, these crusaders prided themselves on their toughness and were not easily reined in. They thus were likely to regard peasant survival strategies, such as converting land to the cultivation of fruit and vegetables – which were exempted from razverstka – as sabotage, and to punish peasant-horticulturalists accordingly.

A second line of analysis would focus on the center where, after all, decisions about continuing the razverstka system and the allocation of quotas were made. Here, quite clearly, ideological considerations are important especially in relation to the question of alternatives. Bolshevik leaders were well aware of the fact that the original basis for razverstka, namely collective commodity exchange (tovaroobmen), had been eroded to the point of nullitude. "We know that in our devastated country the peasant economy has been destroyed," Lenin told the rural soviet ispolkom chairmen, "and that the peasant needs goods, and not the paper money which is being showered on him in such profusion."[5]

But he refused to acknowledge that razverstka was the problem or that another means of surplus extraction such as a fixed tax in kind might be preferable.

Why? Surely, part of the answer lies in the Bolshevik animus against the market and the assumption that a fixed tax would enable the peasants to indulge their "petty bourgeois" instincts for trade. "Freedom to sell bread in a hungry country," Lenin had remarked to the Seventh Congress of Soviets in February 1919, "is freedom of speculation, is freedom of profiteering for the rich. We shall never allow this. Sooner will we all die than yield on this point." The "replacement of trade by a purposive distribution of goods" was duly enshrined in the party's program, adopted by its Eighth Congress, the following month. Even while the black market flourished, Bolshevik officials were expressing the conviction that "buying and selling" was part of the "unreturnable past," and that "as long as Soviet power exists we will never have free and private trade."[6]

But it was not ideology alone that blocked a change of course in 1920. For despite the alarming news from the countryside and rumblings of discontent in the cities, there was reason to believe that the worst was over and that recovery had begun. The removal of the Whites from Soviet territory opened up new prospects for grain collection in Siberia, the Caucasus and Ukraine. In September, some 20,000 workers and peasants from the "hungry" provinces were dispatched to Siberia for this purpose. Even while Makhno's army and other "bandits" made grain collection in Ukraine an impossibility, it was expected that 220 million puds could be extracted from the other two areas. With these additional supplies, a food fund could be accumulated to supply the needs of workers in the factories and to assist poor peasants. Food for industry – oil from Baku, coal from the Donbass and cotton from Turkestan – could now be supplied as well. Moreover, the international situation seemed to be improving. In September, nearly 2,000 "delegates" attended a Congress of the Eastern Peoples in Baku, organized by the Comintern. Summoned to a "holy war" against imperialism, the delegates proclaimed the brotherly union of the peoples of the east with the Red Army and the Communist International.[7] At the same time, the initiation of trade negotiations with the very imperialist powers against which the Baku Congress had pledged itself augured a lifting of the economic blockage imposed in 1918.

Confident of being able to supply urban residents with goods, the government moved to extend its control over the remaining islands of free enterprise. In November, small-scale (cottage) industry was taken over by Vesenkha thus at least nominally adding several tens of thousands of enterprises to its vast empire. Shortly thereafter, the police closed the infamous Sukharevka market in Moscow as well as other bazaars where illegal trade previously had been tolerated.

In the meantime, Sovnarkom was busy laying the groundwork for longer-term economic recovery. Three projects emerged in this connection: the securing of international recognition for the Soviet government as well as trading agreements and foreign concessions; electrification; and compulsory sowing in the form of sowing committees. (A fourth "project," embodied in the First All-Russian Initiative Conference on the Scientific Organization of Labor, did not originate with Sovnarkom but otherwise shared the characteristics of the other three; it is discussed in chapter 3). Each was designed to overcome the problem of economic "backwardness" that had been exacerbated by civil war. Each, in a sense, sought to compensate for the revolutions that did not happen – the proletarian revolution abroad, and the industrial and cultural revolutions in the Russian hinterland. Finally, it must be said that while each promised bountiful returns, not a single pood of grain or arshin of cloth eventuated from these projects during the winter of 1920–1.

To be sure, it was difficult to generate much enthusiasm for trade agreements and foreign concessions, but Lenin did his utmost. Entering into such relations by no means meant capitulation to the imperialists, he assured a gathering of Moscow party activists, it is not they who will be taking advantage of us, but the reverse. They need our resources as much as we need their capital and expertise. Concessions would not mean the selling of the Motherland, but rather the development of its resources located in out of the way parts of the country. Of course, there were dangers, but "we must be able to distinguish between big dangers and little dangers, and incur the lesser dangers rather than the greater."[8]

Electrification entailed no such dangers, not, at least according to Lenin. Speaking to the Eighth Congress of Soviets in December, Lenin outlined the significance of the plan drawn up by the State Commission for the Electrification of Russia (GOELRO) in the following terms:

Anyone who has carefully observed life in the countryside . . . knows that we have not torn up the roots of capitalism and have not undermined the foundation, the basis, of the internal enemy. The latter depends on small-scale production, and there is only one way of undermining it, namely, to place the economy of the country, including agriculture, on a new technical basis, that of modern large-scale production. Only electricity provides that basis.[9]

Electrification was an example of what Roger Rethybridge called large-scale theory confronting small-scale reality, or, as Richard Stites has termed it, "city light and rural darkness . . . the Soviet metaphor for Marx's 'idiocy of rural life.'" It was a vision of a Russia covered by "a dense network of electric power stations and powerful technical installations," a Russia in which every power station would be converted into "a stronghold of enlightenment to be used to make the masses electricity conscious, so to speak," a Russia that would be "a model for a future socialist Europe and Asia." Not for nothing did Lenin consider electrification "the second program of our Party." For, as he intoned on several occasions, "Communism is Soviet power plus the electrification of the whole country."[10]

The plan devised by GOELRO, which Lenin insisted should be made available in every library throughout the country, actually entailed much more than the construction of power stations. It was nothing less than an "integrated economic plan," "a great economic plan designed for a period of not less than ten years and indicating how Russia is to be placed on the real economic basis required for communism." But not everyone within the party was comfortable with 200 (mainly non-party) scientists and engineers determining what was required for communism. Was this uneasiness an expression of what Lenin condemned as "Communist conceit" typical of "the dabbler and the bureaucrat," or did it reflect popular distrust of technocratic fixes to economic and social problems?[11] Probably both. If for Lenin, (electric) power would bring knowledge, then for critics of GOELRO's project, the possessors of scientific knowledge threatened the power that was vested in the party. Such tension between "bourgeois specialists" and communists would persist throughout the 1920s before exploding in the Cultural Revolution that capped the decade.

The third project presented to and approved by the Eighth Congress of Soviets called for the formation of sowing committees (*posevkomy*), whose primary purpose was to raise the productivity of agriculture in the shorter term and by less extravagant means. As conceived by V. Osinskii, at the time a member of the collegium of Narkomprod, the sowing committees were to consist of local food-supply officials and representatives from soviet executive committees. Along with village committees, elected by the village community, they were to administer the registration and redistribution of seed, encourage the maximization of sown acreage, and improve methods of production by establishing obligatory rules for early plowing.

The project has not enjoyed a very good reputation in the west. To

Michael Farbman, writing in 1923, it was "a most fantastic scheme," the prime example of "communism by compulsion." To Alec Nove, it represented "a significant index to the party's mentality at the time," which he characterized as extremist. To Paul Avrich, it was "not merely the retention of War Communism but its reinforcement in virtually every phase of rural life," and in Moshe Lewin's view, it comprised the "fully fledged practice and ideology of 'statism.'" Even the usually more circumspect E. H. Carr considered it an "illusion," drafted "in defiance of all experience."[12]

There is no denying that the sowing committees were a crash or "shock" campaign, involved state compulsion (*povinnost'*) and provoked criticism both within but especially outside the Communist Party. But there was another dimension in the scheme. This was the modestness of its architects' ambitions. The animus of the committees was economic recovery rather than "socialist construction"; their ideological underpinning was partnership with the peasantry rather than class struggle; and to the extent that coercion was involved, it was to be directed against the "idler" who sowed only what he needed for his own family's consumption rather than the kulak. Finally, neither Osinskii nor Lenin, who strongly supported the project, linked it with state or collective farming. On the contrary, Lenin had become quite insistent that "we must rely on the single-owner peasant – that is the way he is and he won't be any different in the near future, and to dream of a transition to socialism and collectivization won't do." Lenin actually went so far as to characterize the project as a "wager on the industrious" (*stavka na staratel'nogo khoziaina*), a phrase strikingly similar to the one used by Stolypin more than a decade earlier. In all these respects, there was more than a whiff of NEP.[13]

However, to many delegates at the Soviet Congress, the project smelled more strongly of coercion and the unwillingness of the authorities to face up to the necessity of replacing the hated razverstka with a less arbitrary and oppressive food supply tax. Peasant delegates' demands for the abolition of razverstka rang out loud and clear and were echoed in resolutions proposed by SR and Menshevik delegates.[14] But precisely because such a step was being advanced by their political opponents, the Bolsheviks could hardly accept it without losing face with and otherwise demoralizing the cadres.

Taking the measure of Bolshevik food policy between September 1920 and March 1921, we can see a nearly constant tension between ideological principle (or less generously, dogma), and expediency. The tension produced both scapegoating – primarily directed at

Mensheviks and SRs, but also at "speculators" and less often, "kulaks" – and evasions in the form of long-term utopian "planning." Among the peasants, as discussed in a previous chapter, the tension produced a variety of strategies, ranging from cut-backs in the cultivation of certain food and fodder crops in favor of others, petitions and resolutions, and, particularly where demobilized soldiers provided the wherewithal, armed resistance.

The regime thus found itself on the horns of a dilemma, one that was neatly summarized by I. A. Teodorovich, a high official in the Agricultural Commissariat. "In order to revive the country," he told the Soviet Congress, "it is necessary to supply it with goods from the town in normal quantity; but in order in its turn to produce these, the town must be supplied with a definite quantity of raw material and food." "How," he asked, "are we to escape from this vicious circle?" Long-term projects were all well and good, but whether the short term could be survived seemed increasingly problematic. The expected relief from outlying areas did not arrive, not only because of peasant resistance, but because there was so little fuel, operative locomotives and even bags in which to load the grain. As for the central Russian provinces, even the most battle-hardened Bolsheviks were aware that there was little grain or livestock to be had.[15]

What was to be done? Was there a middle way between requisitions and free trade? Trotsky had thought there was, but his proposal for a tax-in-kind had been rejected by the Politburo in February 1920. The same idea cropped up again in October in an article by the economist, S. G. Strumilin. According to his version, the state would collect one-half of what it needed, the other half being attracted through premiums of industrial goods or via commodity exchange (tovaroobmen). "There is no basis for fearing that word," he wrote. "*Tovaroobmen* in no way threatens us with a return to free trade."[16]

Lenin, too, was coming around to the same idea. In late November, he instructed Sovnarkom to devise a method for converting local monetary taxes (which inflation had robbed of any purpose) and razverstka quotas to a tax in kind. A month later, he jotted down some "notes on the tasks of economic construction," which included the formula – "relation to the peasantry: tax + bonuses." Soviet historians have attributed great significance to these two documents (as well as to the notes he took of conferences of "non-party peasants"), interpreting them as evidence that Lenin was already thinking in NEP-like terms. If this were the case, though, it would be difficult to explain the formula that immediately follows the one quoted above, namely, "tax

= *razverstka*." Perhaps, as Alec Nove believes, Lenin was "overwrought, or just not thinking." Perhaps, under the stress and strain of a policy that clearly was not working, he had "gone right off the rails(!)."[17]

Rather than attributing the contradictoriness of Lenin's jottings to overwork or a temporary lapse of sanity, we would do better to contextualize them. For with the end of the civil war, Lenin was finally beginning to grapple with the full implications of "the premature revolution." The problem of how to sustain the post-capitalist state in conditions that, from his perspective, were the breeding ground for capitalism, was as complex as it was unique. Recognizing the futility of continuing requisitions, he thrashed about for a formula that would accommodate the peasantry but stop short of the state's complete capitulation to market forces.

A significant benchmark in this rethinking were the "theses concerning the peasants" which Lenin presented to the Politburo on 8 February 1921. The theses called for "[s]atisfy[ing] the wish of the non-Party peasants for the substitution of a tax in kind for *razverstka* (the confiscation of surplus grain stocks)," reducing the amount of the tax compared to the previous year's appropriation, and granting peasants the freedom to use their after-tax surpluses "in local exchange." The last of these theses was potentially the biggest concession, but was sufficiently imprecise as to keep several options open. Although the word Lenin used, *oborot*, can be translated as "trade" (as indeed it is in the English edition of Lenin's *Complete Works*), it actually lay somewhere between *obmen* and *torgovlia* in the Bolsheviks' moral economy. Whereas *obmen* implied the retention of centrally organized distribution, *torgovlia* easily shaded into speculation, as illustrated in Lenin's remarks to the Seventh Congress of Soviets cited above. Then, there was the question of what "local" meant in practice. How, after all, was grain to get from surplus to deficit areas if "exchange" was to remain local? And who was to be allowed to exchange goods – state agencies, the cooperative network, individuals, or all three?[18]

Lenin's formula was essentially reproduced, with all its ambiguities, in the resolution that was approved by the Central Committee of the party on 24 February and presented to the Tenth Party Congress which opened on 8 March. Before considering the denouement of the party's deliberation of this and other issues, it is necessary to introduce some additional actors who stormed onto the stage just prior to and during the Congress. These were the very masses – workers and soldiers – who had brought the Bolsheviks to power in the first place. On 22 January 1921, owing to the paucity of supplies on hand and the small number of freight trains arriving from the hinterlands, the bread ration in Moscow, Petrograd and other industrial centers was cut by a third. But even then, there was not enough to go around. During the early part of February, not a single food shipment reached Moscow. Yet, workers who journeyed to the surrounding countryside to exchange goods with obliging peasants ran the risk of being stopped by roadblock detachments posted on the outskirts of the major cities. Prisoners of starvation, the urban population also suffered from the lack of heating, warm clothing and footwear.[19]

Depleted and exhausted, what was left of the urban working class registered its disillusionment with Communist Party policies (if not the Communist Party itself) in the form of resignations of party members, strikes, demonstrations and resolutions passed at meetings of "non-party workers." Little is known about the provenance of these meetings except that they appear to have been inspired by earlier gatherings of peasants. According to one historian, they were "organized spontaneously," which would make them the last such mass gatherings to occur on Soviet soil until those of recent years. Another source indicates that in the early months of 1921 they were held frequently, were well attended and "in many cases . . . violently howled down" official speakers who were despatched to justify official policy. The one held in Moscow on 2–4 February brought together metalworkers from Moscow *guberniia* and was addressed by Kamenev (Chairman of STO), Lozovskii (from Narkomtrud), Kuraev (from Narkomzem) and Vyshinskii (from Narkomprod). The mood of the workers, as reported by Vyshinskii, was bitter. "The workers are tired of privileges. They don't want inequality in anything, and first and foremost not in food rations . . . By their words, one could sense a complete breach between the masses and the party, between the masses and the unions." Resolutions called for the abolition of all special rations (e.g., the academic ration, Sovnarkom ration, Red Army ration), the withdrawal of the glavki from distribution, the replacement of razverstka by a fixed tax-in-kind, and the sale of surpluses by agricultural cooperatives to workers' organizations.[20]

Faced with such demands, Sovnarkom sought to remove the most egregious features of the state's food policy. In the course of February, it resolved to eliminate privileged rations for certain categories of soviet employees and soldiers, and tighten up on the administration of the academic ration, to establish a commission to assist the "starving peasants" of five central Russian provinces, to chastise provincial food committees for engaging in "illegal forms of coercion," and to instruct the agricultural and food supply commissariats to provide the means for expanding kitchen gardens. On 28 February, the Council of Labor and Defense allocated 10 million gold rubles to the Commissariat of Foreign Trade for the purchase of food and other basic necessities for "needy workers."[21]

Whatever effect these measures had in Moscow, they were either too little or too late to avert massive protests by workers in Petrograd. On 12 February, sixty-four of Petrograd's largest factories closed for ten days due to the catastrophic fuel shortage. No sooner had the factories reopened, than workers walked off their jobs, first at the Trubochnyi factory, then at others. With the escalation of strike activity, Menshevik and SR organizations issued proclamations denouncing the Bolsheviks, and their agitators received sympathetic hearings at workers' meetings. On 24 February, the Executive Committee of the Petrograd Soviet, chaired by Zinoviev, proclaimed martial law throughout the city. Only after a week, however, was order restored.

It would appear that workers' hostility toward communist authorities was as intense as it had been four years earlier with respect to the tsarist regime. Why, then, was the outcome of their protests so different? Four factors may be cited. First, unlike in February 1917, the authorities successfully isolated workers from the regular troops stationed in the city, relying instead on the Cheka and the communist officer cadets (*kursanty*) who were called in from neighboring military academies. The Cheka was a particularly loyal instrument of repression, rounding up thousands of dissident workers, students, intellectuals, and especially, Menshevik activists. Second, the Communist Party organization, under Zinoviev's leadership, rose to the occasion with an impressive display of unanimity and discipline. And, while the party's claim to revolutionary legitimacy was undoubtedly tarnished, it still could plausibly represent itself as the most effective bulwark against a resurgence of White counterrevolution. Third, a number of timely concessions were made in the form of extra rations to workers and soldiers, the removal of the confiscatory roadblock detachments from Petrograd province, and the demobilization of Red Army labor units. Finally, one can hardly underestimate the difficulty of sustaining political activity in circumstances where the natural, biological response to desperate hunger is apathy.

So much for Petrograd. But at Kronstadt, located on Kotlin Island some twenty miles away, the insurgency among the naval base's soldiers, sailors and civilian workers was not so easily subdued. The Kronstadt rebellion of March 1921 and its bloody suppression have been almost universally regarded as a black stain upon the communist government. For here were "the pride and glory of the revolution," proclaimed as such by Trotsky in 1917, organizing a Provisional Revolutionary Committee and, under the banner of "Down with the commissarocracy" and "All power to the soviets but not the parties," calling for a "third revolution." The authorities on the mainland met this challenge first with appeals, then calumny, dire warnings, and a blockade. When these efforts proved futile, Kronstadt was bombarded and Red Army infantry and communist volunteers, including 279 delegates to the Tenth Party Congress, assaulted the island fortress across the ice.[22]

Echoing the bewilderment of many Bolsheviks, Isaac Deutscher characterized the Kronstadt rebellion as "the strangest of all Russian insurrections," and William Chamberlin (inaccurately) referring to Kronstadt as "a stronghold of Bolshevism in 1917," claimed the rebellion was "sudden and unexpected." In fact, the Kronstadters' militance and volatility, so much in evidence in 1917, remained nearly undiminished thereafter. Paul Avrich wrote:

Over the years one finds the same loathing of privilege and authority, the same hatred of regimentation, the same dream of local autonomy and self-administration. One finds, moreover, a powerful antagonism that was deeply rooted in the anarchist and populist traditions of the lower classes, dating from the rise of a powerful bureaucratic state during the seventeenth and eighteenth centuries. Isolated from the mainland, Kronstadt, even more than its sister bases on the Baltic, became a stronghold of primitive anarchic rebellion.[23]

Deeply rooted anarchist and populist traditions, which, incidentally, contained more than a dose of anti-semitism, did not in themselves "cause" the Kronstadt rebellion. They were, rather, the cultural medium through which the Kronstadters interpreted the regimentation to which they were subjected and what was going on around them. In 1917, Bolshevism coincided with the sailors' "loathing of privilege and authority"; by 1921, it had become identified with those negative qualities. Thus, in a sense, the Bolshevik revolution had come full circle. To the "crisis of the peasantry" which Sovnarkom had acknowledged as early as September 1920, was added a "breach between the party and the masses" and now open rebellion within the armed forces.

There was yet another dimension to the crisis of 1920–1. This was the struggle, or rather, struggles within the Communist Party itself. As we have seen, the expression of widely differing points of view and the formation of factional groups punctuated the party's life even in the midst of the civil war. But in January 1921, as he sized up what he called "the party crisis," Lenin urged his comrades "to face the bitter truth. The party is sick. The party is down with a fever." The issue that raised the temperature of the party was the status of the trade unions.[24]

Beginning in early November when Trotsky referred to the need to "shake up" the unions – this, at a trade union conference (!) – and extending right up to the Tenth Congress, party committees were deluged with position papers, pamphlets, theses, and platforms on the issue. Oblast' and provincial party conferences discussed little else. Positions ranged from Trotsky's insistence on transforming trade (professional'nye) unions into "production unions" which would be part of the state apparatus, to the syndicalism of the Workers' Opposition, and at least two intermediary formulations – Bukharin's "buffer" position and the "Platform of Ten" which included Lenin, and which eventually prevailed.[25]

By and large, historians have interpreted the trade union controversy and the vituperation it aroused as reflecting (or deflecting) other issues. Placing the controversy in the broad context of Soviet history, Isaac Deutscher saw it as a struggle between "proletarian democracy" and "the monolithic state," with the outcome indicating that while "Bolshevism" had abandoned the former, it was not yet prepared to embrace the latter. Robert Daniels also took a broad view in seeing it as marking "a further stage of Soviet political development in relation to Communist theory," with the outcome turning on "the estimate of the degree of socialism which the Russian Revolution had attained or could soon reach." To Leonard Schapiro, it was symptomatic of dissentions within the party over "bureaucracy, abuse of power and privilege, and the indifference of some leaders to the masses," but was ultimately driven by "the personal struggle, aimed at the control of the party apparatus." Finally, there is the even more jaundiced view of Stephen Cohen that "[t]he controversy was a model of obfuscation, only peripherally related to the real crisis in the country, and serving mainly to reveal the confusion, indecision and dissention that permeated the party on the eve of NEP." The implication here is that the party leadership had a weakness for theoretical disputation not unlike Nero's for fiddling.[26]

Characterizations of the protagonists' positions do not vary nearly as much, with the exception of Daniels' rendition of the Trotskyists as comprising the "moderate Left," which by implication would place Lenin on the Right. This is not so strange as it might seem, for the role of the trade unions as posited by the Platform of Ten was "to shield the masses against the possible abuses of [a] 'state capitalism'" that neither

Trotsky nor the Workers' Opposition were prepared to contemplate. The scholarly consensus on the Workers' Opposition has been that it represented an ultra-left current, its emphasis on egalitarianism, the spontaneity of the masses and their capacity to manage the industrial economy being reminiscent of Lenin's writings of 1917–18. Whether this current had taken its adherents outside the orbit of what Bolshevism had become by 1921 is debatable. Both of its principal leaders, Shliapnikov and Kollontai, vehemently denied that it did, and their protestations have been endorsed by Schapiro on the grounds that they never questioned the principle of the dictatorship of the proletariat. But in asserting that their "stand was in direct violation of the most fundamental organizational principle of Leninism – the role of the party apparatus as the exclusive leader of all revolutionary forces," Daniels has expressed a more widely held view.[27]

Although evincing agreement with the Workers' Opposition's critique of party policy, western historians generally have been dismissive of the faction's alternative agenda. E. H. Carr, for example, refers to its program as "a hotch-potch of current discontents, directed against . . . the growing efficiency and ruthlessness of the machine." "Fired by utopian optimism," "the real Levellers of this revolution . . . Utopian dreamers . . . enveloped in such fumes of fancy," "unrealistic," and "impractical" are the terms with which other historians have expressed their condescension.[28] One might also note a certain condescension toward Kollontai, who in one account is said to have abandoned "the harmless subjects of free love and communist family life" to enter the fray, and whose "close friendship with Shliapnikov" is cited as giving "extra zest to her advocacy of *his* views."[29]

Exceptions do exist. Two sympathetic biographies of Kollontai provide detailed information on her belated involvement in the Opposition, correctly citing her pamphlet, "The Workers' Opposition," as the movement's most important document, and underscoring the inherent links between her advocacy of women's emancipation and that of workers. And at least one scholar has characterized the Workers' Opposition as "the sole group of internal critics who looked the party's problems squarely in the face."[30]

What the Opposition found was "growing influence in the Soviet institutions of elements hostile in spirit . . . to Communism," for which it held the party responsible. "In order to do away with the bureaucracy that is finding its shelter in the Soviet institutions," wrote Kollontai in support of the Opposition's theses, "we must first get rid of all bureaucracy in the Party itself." Shliapnikov was no less blunt: "The party, as the managing and creative collective, has become a sordid bureaucratic machine."[31]

In taking aim at "bureaucracy," the Workers' Opposition was reiterating complaints voiced by the Democratic Centralists and the Ignatov group, two other dissident factions whose primary base was in the Moscow party organization and particularly its district (*raion*) committees. Their objections were not so much against red tape or the regularization of administrative procedures as what was perceived as the subversion of local party and soviet autonomy by the Central Committee's resort to "appointmentism" (*naznachitel'stvo*) and its frequent (and often politically motivated) shuffling of personnel. This "bureaucratic centralism," as T. V. Sapronov (a leading Democratic Centralist) termed it, was seen as both cause and effect of the estrangement of the upper echelons (*verkhy*) from the masses (*nizy*).[32]

Although overshadowed by the trade union controversy, this attack on the internal structure of the party raised more fundamental issues. To some historians it represented nothing less than the last sustained and principled (though inherently flawed) effort to preserve what was left of "party democracy." This interpretation recently has been criticized as "reflect[ing] the historians' values more accurately than . . . the Bolsheviks'." What was at the center of the factional struggles, it has been argued, was a class struggle between worker-Bolsheviks and those with an intelligentsia background. While the former invoked the self-initiative of the proletariat and condemned the party for suppressing it, the latter responded with accusations of "Makhaevism," that is, the heretical idea that the intelligentsia had climbed on the backs of the proletariat to exercise its own class rule.[33]

The two interpretations are not mutually exclusive. Not all those advocating greater autonomy for provincial committees and freedom of discussion were committed to a "workerist" agenda; and not all Workers' Oppositionists were against the hierarchical structure of the party. At the same time, neither interpretation has adequately addressed the relationship of the factional struggles to the very fluid social circumstances in which they took place. As already noted, the Communist Party and the Soviet state consisted not only of workers and intellectuals, but of other social groups which were capable of proclaiming their "proletarianness" even if their credentials were sociologically dubious. Thus, as Daniel Orlovsky has pointed out, the Workers' Oppositionists' syndicalism can be interpreted as objectively favoring "white-collar social strength," since "most unions had mixed white-collar and blue-collar membership and the bureaucratized unions themselves were chief suppliers of new upwardly mobile cadres for the state and party administrations." Similarly, in criticizing the excessive centralization of the party apparatus, the Democratic Centralists "were advancing the social and political agenda of the provincial lower-middle strata in the soviets and other organs of power." The extent to which these groups survived the defeat and liquidation of these factions may well have depended on their exploitation of what Erik Olin Wright has called "skill and organization assets."[34] But this question can only be resolved by further research.

Why, then, did the Workers' Opposition fail? If it was not the inherent utopianism of its program – for many movements with no less visionary programs have triumphed over more pragmatic adversaries, including the Bolsheviks in their rivalry with Menshevism – what other factors were involved? Certainly, Lenin's vigorous response to the challenge posed by the Oppositionists cannot be discounted. Conceiving of the party as an army, he more than once threatened to use machine guns to achieve party unity. Nor was Lenin alone. Service notes that the Workers' Opposition "incurred the wrath of nearly all Bolshevik functionaries and activists," partly because its charges of bureaucratism hit too close to home and partly because of fear that its "programme would simply produce more anarchy and chaos than already existed." Thus, the party apparatus simultaneously and successfully waged a campaign of defamation, blocked the publication and distribution of its opponents' literature, manipulated elections to party and union conferences and removed or transferred recalcitrant leaders.[35]

But this is not the whole story. The demise of the Workers' Opposition also had a social dimension. This was that "[w]hile the Opposition spoke of the power of a working class fueled by numerical strength and political consciousness, the proletariat's number, confidence and *esprit de corps* rapidly eroded." As every student of the 1917 revolution knows, the Bolsheviks had found their most reliable support among literate, skilled metalworkers. So did the Workers' Opposition. The Central Committee of the Metalworkers Union was dominated by Oppositionists, including Shliapnikov, who served as its chairman. But the industry as a whole had been devastated by shortages, the ranks of skilled workers who belonged to the party had been drastically thinned and the needs of other workers were so desperate as to make the struggle within the party an irrelevancy.[36]

Finally, the Opposition's problems were compounded by its own commitment to party discipline. In meetings with rank-and-file workers, Shliapnikov and other Oppositionists scrupulously "avoided the

very items that made the Workers' Opposition distinctive in an ideological and programmatic sense. Rather than discuss institutional
guarantees of workers' democracy, they seemed content with appeals
for food, clothes, housing, discipline, and vague proposals for the
appointment of workers to managerial and administrative positions."[37]
Here, one can discern the same ambivalence towards workers that
Lenin and other leading Bolsheviks exhibited. In this sense, they
remained true Bolsheviks, even if their faith in the vanguard party was
not repaid by its leaders.

Conclusion

The crises that strained the Soviet state and society to the breaking point
climaxed in March 1921 with the Kronstadt rebellion and the Tenth
Party Congress. The suppression of the rebellion and the decisions
taken by the congress did not so much resolve the crises as radically
alter the terms in which they were to be handled. Not until the late
1980s would it be possible to publicly advocate soviets without
communists. In this sense, and not only in this sense, the political space
for the articulation of alternative paths to those devised by the
Communist Party was virtually eliminated. By contrast, the space for
economic activities outside of those directly administered by the state
vastly expanded, or rather, much of what previously was illegal
became legalized.

The Tenth Congress is noteworthy chiefly for its resolutions on the
introduction of the food tax, on the trade unions, and on party unity
and the anarcho-syndicalist deviation. Together, they provided the
broad framework within which the New Economic Policy was to be
introduced and elaborated. In speaking to these resolutions, Lenin was
nothing if not blunt. The proletarian dictatorship was confronted by a
"petty bourgeois counterrevolution," a counterrevolution "more
dangerous than Denikin, Iudenich and Kolchak combined." Economic
devastation combined with SR and Menshevik agitation had caused
elements of the proletariat to be "infected" with the petty bourgeois
slogan of free trade and other ideas inimical to the proletarian dictatorship. The only way out, the only way to achieve "economic breathing
space" analogous to the Brest peace, was to reinstitute state capitalism,
granting foreign capitalists concessions (compromise from above) and
peasants freedom to engage in local exchange (compromise from
below). There is no getting around the fact that "freedom of exchange
means freedom of trade and freedom of trade means back to

capitalism." The party cannot close its eyes to the likelihood of kulaks taking advantage of this situation, "but they should be combatted not by prohibitive measures" but rather by giving machines and electrification to the peasantry and in the meantime, goods. Above all, "we must satisfy economically the middle peasantry and introduce freedom of exchange, for otherwise, given the retardation of the international revolution, it will be impossible to preserve proletarian power in Russia."[38]

But concessions to the middle peasant majority in Russia and foreign capital was only one half of the equation. In his notes to the speech on the food tax, under the characteristic heading of *Kto kogo?* (Who defeats whom?), Lenin wrote: "in politics: more cohesion (and discipline) within the party, more struggle with the Mensheviks and Socialist-Revolutionaries." More cohesion within the party meant an end to factions and factionalism as prescribed in the resolution on party unity. Criticism of the party's shortcomings, "which is absolutely necessary," must nevertheless "take account of the position of the party, surrounded as it is by a ring of enemies." Criticism leading to the formation of groups with their own platforms is impermissible and non-observance of this stricture "shall entail unconditional and instant expulsion from the party." This was to apply to members of the Central Committee whose breach of discipline or toleration of factionalism were sufficient grounds for demotion or expulsion as determined by a plenary session of the said committee.[39] More struggle against the "petty bourgeois" parties essentially meant police action. Even before Lenin in his pamphlet on the food tax (issued in May 1921) publicly prescribed prison or forced emigration, thousands of Mensheviks and SRs were being consigned to one or the other of these fates. The retreat of the party-state on the economic front was thus accompanied by a consolidation on the political. Many activities constituent of civil society were to be permitted but not their articulation in political society. How long the retreat would last and how much ground had to be conceded could not be foreseen. But it was clear from 1921 onwards that political society was to be the exclusive preserve of the Communist Party.

3   The perils of retreat and recovery

It is not we who are directing the new economic policy; just the opposite; the new economic policy is directing us. (A. Sviderskii, *Pravda*, 24 November 1921)

Where and how we must now restructure ourselves, reorganize ourselves, so that after the retreat we may begin a stubborn move forward, we still do not know. (Lenin, "Speech at a Plenary Session of the Moscow Soviet, 20 November 1922," *PSS*, vol. 45, p. 302)

The decision of the Tenth Party Congress to abandon razverstka in favor of a tax-in-kind is normally associated with the inauguration of the New Economic Policy, and I have already referred to the tax as NEP's founding charter. But this is a retrospective view that does not account for the tentative and piecemeal nature of subsequent decrees. Rather than the product of purposeful planning, we would do better to see NEP as emerging on the basis of unexpected contingencies and the policy-makers' attempts to adapt to unforeseen circumstances.

This is not to say that there was no strategy, that NEP was simply the sum of its parts or that those parts bore no relation to each other. In speaking of the tax-in-kind and defending other new policies, Lenin repeatedly resorted to the military metaphor of "retreat." The state would have to retreat, he insisted, because it could not advance directly to socialism; it had overextended itself in the course of the civil war, had taken on more than it could handle and the workers and peasants could tolerate. With peace reestablished, it had the opportunity, indeed the obligation, to call on other forces – even those with whom it previously had been at war – to restore the economy. Under the revived (but also revised) notion of "state capitalism," Lenin stressed the paramount importance of reestablishing the link (*smychka*) between town and country on the basis of market relations. The state would regulate the exchange of commodities, educate the masses of small producers, the peasants, in the advantages of soviet power, and invigilate against those who might seek to take political advantage of the state's retreat. It would turn over small-scale manufacturing to cooperatives and private producers and invite foreign investors to help restore its fuel industries. What else it would do, what else would be necessary to restore the national economy, could not be foretold but had to be worked out in practice.[1]

NEP fostered recovery but also a great deal of unease within the party about the compromises that recovery entailed. For if recovery involved the restoration of capitalism, as Lenin acknowledged it did, was there not the danger that Soviet Russia would continue to grow *into* capitalism rather than out of it? The idea of using capitalism to overcome what Lenin referred to as "small proprietary disintegration" made a certain amount of sense in the context of the crisis of 1921. Indeed, it may have been the only possible recourse for the beleaguered state. But the effect of NEP was to strengthen small proprietorship in the form of some 20 million tiny household plots and to permit the re-formation of a *kulak* class in the countryside and a private entrepreneurial class, the nepmen, in both the villages and the towns. By the middle of the decade as the limits of recovery were reached, the old Bolshevik question of *kto kogo*, of who was using whom, became increasingly urgent. If, as Lenin insisted, NEP was to be pursued "seriously and for a long time," at what point did it become possible to dispense with it, to cease regrouping and go over to the offensive?

These were complex, even daunting questions around which revolved much of the politics of the NEP years. Although in his last writings Lenin imparted to NEP an ideological legitimacy that went beyond more tactical considerations, he could not oversee the implementation of his recommendations. It thus was left to his successors to borrow, ignore, emphasize and distort what they chose in advancing their respective programs. These, the program of the Left Opposition as developed by Trotsky and its most capable economic theorist, E. A. Preobrazhenskii, and Bukharin's prescriptions – dubbed "Rightist" by the end of the decade – represent a high water mark in Marxist discourse on the transition to socialism. But all the while, there was "a constant narrowing of the apex where the decisions were taken, making the party dependent on the vagaries of kitchen political maneuvering."[2]

Complicating still further the discussion and resolution of these questions within the party was the fact that the party leadership was not alone in posing questions and seeking answers to them. If peasants, shopkeepers, and petty traders were vitally concerned about the genuineness of the state's concessions, workers questioned whether in its quest for recovery the party had abandoned them. The intelligentsia, meanwhile, oscillated between pessimistic visions of collectivism gone mad and "revolutionary dreams" that incorporated the latest in western technological developments and modernist cultural perspectives. It thereby reflected the existential uncertainty not only of Soviet conditions but of the postwar aftershock experienced by western intellectuals with whom it had strong affinities and personal contacts. And abroad, as the immediate threat of the spread of Bolshevism subsided (thanks in no small part to severe repression), statesmen, journalists, and private investors began to speculate about whether Bolshevism was a spent force in the land of its germination.

The present chapter focuses on the emergence of NEP and the tensions between "retreat" and "recovery" in the years 1921-3. While exploring the diverse dimensions of these categories, it also interrogates their usefulness and limitations in understanding such developments as the emergence of a plethora of revolutionary projects within civil society, the consolidation of soviet republics into a Union of Soviet Socialist Republics, and the strengthening of the Communist Party's own administrative apparatus. Taken as a whole, this period reveals the complex and contradictory currents within the Soviet state and society as the bequeathals of the revolution were refined and redefined.

The peasants in triumph

Once the Tenth Party Congress resolved to introduce a tax-in-kind, its implementation became a matter of urgency. "We must muster our whole administrative apparatus," Lenin told the delegates, "for the sowing season is almost at hand." On 21 March, VTsIK issued the decree that had been approved by the Politburo and two days later published in *Pravda* an appeal "To the Peasants of the RSFSR." The appeal noted that the tax would be smaller than the requisition quotas, that responsibility for its payment would fall on individual households "so that a careful and industrious proprietor will not have to pay for a defaulting fellow-villager," and that what remained would be left to the peasants to dispose of at their will. "Every peasant now must know," it continued, "that the more he plants the greater will be the surplus of grain which will remain in his full possession."[3]

Sovnarkom set the grain tax for 1921-2 in RSFSR and the Belorussian republic at 240 million puds, considerably less than the previous year's requisition quota of 423 million (of which no more than 300 million were collected). Taxes were subsequently assessed on other farm produce as well. The replacement of requisitioning by a tax, although psychologically important, was a relatively minor concession in itself. More significant was what it implied, namely that peasants could "dispose of" (note, still not "sell") their remaining surpluses. The state's initial retreat, then, was not so much in converting Narkomprod's food detachments to tax collectors, but in abandoning its monopolistic claim over the distribution of goods and in legalizing market transactions that previously had been "black."

Still, given the importance attached to the introduction of the tax by both contemporaries and historians, it is surprising how little attention the latter have given to its fate.[4] This was, after all, a major operation deemed by Lenin to be one of "two main criteria of success in our work of economic development on a nation-wide scale." During the spring he called repeatedly for the speedy, full, and "from the state point of view, proper collection of the tax," urging collectors not to dispense with coercion or "hover over the peasant for long."[5]

How the agents of Narkomprod, many of whom undoubtedly had served in the razverstka campaigns, fared in the field is a question that can only be answered by further research. Such research would have to take account of the pre-revolutionary experience of taxation (soul tax, zemstvo taxes, redemption payments, etc.), peasant understandings of the initial soviet land decree (apparently quite different from that of the government), and the persistence of other tax obligations including cartage and other labor services.[6] It must also consider regional and even local variations not only with respect to tax paying capacities, but the disposition of the peasantry toward soviet power and that of officials toward the peasants. How easy could it have been to collect taxes in Ukraine, where poor peasants' committees (komnezamy) were expropriating kulak land, livestock, and produce and where guerila activity was rife? During the first five months of the year, the Red Army suffered 1,923 casualties trying to suppress dozens of guerila "bands," whose strength was estimated as at least 10,000 armed men. Apparently, even where peasant rebellion had been repressed, as in Tambov province, tax collection was no easy matter. Oliver Radkey spoke of "a surprising degree of resistance to collection of the new tax despite suppression of the uprising," and cites a provincial party conference resolution of August 1921 that collection of the tax must "proceed as in war, in the full sense of the word." That war did not go well for the authorities, for by late November, Tambov was "well down in the list [of provinces] with only twenty-five to fifty percent of the tax collected as against docile provinces like Tula, Moscow, Ivanovo-Voznesensk and Briansk in the category exceeding seventy-five percent."[7]

Meanwhile, in the "docile" provinces, all did not go smoothly. As A. M. Bol'shakov noted with respect to his native volost of Goritsy (Tver' province), "the machinery for collecting the tax in kind was extremely unwieldy . . . Since the countryside had no clear conception of how much and just what had to be paid, the multiplicity of payments, sometimes in minute quantities (for example, 5 eggs per farm, a half or a third of a chicken), had an oppressive psychological effect on the payers: there seemed to be an endless chain of taxes of which you could never be free." Indeed, it was not uncommon for peasants to barter for or buy produce to meet tax obligations.[8]

But far more important in limiting the collection of the tax was the second successive year of drought which caused major crop failures in the producing provinces of the Volga basin, the southern Urals and to a lesser extent, Ukraine. The grain harvest for 1921 was half of that of 1913, and nearly 20 percent less than in 1920. In June, Lenin acknowledged the situation as "menacing," and by early July, M. Frumkin, a leading Narkomprod official, was predicting an "ideal" of only 150 million puds from the tax and a total procurement from all sources of 240 million (140 million plus 50 million via exchange plus 40 million from Ukraine). In fact, the estimated amount of grain obtained by the state via tax collection and exchange in 1921/2 was 222.8 million puds, of which 138 million was in the form of taxes collected in RSFSR.[9]

Instead of the peasantry relieving the cities, millions of peasants themselves became objects of relief. Grain was purchased from abroad with scarce foreign currency as well as gold melted down from objects that had been confiscated from churches; aid from the American Relief Administration (ARA), the Red Cross, and other relief agencies was gratefully accepted; the tax was waived in the most severely affected areas, while in others, as Kamenev put it, the hungry were taxed to feed the starving. But for an estimated 3 to 4 million, it was not enough. As one ARA investigator reported from Elizavetgrad in the Ukraine: "Many are dying here daily. In the mortuary I found several score bodies, stripped naked, thrown in helter-skelter, men, women and children, their limbs and features twisted and distorted just as the death agony had left them. It was not a pleasant Christmas experience."[10]

The Russian and Ukrainian peasants had experienced Christmases like this before, most notably in 1891, and they would do so again in 1932. Every famine is different but every famine is the same. Unusually severe winters, droughts and crop failures are the precipitants but the underlying causes are social. The last great famine of the tsarist era has been attributed to the fiscal policies of the regime and associated pressures to maximize grain exports. That of 1932–3 was a direct consequence of collectivization and the accompanying removal from the villages of all grain including seed and fodder. The famine of 1921–2 had its own peculiarities but also similarities with these other two demographic catastrophes: epidemics of cholera and typhus, death agonies of the very old, the very young and the feeble, wanderings and apocalyptic visions among the survivors.[11]

Shortages of food persisted well into 1922, not only in famine-stricken provinces but in areas where surpluses had been collected for relief. The following extract from a report by the director of the Iuzovka State Factory and Mines (the former New Russia Company), dated 28 March 1922, is suggestive of conditions in a town *outside* the famine zone:

There is only bread for two days and no more is expected; there is almost no timber and the mines are in a catastrophic state. There is a huge shortage of horses. Butter, sugar and meat the workers have not seen for three months and they cannot afford to buy what is in the market at existing prices. As a result, workers are dying every day at their benches or on their way from work to home. A year of famine riot (*golodnyi bunt*) and complete cessation of work.[12]

In the face of appeals by provincial party secretaries to release stocks of supplies for local consumption and protests by workers over rationing inequities, Narkomprod struggled mightily to maintain its priorities. By the summer of 1922, the worst was past. The grain harvest was nearly 40 percent above the previous year's level and the average yield per hectare rose by 44 percent.[13] The tax burden correspondingly fell from 17.8 percent to 15.5 percent of net income, notwithstanding the fact that the state received 366 million puds of grain in tax, or almost three times as much as in 1921/2. By the time the next year's taxes were collected, money had inserted itself into rural life to the extent that it comprised over 60 percent of tax payments, and by 1924/5 was the exclusive form in which taxes were paid. How much tax was evaded, what methods of evasion were employed and by whom are questions requiring further research.[14]

The rapid recovery in agricultural production was matched by improvement in the material condition of the peasantry. The necessity for industry to acquire liquid assets by selling off stock and the general hunger for food in the towns swung the terms of trade dramatically in favor of the sellers of food crops. Growing and selling more, the peasants also had more to consume. Whereas, early in 1922, peasants in the producing region were eating less than half as much grain as before the war, by the autumn, "grain consumption had rebounded everywhere almost to prewar levels." By October 1922, rural dwellers in the consuming provinces were consuming on average a third more by weight than urban inhabitants, while consumption in the producing region was 15 percent higher.[15]

All this appeared to vindicate the new relation of Soviet power to the peasantry and to enhance the possibilities for the success of the smychka. Addressing the Comintern's Fourth Congress in November 1922, Lenin could exult that "The peasantry is satisfied with its present position . . . This has been achieved in the course of a single year." E. H. Carr, who cites Lenin's remark, went even further by claiming that "Both the avowed purposes and the hidden implications of NEP were suddenly realized to an extent which had scarcely been foreseen: partly by design, partly by accident, the peasant had become the spoilt child of the proletarian dictatorship." There is little direct evidence of what peasants themselves thought about the new relation. To be sure, armed rebellion had all but ceased. But it is highly unlikely that many peasants regarded themselves as objects of governmental favoritism, or would have appreciated the irony in Carr's assessment. The mere fact that they were able to legally market their produce endeared them no more to the Soviet government than it had to the tsarist regime.[16]

Illustrative of both the state's efforts to strengthen the smychka and the contradictions inherent in that enterprise was the new legal framework for land tenure. This was embodied in a Fundamental Law on Land Use for the RSFSR – more commonly known as the Land Code – that was approved by VTsIK in October and came into effect on 1 December 1922. The Land Code has been termed "the high point" in the study and formalization of Russian customary law and "little more than a codification of nineteenth-century peasant legal custom."[17] It mattered little (at least at the time) that all land was declared the property of the state. For, in practice, the prohibition against selling and purchasing land corresponded to the "philosophy of the commune and widespread peasant opinion, [that] land belonged 'to nobody' and the state should play the mainly supervisory role of ensuring the good working of the 'national commune' and seeing to it that every peasant got the share of land that was his due." This, as Moshe Lewin has noted, was "a concept which was more archaic in one sense, but at the same time nearer to certain modern socialist ideas."[18] According to the principle of "juridical neutrality," households could hold, cultivate, and under certain circumstances, lease land in consolidated holdings (*khutors* and *otrubs*), in traditional communes, or in collectives (*kolkhozy*). The overwhelming majority opted for communal tenure.

The contentious issue of whether to recognize the commune as a juridical person was fudged by the framers of the Land Code who referred instead to the "land society," analogous to the Emancipation Act's "rural society." Like "turnover" instead of "trade," the land society was a legal fiction that fooled no one, leastwise the peasants. The governing body of the land society was, after all, nothing but the old communal assembly (skhod) which, given the elimination of the zemstvos and the weakness or non-existence of village soviets, assumed a broad range of responsibilities. To the question, then, of what was recovered during these years, the answer would have to be the self-governing powers of the village commune.[19]

The "traditionalization" of peasant life was given another boost by the Land Code's acknowledgment of the household – rather than the individual – as the legal economic entity. The aim here was apparently to give socialist content to a traditional institution by interpreting the household as a "family-labor association of people farming together." The role of the household head was accordingly redefined as the elected "representative of the family household in its household affairs." Although the representative function of the household head corresponded to customary practice, the elective principle did not. Danilov claims it "proved unsuccessful" and cites the statement by a village correspondent that "no elections take place. I find this question funny. The change takes place naturally." In two major departures from customary law, women were to be considered equal members of the household with equal claims in the event of partitioning, and all adult household members were to have the right to participate in communal assemblies. To what extent these guidelines were observed remains in doubt.[20]

Finally, the Code addressed the ticklish subject of household partitioning, but only to the extent of granting peasants the right to declare their households "indivisible," and empowering local bodies to establish a fixed minimum of land and tools for each household. As was generally the case, however, even this modest attempt at state regulation was dependent on the commune for its enforcement and thus was prey to customary definitions of household viability. Later in the

decade, restrictions against partitions were tightened, but their impact
on the rate of partitions appears to have been relatively small.

We will have occasion to consider the debates that arose in the party
in connection with the reinforcement of the rule of the commune and,
within it, the law of the household. For now, it is important to note
other dimensions of the state's retreat from the countryside. Ironically,
not only did the introduction of NEP mean a diminution of the state's
coercive power, but it also weakened the struggle for political and
cultural hegemony. As indicated previously, that struggle had been
carried on throughout the civil war years via a mass literacy campaign
and political education in the Red Army and the villages. With
demobilization, the army "went from being the 'petted child of the
government' in the civil war to the regime's unwanted orphan," and its
access to and education of young peasant males correspondingly
diminished.[21] At the same time, the precipitous decline in state revenue
occasioned by the revival of private trade, combined with the return to
such orthodox financial policies as balanced state budgets, meant a
slashing of Narkompros' funds and staff and the adoption of the
principle of local self-taxation to support cultural and educational
institutions.

The result was an immediate and sharp reduction in the number of
such institutions, termed "catastrophic" by one Soviet historian. By
January 1923, there remained only 3.8 percent of the literary bases,
16.1 percent of the reading rooms, and 47.7 percent of the libraries that
had been functioning two years earlier. The proportion of children aged
8–11 who attended school in the RSFSR also shrank from 74.3 percent
in 1920/1, to 61.1 percent in 1921/2 and 46.0 percent in 1922/3. Or to
put it another way, six years after the October Revolution there were
fewer pupils in primary school than in 1914. Little wonder, then, that
Nadezhda Krupskaia, head of Glavpolitprosvet (Main Administration
for Political Education), bitterly characterized the new economic policy
her husband had introduced as having "brought with it to the countryside an upsurge of darkness."[22]

The same thing happened to the provision of medical care. The
impact of the government's decision to transfer the funding of public
health to local budgets was an overall reduction in rural medical
services in 1922 of 20 to 25 percent. As there were few physicians
working in rural areas – no more than 4,000 – feldshers bore the brunt
of lay-offs. "This retreat," we are reminded, "occurred during one of the
worst periods of famine and epidemic in modern European history."[23]

Financial constraints also severely hampered the rural soviets (*selsovety*). Lacking the power of taxation, they were dependent on whatever volosts could spare or the communes were willing to allocate, which in both cases was not very much. But this was not the main problem. Although an elective body, the selsovety were actually the lowest organ of the soviet administration, or as one contemporary author put it, "executive bodies carrying out tasks delegated to them by various administrative and juridical organizations (the issuing of summonses, help in the work of tax-collection, etc.)."[24] They thus failed to sink roots in, or gain legitimacy among, their village constituencies. Before 1924 when the party organized a boisterous campaign to "revitalize" the soviets, rural voter turnouts were embarrassingly low – 22 percent in 1922 and 37 percent in 1923 – as was the level of participation by those elected. The prohibition against certain categories of people (priests, ex-tsarist officials, agriculturalists who used hired labor, etc.) taking part in soviet affairs – a rule that did not apply to communal assemblies – thus had little real consequence.

As for the party, it was hardly present in the villages. Summarizing the results of investigations conducted in the mid-1920s, Shanin writes:

A typical rural party branch would be set in the centre of a *volost'*, and consist of twelve to fifteen members, at least two of whom would hold administrative posts – e.g. the chairman and some members of the V.I.K. [volost' *ispolkom*], the judge, the head of the militia, the heads of the local departments of education and propaganda, tax inspectors, and so on. Of this group, not less than one-third would be newcomers, with no roots in the locality, sent in to carry out various administrative duties.[25]

In some places, the party branch was indistinguishable from soviet administrative organs; in others, neither existed. Viriatino, a village in Tambov province, was more heavily represented with party members than many others. In the early 1920s it contained two communists, one of whom was a seasonal miner and Red Army veteran. In Bol'shakov's *volost*, as of 1923 the party cell consisted of four members (as compared to eighteen in 1918), of whom only one was a "proper peasant."[26]

As suggested earlier, youths and, among them, Red Army servicemen were more apt to identify with soviet power than their elders did, and this would explain why in many rural districts the Komsomol was more active than the party itself. (It would also explain why approximately half of all rural soviet chairmen in 1925–6 were ex-servicemen.) But far from necessarily challenging the cultural hegemony of the communal order, it was just as likely that the longer these cohorts remained in the villages, the more they would be absorbed within them.[27] The extent to which urban modes of dress, speech and leisure activities penetrated the villages via veterans, school teachers, village correspondents (sel'kory) and anti-religious activists requires further investigation.

Cooperative socialism?

There was one institution whose fate was bound up with NEP that did sink roots in the countryside. This was the agricultural cooperative, an institution (or rather a myriad of small credit, commercial, and production institutions) that according to Danilov, "formed part of communes," or at least was formed by the communes. Much of what has been written about these associations has to do with Lenin's assessment of them. To a lesser extent, attention has been focused on the politics surrounding the All-Russian Union of Agricultural Cooperatives, the Sel'skosoiuz, which was founded in August 1921. Here as well as in the constituent "centers" ("Soiuzkartofel'," "L'notsentr," etc.) and provincial unions there was no question of retreat by the party. Rather, party organizations waged a protracted campaign of intimidation (or in the parlance of the day, "administrative methods") and electoral fraud to "neutralize the influence of the old cooperators." The result was that by 1923, the last bastion of SR and to a lesser extent, Menshevik influence fell.[28]

But these struggles hardly affected the thousands of "simple" cooperatives that sprang up after the introduction of NEP and were only partially or not at all connected with the provincial or national centers. According to Lewin, "[i]t was unquestionably in the 'wild' associations, or in other words the 'simple associations' and many of the kolkhozes, that the people's co-operative activities found their most authentic expression." These activities included obtaining credits to purchase machinery or high-grade seed for communal use, selling and processing particular crops and handicraft goods, and, as in the TOZ (Tovarishchestvo po obshchestvennoi obrabotki zemli), collectivizing portions of communal land for the period of production.[29]

All this was perfectly compatible with the retreat to "state capitalism," as defined by Lenin. As early as April 1921, he foresaw that "small commodity producers' cooperatives" would "inevitably give rise of petty-bourgeois, capitalist relations," since "freedom and rights for the cooperative societies mean freedom and rights for capitalism." But under the Soviet system, this "cooperative capitalism" would be more advantageous and useful than private capitalism in that "it facilitates the association and organization of millions of people, and eventually of the entire population, and this in its turn is an enormous gain from the standpoint of the subsequent transition from state capitalism to socialism."[30] In other words, while not socialist institutions in themselves, agricultural cooperatives laid the groundwork for joint production-collective farms which would be socialist.

Lenin's view remained the prevailing interpretation of the peasant cooperatives until he himself revised them in January 1923. Confined to bed after having suffered a second stroke, he dictated two short articles under the heading "On Cooperation." He now declared that

With most of the population organized in cooperatives, the socialism which in the past was legitimately treated with ridicule, scorn and contempt by those who were rightly convinced that it was necessary to wage the class struggle, the struggle for political power, etc., will achieve its aim automatically.

For,

the power of the state over all large-scale means of production, political power in the hands of the proletariat, the alliance of this proletariat with the many millions of small and very small peasants, the assured proletarian leadership of the peasantry, etc. – is this not all that is necessary to build a complete socialist society out of cooperatives, out of cooperatives alone, which we formerly ridiculed as hukstering and which from a certain aspect we have the right to treat as such now, under NEP?

To be sure, it would take "a whole historical epoch" for cooperators to undergo a cultural revolution and become "civilized cooperators," learning to trade "in the European manner." But even so, "we are entitled to say that for us the mere growth of cooperation . . . is identical with the growth of socialism . . . "[31]

This was not only a "genuine revolution in the evaluation of the social nature of cooperation," but, as Lenin himself put it, "a radical modification in our whole outlook on socialism." Unfortunately, Lenin did not have the opportunity to elaborate on this modification, and thus, "On Cooperation" stood as "a legacy from Lenin, his final injunction."[32] And a confusing legacy it was. What came to be referred to as "Lenin's cooperative plan" was invoked by both Bukharin in defense of maintaining the link between workers and peasants through "cooperative exchange of goods," and his leftist antagonists (e.g. Preobrazhenskii), who professed to see in it the recipe for converting commercial cooperatives to production collectives. By the time the Left had been defeated and Stalin squared off against Bukharin, "Lenin's cooperative plan" had become inextricably linked with the policy of collectivization. What essentially distinguished the Left from the Stalinists in this respect was that the former assumed the conversion to cooperative farming would be a gradual process facilitated by the application of the state's increased economic leverage, whereas the latter were in much more of a hurry and willing to countenance the use of violence.[33]

But all this was in the future. The problem in the early 1920s was to convince local party organs of the importance of agricultural cooperatives to the success of the NEP, that is, to prevent the cadres from using administrative measures against them. This problem was compounded by the fact, readily acknowledged at the Twelfth Party Conference (August 1922), that the cooperatives were dominated "primarily by better-off (zazhitochnye) elements of the countryside." And if the "better-off" were taking advantage of new opportunities to secure credits and market produce, how long would it be before they allied themselves with, or merged into the kulaks? It was one thing for the Central Committee to mandate that cooperatives should be open to better-off peasants "unless they assumed a clearly kulak character." It was quite another for local bodies to distinguish between these two categories on the spot.[34]

The issue of peasant differentiation, which eventually was to assume major and tragic proportions, could be ducked in the early 1920s because of the overriding concern to stimulate the rural economy and its links with the "commanding heights." When, in March 1922, Preobrazhenskii attempted to draw attention to the emergence of an "agricultural bourgeoisie" amidst the general impoverishment of the countryside, Lenin dismissed his alarm as being based on supposition and lack of concrete experience. "What we must fear most of all," he wrote to Osinskii (who as Narkomzem official had become a convert to agricultural cooperation), "is clumsy interference; for we have not yet made a thorough study of the actual requirements of *local* agricultural life and the actual abilities of the machinery of local administration (the ability not to do evil in the name of doing good)."[35]

The accursed nepmen

There was much to study in the early 1920s, much for which the regime found itself ill prepared – not only the requirements of agricultural life, but the lifeblood of commerce, the real, material link between the peasantry and the state. Lenin's famous dictum about Bolsheviks needing to learn how to trade probably caused as much consternation among the cadres as it has bemusement among latter-day western historians.[36] For who else was there to teach them except private traders, the accursed nepmen?

Initially, it was hoped that commercial transactions could be limited to bartering or direct exchange of goods (tovaroobmen) between town and countryside, with the consumer cooperatives serving as conduits. This hope did not survive the spring of 1921. With the state possessing only a "tiny supply of desirable consumer goods," and in the absence of controls over transport, "a wave of private buying and selling had rolled into the void."[37] As one decree followed another, each further loosening controls on prices and exchange, tens of thousands of private traders – including the civil war era bagmen – emerged from the underground to compete successfully with the generally inefficient state and consumer cooperative networks. In many rural areas, the nepmen were the only sellers of manufactured goods. Even the state-owned industrial trusts relied on them to obtain raw materials and find buyers for their products, despite the official policy of giving preference to cooperatives. Throughout the country, private entrepreneurs handled over three-quarters of all retail trade in 1922/3; in Moscow, they controlled over 80 percent of retail, 50 percent of mixed retail-wholesale, and 14 percent of purely wholesale trade. In more outlying areas where soviet power had been more recently established, the proportions were higher still.[38]

The term "nepmen" applied not only to private traders but also to those who took advantage of the legalization of small-scale private manufacturing. Some reacquired businesses that had been nationalized in 1920, but the majority – approximately 70 percent – operated on a leasehold basis. The largest firms, employing upwards of twenty workers, tended to be located in cities. The more rural-based artisan and handicraft (kustar') producers comprised the largest category of private manufacturers. According to the 1926 census, they numbered nearly 2 million, not counting those who practiced crafts and artisan trades as a side occupation. Often dependent on nepmen for raw materials, credit, and marketing but also (at least in some instances) for training apprentices and employing hired labor, kustari occupied the intermediate and unstable social ground between nepmen proper and peasants or industrial workers. The government preferred that they band together in industrial (promyslovye) cooperatives or artels, but in the rural areas where they often were separated by considerable distances, few did so in the early years of NEP.[39]

Nepmen and kustari never accounted for more than a small fraction of total industrial production. But they were extremely important in certain branches of industry, particularly in the early years of NEP. In 1923 private establishments accounted for nearly 90 percent of all baked bread and only slightly lower proportions of processed foods, footwear, clothing, and furs. Thus, private manufacturing operated not so much in competition as in tandem with "the commanding heights", providing a not inconsiderable component of consumer goods production and thus freeing the state to concentrate its investments in the capital goods sector.[40]

Indispensable though they were, the nepmen were an affront to communist sensibilities. The very term was laden with negative connotations (which spilled over into popular associations with the policy that had brought forth this particular social type). Never were they referred to in party discourse as "commercial specialists," though their services in reviving commerce were arguably no less critical than those provided by engineers and former tsarist military officers in their respective fields. In this sense, the Bolshevik moral economy coincided with – or perhaps grew out of – the traditional Russian antipathy (evident in nineteenth-century *belles-lettres* and folklore alike) toward the *torgash*, the petty tradesman or huckster, as well as the *bogatei*, the (stereotypically fat) rich man who got that way by taking advantage of general shortages and the hardships of hard-working people. Satirized in the theatre, caricatured in newspaper cartoons and reviled at party meetings, the nepmen easily became lightning rods for popular frustrations. Given the heavy concentration of Jews in private trading, particularly in Ukraine, popular antipathy toward nepmen could not but be tinged with anti-semitism.[41] In the late 1980s and into the present decade, as the Soviet Union lurched towards a market economy, the same attitudes with respect to *kooperativchiki* became apparent.

Thanks to Alan Ball's book on which I have based much of this discussion, we know a great deal more about the contradictions and social tensions stemming from the attempt "to build socialism with bourgeois hands." However, there is a good deal that remains elusive about "Russia's last capitalists," including their social consciousness, business practices, and disposition toward soviet power.

Even less is known about "nepwomen," although a sizeable proportion of licensed private traders as well as producers and distributors of illegal homebrew (*samogon*) were female.[42] The standard representation of the "bourgeois woman" of these years was not, however, of a crafty entrepreneur, but rather the embodiment of parasitism and moral degeneration. Contemporary accounts contain many unflattering descriptions of fashionable "ladies" (*damy*) flaunting their husbands' new found or recovered wealth, of "daughters of joy whom NEP had hatched in flocks," and of singers and actresses with loose morals or no morals at all. Fears that such women would spiritually and physically infect proletarian males were real.[43]

Finally, there was the perilous type portrayed by E. Iu. Kviring, first secretary of the Ukrainian party organization and former secretary of the Donetsk party gubkom. This was the woman of bourgeois background who, having been "brought up to regard her main aim as landing 'a good catch' . . . has learned how to manipulate her 'charms' sufficient to charm, win over, and subdue even the most ardent revolutionaries." The result was that "the bourgeois way of life (*byt*), the Philistine way of life, flows over the families of many Communists like insurmountable lava." Invoking the "admittedly extreme" example of Stenka Razin, who in peasant mythology threw a Persian princess into the Volga rather than succumb to her wiles, Kviring insisted that the party had the right to demand "that spiritual supremacy (*verkhovenstvo*) in the family belong to them – to Communists."[44]

How representative this view was is not clear. But it is not hard to detect the presence of a fairly strong misogynist current in party discourse, one that perhaps reflected the persistence of the civil war experience and the fear that in conditions of civil peace, communists were in danger of losing on the domestic front.

Workers and industrial recovery

The configurations of retreat and recovery only partially coincide with those of state and society. While peasants and nepmen clearly were not part of the state apparatus and, as we have seen, experienced recovery in conjunction with the state's retreat, industrial workers represent a more complicated case. It was not only that the state's retreat to the commanding heights of large-scale industry left those employed in smaller establishments either without work or exposed to the tender mercies of private owners or leasees. For even within the state-owned sector, the restoration that workers experienced was that of relations of production which bore many of the classical features of capitalism. To what extent this restoration/retreat was acknowledged and contested within the party, by the trade unions and among rank-and-file workers, and whether it was mitigated by developments outside the workplace are questions that need to be examined.

What Carr refers to as the "cornerstone of the industrial policies of the new economic order" involved the denationalization of small-scale enterprises, defined in terms of the size of the work force and degree of mechanization, and the devolution of responsibility for supplying, financing, and marketing operations of large-scale industry to individual enterprises or combinations of them – initially called "unions" or "bundles" (*kusty*) and eventually trusts – according to the principle of commercial accounting (*khozraschet*). This policy, first set out by Sovnarkom in an instruction of 9 August 1921, was intended to relieve the state of financial and administrative burdens that had become, quite literally, incalculable under the glavk system (see chapter 1). The instruction contained, as Nove puts it, "stern medicine." Materials and fuel had to be bought. Workers had to be paid. The necessary resources would have to be obtained from sales. No more spoon-feeding, and no easy sources of credit."[45]

Trustification was thus a strategy for the survival of industry in the harsh newly marketized economic conditions. Organized along branch and in some cases regional lines, trusts became major players in the economic field. By October 1922, there were 430 of them combining 4,144 enterprises in which 977,000 workers were employed. The size of the trusts varied a great deal, ranging from relative giants such as "Gomza" (State Union of Metalworks Factories) with 39,500 workers, "Iugostal'" and the Orekhovo-Zuevo Cotton Trust, down to "dwarfs" such as Moscow's "Compressed Gas" which employed twenty-two workers or Belorussia's ceramics trust with sixty-three. Most of the larger trusts answered directly to Vesenkha and in some cases (tea, sugar, rubber) they were merely converted from pre-existing glavki; the smaller ones were attached to provincial sovnarkhozy. Soviet historians used to make a point of distinguishing the trusts of the NEP period from their namesakes in the capitalist world, but in several critical respects, including their object of earning a profit, they were identical.[46]

Before the trusts could become profitable, though, they had to find some way of compensating their constituent enterprises for the loss of state credits and state supplies of raw materials and foodstuffs, the latter being a critical factor in retaining a work force. The method they resorted to was selling off whatever stocks of equipment and finished goods were at hand, a procedure that involved setting up shops or stalls in marketplaces (or hiring agents on commission) and went by the colorful name of *razbazarivanie* (bazaar sales). But in the famine conditions of 1921–2 buyers were scarce and competition was stiff. The result was a depression of industrial prices relative to those for agricultural goods. In May 1922 when this process was at its most extreme, industrial prices had plunged to 65 percent of their 1913 value, while agricultural prices rose to 113 percent. Thereafter, the different trusts in each branch of industry rationalized their marketing by forming "syndicates" – evidently again without qualms about using a term so redolent of monopoly capitalism. With increased quantities of food and raw materials coming into the market, the disparity of prices quickly disappeared. Indeed, by the spring of 1923, price structures had moved far apart in the opposite direction. The "dictatorship of grain" had been replaced by the "dictatorship of manufactured goods" and the "scissors crisis," so dubbed by Trotsky, was upon the nation.[47]

Rationalization of another sort proceeded throughout this period. At the same time that trusts sought to realize their production, they also engaged in cutting costs by concentrating output in the most viable enterprises. This amounted to industrial triage, the closing down or leasing out of many factories that had ceased production in any case, and cannibalizing their capital stock. Of the more than 1,000 enterprises in the leather industry previously administered by Glavkozh, only 124 were taken over by the trusts, the remainder being leased or abandoned. Whereas 969 mines were operating in the Donbass in 1920, the coal trust, Donugol', took over less than 300. By October 1922 the number was down to 202 and a year later stood at 179. Only in a few instances did central authorities intervene to prevent the closure of individual enterprises. A case in point was the Putilov Works which was kept open by order of the party's central committee on the grounds of its "political significance . . . for the life of Petrograd."[48]

As for the revival of industrial production, a great deal depended on overcoming the shortage of fuel. Toward this end, "the whole energies of the party personnel were mobilised." This is only a slight exaggeration, for throughout 1921 and into 1922 sizeable quantities of food, equipment, and personnel were mobilized to reverse the catastrophic decline in coal and oil production. At the same time, no little effort was made to revive railway transportation which suffered not only from a lack of fuel, but "healthy" locomotives. As suggested in Table 3.1, it took several years before substantial increases in output were achieved.[49]

A closer look at the table will reveal that recovery was swiftest in cotton fabrics, and this was generally the case in what is referred to as light or consumer goods industries. Given the importance that the party attached to the smychka with the peasantry and the critical role that textiles played in developing it, this was a significant index of NEP's

Table 3.1. *Industrial output and transportation, 1913–1926*

	1913	1920	1921	1922	1923	1924	1925	1926
Industrial (factory) production (million 1926–7 rubles)	10,251	1,410	2,004	2,619	4,005	4,660	7,739	11,083
Oil (million tons)	9.2	3.9	3.8	4.7	5.3	6.1	7.1	8.3
Coal (million tons)	29.0	8.7	8.9	9.5	13.7	16.1	18.1	27.6
Electricity (million kwhs)	1,945	—	520	775	1,146	1,562	2,925	3,508
Pig iron (thousand tons)	4,216	—	116	188	309	755	1,535	2,925
Steel (thousand tons)	4,231	—	183	392	709	1,140	2,135	3,141
Cotton fabrics (million meters)	2,582	—	105	349	691	963	1,688	2,286
Rail freight (million tons)	132.4	—	39.4	39.9	58.0	67.5	83.4	—

Sources: Alec Nove, *An Economic History of the USSR*, p. 87; figures for oil from Robert A. Clarke, *Soviet Economic Facts, 1917–1970* (London, 1972), p. 54.

success. But at the same time, the relatively slow pace of recovery in heavy industry was disturbing. Why it should have been so regarded may be less obvious in our post-industrial age than in an era when industrial power was considered the *sine qua non* of a modern civilized state, no less a socialist one. But over and above this association was another, namely the historical but also ideological association of the "real" (i.e. experienced, predominantly male, and skilled) proletariat with heavy – and in particular, the metalworks – industry. If Russian workers generally tended to fall short of the Bolshevik conceptualiz-ation of the ideal proletariat, workers in light industries fell furthest – partly because many were rural-based or maintained strong ties to the village and partly because of the gendered definition of "skill," accord-ing to which most female operatives were classified as unskilled or at best semi-skilled. These were the reasons why Lenin, for one, always regarded heavy industry as "indispensable," and why Carr refers to the sluggishness of its recovery as "the fundamental problem created by the first two years of NEP."[50]

How then did the new course impinge on industrial workers? As we have seen, the state's labor policy until 1921 was based on the reciprocal principles of compulsory service (*povinnost'*) and social maintenance via rations supplied to all who rendered such service. The dismantling of the bureaucratic machinery of povinnost' actually proceeded faster than the abandonment of rationing. But by September 1921, when a decree was issued setting forth the "Basic Rules on Wages," the distinction between payment for work done and social relief was complete, at least in theory. Henceforward, compulsory labor became synonymous with enterprises run by the GPU and the chief alternative for workers to "free" wage labor was unemployment.[51]

Keeping track of the number of unemployed was a growth industry in the 1920s. Both the labor exchanges administered by Narkomtrud and the trade unions compiled data. These were approximate and never coincided, for if the exchanges only counted those actively seeking work (i.e., registering with an exchange), the unions restricted their calculations to dues-paying members. Abuses of the labor exchange system were notorious and led to periodic attempts to remove from the books those who had registered to avoid taxation, "dead souls" and other simulators. But there is no doubt that throughout the early years of NEP unemployment rose dramatically. According to the labor exchanges, the number of unemployed shot up from 160,000 on 1 January 1922 to 407,500 by July 1922, 641,000 on 1 January 1923 and 1,240,000 a year later. Unemployed trade union members numbered 427,600 on 1 July 1923, 657,700 on 1 January 1924 and 676,000 on 1 July 1924. The latter figure represented 13.8 percent of all union members, whereas the number registered with the labor exchanges as of July 1924 (1,344,300) comprised 18 percent of all hired labor.[52]

Aside from the scaling down of the work force in connection with khozraschet and rationalization, two additional factors contributed to these soaring rates. One was short-term, namely, the demobilization of the army which in the course of 1922–3 threw several million men onto the labor market.[53] The other was rural to urban migration, a process that had been interrupted, indeed reversed, by the implosion of the urban economy during the revolution and civil war. In 1921–2 migrants consisted mostly of refugees from the famine and former urban residents. Thereafter, landless peasants and seasonal workers (otkhodniki) comprised the main contingents. The combined effect of this increase in labor supply was to produce the paradox of unemployment rising at the same time as the number of workers employed also was increasing.

In these circumstances of intense competition for jobs, certain workers were more vulnerable to unemployment than others. Pressure exerted by party organizations on the exchanges to find work for war veterans combined with protective legislation covering the conditions of employment for women and juveniles worked against the latter two groups. Women accounted for 31.1 percent of those registered with the Moscow labor exchange in January 1922 but 62.2 percent by June. Nationally, women accounted for 42.8 percent of the unemployed in January 1924 and 47.5 percent a year later, figures far in excess of their proportion in the work force. As for juveniles, the number employed in industry plummeted from 120,000 in 1921 to 5,000 two years later. A 1922 decree mandated that at least 7 percent of an enterprise's work force consist of juveniles, but enforcement was lax.[54]

Until 1925 and again after 1927, all hiring was to be done through the labor exchanges. But even before their monopoly was (temporarily) abolished by decree, it was widely breached in practice. This was a sore point with the trade unions which sought to protect their members, and particularly the skilled among them, from competition by peasant migrants. The latter found work most readily in transport and construction where they were usually hired on sight. Otherwise, available statistics indicate that those designated as unskilled fared badly, whereas in certain industries there was a shortage of skilled workers.[55]

Finally, it should be noted that in the early years of NEP the ranks of the unemployed were swelled by hundreds of thousands of office, service, and clerical workers. For just as the state cut back on its rural outreach activities, so it drastically reduced staff in urban-based institutions and enterprises. If in April 1921 employees of Soviet institutions comprised 12 percent of all hired workers, then in October 1922 their share had fallen to 9 percent. During 1923 and 1924, approximately one-third of the unemployed consisted of those classified as "intellectual workers."[56]

The historical literature has fairly well covered the dimensions of unemployment and their sectoral and regional variations. It also has detailed the state's efforts to organize public works projects, encourage the formation of artels or cooperatives of unemployed workers, and provide social insurance. What remains ripe for social historical investigation is how Soviet workers coped with unemployment. A few tentative leads are provided in recent works. William Chase argues that "unemployment wracked the proletariat," uniting urban workers against rural migrants at the same time as it intensified "centrifugal tendencies" within that class. On an individual level, unemployment was an "alienating" experience. It drove some to sell samogon, others to sell their bodies and still others to thievery, petty and otherwise. The Soviet historian Iu. P. Kokarev has noted a close correlation between the number of unemployed and the rise of suicides in major cities. In the longer run, fear of unemployment and resentment against nepmen and "bureaucrats" who seemed immune to its miseries "consciously or unconsciously helped to forge a tacit alliance between urban workers . . . and the party's radicals in the late 1920s."[57]

All this is as one might expect, which is to say it is reminiscent of patterns familiar from the history of western capitalist societies. Much less so is the discussion of unemployment in Chris Ward's *Russia's Cotton Workers and the New Economic Policy*, the first western monograph on a specific occupational group. Mapping the local distribution of unemployment among operatives, Ward notes that mills in the Central Industrial Region (CIR) – as opposed to Petrograd's larger and more efficient enterprises – "bore the brunt of the concentration of production" and the scissors crisis. But he also emphasizes with reference to the CIR's provincial mills the "blurred . . . distinction between peasants with sources of off-mill income and jobless proletarians reliant on wage labour . . . During summer shut-downs in 1922 and 1923 the [Ivanovo – LS] guberniya's operatives frequently occupied themselves with farm labour or handicrafts, but because such work was precarious they often registered at the exchanges in order to find a place on the shop floor later on." Unemployment was thus a "construct," the registration of which "was a function of stop-go production in the cotton industry intermingled with local perceptions of the job market."[58]

Ward deconstructs not only "unemployment," but "worker" as well. He points out that the complex symbiosis between field and factory, a commonplace of pre-revolutionary social historical analysis, persisted throughout the 1920s, being strengthened by the insecurities associated with NEP. What was true of cotton workers did not necessarily hold for other occupational groups, though the rhythms of employment in construction work, timber felling, peat cutting, and coal and iron ore mining bear a strong resemblance. In each case, the "peasant–worker continuum" was maintained by the complementarity between agricultural and industrial calendars and the informal institution of the artel (and, in the cotton industry, the *komplekt*) which drew upon kinship and local ties to facilitate obtaining a job, finding accommodation, and learning a trade. Many parallels with the experiences of industrial workers in other countries are suggested by these patterns.[59] Exactly how they worked in the early Soviet context and what implications they had for employment patterns, wage levels, and ethnic, trade and class identities should be high on the agenda of labor historians.

If generalizations about unemployment need to be qualified, so too does the impact of NEP on wage structures. To be sure, the thrust of the state's wage policy was clear and universal. To replace payments in kind by monetary wages, to establish a contractual relationship between hired labor and employers through collective agreements between trade unions and trusts, and to link wage rates with skill and productivity – these were the state's main objectives. None, however, was easily obtainable.

Not until the financial reform of February 1924 did payments in kind completely disappear. Their persistence was partly a function of institutional inertia, for Narkomprod was still collecting sizeable quantities of foodstuffs via the tax-in-kind and was slow to abandon the principle of social maintenance. They also figured in the practice of "piece-selling," whereby factories, in lieu of their shortage of liquid assets, set aside a portion of their output for workers to exchange with cooperatives or in bazaars. But the key factor here was the reluctance of workers to subject themselves to the vagaries of a rapidly depreciating currency and the strong support they received from their trade unions.[60] Indeed, it is far from clear that workers favored the abandonment of the "iron-clad" ration, even if prominent trade unionists recognized the necessity of doing so. What they had objected to, after all, was not rations as such, but inequities and abuses in the ration system as it was practiced in 1920–1. Such an attitude, where it was acknowledged at all, was interpreted as reflecting workers' "consumerism" and/or residual egalitarianism. It may just as well have been their pragmatic sense.

The concept of the "goods-ruble," according to which wages were calculated in terms of a price-index based on 1913 prices, emerged as an attempt to insulate wage earners from the worst of inflation. Despite wrangles about what goods should be included in the "basket," the logarithmic nightmares of converting the paper rubles in which workers were paid to the price indices, and a certain amount of manipulation of the indices by local authorities, it appears that real wages rose across the board throughout 1922 and into the following year. Here again, though, the consumer goods sector showed the way partly because of its more rapid recovery and partly because of competition from private enterprises. It must have scandalized delegates to the party's thirteenth conference to hear that in December 1922 "girl workers in tobacco factories packing cigarettes were getting more than a coal-hewer or a fitter." Only with the onset of the scissors crisis, which primarily affected consumer goods, was a "saner balance between wages in different sectors of industry" achieved, though more as a result of levelling down the wages of girl workers than levelling up those of their heavier brothers.[61]

Collective agreements should have standardized wages, but did not. Since retail prices varied across the country, so did the purchasing power of the same amount of rubles. The substandard and idiosyncratic nature of machinery, frequent breakdowns and shortages of spare parts made a mockery of standardized piece rates which figured in many agreements. Local negotiations with union branches generally had the effect of pushing wages upward, whereas on-the-spot adjustments of output norms and the late payment of wages had the opposite effect.

Collective agreements did, however, provide "a legitimate arena for open conflict with enterprise and trust management." Available data from Moscow indicate that most conflicts in the early 1920s concerned wages (and particularly their late distribution), followed by assignments to technical courses and rest homes, and then more distantly by labor protection and hiring and firing practices. Most of these disputes were handled by assessment and conflict commissions (RKK), which were jointly staffed by union and management representatives, and where the RKK had failed to reach a decision satisfactory to both parties, by conciliation courts and arbitration tribunals. These mechanisms did not, however, prevent workers from resorting on occasion to their most powerful weapon, the strike.[62]

No statistics are available on the incidence of strikes before 1922. In that year, which saw a reported 446 strikes involving 192,000 workers, those employed in textiles comprised the largest number – yet another indication of the perils of recovery. The peak of strike activity, what is usually referred to as a "strike wave," came a year later at the height of the sales slump occasioned by the scissors crisis. Indeed, these strikes, which affected some of the country's largest factories (for example, Sormovo in Nizhni-Novgorod; Trekhgornaia in Moscow) were a critical factor in focusing the Politburo's attention on resolving that crisis.

The most spectacular example of friction between workers and management, strikes also pitted workers against their unions and the party. However much sympathy the plight of labor might evoke among individual unionists or the party leadership, the resort to the strike violated the productivist orientation that was a cardinal principle in the latter's strategy for economic recovery. More than that, it challenged the Bolshevik shibboleth of the proletarian state and the claim of unions to represent workers' interests. Consequently, strikes tended to be local, short-lived affairs, and while often at least partially successful, could be accompanied by expulsion from the union, arrest, dismissal, or other forms of victimization of those identified as instigators.

Strikes thus highlighted the fact that the breach between the party and workers and between workers and "their" unions – a breach that was noted on the eve of NEP – had not been healed by the adoption of that policy. As William Chase has argued, "The NEP's (sic) policies of rationalization, tying wages to productivity, reducing costs, intensifying labor, and one-man management were not the means by which workers hoped to enact their revolutionary agenda. They were the problems. They smacked of a return to the old order." Yet, one must be cautious about interpreting strikes as evidence of anti-party or anti-union sentiment, even among those who took part in them. For, "what spared the party from feeling the full force of workers' discontent was that the NEP, by its very nature, absolved the party from direct responsibility for many of the problems of factory and economic life. Impersonal market forces increasingly determined the course of the economy." It was management, forced to operate within the constraints of those forces and periodically the object of the party's anti-bureaucratic rhetoric, that bore the brunt of workers' discontent.[63]

For their part, the trade unions found themselves reduced to decrying the "excesses" and abuses of the above-mentioned policies that they were otherwise compelled to boost. This was an unenviable position. One can sense the discomfort of a union leader who in supporting multi-machine working, observed that "In the time of the tsar we took strike action against such measures, now we ourselves are carrying them out in order to show the peasants that we mean to increase [supply] and cheapen the cost of manufacture."[64] Such were the ironies and contradictions of recovery.

No longer part of the state apparatus, the unions also lacked an autonomous civil status apart from the state. In official discourse, they became "transmission belts" of party policy, "a subordinate participant in the formulation of industrial policy, and the mechanism through which centrally determined policy was implemented." Did this mean that they had forfeited their claim to being genuine trade unions? Such a judgment seems excessively harsh. Aside from begging the question of how often unions in the western world have deviated from their "genuine" role under different sorts of constraints and compulsions, it ignores other dimensions of unions' activities during the 1920s. Indeed, it could be argued that the anomalous civil status enabled the unions to function not only as transmission belts of party–state policies, but as social mediators. In the latter capacity, they provided a broad range of cultural activities, access to secondary and higher education, and even an identity alternative to the narrow "shopism" to which many workers were inclined or the much broader but increasingly vague and problematic identity of class.[65]

As for unionists themselves, there was no shortage of bureaucratic functionaries. But there were also activists who, while accepting the necessity for raising productivity, tried to minimize workers' sacrifices, and others who saw in the ethos of productivism and the new production techniques it extolled an opportunity for unions to reacquire functions appropriated by management. In short, the language of productivity was sufficiently broad at this stage to be appropriated by several different groups, each with its own agenda. The controversies surrounding the "scientific organization of labor" (*nauchnaia organizatsiia truda* – NOT, or as western historians refer to it, Soviet Taylorism) are a good illustration. Already at the all-Russian initiative conference convened by Trotsky in January 1921, a division between "engineers–Taylorists" and the "social minded" was apparent. In subsequent years, as public discussion about how to raise efficiency and increase productivity grew in volume, there was further fractioning. For the Central Institute of Labor and its visionary director, A. K. Gastev, NOT constituted a culture of work consisting of a series of gradated stages that workers could learn through conditioning (*ustanovka, trenirovka*). Although sponsored by VTsSPS, the institute and its self-proclaimed "narrow-base" approach to NOT came under attack by many trade unionists as well as Proletkultists for ignoring workers' creativity and all-round development. By the time the second NOT conference was held in 1924, there were at least four distinct though overlapping loci of NOTism: Gastev's institute and its branches throughout the country; various psychophysiological, psychotechnical and labor hygiene institutes promoting the "scientific" basis of their research; a council (SovNOT) sponsored by the Workers' and Peasants' Inspectorate as well as that commissariat's own Directorate for Improvement of the State Apparatus; and the Time League (later, League-NOT), a mass movement headed by a former Proletkultist and theatrical journalist, P. M. Kerzhentsev.[66]

Employment and wages, unions and management, rationalization schemes and the petty negotiations that took place on the shop floor all structured working-class life in important ways. But they did not fully consume it. Workers did not live in factories, although many depended on workplace-based housing associations for accommodation. Nor were their cultural pursuits bounded by the factory gates, though the workers' clubs that were jointly sponsored by the Main Committee on Political Education (Glavpolitprosvet) and the trade unions were supposed to reflect all production life, and many informal – and officially frowned upon – activities such as smoking breaks, skill acquisition celebrations and post-shift drinking sessions were defined by the rhythms of work. That most workers have families, that family members partake of and reproduce popular culture, and that their attitudes toward politics and government and toward each other critically depend on age, gender, state of health, and family status – as well as occupation, work experience, and skill – have long been recognized by historians of other working classes.

In the Soviet case, acknowledgment of the importance of these attributes of working-class life has come slowly, no doubt because of the weight attached by communist discourse to other factors and the extent to which that discourse has consciously or unconsciously shaped the kinds of questions historians ask. Here, it is only possible to suggest a framework for analyzing some of the features and forces that were peculiar to, or unusually evident in, the early 1920s.

Mention has already been made of the peasant–worker continuum, a concept which stands as an important corrective to the hypostatization of class categories. The economic dimension of the continuum is amenable to certain kinds of quantification specifying fluctuations in seasonal migration, which workers owned land, and who sent money back to the villages. But these kinds of data need to be supplemented by a cultural dimension that includes consideration of pre-revolutionary and indeed pre-capitalist traditions (religious practices, for example), spontaneous adaptations to the material uncertainties of NEP, *and* the formidable efforts of party, Komsomol and trade union activists to promote the new "proletarian consciousness."

Considerable work has been done on unpacking this "consciousness." Fitzpatrick defines it as "a powerful Soviet myth" which conveyed "a sense of aggressive collective identity, comradeship, identification with Soviet power and the Bolshevik Party." As she and others have demonstrated, it not only contended with the other cultures available to workers but was itself the object of contention among Proletkultists, the Komosomol, Narkompros' pedagogical theorists, and productionists scattered throughout party and state institutions. What was involved here was nothing less than the search, conducted in highly polemical terms, for a definition of "class." This definition had to be adequate to both the complex, multi-layered reality of social relations and capable of mobilizing support among and imposing a degree of discipline on potential cadres. In short, it had both descriptive and prescriptive dimensions.[67]

Recognizing that workers moved in and out of new and old cultures, even on a daily basis, it must also be acknowledged that receptivity to new cultural impulses was not restricted to industrial workers. To cite Fitzpatrick again:

Urban blue-collar and white-collar youth of the NEP period shared similar interests and aspirations, dressed in the same way for their nights out, liked the same dances . . . saw the same movies, and read the same books and journals. Their culture was strongly influenced by the Komsomol press, and in many respects constituted a popular version of the "high" culture of the young Communist intelligentsia . . . It was characterized by romanticism about the revolution and civil war, liberated attitudes to sex (and anxieties about liberation), contempt for "bourgeois" conventions, fascination with modern machines and the idea of "Soviet America," hope for adventure, enthusiasm for the task of "building a new world" and confidence about the future, especially the future prospects of the young.

This may have been why "'youth' was often treated as the equivalent of a class category by NEP commentators."[68]

But this too was a highly inflected category. If the above-cited definitional force-field helped to identify the children of the revolution and not incidentally swelled the ranks of the Left Opposition, it necessarily excluded a large segment of Soviet youth, namely, the *besprizorniki* (orphans, or literally, "untended ones"), the real stepchildren of the revolution. Offspring of poor peasant and working-class households that had ceased to exist or could not otherwise support them, these youths thronged the cities in search of survival, often resorting to begging and brigandage. The besprizorniki were a legacy of war, revolution, and civil war. But far from alleviating the problem, NEP and its associated economies on state expenditure actually had the opposite effect. Between 1921 and 1924 the capacity of children's shelters fell from "an already inadequate" 540,000 to 280,000.[69]

Along with the related phenomena of unemployment and hooliganism *besprizornost'* was a blight on Soviet urban society. Whether it was a blight on NEP as well, that is, whether NEP was part of the problem or the solution to problems inherited from the years of war, revolution, and civil war, was a question to which there was no definitive answer, at least not in the early 1920s. What is apparent is that during this period of indefiniteness, experts of all kinds came forward with claims of special knowledge to alleviate social ills. In this respect, the besprizorniki served as a social laboratory for psychologists, hygienists, criminologists, pedagogues, and other specialists to experiment with various and sundry theories of "defectology" and social rehabilitation. Thus were spawned the famous labor communes for children sponsored by Narkompros (and later OGPU) and a rich literature, itself reflective of the creative tension between appalling social conditions and bold, often utopian, thinking.[70]

The intelligentsia in limbo

I am looking at a reproduction of "Communal House," a pencil and ink drawing by Vladimir Krinsky. The catalog in which the drawing appears describes it as one of the "highly speculative, gravity-defying arrangements of abstract shapes," turned out by the Moscow-based group of architects and artists known as *Zhivskulptarkh* (Paint-Sculpt-Arch). In the early years after the revolution, Soviet Russia was awash with such imaginative drawings and models – Tatlin's Monument to the Third International, a model of a leaning tower that was to stand 400 meters high, is perhaps the best known – none of which was ever built. If the pedagogues who sought to fashion a new collective-minded individual out of the besprizorniki were metaphorical "architects of the future," real architects also had their vision squarely (or gravity-defyingly) on the future as well. Urged by Maiakovskii "to cover the sites of yesterday's conflagration" with "fantastic structures," the architects gave full reign to their artistic impulses.[71] But, as Bukharin was to note later in querying the rationality of the First Five-Year Plan, one can't build today's factories with tomorrow's bricks. Or was it because of the critical shortage of building materials that architects, knowing their designs could not be realized, liberated them from the constraints of gravity?

Liberation from the constraints of space and time figures prominently during these years not only among avant-garde architects but also among artists, writers, and scientists. Kazimir Malevich who fancied himself as much an architect as an artist and theorist of art, announced in an essay entitled "Futurism-Suprematism, 1921" that "In the future, not a single grounded structure will remain on Earth. No thing will be fastened or tied down." Taking seriously the revolution's cosmic potential, such dreamers sought to project it into the future, throughout the world and to the heavens. Stites' book on *Revolutionary*

Dreams is chock full of examples of such "utopian visions" – stateless societies without classes or exploitation, technological fantasies of all-world cities, nostalgic utopias without cities at all. He is surely correct to link this "futuristic speculation" to the "pathos of the period and the reality from which it arose: immortality yearned for in a land still groaning from a decade of holocaust; space flight, in a land where wooden plow and horse-cart were everyday sights."[72]

But revolutionary dreams based on notions of leveling, egalitarianism, and revolt against deference were not only projected; they were also practiced. Furniture designed under the auspices of VKhUTEMAS (Higher State Artistic and Technical Workshops) was typically simple, made of standardized parts and multi-functional. Leading Constructivists such as Popova, Stepanova, Tatlin, and Exter designed functional proletarian costumes (*prododezhda*) that could be worn for working, relaxation or sport.[73] Others, notably the "Down with Shame" movement that held evenings of the Denuded Body in Moscow in 1922, advocated wearing no clothes at all! Then there was Persimfans, the First Symphony Orchestra without a Conductor, a "practicing utopia" organized by Lev Tseitlin in 1922. Persimfans explicitly took aim at the egotism and autocratic power of conductors (whose ranks were depleted through emigration). It thereby implicitly challenged Lenin's rationale for one-man management in industry which had been based on the analogy with orchestral organization and discipline.[74]

What did all this have to do with retreat and recovery? Absolutely nothing, it would seem. While communist leaders and economists set their sights on restoring production to pre-war levels, the avant-garde's benchmarks were more lofty and less quantifiable. What the latter wanted was not to retreat, but to move forward, "From the Left/ As one/ Begin!" as the journal *LEF* put it. Yet, it was still possible in the early 1920s for both political authorities and avant-gardists to assume a compatibility of interest based on mutual contempt of the bourgeoisie. Under Lunacharskii's protective wing, many avant-garde artists found employment in Narkompros' Department of Fine Arts, received commissions and organized exhibitions.[75]

Matters stood differently with those who represented older cultural and political values, who for one reason or another had not emigrated but who despised the Bolsheviks and all they stood for just as fiercely as their former colleagues who had taken up residence in Prague, Paris or Berlin. At a time when civil war induced traumas and insecurities were still fresh and "revolutionary justice" was still a very live concept, the arbitrary repressiveness of the State Political Administration (GPU) was bound to be visited upon those who resisted or simply mocked the state's definition of what was necessary for its survival and that of Soviet society. The executions in 1921 of the Acmeist poet, Nikolai Gumilev, the chemist Tikhvinsky and other engineers employed by the Main Fuel Administration were a clear indication of this nervousness and intolerance. The arrest and expulsion in August 1922 of 160 philosophers, sociologists, linguists, and university administrators, most of whom had been involved in a professorial strike the previous year, perhaps more effectively conveyed the message that the state's retreat was not to be construed as a rout.[76]

It would not do, however, to treat relations between the state and the intelligentsia in simple bipolar terms. The boundaries between the two were too fluid and divisions within each too severe to sustain such a framework. Within the professions, young vanguardist communists crossed swords with both their pre-revolutionary trained elders and their non-communist contemporaries. But they did not necessarily have official backing. The unsuccessful campaign by RAPP (Russian Association of Proletarian Writers) to establish its hegemony over literary production and criticism is a case in point. RAPP did enjoy the support of the Komsomol and its journal *Molodaia gvardiia*. But the "thick" journal, *Krasnaia nov* (Red Virgin Soil), which published the works of Boris Pilnyak, Vsevolod Ivanov and other non-communist, non-proletarian writers, was more characteristic of the official party attitude towards literary expression. So too was Trotsky's term for such writers – "fellow travelers" – which he coined in 1923.[77]

This too was part of the retreat. By sustaining a rich café culture, dozens of private publishing houses, and heavy cultural traffic with the West, NEP made fellow traveling possible, even attractive. It was even possible to think that "It is not the non-Russian revolutionaries who govern the Russian revolution, but the Russian revolution which governs the non-Russian revolutionaries, who have assimilated themselves, externally or internally, to 'the Russian soul' in its present condition." This, in any case, was the view of N. Ustrialov, a leading figure in the *émigré* movement known as *Smena vekh* (Change of Landmarks), the name of which came from a volume of essays published in Prague in 1921. Like the fellow travelers within Soviet Russia, the *smenovekhtsy* were prepared to accept the revolution as both inevitable and a peculiarly Russian national phenomenon. Although the movement evoked wariness among Communist Party leaders, Carr makes the interesting observation that it "helped to prepare the way for the reconciliation of the revolutionary and the national tradition which was a condition and concomitant of 'socialism in one country.'"[78] The history of *Smena vekh* remains to be written.

The scientific-technical community was faced with a different set of circumstances. As already has been pointed out, the Soviet government, and Lenin in particular, was keen to tap the expertise of scientists and engineers. Thus, more so than the cultural intelligentsia, the elite of the technical intelligentsia was provided first-class accommodation in its fellow traveling. By 1921, it had achieved a high degree of professional autonomy and at least in numerical terms dominated such state agencies as GOELRO, the State Planning Commission (Gosplan), and Vesenkha. The restoration of industry presented huge opportunities for specialists to influence such critical decisions as which enterprises and rail lines to keep operational, what kind of equipment to purchase abroad, and how to implement cost accounting and efficiency procedures in state and industrial administration.

To at least some of them, NEP represented nothing less than salvation. Nikolai Valentinov – himself a "non-party specialist" – remembers several engineers referring to NEP as having changed everything:

It was at that point that we came out of the airless crypt and began to breathe. Then we rolled up our sleeves and got down to real work . . . Many of us felt that, thanks to NEP, we had finally returned from the moon to the earth. The energy of the intelligent and useful strata of the country, which had been repressed up to this time, was now released . . . In our Commissariat [Ways and Communications – LS] we are not limited simply to the restoration of transportation; we dream about more – about its complete and rational reconstruction, about the great construction of new railway lines, additional locomotives, and cars, the reconstruction of railroad lines and automatic coupling.[79]

Of course, mutual doubts and suspicions between technical specialists and Soviet authorities were bound to persist. In a survey conducted in 1922 among 230 engineers employed in Moscow area trusts, only 28 expressed sympathy with the "soviet platform," while 46 claimed indifference and 110 supported the *Smena vekh* position. The party used five categories in its assessment of engineers' political orientation. These ranged from "*spets*-communist" to "*spets*-white guardist," with the majority being in the "wait and see *spets*" category. Bukharin was undoubtedly correct when, in December 1924, he referred to the smychka between engineers and leading party cadres as an ideal rather than something that had been achieved.[80]

More strained still were relations between technical specialists and workers. The former, after all, not only staffed the government's commissariats, commissions and institutes, but occupied the directorships of most large industrial enterprises. This, the replacement of "commissars" by *spetsy*, was a new development associated with the adoption of khozraschet. It was yet another example of retreat, as much a personification of NEP as were the nepmen. What workers thought about it was summed up by Tomskii, chairman of trade unions' central council, in the following terms: "The *spets* live better, gets paid better, he gives the orders, makes demands; the *spets* is an alien person, the *spets* did not make the October Revolution."[81] Tomskii and others attributed such an attitude to a lack of understanding on the part of "the backward strata" of workers, but it is unlikely that "*spets*-baiting" was restricted to the politically illiterate.

In 1923, thanks largely to the intervention of the party Secretariat's Records and Assignment Section (*Uchraspred*) in the appointment of leading state and economic officials, the proportion of specialists among factory directors began to decline, while that of party members of proletarian origin increased.[82] This trend, which continued throughout the remainder of the 1920s, had little effect on industrial policy, since the so-called "Red directors" remained heavily dependent on technical directors and other specialists working in line and staff positions. It was, though, an important indication of the aggrandizement of power by the Secretariat and particularly, the General Secretary, I. V. Stalin.

The in-gathering of nations

The year 1921 was a turning point in Soviet history in many respects not the least of which was the relationship between Moscow and the non-Russian peoples of the former tsarist empire. If during the civil war the major question was which parts of that empire would remain within the soviet orbit, then its aftermath brought different issues to the fore. These revolved around how to weld together the newly created soviet republics and in the process foster a common consciousness based on class as opposed to pre-existing and/or competing national, religious, or ethnic identities. If military conquest was the primary means for the establishment of these republics, other methods would have to be sought to consolidate the military victory.

By February 1921 when a soviet republic was proclaimed in Georgia, there were six such republics: the RSFSR which itself was federative in the sense of incorporating a number of autonomous republics and territories, Ukraine, Belorussia, Georgia, Armenia, and Azerbaidzhan. In addition, there were two "soviet people's republics" – Khorezm (the former Khiva) and Bokhara – and a "democratic republic" of the Far East, each of whose status was declared to be provisional. Between September 1920 and May 1921, bilateral treaties were signed between the RSFSR and each of the other five soviet socialist republics committing each side to a "close military and financial-economic union." While explicitly concluded between independent sovereign states, the treaties, in Carr's view, "had some features of an alliance, some of federation and some of a unitary state." Thus, in the case of the Ukrainian treaty, the preamble asserted both "the independence and sovereignty of each of the contracting parties" and "the necessity to unite their forces for purposes of defense and also in the interests of their economic construction." This meant, among other things, that "unified commissariats" would be created for military affairs, the national economy, foreign trade, finance, labor and ways and communications but not for agriculture, education, justice or foreign affairs.[83]

What is surprising here is not so much the asymmetries and vagueness built into these treaties, as the attention that was paid to diplomatic formalities. A number of factors may account for this. First, at a time when Soviet Russia's relationship with the European powers was in transition from open hostility to securing diplomatic recognition and commercial ties, it is likely that international approval figured in the formulation of the treaties. But the treaties had other potential audiences as well. To the inhabitants of these republics as well as the colonial peoples of the rest of the world, they could demonstrate the respect that communists had for the national independence of formerly subject peoples. Indeed, the first of the treaties, with Azerbaidzhan, was signed only a few weeks after the Congress of the Peoples of the East had been held in Baku.

Over and above such considerations, it may be surmised that at this stage and for some time to come, the communist authorities in Moscow were feeling their way, were not at all sure of what kind of constitutional framework best suited their purposes, and were divided about how to achieve them. The creation of autonomous republics and regions within the RSFSR was an obvious precedent, but none of those areas had had the experience of internationally recognized independence or, with the possible exception of the Volga Tatars, a sufficient quotient of intellectuals and other resources necessary to sustain a state apparatus. The treaties concluded in 1920–1 thus reflected Moscow's awareness of this difference, its recognition that Belorussia, Ukraine, and the Transcaucasian republics constituted "nations," albeit ones that required the presence of the Red Army and proconsuls dispatched from Moscow to ensure that they remained within the soviet orbit.

Aside from the coercive machinery of the Russian state and the party's regional bureaus, the Commissariat of Nationalities Affairs (Narkomnats) and its commissar, Stalin, played an important role in keeping Moscow in touch with the non-Russian peoples. Unlike many other high-ranking communists, Stalin had never flirted with the doctrine of proletarian internationalism associated with Rosa Luxemburg. Nor did he accept the Austro-Marxists' interpretation of the nation as an eternal category unrelated to its political configuration. As elaborated in his 1913 essay, *The National Question and Social Democracy*, Stalin defined the nation in historically contingent terms, associating its rise with the era of bourgeois revolutions and its super-cession with the gradual development of the international solidarity among workers.

This indeed became party doctrine, but much hinged on the definition of where on the historical continuum any one nation stood. As commissar, Stalin presided over an assortment of national sections (or "commissariats" as they were known at first) that were less the conduits for the expression of particular national concerns than channels for translating and disseminating the legal framework of soviet power, first among the non-Russian peoples of the RSFSR and later, the national republics. This and Stalin's previous experience of dealing with the ethnic minorities were critical to the way he conceived of future relations with the formally independent soviet republics. The only distinction he made between, say, the Bashkir or Volga Tatar autonomous republics and the Ukrainian SSR was of degree of autonomy. The bilateral treaties notwithstanding, there appeared no reason why the republics could not be absorbed within the existing framework of the RSFSR. It was this scheme for "autonomization" of the republics that Stalin adumbrated in October 1920 and took up again in 1922 when he tried, unsuccessfully, to gain the approval of Lenin and the Politburo.[84]

Lenin no less than Stalin was – and long had been – the advocate of a strong central state, guided by a strong central party dedicated to fostering working-class solidarity. As he had argued before the revolution, "the right of nations to self-determination implies exclusively the right to independence in the political sense, the right to free political separation from the oppressor nation."[85] Since the ruling Communist

Party stood for "real" (i.e., economic) and not merely formal equality among different peoples and was prepared to apply this principle by providing material and cultural assistance to "backward" areas in order to overcome the legacy of national oppression, there could be no question of the Soviet state being an oppressor nation.

But, though removed from day-to-day affairs by illness, Lenin seemed more aware than Stalin (and other assimilated non-Russians within the party) that because the Russian Revolution had been extended to the borderlands by the sword, the establishment of soviet law and institutions in these areas had to be handled with delicacy and with due consideration to national sensitivities and peculiarities. While insisting on a unitary party structure, he was willing to concede that a federative state – a union of soviet socialist republics in which the Russian republic would be one of several established on the basis of formal parity – more closely corresponded to such sensitivities. Stalin, in a rare instance of criticism of his mentor, equated Lenin's plan with "national liberalism," but signed the Orgburo's resolution incorporating Lenin's amendments, which were then approved by the central committee.[86]

During the two months of active work left to him (mid-October to mid-December 1922), Lenin pushed ahead with the project for the political integration of the soviet republics. In mid-December, resolutions in favor of joining the union were secured from the congresses of the newly formed Transcaucasian Socialist Federated Soviet Republic (ZSFSR) as well as the Ukrainian and Belorussian republics. This was preliminary to the convening of the Tenth All-Russian Congress of Soviets at which a resolution, proposed by Stalin, was passed creating the Union of Soviet Socialist Republics. The Congress thereupon reconstituted itself as the first All-Union Congress of Soviets with delegates from each of the four union republics.

In the meantime, however, Lenin had suffered a second stroke and it was in a condition of semi-paralysis that he learned about the unsavoury tactics employed by Stalin and his supporters against the Georgian Communist Party's central committee to secure Georgia's entry into the Transcaucasian Federation. (The term "party," though conventionally used, is something of a misnomer since there was only one party, the Russian Communist Party (Bolsheviks), of which the Georgian, Ukrainian and Belorussian "parties" were regional committees. At the Fourteenth Congress (1925), the name of the party was changed to All-Union Communist Party (Bolsheviks)). This, the so-called "Georgian Affair," has brooked large in western historiography not only because of its implications for nationality policy, but because it appears to have confirmed Lenin's worst fears about Stalin's Great Russian chauvinism and "administrator's impulses."[87]

While the Soviet Congress was in session, Lenin dictated several anguished memoranda. The first of these was his so-called "Testament," in which he expressed his alarm about the possibility of a split in the party arising out of tensions between Stalin and Trotsky. He also gave rather unflattering capsule assessments of both of them (but especially Stalin) as well as of Zinoviev, Kamenev, Bukharin, and Piatakov. To this he added a postscript in early January calling for "the comrades to find a way to remove Stalin" from the office of general secretary. More relevant to the current discussion were his "Notes" on the nationality question in which Lenin, "full of heart-searching, passionate remorse and holy anger," denounced Stalin, Ordzhonikidze, and Dzerzhinskii for their rough handling of the Georgians.[88]

The fate of these missives has evoked much hand-wringing among historians who argue that had they been more widely publicized and/or if Trotsky – to whom Lenin entrusted the defense of the Georgian communists in March 1923 – had used them more effectively than he did, Stalin could have been removed from his post as general secretary and the subsequent course of Soviet history would have been very different.[89] Be that as it may, fealty to an ailing leader was no match for personal jealousies and suspicions which for the most part were directed not at the uncharismatic and hard-working Stalin but the mercurial Trotsky. In this sense, Lenin's "last struggle" came both too early and too late to have had much chance of succeeding – too early because Stalin generally was not perceived to have amassed the power that Lenin claimed he already possessed or to have been capable of using what power he had in ways detrimental to the interests of the party, and too late because these perceptions were based on a vision of the party that already was becoming anachronistic.

From January 1923 a special commission, appointed by VTsIK, was engaged in drafting a "fundamental law" or constitution for the USSR. But it was the party, specifically its Twelfth Congress meeting in April, that resolved the key issues associated with that process. The national question was the subject of a special session at which Stalin delivered the main report. Stung by Lenin's criticisms, Stalin forthrightly condemned Great Russian chauvinism but, interestingly enough, connected its spread with "what is known as [in 1923! – LS] the NEP" and the slowing down of the international revolutionary movement. He also attacked "local chauvinisms" particularly in republics with several nationalities (i.e., Georgia, Azerbaidzhan and Turkestan) and hit back at those who, in his view, would "exaggerate the importance of the peasant borderlands, to the detriment of the proletarian regions." This was an obvious reference to the "national communists," delegates from the non-Russian republics who challenged Stalin's theses and recommendations on several grounds, but whose counterproposals the congress overwhelmingly rejected.[90]

Still, there was some unfinished business. In June, a special Central Committee conference attended by representatives from the borderland republics was convened by Stalin for two purposes. One was to discuss the case of Mir-Said Sultan Galiev, a Tatar who, as the most prominent Muslim national communist, had articulated the heretical notion that the USSR was a new mask for Russian exploitation of the eastern "proletarian nations" and had been arrested on charges of having collaborated with the Basmachi insurgents. The discussion was obviously designed to set the limits beyond which other national communists risked the same treatment. The other item on the agenda consisted of specific directives drafted by Stalin and sanctioned by the Politburo for forwarding to the constitutional drafting commission. These called for a two-chamber central executive committee: a Council of Nationalities, consisting of an equal number of delegates elected by the executive committees of each union and autonomous republic and a much larger Council of the Union which, given the RSFSR's disproportionate share of the population, inevitably would be dominated by representatives from that republic. In other respects, including the distribution of commissariats, the RSFSR Constitution of 1918 served as a model, with the "central institutions of the RSFSR . . . converted, with some accretions of personnel but in substance unchanged, into central institutions of the USSR." The final draft of the constitution was approved by VTsIK in July 1923 and on 31 January 1924 the Second All-Union Congress of Soviets ratified it.[91]

Historians' assessments of the manner in which the USSR was formed have varied a good deal. Expressing one widely shared view, Richard Pipes has argued that "[t]he Soviet Union, as it emerged in 1923, was a compromise between doctrine and reality." The doctrine centered around a "monistic class interpretation of world events" which precluded acknowledgment of "the fact that nationalist movements represented in many cases genuine social, economic and cultural aspirations." Reality was accommodated to the extent of granting linguistic autonomy and establishing the national-territorial principle as the basis of the state's political administration. But, notwithstanding

Lenin's late conversion to the cause of national rights, the key issue of "self-rule versus centralism on the administrative level was decided in favor of the latter," and it is in this sense that the debate surrounding this question "ended in the complete triumph of Stalin."[92]

Another, more recent approach interprets the gathering of nations into the USSR as having been accomplished on the basis of a series of "national contracts" of which the 1923 Constitution was the "finalized" version. In this interpretation, nationality policy was tied up with NEP which "was aimed at placating the peasantry and consolidating Soviet rule. Because the non-Russian nations were largely composed of peasants, the inauguration of the NEP inevitably had implications for Soviet nationalities policy . . . The more liberal approach in the economic sphere was therefore translated into the area of nationality policy."[93]

As appealing as it might be to western legal minds, the concept of a national contract would have been quite alien to Bolshevik political culture. It certainly obscures the entrenched and sometimes violent opposition to sovietization that is best exemplified by the mullah-led Turkic Basmachi. One wonders in any case how useful it is to think of nationality policy in terms of a contract that simultaneously was being elaborated and subjected to "frequent and blatant" breaches by the same individual, namely, Stalin.[94] Rather than counterposing doctrine to reality, disembodied communism to ur-nationalism, or contractual agreements to their violation, it makes more sense to view the formation of the USSR as involving two separate but related issues, each with its own protagonists and chronology. One was what kind of a federative system would be constructed and was essentially political-administrative. On this level, boundaries were fixed and institutional and legal frameworks largely replicating those for the RSFSR were established. The major players in these matters were the central organs of the party and those of the republics. The other was the issue of socio-cultural transformation. Here, party officials were confronted by the power of religious and secular elites, by deep-seated local solidarities, and by economic rivalries and contradictions between different nationality groups.

The 1923 Constitution represented a major step toward the consolidation of Soviet state power. But, as Carr has emphasized by referring to "the haze of empirical ambiguity which surrounded the mutual relations of the central organs of government," the "obscure and mutually frustrating provisions," and even the "somewhat unreal framework of the constitution," there were many issues that remained unresolved in law. These, he adds, would have been "quite unworkable without the reality that lay behind them: the overriding power of the party." A. Enukidze, who had been intimately involved in drafting the Constitution, admitted as much when he noted in October 1924 that "Our unity is sealed not by constitutional laws, not by this or that paragraph, but the common interests of the workers and peasants of all the union of republics."[95]

There were, however, formidable obstacles to persuading the non-Russian peoples of the advantages of this new political arrangement. For them, "the arrival of Soviet forces in the urban hubs . . . could indeed be regarded as still another exchange of urban masters." While such masters might elicit outward signs of obedience (e.g., payment of taxes, participation in local soviets, enrolment of children in schools), "what Soviet victories ultimately attained . . . was a peace of well-nigh universal withdrawal [and] a vast conglomeration of self-imposed insularities."[96]

We have seen something like this response in the case of the Russian peasantry, but the problem of breaking through local insularities in the borderlands was compounded by linguistic and ethnic barriers. At the time of the formation of the USSR, those identifying themselves as Great Russian comprised 72 percent of the membership of the ruling Communist Party. With the sole exception of Armenia, titular nationalities were less well represented within the party than in the general population of the union and autonomous republics. In many cases (e.g., Ukrainian SSR, Belorussian SSR, Azerbaidzhani SSR, Bashkir ASSR, Tatar ASSR), they made up far less than half of the party membership and a still smaller proportion by language. So far as I am aware, no comparable survey on the ethnicity of state officials was conducted, but several authors claim that Great Russians, drawn largely from the bureaucracy of the old regime, predominated.[97] All of this could be explained in terms of the dearth of native-born intellectuals with the skills and desire to serve the new regime. But the fact in itself is a measure of the gap separating the "proletarian dictatorship" from those to whom it hoped to appeal.

Lack of familiarity with indigenous languages and cultures often bred contempt for the societies from which they sprang. Not for nothing did terms such as "primitive," "backward," and "stagnant" figure in the official discourse. Even (or especially?) assimilated non-Russians thus expressed themselves, much as western educated colonials did in other parts of the world. In short, there was a good deal of Great Russian chauvinism, as there was of what Stalin labeled "local chauvinisms." The latter existed particularly in Transcaucasia where sizeable minority communities lived cheek by jowl with the titular nationality and where maladministration, favoritism, slights of the past and apprehensions toward the future bred not only contempt but inter-ethnic violence.

It was in this context that the party committed itself to staffing the "organs of the national republics and regions . . . primarily with local people who know the language, mode of life, values and customs of the corresponding peoples," and guaranteeing "the use of the native language in all state organs and institutions serving the local population and national minorities." This policy of "indigenization" or "nativization" (korenizatsiia) has been likened to the adaptation of the medieval Catholic Church to rural paganism.[98] It also has obvious similarities, including opposition from within the dominant nationality group, with Affirmative Action in the United States.

Within the context of party politics, korenizatsiia represented a victory or at least partial compensation for the national communists who had been urging the party to make itself and the new political order more comprehensible, accessible and therefore legitimate in the eyes of the non-Russian peoples. By the time the party conducted its next census in 1927, substantial increases were registered in the proportion of party members belonging to the titular nationalities – from 23.6 percent to 47.0 percent in Ukraine; from 21 percent to 46.7 per-cent in Belorussia; and from 19.8 percent to 32.4 percent in the Tatar ASSR.[99]

But the policy went beyond transforming the ethnic composition of the party and state apparatuses. It was national liberation, Soviet-style. In Central Asia, it encouraged emissaries from Zhenotdel to reach out to and seek to mobilize their sisters, "the lowest of the low" – in effect, a surrogate proletariat – within Muslim society. In Ukraine, where it was known as "Ukrainization," it turned the tide against the "theory of the struggle of two cultures," according to which the party should side with the Russian culture of the urban proletariat against that of the relatively backward Ukrainian peasantry. The active promotion of the Ukrainian language in all spheres of public life encouraged a Ukrainian Smena vekh. By the mid-1920s, the historian Mykhailo Hrushevskyi and many other émigré intellectuals had returned to their native land where they contributed to a national cultural revival or renaissance. Among Jews, the special concern of the party's Jewish sections (Evsektsii), korenizatsiia was associated with the spread of Yiddish secular culture as opposed to Hebrew, the training of Jewish youths in industrial and agricultural trades as opposed to commerce, and Soviet socialist as opposed to Zionist consciousness. Elsewhere, korenizatsiia was a major factor in the preservation, if not transformation, of languages and cultures in danger of extinction, contributing to the making of nations where there was little sense of them having existed previously.[100]

It also was a major gamble on the part of the Communist Party and its national branches. Although it was supposed to promote the development of a consciousness that was "socialist in content and nationalist in form," the danger always existed of that formula being reversed, as it undoubtedly was in many small ways throughout the 1920s. Who really occupied the commanding heights, or to put it another way, who was fellow traveling with whom may have been decided in the political-administrative sense. But in many others – cultural, educational, even economic – it remained unclear and contested for the rest of the decade. Only the repression of the national intelligentsia and many of their brokers within the party during the first two Five-Year Plans removed the spectre of this particular peril.

Rises and falls within the party

All sectors of Soviet society experienced retreat and recovery but in different ways and degrees. For peasants who survived the great famine of 1921–2, the state's retreat meant relief from its primitive method of extraction but no relief from the perils of subsistence farming and a highly unstable price structure. For nepmen and specialists, opportunities may have outweighed risks, but the legal and social foundations on which to establish and run businesses, assume managerial responsibility and maintain professional autonomy were anything but firm. For others, notably industrial and clerical workers, the risk of unemployment was ever-present. And for still others, such as the besprizorniki who dwelt in the urban underworld or the remnants of guerilla armies who roamed the borderlands of the country, day-to-day living was risky.

It was the party, however, that seismically registered the perils of the new economic order. NEP, after all, was the party's policy and while party discipline required that it be propagandized and defended, rank-and-file resentment of its strictures and the center's fears of it unleashing uncontrollable forces were never far from the surface. For the party, the period of retreat and recovery opened with the explosion at Kronstadt and the momentous decisions of the Tenth Congress and closed with another *éclat*, namely Trotsky's letter to the Central Committee announcing his break with the Politburo's triumvirate of Zinoviev, Kamenev, and Stalin. This was followed shortly by the circulation of the "Platform of the 46," which further divided the party's upper echelons and set the stage for a major confrontation at the Thirteenth Party Conference in January 1924. In the course of these not quite three years, the party experienced numerous stresses and strains as it consolidated its role as the administrative whip of the entire Soviet system. At the same time, a process of administrative consolidation was also occurring within the party itself, closely associated with the expansion and consolidation of the party apparatus. Challenged by various oppositional groups in the name of party democracy, the apparatus and mechanisms and procedures by which it functioned were to remain in place for a very long time, surviving Stalin's use and abuse of them.

In charting the rise of the apparatus it is well to remember that most of what we know about this process comes from those who opposed it. The reasons why this is so are not hard to fathom. While secretaries and other *apparatchiki* were loathe to advertise the aggrandizement of their power and associated privileges, it was still possible for critics to voice their objections at congresses and other meetings, as well as in the party press. And what was not published in the Soviet Union often found its way abroad, appearing in the Menshevik journal, *Sotsialisticheskii vestnik*, or other publications.

Such sources typically associated the rise of the apparatus with "bureaucratization" or "degeneration," and drew implicit or explicit contrasts with an earlier more open, dramatic, and comradely party. Thus was born the rhetoric of the Fall, a rhetoric that later was to figure centrally in Trotsky's critique of Stalinist betrayal, of Thermidor, of heroic, self-sacrificing revolutionaries being replaced by faceless, self-seeking functionaries and of the corresponding political expropriation of the working class.[101] Powerful and, in certain renditions, persuasive, the interpretation of the rise of the apparatus as the Fall crept into much of western historiography, even where the notion of a retrospective period of grace or bliss was absent. The contrast with what until recently was standard history in the USSR is absolute. There, the narrative was about organizational strengthening, party construction (*partstroitel'stvo*), the training of cadres, the redeployment of party forces, and the struggle against fractionalism and the Trotskyist revision of Leninism. The rise of the apparatus in this version was no

Fall but rather a major factor in facilitating the realization of tasks which Lenin had set for the party.[102]

But perhaps it is not fair to cite the now much discredited official Soviet version. To better illustrate the point that the evident change in the character of the party during these years can lend itself to divergent readings, let us listen to the memoir of an Old Bolshevik, one Aleksandr Ilin-Zhenevsky, who had served as a leader of the party's Military Organization in 1917. Writing in the mid-1920s, Ilin-Zhenevsky recalled the Central Committee in the months preceding the October Revolution and contrasted it with what it had become:

Just about every day I used to go [to Central Committee headquarters] . . . and I frequently encountered a serene family scene. Everyone sits at the dining table and drinks tea. On the table, a large samovar steams cozily. L. R. Menzhinskaia [one of the secretaries], a towel over her shoulder, rinses glasses, wipes them, and pours tea for each arriving comrade . . . Involuntarily, a comparison with the present headquarters of the Central Committee comes to mind. [We have] a gigantic building with a labyrinth of sections and subsections. Bustling about on every floor are an enormous number of employees, feverishly completing urgent tasks.

Intimacy as opposed to impersonality; serenity as opposed to feverishness; a modest apartment contrasted with a "gigantic building"; the Central Committee as a family affair compared to one with "an enormous number of employees." These contrasts seem to point to a nostalgic, even tragic, reading of the change. The author himself confesses to "a certain sadness in the fact that the time when simple and unpretentious, yet profoundly comradely and united effort was possible, has gone and will never come again." Yet, it is possible to make the same contrasts using quite different imagery: amateurishness as opposed to professionalism; leisureliness as contrasted with punctuality; a cottage industrial Central Committee compared to a modern factory or machine. It is as difficult to deny the plausibility of these images as it is to dissociate them from Lenin's vision of the party and indeed the kind of society he wished to create. In addition to a tragic reading of the rise of the apparatus, one could acknowledge the possibility of a "realistic" one. This, indeed, is implied by Ilin-Zhenevsky, albeit perfunctorily. "Naturally," he writes, "with its functions so expanded today, there is no possibility of the Central Committee operating in any other way."[103]

The statement attests to what students of organizational theory have always known, namely that there is a dynamic interplay between the accretion of responsibilities and the necessity for increased administrative resources, data banks, procedural rules, and staff. But why were the functions of the Central Committee, or rather its "sections and subsections," "so expanded"?

To answer this question we need to recall that throughout the party's history, first as an underground conspiratorial body, then as a more fluid mass organization, and after 1917 as the political core of the Soviet state, elective and appointive practices coexisted uneasily. While committees functioned at least to some extent on the basis of free discussion of issues and majority votes, the Central Committee always reserved the right to make final decisions in the form of directives and to appoint, coopt or reassign members as it saw fit. Following the Eighth Congress in March 1919, these latter functions accrued to the Secretariat's Records and Assignment Department (Uchraspred). In the disorganized conditions of the civil war, it was all the tiny staff of this department could do to dispatch thousands of party members who were displaced and needed a party job or those who were mobilized for one or another front. At the same time, however, appointments of a different kind were being made, sometimes by the Orgburo, sometimes by the Secretariat, to break up localist cliques (*mestnye gruppirovki*), resolve conflict between local groupings, and counter the influence of provincial leaders with oppositional leanings. Occasionally, as in the case of the Nizhni-Novgorod gubkom, the center's "nominee" encountered stiff opposition from provincial authorities and much of his time was taken up with in-fighting. But these were teething problems. Local communists discovered soon enough that there was no future in open defiance of the center and began to engage in *pokazukha* (putting on shows), currying favor with would-be patrons, and other tricks not unknown in tsarist times.[104]

The growing strength of the center at the expense of local autonomy was already well advanced before the party's Tenth Congress and, as we have seen, was among the complaints registered by the Democratic Centralists and Workers' Opposition. It was, however, in the wake of the Congress and the defeat of these factions that, according to Merle Fainsod, "the welding of the Party apparatus into a homogeneous, disciplined and tightly controlled machine was achieved." Fainsod identifies three constituent "instruments" of the machine – Uchraspred, the Organization-Instruction Section, and the control commissions, central and local. The first two of these were under the aegis of the Central Committee and under the direct authority of the Secretariat; the third had been created in 1920 as independent tribunals to hear complaints about overbearing and "bureaucratized" party officials, but following the Eleventh Party Congress in 1922, was transformed "into a second highly centralized hierarchy, paralleling the hierarchy of party secretaries."[105]

One can easily exaggerate the extent to which, at this stage, the instruments functioned harmoniously or, to extend the musical metaphor, played Stalin's tune. Yet, it would be foolish to deny that personnel management and control over local party organizations were becoming systematized or that as the only Politburo member also serving on the Orgburo, Stalin was already the dominant individual within the apparatus. We have it on the authority of Anastas Mikoian, who had outmaneuvered the Workers' Opposition in the Nizhni Novgorod gubkom, that on the eve of the Eleventh Congress, Stalin had dispatched emissaries to the provinces to ensure that "Leninists" (that is, neither supporters of the Workers' Opposition, the Democratic Centralists, nor allies of Trotsky) were elected as delegates.[106] This was *before* the newly elected Central Committee appointed him General Secretary.

Upon taking office, Stalin recalled L. M. Kaganovich from Central Asia and placed him in charge of the Organization-Instruction Section. The functions of this section were extremely broad, essentially involving supervision of local committees, "the strengthening and improvement of Party organization, liquidation of disputes, [and] improvement of methods of general Party work." Its reports were used by Uchraspred to work out assignments of personnel. By the time the Twelfth Congress convened in April 1923, some 10,000 party members had been assigned in this manner to various party and governmental positions, with another thousand or so senior appointments, including forty-two gubkom secretaryships, having been filled by "nominees" of the Secretariat and Orgburo. "In this way, entrenched local cliques were broken up and the odd nest of oppositionists dispersed, and leaders installed on whom Stalin could rely." Within a few months, the Orgburo announced the regularization of these procedures, a resolution that T. H. Rigby considers to have represented the birth of the *nomenklatura* system. In the meantime, the Central Committee, twice enlarged by decisions of successive congresses and meeting less frequently, was being transformed from "the main working organ of the party into a grand council of party chiefs."[107]

All this was occurring with the complicity or at least knowledge of the other members of the Politburo, Zinoviev and Kamenev in particular. Like Lenin, they were aware of the "immense power" that Stalin was accumulating. But they were relatively unconcerned about the possibility of Stalin translating such power into authority, relative, that is, to the prospect of Trotsky extending *his* authority as architect of the Red Army's victory in the civil war and the party's best known leader after Lenin. Thus was cemented the triumvirate, an alliance at the top that gave the party at least the outward appearance of unity and strength during the period of uncertainty associated with the "interregnum."

But what the triumvirs determined to be necessary for the "strengthening and improvement of party organization" struck dissident forces as a catastrophic retreat from the principles of democracy within the party and its further alienation from the working class. That the leadership itself was acutely sensitive about such charges is evident from its sponsorship of resolutions – but not concrete measures – against bureaucratism, and the terms of the purge which was carried out in the latter half of 1921. The purge was explicitly directed against "petty bourgeois elements" and former members of other parties, both of whom were made scapegoats for the political crisis that had erupted earlier in the year and continued to simmer. The verification commissions that conducted the purge were to pay special attention to the credentials of those in government service or of bourgeois, white-collar and intelligentsia origin, and to expel anyone found guilty of passivity, careerism, drunkenness, failing to carry out party instructions, or practicing religion. In the end, nearly one-quarter of the entire membership was expelled, including one in three of white-collar origin, two-fifths of all peasants, but only one in six who were registered as workers.[108]

All in all, though, the proportion of workers (as defined in terms of pre-revolutionary occupation) increased only slightly during 1921 and remained unchanged for the next two years at 44 percent. Why was this so? We know that there were mass resignations of workers, some in connection with the crisis that enveloped the party and society in late 1920 to early 1921, some as a result of disillusionment with the way the crisis was resolved. Subsequent difficulty in recruiting workers was attributed by the leadership to the dilution of the class by non-proletarian elements. This explanation was ridiculed by oppositionists along the lines of Diane Koenker's arch comment that "when Bolshevik party leaders saw support slipping away, they blamed the physical disappearance of their supporters rather than changed attitudes."[109]

Whatever the case, the party census of 1922 could not have been comforting to party leaders. This showed that only 15 percent of all members were working in manual industrial jobs, 22 percent were peasants "engaged in physical labor," and the remainder were employed in white-collar work. In other words, most party members of working-class origin had been absorbed by the burgeoning party and state bureaucracy, this at a time of spiraling unemployment among both blue- and white-collar workers. As for new recruits, only 12 percent in 1922 were workers by actual employment. It would indeed appear that,

despite the most varied and determined countermeasures, the tendency of the party to become the preserve of the more powerful and privileged strata of the emergent postrevolutionary society, a tendency which was somewhat moderated in the later stages of the Civil War, became more marked than ever during the first years of NEP.[110]

The evident deproletarianization of the party seemed to confirm the dire warnings of the Workers' Opposition, but the oppositionists were no longer in a position to influence the party, or for that matter, the working class. In the course of 1922, their strongholds in the provinces and the trade unions fell to appointees of the apparatus, and their leaders were effectively silenced by the threat of expulsion from the party or via diplomatic postings. However, the more incorrigible critics of the party regrouped to form two new organizations, the Workers' Group and Workers' Truth. Most of what is known about these "fringe," "Ultra-Leftist" groups comes from their manifestoes which echoed the syndicalist line of the Workers' Opposition, condemned NEP as the "new exploitation of the proletariat," and called for the removal of Zinoviev, Kamenev, and Stalin from the Central Committee.[111] In the context of party politics, what is most significant about them is their marginality, that is, the extent to which the articulation of a "left" alternative now involved working outside the party and in violation of its strictures. Neither group survived the GPU's dragnet which apprehended most of the leaders just as the strike wave of 1923 was peaking.

Hence, when Trotsky launched his attack on the triumvirate, it was a very different kind of initiative, basically intended to recall the Central Committee from the errors of its ways. While denouncing "secretarial bureaucratism," and calling for the restoration of party democracy, Trotsky's letter stopped short of making any specific recommendations. The alarm it expressed was that of an insider appealing first and foremost to the revolutionary conscience of his wayward comrades. The "Platform of the 46," signed by such prominent party members as Preobrazhenskii, Antonov-Ovseenko, Piatakov, Sapronov, and

Osinskii, was only slightly more strident. Much like Robert Michels' diagnosis of the "iron law of oligarchy," it attributed the party's ills to "a progressive division of the party, no longer concealed by hardly anyone, into the secretarial hierarchy and the 'laymen,' into the professional party functionaries, selected from above, and the simple party masses, who do not participate in its group life."[112]

Space does not permit a recitation of the ensuing maneuvers by the party elite and the accompanying flurry of accusations. Suffice it to say that this new Left Opposition was no match for the apparatus, which not implausibly characterized its agitation among the rank-and-file as a violation of the party's ban on factions. The absence of visible support for the Opposition among working class communists and non-party workers may or may not have stemmed from their memory of Trotsky as the prime advocate of the militarization of labor and his position in the trade union controversy. It is just as likely that his call for stepping up investments in industry made them apprehensive about further sacrifices or that they shared Shliapnikov's suspicions that "[i]n the present controversy the only goal of Comrade Trotsky and the Opposition is simply to seize the apparatus."[113]

Support among educated youth and within the army hardly compensated. One cannot escape the conclusion that irrespective of Trotsky's mysterious and untimely illnesses, his inexplicable silences at critical meetings, and his notorious imperiousness – or for that matter his intellectual brilliance as well as that of many of his leading supporters – the Opposition was doomed from the start. In a polity where loyalty and opposition were generally considered incompatible, and where forming another party was out of the question, the real option confronting middle and low-echelon communists to whom both sides appealed was between unity and chaos.

There remains one final issue to settle in regard to these rises and falls within the party. This has to do with Lenin's responsibility. It has often been noted, correctly, that both the apparatus and its opponents cited Lenin's authority with more or less equal justification. After all, the same Lenin who could threaten the Workers' Opposition with machine guns was sickened by the spreading cancer of bureaucratism. It is true that in his last writings Lenin strove mightily to find a way of curbing the abuse of power and personal privilege by party and state functionaries. But is also seems evident that the solutions he urged were inadequate if not misguided.

Typically, Lenin viewed the problem of bureaucratism in class terms, tracing the defects of the state and party apparatuses to survivals from the pre-revolutionary past. The solution to the problem therefore was not so much institutional as personal, or rather, personnel. It centered around the recruitment of pure, incorruptible workers and peasants, "human material of a truly contemporary kind" into the apparatus. Initially, he thought of adding fifty to seventy-five of them to the Central Committee, but in the published version of his article substituted the Central Control Commission which was to be amalgamated with the Workers' and Peasants' Inspectorate. Some of the details of the scheme are rather hazy – for example, the notion that these new people would enjoy "the same rights as the members of the Central Committee" – and only parts of it were realized. The main point, however, was not to curb the powers of the apparatus and still less to disband it. Rather, Lenin sought to make it more authoritative by relying on these professionally trained proletarians to serve as a living link between the top echelon of the party and "an 'ordinary' People's Commissariat."[114]

In one sense, Lenin was responsible for everything – the rise of the Bolsheviks to power, the policies that saw the party and the infant Soviet state through civil war, the retreat to NEP, in short, virtually all the decisions to which he appended his signature as chairman of Sovnarkom and party leader. In another, Lenin, even Lenin, was not a free agent in the sense of being able to impose his will on a recalcitrant reality. As to the future course of Soviet history, if it makes little sense to hold Lenin accountable for the crimes of Stalin, using Lenin's "Testament" as evidence with which to convict his eventual successor is no less problematic.

Time and distance allow us to perceive that for all their vanguardism, revolutionary Marxist regimes are no less subject than other political formations to their own ritualization, routinization, and eventual supercession. While he fretted over the functions of the Workers' and Peasants' Inspectorate, Lenin was aware that only "cultural revolution" could provide an effective antidote to these processes. The Soviet Union was to get its cultural revolution, but in circumstances that were different from those prevailing at the time of Lenin's death and with results that he could not have anticipated.

4   Living with NEP

We cannot celebrate the supposed victory of non-capitalist evolution in agriculture at the very moment when we are having to make supplementary concessions precisely to the capitalist elements in agriculture. (G. Zinoviev, *Leninizm* (1925) cited in E. H. Carr, *Socialism in One Country, 1924–1926*, vol. 1, p. 326)

You see, down in the district Soviet they think of me as a bourzhui, because I have built a decent house and have cultivated this fine orchard. I have been told that they are planning to lay a special tax on the orchard, twenty gold roubles . . . That's what Russia is coming to, my friend. A man cannot even work his head off to improve himself a bit without being called a bourzhui or a *koulack* and burdened with taxes that break his back. (The "richest man in the village" cited by Maurice Hindus, *Broken Earth* (New York, 1926), p. 142)

Every worker and peasant in a car within fifteen to twenty years! (V. Osinsky in *Pravda*, 20 July 1927)

After three years of NEP, most of the institutions and practices introduced or adumbrated in 1921 were in place. Agricultural products and industrial goods were being marketed through an extensive network of state and cooperative institutions as well as private traders. Direct taxes, initially paid in kind, reverted exclusively to monetary form in 1924. The return to freedom of trade and a monetary economy found their logical corollary in the establishment of a stable currency based on the universal gold standard. While common or collective cultivation of land was a rarity, agricultural producer and credit cooperatives took advantage of favorable credit opportunities to expand their operations and enroll new members. In industry, state-owned enterprises dwarfed those leased to private individuals or cooperatives in terms of output and numbers of workers. But production levels of all three forms as well as small-scale rural and artisan concerns registered significant annual increases. Having been made voluntary at the outset of NEP, membership in trade unions fell off sharply but then rapidly recovered, reaching 6.9 million by 1925 of which 2.7 million consisted of industrial workers.[1]

It was not just in the economic sphere that associational activity assumed impressive variety and vigor. The mid-1920s witnessed the founding of a myriad of unions, leagues, societies, and institutes promoting one or another cause – contemporary music, "massism" in literature, cinema attendance, conservation, militant atheism, support for the fledgling air fleet, labor hygiene, physical culture, support for the blind and deaf, and so on and so forth. Some of these public organizations and movements were run by communists and were dedicated to promoting a particular aspect of the party's program; others were composed primarily of non-communists and were essentially apolitical. Some were short lived, barely surviving beyond the end of the decade; others persisted albeit with their sails trimmed until the Great Patriotic War, while a few exist to this day. Whether they comprised the elements of an autonomous "civil society" or functioned as extensions or front organizations of the party-state is an important question to ask, even if a satisfactory answer would require a close examination of the life history of each organization and a clear definition of "autonomy" or degrees thereof. But however guided or otherwise circumscribed civic life was in the mid-1920s, it surely was less so than by the end of the decade.[2]

We are dealing, then, with a rather brief period. Conventionally known as "High NEP," it lasted no more than three years. Though relatively crisis-free, it was a period of much restlessness and contestation. The party had weathered the perils of retreat and recovery, but was no closer to resolving the central issue of NEP – whether that policy was strengthening the forces of capitalism or socialism. Its ambivalence was reflected in the contradictory signals sent out to the countryside. What it gave with one hand, it seemed to be taking back with the other. Peasants responded in kind. Meanwhile, the necessity of supplying a predominantly peasant market with cheap goods and industry's dependence on the irreplaceable skills of the specialists placed severe constraints on workers' status and standard of living and the party's ability to assist them. Urged by "their" trade unions to tighten labor discipline and raise productivity, workers were well aware of the high salaries and privileges of specialists and the intelligentsia and the high living of nepmen and certain officials. Within the professions, young communist militants chafed at the hegemony exercised by their non-communist "bourgeois" elders, a hegemony that the party leadership seemed unwilling to contest. Finally, over and above these internal tensions was the possibility of a renewal of hostilities with the European capitalist powers and the corresponding rhetoric of "capitalist encirclement."

In short, as Soviet society grew into NEP, there were real anxieties about the implications and consequences of the policy itself. If, in the 1920s, western Europe was "in search of stability," and the "return to normalcy" appealed to large sections of the American public, the prospect that the relative stability achieved under NEP would become normal worried many whose thirst for revolutionary transformation had been unquenched or who were simply dissatisfied with where the storms of revolutionary upheaval had tossed them. This was the context in which sharp debate arose, both within and outside the party, over a range of issues that touched on the lives of all Soviet citizens. An examination of these debates can shed light not only on the civic life of the mid-1920s but on the viability of NEP.

Agrarian debates

The Soviet state inherited from its tsarist predecessor not only an overwhelmingly peasant society, but a tradition of rigorous and detailed research on the socio-economic condition of the peasantry. Conducted mainly under the auspices of zemstvo statistical departments, this research took the form of household and budget surveys concerning a wide range of subjects – family size, land usage, inventory, craft activities, hiring of labor, and income and expenditures. It revealed significant regional variations, but also differences in the distribution of factors of production within the same region, which through "dynamic surveys" could be charted over time. Debates among zemstvo researchers and other students of the peasantry in the late nineteenth century centered on two issues. One was methodological and had to do with whether the amount of sown area was the best indicator of peasant wealth and poverty. The other, more politically charged issue, was interpretive, namely, whether differentiation among households was to be understood as characteristic of peasant society and internal to it, or was progressive, leading to the dissolution of the peasantry and the formation of new classes in the countryside consistent with capitalist development. The former interpretation was dominant among agricultural economists and was central to populist ideology; the latter was the main theme of Lenin's *Development of Capitalism in Russia* (1899).[3]

What has become known as the "differentiation debate" continued along these lines into the twentieth century. The Stolypin reforms, designed to combat the equalizing functions of the village commune and ultimately create a class of independent, conservative-minded yeomen farmers, seemed to accelerate differentiation and thus confirm Lenin's prognoses. But, as already indicated, the revolution and civil war reversed this process, resulting in a leveling down of the peasantry. By the early 1920s, the situation in the countryside had returned to the *status quo ante*, except, of course, that large-scale, market-oriented agriculture in the form of the landed nobility's estates had been abolished.

According to the Central Statistical Administration (TsSU), which had assumed responsibility for carrying out surveys previously conducted by the provincial zemstvos, some 85 percent of peasant households in the RSFSR sowed four or less desiatina of land in 1922, and 87 percent possessed less than two draught animals. Farming typically was done with wooden ploughs, sickles and scythes over widely scattered strips subject to periodical communal redistribution. Most peasants lacked the means or inclination for manuring and crop rotation, mechanized equipment was almost non-existent and storage facilities were few and far between. Harvests were well below pre-war totals, and so too was the proportion of the diminished crop that was marketed. "Thus," remarks Alec Nove, "the effect of the revolution was in a technical sense, reactionary."[4]

In such circumstances, it was all the party could do to encourage diligence and entrepreneurship among the peasantry. Even while lip service was paid to collective forms of farming (sovkhozy and kolkhozy) and much was made of Lenin's notion of peasants growing into socialism through cooperation, the prevailing view seemed to be that expressed by a Narkomzem official who remarked in 1924 that "The role of the well-to-do peasantry in the growth of the production of grain and cattle is acquiring an exclusive significance in the national economy. On these strata of the peasantry, as well as on the agent who brings the commodities to the foreign or domestic market, rests the task of rebuilding the economy."[5]

But on this, as on most other policy questions, there was no unanimity. In 1924, Preobrazhenskii, who two years earlier had expressed his alarm at the revival of differentiation, formulated "the fundamental law of socialist accumulation." Making the analogy with the process that Marx had called "primitive capitalist accumulation," Preobrazhenskii asserted that before the socialist economy could develop its economic advantages, it had to pass through a preliminary stage of "primitive accumulation." This, perforce, had to be done from above, by the state. It involved the exploitation of small-scale production via non-equivalent exchanges – taxation, loan restrictions, and a pricing policy that would favor industrial goods (that is, opening up of the "scissors" again). Either the state would have to utilize these mechanisms and the anticipated advantages of planning or it would succumb to the "law of value" whose logic was antithetical to the state's accumulation of resources for industrialization.

In essence, Preobrazhenskii's understanding of the transition to socialism was based on his identification of a series of antitheses – from above vs. from below; large-scale industry vs. small-scale agriculture; planning vs. the market; and the proletarian state vs. the surplus-producing peasantry. Whether such an understanding contradicted NEP, as Bukharin contended, is doubtful. As already suggested, NEP was open to a number of interpretations, and there is nothing – except party resolutions – to say that the positing of a protracted war of maneuver was any less appropriate than a more sanguine view of peasant–state relations.[6]

Preobrazhenskii's "ambitious medley of far-sighted analysis, grand historical analogy, theoretical innovation, and economic policy" could not go unanswered, and it fell to Bukharin, the most formidable economic thinker within the leadership, to respond. He did so by characterizing the views of his one-time co-author as "the economic foundation of Trotskyism," which he considered "anti-Leninist." This was the political import of Bukharin's response which, couched in highly polemical if not demagogic terms, represented another nail in the coffin to Trotsky's ambitions and the fate of the Left Opposition. But there were other dimensions as well. These came to the fore over the next two years as Bukharin developed the most sophisticated defense of the party's strategy with respect to the peasantry and the "road to socialism."[7]

He explicitly rejected the Left's premise of antitheses and contradictions on both pragmatic and ethical grounds. Squeezing the peasantry, he asserted, risked igniting internal war, something that the nation could ill afford, surrounded as it was by hostile capitalist countries. For Bukharin, the proletarian state could escape from its isolation on the fortified peaks not by the conquest and colonization of the lowlands, but by fostering "the development of a Soviet "civil community (obshchestvennost') based on "all types of voluntary circles, societies . . . and groups for agricultural propaganda, for fighting alcoholism, against smoking, societies for rural amenities, for cooperative assistance and so forth." Bukharin particularly stressed the role of cooperatives, understood in the terms Lenin had described in his last writings. They were "the organizational footbridge" linking state industry and the peasant economy, and thereby overcoming both the "pettiness" (*melkost'*) from which the peasant economy suffered and the dangers the party associated with kulak exploitation. Class struggle was involved here, but not violent class war.[8]

Since this is ground that has been well covered by many historians, it will suffice to make three brief points about Bukharin's views. First, they were not a brief for what has come to be known as "market socialism." The notion that markets had a place in a fully socialist economy was no less alien to Bukharin than it was to the Left or Lenin for that matter. What Bukharin stressed – and not merely conceded – was the vital role that markets would play throughout the transitional period to socialism, that is, for the duration of NEP. He wrote, "we believed that it was possible to destroy market relations by one stroke and immediately. It turned out that we shall reach socialism *precisely through* market relations." The market was thus the mechanism or lever (*rychag*) that would propel peasants across the bridge. It would only do this, however, if state industry successfully competed with private industry and if peasant cooperatives were provided with a legal framework and other inducements to expand.[9]

Bukharin was cognizant of the fact that involvement in the market tended to accelerate differentiation among the peasantry by favoring those who could exchange their surpluses for machinery, infrastructural improvement or hired labor. Here, he was walking the thin line between wagering on the peasant and wagering on the kulak. His epithet, "peasants . . . Enrich yourselves," may well have crossed that line, and ultimately proved as damaging to Bukharin as its counterpart, "primitive socialist accumulation," was for Preobrazhenskii and the Left. But at the time it was uttered, in April 1925, the Politburo had just decided in favor of lowering the tax rate and extending the provisions for hired labor and land leasing in the countryside, measures that amounted to major concessions to the peasantry and particularly its better-off strata. Moreover, other leading members of the party and government (notably, Rykov, Kamenev and Kalinin) were no less explicit in urging well-to-do households to take advantage of them as a means of developing the productive forces of agriculture. "Facing to the countryside," the party relied on the rural-based economy to fertilize state industry. Industry would produce for an expanding peasant market, the "enrichment" of which would provide a fund for the accumulation of capital by the state via tax receipts, access to bank deposits, etc. This was truly "the high-water mark of the campaign to support the efficient and well-to-do farmer."[10]

Finally, it is worth noting that however friendly he appeared toward the immediate aspirations of peasants (or at least its more substantial strata), Bukharin did not idealize the peasantry or concede anything to it politically. His attitude was that of the enlightened missionary who had come to transform the benighted into citizens worthy of being partners of the proletariat, or more accurately, of ceasing to be peasants. In a revealing but hitherto overlooked passage from his "Road to Socialism," he refers to the working class using "all its powers" to "recast the peasantry," "reeducate it" and "re-fashion its nature" so that it could "acquire the skills necessary for the business of state administration." At this point, the furrow between the working class and the "advanced strata" of the peasantry would be breached, the peasant economy would "pour into the single planned socialist economy" and the peasantry correspondingly would be "poured together with the working class in a single socialist society," thus marking the end (or "withering away") of the proletarian dictatorship. Perhaps rather than a missionary, Bukharin's vision could be likened to that of an hydraulic engineer.[11]

The debate outlined here under the rubric of "agrarian" thus involved a multitude of issues, political as well as economic, domestic as well as foreign. Pricing and credit policies, the party's recruitment drive, the state of the Red Army and political education within it, even literary politics were all grist to the mill of one side or the other. The debate was conducted in the party press and technical/economic journals, in speeches before the Communist Academy, at sessions of the Comintern's executive committee and at party conferences and other mass gatherings. It has since been replayed in the west by scholars who have counterposed both Preobrazhenskii's and Bukharin's positions to that eventually adopted by Stalin. More recently still, it has been revived in the Soviet Union where the "Bukharin alternative" informed much of the rethinking invested in perestroika.

But however broad its implications, the party's High NEP strategy kept coming back to – or up against – the peasantry.[12] This was largely because the procurement of grain was still the linchpin of NEP and because the party was a long way from resolving the problem of how to maximize procurements without capitulating entirely to peasants with grain to sell. The different, but from the state's point of view equally unhappy, experiences of the harvests of 1924 and 1925 are instructive.

Despite an increase in sown area, less grain was harvested in 1924 than in the previous two years and a still smaller proportion was marketed. Prices soared. By August 1924 they were twice as high as a year earlier. The newly created Commissariat of Internal Trade saw fit to set maximum prices for state purchases, and exports of grain, which had been expected to exceed the 1923 level, were halted. But private traders were not bound by state prices and moved in to offer peasants more lucrative deals. With procurements well below anticipated levels, the state was compelled to abandon price fixing. Industry thereupon experienced irresistible pressure for wage increases, which, as we shall see, led to concerted though not very successful efforts to raise productivity. This, then, was the context in which a series of measures to stimulate the peasant economy was introduced, measures which some have termed "neo-NEP."

The 1925 harvest was the most bountiful since 1913. To cushion an anticipated fall in the price of grain and avoid a recurrence of the scissors crisis, the state now introduced "directive prices" to its purchasing agents. But peasants had their own way of dealing with the situation. Taking advantage of lower tax rates and what Kamenev angrily referred to as a "bacchanalia of competition" among different state agencies and Tsentrosoiuz, those with the largest surpluses withheld them from the market in hopes of driving prices upward. This strategy paid off – for surplus producers – as early rains cut into the harvest. "The bumpkins got the best of us," was the way Kamenev put it. Once again, the state had to lower its expectations of procurements and suspend exports.[13]

In two successive confrontations, the state backed down. But whom did the state confront? Surely not all the peasants, for not all peasants were grain producers and fewer still were sellers. In 1925 it was estimated that 14 percent of peasant households harvested 33 percent of the grain crop but 61 percent of the amount destined for the market. Even among those with surpluses, many had to sell immediately (when prices were at their lowest) to meet tax and loan payments.[14]

Was Carr then right to conclude that it was the kulak who "had shown himself master of the situation" and "had proved victorious"? Such a conclusion seems at best misleading, and, in light of the subsequent repression and suffering of those labelled as kulaks, at worst pernicious. By subsuming under the category of "kulak" all households that played the market or otherwise benefited from high grain prices, Carr not only suppressed distinctions that both he in other contexts and party officials at the time tried to make, but could be construed as providing retrospective justification for later "dekulakization." To be fair, Carr was writing in the late 1950s when peasant studies were not even in their infancy. It was to be another ten years before Moshe Lewin demonstrated on the basis of his own prodigious research and acute awareness of the complexities of peasant society the extent to which the kulak was a discursive category.[15]

There were really two discourses that developed around the kulak. One was the peasants' own, as applied to village extortioners, userers, cut-throat traders, or others who drove hard bargains or otherwise violated culturally determined norms of fairness. Peasant letters to the newspaper *Bednota* in the mid-1920s revealed an even broader applicability which included those who were sober all the time, had supported the Whites during the civil war or were perceived as out-siders (e.g., non-agricultural craftspeople or rural *intelligenty*). These types may or may not have been wealthy, but that was not the point. "Kulak" (in Russian, "fist") was a moral economic category which had little to do with either sociologists' or politicians' definitions.[16]

The other discourse emerged out of the late nineteenth-century definition debate. Roughly corresponding to the Marxist category of merchant capital, the term took on a broader and less precise meaning during the civil war when the Bolsheviks used it to mobilize support among poor peasants (*bedniaki*) for the kombedy and later among middle peasants (*seredniaki*) for requisitions. By the mid-1920s, when social differentiation was reappearing in the countryside, it gained additional currency and potency, becoming something of a lightning rod for intra-party conflicts. As suggested by Maurice Hindus' informant and other evidence, there was some spillage from the party's categorization into the villages in the 1920s, kulak becoming inter-changeable with "burzhui" in certain circumstances. But the reverse process whereby village definitions influenced the party does not appear to have been the case.[17]

Why this near obsession in the party with kulaks? For one thing, they were part of the heritage of Lenin's class analysis. According to the formula coined in the civil war, the party was committed to supporting the poor or weak peasants, establishing an alliance with the middle peasantry and combatting the kulaks. Even if "this 'threefold' formula can scarcely be said to have borne any relation to the realities of NEP" or the Soviet countryside, party officials liked to think it did as evidenced by the frequency with which they invoked it.[18]

Also, identifying and struggling against kulaks in the countryside and nepmen and "bourgeois intellectuals" in the towns was a way in which rank-and-file communists identified themselves. That is, it was an index of their own class consciousness irrespective of their own class origins, or even the party line at any one time. Thus, in late 1925 at the height of the party's conciliatory policy towards the peasants, Stalin could assert that "of every 100 communists, 99 would say that the party needs to prepare itself more for the slogan: beat the kulak." He condemned such an attitude, arguing that overestimation of the kulak danger was a more serious deviation than its underestimation.[19]

But irrespective of fealty to dogma, the identification of self, or Stalin's animadversions, the obsession with kulaks betrayed a genuine and persistent anxiety about NEP fostering a capitalist class that would constitute a counterweight to the party's meagre influence in the countryside. Kulaks were thus both a projection of party leaders' fundamental distrust of the peasantry and the mirror image of the party's failure to penetrate or fully comprehend the laws of motion of peasant society. This is not to deny the reality of social differentiation or the existence of exploitative relationships in the countryside. The question remains, though, how significant was the exploitative class in peasant society? When party officials turned to the experts for an answer (or confirmation of their suspicions), they met conflicting criteria, equivocations, and a wide range of estimates.

Part of the problem was that even the uppermost stratum of the peasantry was considerably less well endowed than its pre-revolutionary equivalent. To cite merely one example, peasants in Bashkiria who were defined as kulaks possessed on average 4.1 animals and 17.5 desiatina of sown land in 1913, but only 2.2 animals and 11.9 desiatina in 1923. Elsewhere, it was possible to find households with large tracts of land, many horses and cows and three or four permanently hired workers. But, "[s]uch cases were rare . . . The average kulak (or rather the average farm among those classified by authorities as kulak) had little in common with these," for, "[a]ll things considered, the dimensions of the so-called *kulatskoe* farm were modest." Adding to the difficulty of distinguishing kulaks from seredniaki (and particularly those sometimes classified as "strong" or "well-off") was the fact that well-to-do households resorted to a variety of strategies – e.g., fictitious marriages with widows; phony cooperatives – to conceal their wealth lest they excite the envy of fellow villagers or the attention or tax collectors.[20]

But such considerations relate more to stratification than economic relationships betokening exploitation. Among the latter, the hiring of labor was considered an important, if not the most important, index. But problems arose in this connection as well. According to the all-Union census of 1926, there were 754,000 labor-hiring households in the countryside (3.2 percent of the rural population) of which 714,500 were engaged primarily in agriculture. Danilov, the dean of Soviet agrarian historians, tells us that they "may be regarded as the kernal of the rural capitalist class," but notes in the same paragraph that one-quarter of these households were headed by women who could not be considered kulak householders and were "more exploited than exploiting." "It was very common," he adds, "for labour-hiring to form part of the system of neighbourly cooperation. The rich peasant reasoned to his poorer neighbour: 'in the spring I gave you grain' (or 'I ploughed your land,' or 'I gave you a horse and plough,' etc.); 'so this summer your lad (or your girl) will work on my land. We are neighbours and she has nothing to do on your land.'"[21]

Under the old regime, as Geroid T. Robinson noted:

[s]ome of the peasants were "capitalists," to be sure, in that they were employers of labor (and if day-labor be included, no one may say how many such there were), but even among these "capitalists" nearly all were laborers too, in that they still knew the jerk of an unruly plow-handle and the drag of a sackful of grain between the shoulders.

This was still more the case in the 1920s when, according to Kritsman, only 1 percent of farms employed more than one paid worker.[22]

It is little wonder that researchers resorted to such terms as "small capitalist" or "semi-capitalist" to express the subtleties and complexities of household relationships, or that they differed on the proportion of households falling into these categories. On the basis of a sample survey of 835 households in one area of the Urals, V. S. Nemchinov found that only eight (0.96 percent) were both "well-to-do" and more than 15 percent entrepreneurial in their relations. But a study by A. I. Gaister using budget and household survey data collected by the TsSU for different regions placed the proportion of "entre-preneurial" households in the Urals oblast at 15.4 percent and "semi-and small capitalist" households at 9.3 percent. Factional politics loomed large in these estimates. In the case of Siberian peasants, the Left advertised a study claiming that 15.5 percent of households were well-off. This was considerably higher than other studies which variously estimated the well-off category as comprising 8.8 percent, 6.3 percent and as little as 3 percent of all households. In light of such ambiguities and contradictions, one can but marvel at the boldness or naiveté of Molotov who announced in December 1927 that kulaks amounted to 3.7 percent of all peasant households.[23]

Of vital interest to the party, the whole issue of social differentiation in the countryside was also at the center of a debate among specialists in agrarian economics and sociology. This debate pitted the so-called Organization and Production School represented by A. V. Chaianov, A. N. Chelintsev and their colleagues at the Timiriazev Agricultural Academy against the Agrarian Marxists centered around L. N. Kritsman, M. N. Kubanin and others associated with the Agrarian Section of the Communist Academy and the Central Statistical Administration. Initiated by the Agrarian Marxists (among whom were several former students of the Timiriazev Academy), the debate was a reprise of the pre-revolutionary controversy between Marxists and Populists, which itself echoed the mid-nineteenth-century divisions between westernizers and Slavophiles. It persisted until 1928 when, faced with the radical shift in the party's rural strategy, Chaianov and his colleagues abandoned their research on peasant households and their championing of small-scale agriculture. The victory of the Agrarian Marxists proved short-lived, however. During 1929–30, the party, aided by a new, more party-minded cohort of scholars, mobilized rural studies to celebrate the supposed achievements of collectivization, thus effectively ending the investigation of social dynamics in the countryside. This artificial closure robbed the country of some of its most outstanding thinkers who were to die in prison in the 1930s. Nearly four decades were to pass before the debate was rejoined, this time in the west, where several key texts by Chaianov were published for the first time in translation.[24]

What were the main differences between these two schools of rural scholars? First, they had different research agendas. While the Organization and Production School focused almost exclusively on the internal dynamics of the Russian peasant family farm, the Agrarian Marxists concerned themselves primarily with unequal social relations generated by iniquities in the distribution of resources. What each sought, each found. By studying the family farm independent of market relations or the hiring of labor, Chaianov and his associates came to the conclusion already before the 1917 Revolution that the laws of capitalism as understood by neo-classical and Marxist schools and the categories they employed did not apply. Rather, the family farm was to be understood as an organic unit whose labor–consumption balance varied over the life-cycle of the household and depended in part on the degree to which the household expended effort or engaged in the "self-exploitation" of its members. Most fully elaborated in Chaianov's *Peasant Farm Organization* (1925), this model informed research into the optimal size of peasant farms, the mathematical definition of land use efficiency and the extent to which advanced technology could be successfully integrated into the peasant economy via vertical cooperation.[25]

While not denying the importance of internal household relations, the Agrarian Marxists stressed the critical role of the commodity economy and its corroding effect on the independence and viability of peasant farms. Kritsman analyzed peasant agriculture into six basic elements: own farm, other's farm, own means of production, other's means of production, own labor power, other's labor power. He then hypothesized sixty-four combinations of these elements, of which only (!) thirty-nine were actually possible. Judging the class character of farms within this typological frame of reference required painstaking quantification. Even then, Kritsman cautioned, one had to factor in "possibilities of various lines of development" based on the presence or absence of pre-capitalist forces and cooperatives.[26]

The controversy among these scholars had been evident since 1923, but it entered a new phase in 1927 when each side began to impinge on the other's methodological territory. Having previously skirted the issue of differentiation, the Organization and Production School now insisted that the phenomenon was far more complex and multivariate than the Agrarian Marxists had assumed and that the latter's inferences about the eventual disappearance of the independent family farm (that is, the seredniaki) were groundless. This was because the family farm enjoyed certain economic advantages over capitalist farming, among which was its capacity for absorbing greater costs. Meanwhile, M. Kubanin, a leading Agrarian Marxist, concluded on the basis of a study of the internal dynamics of the family farm that the Timiriazev professors had exaggerated its internal harmony and stability. He discerned elements of a class struggle, with the head of the household playing the role of capitalist and the younger members cast as proletarians. The resultant partitions left the new households with miserably small allotments thus advancing differentiation.

In terms of academic politics and the sociology of research, the debate over the laws of motion of Russian peasant society was analogous to others occurring simultaneously in such fields as jurisprudence, history, psychology, criminology, and pedagogy. In each case, an older pre-revolutionary elite was challenged by younger scholars, determined to establish the legitimacy of Marxism and not incidentally make a name for themselves in their respective fields. Strange as it may seem from a later vantage point, the participants in these debates did not conceive of them as wars to the finish. What the insurgent Marxists were striving for was not so much to crush their opponents as to earn their respect. They did not invoke party doctrine, for in most instances there was none to invoke. That the disputants were playing to a larger audience which included leading party officials did not necessarily mean that the outcome of these disputes was a foregone conclusion. Not for nothing do historians use terms such as *modus vivendi* and accommodation to characterize the relationships among scholars and between prominent scholars and higher party officials during the mid-1920s.[27]

The seminality and broad applicability of the agrarian debate is illustrated by the fact that when peasant studies reemerged, this time in the west, its parameters were largely those established by Chaianov and Kritsman. In this replay of the earlier debate, Chaianov's theory of the peasant economy seems to have come out ahead, although whether this is due to its greater explanatory power or the peasantist proclivities of western researchers is not easy to determine.[28] Whatever the case, what was sown in Soviet Russia in the 1920s was reaped half a century later.

It is only within the last few years that some of the limitations of these debates have been thrown into relief. One has to do with regional variations in terms of land/labor ratios. Another is the role of off-farm income and particularly seasonal migration to towns, mines, forests and construction sites. Both have been recognized as having serious implications for social differentiation, but an assessment of their extent has been hampered by the lack of data. Aside from these lacunae, the heavily economic and quantitative component of the debate has tended to obscure dimensions of peasant society that are less amenable to quantification. Foremost in this respect are gender relations within peasant households and the extent to which they were changing in the 1920s. Both earlier and later researchers tended to assume that the household was a patriarchal unit rather than one in which male and female members led separate lives and were involved in different kinds of production relations. However commonplace, the observation that "male and female worlds do not always harmonize, and frequently . . . do not even touch" has yet to be fully utilized in examining the Russian peasant household in the 1920s or for that matter, succeeding decades. Lending itself to anthropological research, the question of gender relations also can be approached via a debate that arose in the mid-1920s involving not only peasants but workers and Soviet officialdom as well. It is to this debate that we now turn.[29]

The marriage law debate: the gendering of class and the classing of gender

Long decried and even ridiculed for its utopianism, early Soviet policies toward sexual equality and the institution of the family have been examined more recently by feminist historians and have been found wanting for the opposite reason. If earlier generations of scholars perceived the social conservatism embodied in the legal changes of 1936 as a *volte face*, it is now interpreted as the culmination of trends already observable in the 1920s. This shift in interpretation has occurred not so much because of new research. Rather it reflects a paradigmatic change involving a reconsideration of the standard against which Soviet policies are measured. What once was considered the natural or at least proper division of responsibilities both within the household and between it and society has come to be identified as peculiar, if not endemic, to western bourgeois society. Thus, the 1926 RSFSR Code on Marriage, Family, and Guardianship, previously characterized as "the most radical departure from the traditional family law" and a liberalization of the 1918 Code, more recently has been assessed as "an ideological retreat" to a "conservative approach."[30]

Several questions arise here. If the 1926 Code was indeed a retreat, what was it a retreat from? Why in any case was a revision considered necessary? Whose views prevailed in 1926 and what were the alternatives? And finally, what does the outcome of the debates surrounding the new Code suggest about gender roles in the NEP social order? These questions will be addressed in order.

Beatrice Farnsworth was the first to challenge the then existing consensus, judging the 1918 Code as "no more than modern and Western" as distinct from "socialist." By contrast, both John Quigley and Wendy Goldman consider the earlier Code, which recognized only civil marriages, granted the absolute right of divorce, and abolished adoption and illegitimacy as a legal category, as an intensely revolutionary document that reflected "the socialist-libertarian heritage of the Bolsheviks." These different evaluations echo the different assessments of those who participated in the drafting of the Code – Kollontai in the case of Farnsworth, and Brandenburgskii and Goikhbarg in the case of Quigley and Goldman – or perhaps it is the reverse: each historian has found a contemporary spokesperson for her/his own viewpoint.[31]

The 1918 Code did not aim to abolish the rite of marriage but to detach it from the Orthodox Church's clutches; it did not seek to destroy the nuclear family, but to remove its exploitative character; and it did not provide for public maintenance of children, but rather sought to inculcate a sense of civic obligation among parents for their upbringing. In this sense, Farnsworth is right. But it is hard to accept her characterization of the Code as "socially conservative" without radically altering the conventional meaning of that term. After all, in Soviet Russia it was not so much the Victorian bourgeois family that stood in the way of women's emancipation as the traditional patriarchal peasant household. In Muslim Central Asia, where abduction, forced marriage, the payment of *kalym* (bride price) and polygamy were practiced, a "modern and Western" Code had still more revolutionary implications.[32]

The impact of the 1918 Code is difficult to measure. The year 1919 saw an astonishing rise in the number of registered marriages over previous years. This may have been the result of earlier postponements due to the war, the ease of divorce (and therefore remarriage), women's response to their increased vulnerability in circumstances of socioeconomic breakdown, greater efficiency on the part of the local bureaus of vital statistics (ZAGS), or a combination of these and still other factors. A better index of the effect of the Code would be the relative proportion of Church weddings, but unfortunately the data are not available to make such a comparison. It would appear that Church weddings did decline in urban areas, while the marriage rate as a whole remained considerably higher during the first half of the 1920s than before the Revolution.[33]

Far more powerful an influence than the Code itself, however, were the dislocating and disorienting effects of the First World War, the civil war and the return to a market economy ushered in by NEP. The civil war in particular, "broke up families, cast women and children adrift, beckoned some women into new sorts of alliances, and probably convinced others of the wisdom of tradition." In the countryside, it seems to have contributed to the weakening of the extended patriarchal family but left intact, if not increased, the authority of husbands over wives. In the cities, it accelerated the development of "modern" marriage patterns (for example, higher ages of first marriages and smaller families) which already were apparent before the war, even

while it encouraged the belief that the institutions of marriage and the
family were breaking down.

Urban residents did not have to look far to find evidence corrob-
orating such a belief:

Orphaned children were roaming the streets in gangs. The divorce rates were
soaring all over the RSFSR . . . The legalization [in 1920 – LS] of abortion,
condemned even by Bolshevik spokesmen as a necessary but temporary evil,
appeared yet another threat to the survival of marriage. And the threats were
made to seem all the greater by reports of the hedonism of the young, who were
alleged to be preaching a variety of theories of sexual liberation in order to
defend the practice of old-fashioned promiscuity.[34]

The coming of NEP increased pressures on working-class women.
Childcare and other social services were drastically cut back,
unemployment soared, housing remained acutely scarce, and for all
these reasons, pregnancies were frequently aborted. Women in
unregistered or *de facto* marriages were perhaps in the most perilous
situation, for if abandoned by their husbands, they faced utter desti-
tution. The subject of satirical films such as "Bed and Sofa," popular
tunes, and risqué novels by Panteleimon Romanov, Lev Gumilevskii,
and other middle-brow writers, these phenomena were regarded
with dead earnestness by physicians, legal experts, psychologists,
hygienists, and other professionals as well as leading party and
governmental officials. Two solutions were proferred. One stressed the
necessity for expanding and improving the stock of housing, public
dining and catering facilities, organized leisure activities, and other
services to alleviate the burdens of housewives and wage-working
women. The other, representing a clear retreat from the doctrines of
"free love," the "withering away of the family" and other revolutionary
and avant-garde shibboleths, emphasized moral improvement.

Already in 1922, a Komsomol congress heard Bukharin attack
"anarchy in the realm of conduct" with specific reference to lax sexual
morals and excessive consumption of alcohol and tobacco. The following year, Trotsky chaired a conference of party propagandists at which
"some comrades spoke with great and natural anxiety of the ease with
which old family ties are broken for the sake of new ones as fleeting as
the old." Trotsky himself wrote not long after the conference that "there
is no denying . . . that family relations, those of the proletarian class
included, are shattered," and went on to give "examples of such
domestic tragedies" which "could be multiplied endlessly." Interpreting this crisis as symptomatic of the death of the old family and the birth
pangs of the new, he cited approvingly new secular ceremonies and

symbols promoted by the Komsomol and urged the party to work towards heightening "the development of the individual . . . raising the standard of his requirements and inner discipline."[35] Given the inability of the state to alleviate the burdens of childrearing, and a rate of abortion in Moscow and Leningrad that one prominent party official described as "horrifying," it was not surprising that the RSFSR Commissar of Health, Semashko, also recommended inner discipline, or, with a nod toward Freud, sublimation of the sex drive.[36]

This, then, was the context in which the RSFSR Commissariat of Justice prepared a draft of a new Family Code. The draft was widely discussed in the press as well as in regional and district executive committees before being submitted to the TsIK of the RSFSR in October 1925. The new draft code differed from its predecessor in a number of important respects. First and most controversially, it recognized *de facto* marriage as juridically equal to registered marriage, thus extending property and alimony rights to women whose marriages had not been registered. Second, it established joint ownership of property acquired in the course of marriage and its equal division in the event of divorce. And third, it simplified divorce procedures, transferring them from the courts to the ZAGS and providing for notification of divorce via postcard.

The introduction of the draft before the TsIK occasioned extensive debate from among the 434 delegates, nearly three-quarters of whom were party members. The debate touched on a broad range of issues, from the legal criteria for marriage to the disposition of property within the peasant household, childrearing, and the role of law in a socialist society. It also cut across party factional lines: Left Oppositionists and supporters of the party majority could be found among the proponents and critics of the draft. Taking into account the deeply personal nature of the issues, the TsIK decided to postpone a decision until local (uezd and volost') soviets had been given a chance to consider the draft. As pointed out by Iurii Larin, a strong supporter of the legislation, this was a highly unusual procedure, one which went against the tutelary-vanguardist tradition of the party. "Are we creating our laws on the basis of a general vote, a referendum?" he asked. "Are we to place ourselves on a level with the more backward? Or do the working masses elect the best from their midst, elect the advance-guard to lead them forward?"[37]

In the event, over 6,000 village meetings were held. Larin's fears that the meetings would be dominated by "the most backward, long-bearded village elders" were probably heightened by the local soviet elections of 1925–6. Part of the campaign to revitalize the soviets, these elections were widely interpreted as a victory for the kulak element in the villages. But it was not just the grey-beards who were critical of the draft. Most peasants, especially women, did not look favorably upon divorce, associating it with the loose living of urban folk. The clauses relating to alimony evoked criticism on the grounds that the property of the household was indivisible. As one peasant delegate put it: "I divorce my wife. We have children. My wife immediately appeals to the court and I am ordered to pay for the children. Why should my whole family suffer on my account?"[38]

Working-class women also expressed their views in meetings organized by the Zhenotdel and in the pages of the party's journal, *Rabotnitsa* (The Woman Worker). Analyzing their statements, Wendy Goldman has found that married women were generally hostile to the liberalization of divorce and recognition of *de facto* marriage. This was not "because of ignorance, backwardness or irrational attachments to traditional social forms." Rather, "their ideas were a direct expression of their own interests in the context of contemporary social conditions." Given the precariousness of their economic condition, such women "could ill afford the personal freedom inherent in Soviet divorce law."[39]

The drafters of the new code interpreted women's responses differently. "With such points of view we shall never succeed in establishing socialism," intoned a member of the USSR Supreme Court. "In order to set up socialism, we must give women their freedom."[40] But before TsIK resumed its discussion of the new code in November 1926, these would-be emancipators of women were challenged from another direction. Having returned briefly to Moscow from her diplomatic post in Norway, Aleksandra Kollontai, the preeminent Bolshevik feminist, plunged into the debate. To Kollontai it was demeaning to women and a negation of socialist principles to oblige them to plead before the courts for support from their former husbands. She also drew attention to the plight of women who had borne children as a result of "casual" relationships which were not covered at all by the Code. Instead of imposing economic responsibilities on men for the maintenance of the "weaker" sex, Kollontai proposed a General Insurance Fund, based on contributions from the entire adult working population according to a graduated scale.[41]

Kollontai's proposals sparked a lively debate, particularly in the pages of the Komsomol press. While supported by some students and Zhenotdel activists, they were strongly criticized by wage-working women who rejected the principle of collective responsibility. "How can anyone speak of a general taxation of all men?" wrote several from the Dukat factory in Moscow. "What has it to do with *all* men when only *one* man is concerned in the begetting of a child?" "Why should a deserted mother become a burden on society?" several others asked; "if once a man has succeeded in fooling a woman with poetical spells and African passion (sic), and begetting a child with her, then he should pay his 'third.'" Several leading party figures, Trotsky and Larin among them, found some merit in Kollontai's idea of a Fund, but considered it impracticable. The self-styled progressive jurists had their way. The new Family Code was adopted with minor revisions by TsIK in November 1926 and went into effect on 1 January 1927.[42]

Simultaneous with the state's and society's reconsideration of family law was the reversal of state policy with respect to adoption. Overwhelmed by the numbers of besprizorniki and the lack of funds to staff and adequately provide children's homes with food, clothing, and other resources, the state (that is, Narkompros) began to farm out homeless children to peasant and artisan families even before this system of "patronage" was decreed in April 1926. According to official statistics, 210,000 children were so placed in the years 1924 to 1926. Many reportedly were maltreated by their charges.[43]

In assessing the marriage law debate, one issue still remains to be addressed, namely the failure of the party to take a position. Was this because the leadership considered it too unimportant, or, as Kalinin implied in arguing in favor of mass discussion, were the issues regarded as too personal? If the latter was the case, where did the party draw the line between the personal and the public or political?

A fundamental ambivalence dogged the party over this and other issues involving sexuality. Sexual freedom, the notion that each individual is capable of determining the kinds of sexual relationships and living arrangements that suit him- or herself without interference from the state, was an avant-garde rather than vanguardist ideal. Still, both Lenin's condemnation of household bondage and Kollontai's dissection of the shackles of the marriage tie itself were predicated on the desire to make women fully-fledged citizens of the new Soviet republic. It was not merely tradition that thwarted such a desire, but rather the general primitivization of social life associated with the civil war. In such circumstances, the relative security of the household exercised a strong pull, especially on women. This pull was, if anything, strengthened after the introduction of NEP. For the difficulties – again experienced disproportionately by women – of leading an economically independent existence were compounded by the state's withdrawal from responsibilities it had assumed earlier. As the party made its peace with the family, the image of the new communist woman, embodied by Kollontai, increasingly fell into disfavor.[44]

Ambivalence over sexuality, of course, was not confined to marriage and the family. Indeed, there was an "explosion of concern with sex in the mid-1920s" which, it has been argued, "may be read as despair about grander impurities," specifically the corrupting influences of capitalism. Most corruptible were urban youth, "untempered" by class mentality and prone to "hooliganism," a construct that included not only drunkenness, rowdiness and thievery, but also sexual dissipation. Fearful of losing control over impressionable young citizens, the Komsomol and the party publicly acknowledged the need for greater attention to the personal lives of their members. Thus, the cult of the poet, Sergei Esenin (*Eseninshchina*) – replete with imitative suicides – evoked strong condemnation and a counter-campaign in 1926. So too did the much publicized rape of a Leningrad woman by some forty youths, including quite a few *komsomol'tsy*.[45]

Further light on the instability of the party's commitment to sexual emancipation and equality can be shed by looking beyond the boundaries of the Russian republic. The RSFSR was unique among the constituent republics of the USSR in conferring the same legal rights and obligations with respect to *de facto* marriage as to registered marriages. Associating opposition to this measure with "a strong prejudice among the peasants . . . in favor of conventional marriage," Carr explains its incorporation into the RSFSR Code as reflecting "the weight and prestige of the cities in party counsels." "In other republics," he notes, "where peasant influence was dominant, no such recognition was ever accorded."[46] Class, in this case the peasant class, had become gendered. But to conclude that family policy reflected the social composition of the republics would be misleading. For over and above the administrative apparatus of the soviets stood the central party institutions. And in at least one case, they were not content to allow traditional family relationships to perpetuate themselves, but sought to intervene directly in the family to weaken the power of traditional elites.

The case in point was a militant campaign (*khudzhum*, in Turkic) organized in the newly formed Central Asian republics by the Central Committee's Central Asian Bureau (Sredazbiuro) and Women's Section (Zhenotdel) against female seclusion. In Gregory Massell's terms, the campaign relied on both "revolutionary legalism" and "administrative assault" to break the resistance of mullahs, village and clan elders and even local soviet officials who in not a few instances were the same notables. Animated by a missionary zeal and ramified by newly formed women's organizations with such colorful names as "For the New Life" and "Down with Bride Price and Polygamy," it took the form in late 1926 and early 1927 of demonstrative unveiling. On the morning of 8 March 1927, Soviet International Women's Day, a reported 10,000 women burned their veils in Uzbek city squares. This touched off a "revolutionary wave" of such actions, encouraged and supervised by Zhenotdel activists.[47]

The *khudzhum* ran its course for another two years. In its organization and rhetoric, in the violence it spawned and its mixed results, the campaign presaged and overlapped with the "cultural revolution" in the rest of the USSR. That it occurred during an otherwise unmilitant phase of party policy toward the family is revealing of both the peculiar circumstances of Central Asia and the extent to which in this instance gender could be linked to a broader revolutionary strategy. Indeed, insofar as Muslim women were perceived by Zhenotdel activists as "the lowest of the low" and "the oppressed of the oppressed" (or, in Massell's terms, a surrogate proletariat, an interesting variation on Sultan Galiev's characterization of all eastern peoples as proletarians), then it is possible to speak of gender becoming "classed." But it bears repeating that this was an extraordinary case, one in which "the scope and intensity of the Zhenotdel's activities . . . were far greater than in European Russia." Its curtailment in the spring of 1929 thus signified several things: a cost-benefit calculation in which the inevitable "heavy-handed bungling" accompanying the campaign, murders and suicides of heretical women and disruptions to other projects were judged to have outweighed the at best temporary advantages derived from the breaking up of taboos; the uneasiness within the upper echelons of the party about female mobilization in particular and more generally, any social activism that could not be effectively monitored and controlled; and the subordination of sexual emancipation to the imperatives of the Stalin revolution.[48]

Religion, anti-religion and double faith

Relations between soviet authorities and religious institutions were bound to be stormy. As the descendants of western Enlightenment thought and the Russian intelligentsia's own anti-clerical inclinations, the Bolsheviks came to power with a strong commitment to liberate the masses from the thrall of ignorance and religious superstition. For their part, the Christian, Jewish, and Muslim clergy could not but regard Bolshevism as a threat to the spiritual values they sought to inculcate among their respective flocks, to the physical property in their charge, and to their own lives and well-being. Especially vulnerable in these respects was the Orthodox Church, the principal agent of religious indoctrination and ritual observance among ethnic Russians, and moreover, an institution intricately tied to the old regime.

The overthrow of the Tsar provided the Orthodox Church with the opportunity to realize a project long mooted in ecclesiastical circles. This was the convocation of an All-Russian Council or Sobor. Inspired by the need for a strong unifying figure who could provide both spiritual and political guidance, the Sobor resolved in September 1917 to restore the patriarchate, which had been abolished by Peter the Great. Less than a fortnight after the October Revolution, Metropolitan Tikhon of Moscow was chosen as Patriarch.

It was not long before the new ecclesiastical and secular regimes clashed. On 19 January 1918, Tikhon, claiming that "the most violent persecution is begun against the Holy Church of Christ," anathematized the Bolsheviks as "outcasts of the human race." A few days later, the Soviet government decreed the disestablishment and disendowment of the Orthodox Church, in effect, placing it on the same legal footing as all other religious institutions. Disenfranchisement of all ecclesiastical officials soon followed. Beyond this, though, the state was not willing to go. The RSFSR constitution recognized "freedom of religious and anti-religious propaganda," and the party's 1919 program, while calling for "the broadest propaganda in favor of scientific enlightenment and against religion," warned against "any insult to the feelings of believers which can lead only to the strengthening of religious fanaticism."[49]

But like much else at the time, the center's wishes, if known at all, were ignored in the provinces. Persecutions and killings of priests, lootings and desecrations of churches, and liquidations of monasteries – all carried out by, or at least with the approval of, local authorities – were commonplace and were very much part of the civil war. Many in the Orthodox priesthood performed *Te Deums* for the Whites, a few bishops and metropolitans openly sided with one or the other White armies, and some of the Siberian clergy actually formed Holy Detachments to fight the Reds. But there is no evidence that they did so at the behest of the patriarch who, from 1919, maintained a public position of strict neutrality.[50]

The legal framework for church–state relations, established in 1918, was to remain intact until April 1929. Within this framework the state was able to exert various kinds of pressure against religious institutions when it seemed advantageous to do so and to tolerate them when it did not. Pressure was exerted in 1922 when the government ordered that articles containing gold, silver, and precious stones in the Church's possession should be turned over to Narkomfin for sale abroad to raise funds for famine relief. Having already set up a committee to collect money, foodstuffs, and ornamental jewels "not used for the holy rites," Tikhon urged the faithful to resist the decree. For assisting the soviet authorities, clerics faced defrocking and laymen excommunication. However, many did cooperate, either because they feared the wrath of the Cheka or felt that Tikhon was putting material objects above the lives of starving people. Still, there was considerable resistance by both church people and sympathetic laity. Demonstrations, pitched battles with police and soldiers and pogroms against Jews – blamed as the instigators of the decree – were reported in Moscow province, Smolensk and Petrograd. All in all, there were over a thousand separate incidents resulting in the deaths of priests, monks and nuns that may have run into the thousands and the arrest, trial and sentencing to internal exile or imprisonment of several hundred more. The Patriarch himself was indicted and placed under house arrest in May 1922.[51]

All the while, a rebellion against episcopal authority had been brewing among the Orthodox clergy. The arrest of Tikhon provided the insurgents, led by Fathers Kalinovskii and Krasnitskii, with the opportunity to form a Temporary Higher Church Administration. They also founded a journal, *The Living Church*, after which their movement took its name. The sources of this rebellion antedate the restoration of the patriarchate and have been traced back to the reformist liberal impulses of urban priests and lay theologians in the early years of the twentieth century and particularly during the 1905–7 revolution. The rebellion was thus not so much theological as political – a kind of clerical Smena vekh. Long-standing resentment among the white (parish) clergy at the black (celibate) clergy's control of the dioceses figured as well, giving the insurgency something of a trade unionist character. The Living Church called on all clergy to recognize "the justice of the Russian social revolution" and to work to oust the Orthodox Church hierarchy of counterrevolutionaries. This was not the only blow to patriarchal authority from within the Church. Nationalist sentiment surfaced in the form of a national Ukrainian Church under Petliura, and in 1921 a Ukrainian Autocephalous movement.[52]

There is no doubt that in 1922–3 the state departed from its position of strict neutrality among religious organizations, privileging the Living Church in its struggle against the "Tikhonists." By the end of 1922, the soviets had turned over nearly two-thirds of all functioning churches in the RSFSR – almost 20,000 – to the Living Church, or rather to the three Renovationist factions into which the insurgent movement in the meantime had split. Yet within a year, the state reversed itself, releasing Tikhon from imprisonment, and dropping the charges against him in return for a written statement confessing his past crimes against the state and declaring his recognition of soviet power.

Why the reversal? Expressing a hostility typical of Church historians, Dimitry Pospielovsky surmises that "the answer lies in the dismal failure of the subservient Renovationists to attract and keep the masses of Orthodox believers." But in 1923 it was not at all clear that this was so, and two years later Renovationists could still claim approximately 14,000 parishes. Nevertheless, the gradual decline of the movement and its following throughout the remainder of the decade is evident, the number of parishes falling to 6,245 by 1927. This may have been because of internal divisiveness and the maneuverings of Tikhon and his successors. It may have been because Renovationism was too radical and secular for devout Christians, who cleaved to the familiar in unsettled times, and insufficiently so for those who had abandoned ties with formal religion or gravitated to the more syncretic religious sects. The real issue is why the state should have sought a *modus vivendi* with patriarchal authority. Carr sites two plausible reasons: external pressure coming at a time when the government was seeking to establish diplomatic and trade relations with the rest of Europe, and the pursuit of the smychka. Toleration of the national Church was a function of the retreat initiated by the state in 1921 but delayed in this case by two years.[53]

This retreat, as the others, had its limits. While permitting religious institutions to function, the state began to organize anti-religious propaganda to win the minds, if not hearts, of the Soviet people. Among the earliest forms of anti-religious propaganda were exposures of "relic frauds," that is, cases where what were purported to be miraculously preserved remains of canonized individuals turned out to be wax effigies or other imitations of human figures. Otherwise, though, the anti-religious campaign was on a relatively modest scale during the civil war. Lunacharskii, who had been associated with the God-building movement of the pre-war years, was keenly aware of the need to "fight religious prejudice and antiquated beliefs" with a humanistic education stressing the natural sciences and history. But given the absence of funds and textbooks and the uncooperativeness of many teachers, Narkompros' contribution to the effort was limited. More active were the Red Army's Political Administration (PUR) and the Commissariat of Justice, which in addition to initiating criminal proceedings against the perpetrators of frauds, organized anti-religious lectures and published a journal, *Revoliutsiia i tserkov* (The Revolution and the Church).[54]

The party itself paid little attention to organizing anti-religious propaganda until its Twelfth Congress in April 1923. The resolution passed on that occasion called for the training of anti-religious propagandists in party schools, courses and circles, the publication of scientific and popular literature on the origins and class nature of religion and the counterrevolutionary activities of the Church, and the improvement of political educational methods especially in connection with the rural-based reading rooms. At the same time, it recognized that religious beliefs would continue to exist so long as peasants remained dependent on nature and capitalist relations persisted in the towns, and warned against administrative measures or other acts offensive to religious believers.[55]

The resolution, sandwiched between others on work in the country-side and propaganda, the press and agitation, evidently was part of the effort to expand the party's influence among the peasantry. It may also have had a more immediate – and negative – inspiration, namely, the Komsomol Christmas of 6 January 1923. This was a carnivalesque mockery of the religious holiday, replete with processions of students and working-class youth dressed as clowns, singing the "Internationale," and burning effigies of religious "cult" figures. The technique appears to have been borrowed from the party's Jewish Section (Evsektsiia) which organized torchlight parades and free lunches in several cities with large Jewish communities in celebration of "Yom Kippurnik." The mischievousness of the Komsomol Christmas sufficiently outraged the sensibilities of believers and non-believers alike to provoke the party's Central Committee to "recommend" that the forthcoming "Komsomol Easter" be restricted to the organization of lectures, movies and plays.[56]

In the forefront of the more temperate approach to anti-religious activism was Emelian Iaroslavskii, a secretary of the party's Central Committee, with a long personal involvement in the religious question. In December 1922 Iaroslavskii founded a weekly newspaper, *Bezbozhnik* (The Godless) which began serializing his major works on religion including *The Bible of Believers and Unbelievers*. Subsequently, he organized a support group, the Society of Friends of The Godless, which in 1925 became the League of the Godless (Soiuz bezbozhnikov; the adjective "militant" was added in 1929).

Iaroslavskii's approach was based on the assumption that exposure to rationalist explanations of natural phenomena, the wonders of applied science, and ethical, clean-living atheists would demystify religion. It was reflected not only in *Bezbozhnik* and the more high-brow journal, *Antireligioznik*, but the numerous museums of atheism, anti-religious exhibitions and the quite detailed instructions to party and Komsomol cells about how to organize anti-religious evenings, all of which date from this period. More exciting and certainly more accessible to the non-literate population were the public debates (*disputy*), which typically involved an atheist and a priest addressing the theme of God's existence. Some of these encounters were held before audiences numbering in the thousands. On one occasion, Lunacharskii took on the (Renovationist) Metropolitan A. I. Vvedenskii over the issues of "Christianity or Communism" and "Idealism or Materialism." Sometimes, the rival claims of each side were put to the test as in the case of competition between "Godless acres" treated with chemical fertilizers and "God's acres" sprinkled with holy water.[57]

At the same time, the more confrontationalist approach, termed "priest-eating" (*popoedstvo*) by its detractors, refused to die. It lived on in a monthly journal, *Bezbozhnik u stanka* (The Godless at the Workbench), which was dedicated to establishing the "antireligious proletarian dictatorship of the atheist city over the countryside." Edited by M. M. Kostelovskaia, a secretary of the Moscow party committee, the journal carried illustrations by D. Moor lampooning the priesthood and religious faith. One had Christ walking in front of a gigantic cross driven by a devilish capitalist and pulled by toilers in chains; another showed priests, saints and devils being sneezed out of the nose of a peasant as a party man stands by wishing the peasant "Good health!"[58]

The extent to which these efforts were successful in persuading peasants and workers to renounce religious beliefs and practices is unclear. Certainly party committee reports (uncritically reproduced by Soviet historians) of so many people listening to lectures, attending meetings, and viewing "The Cross and the Mauser" and other anti-religious films are not convincing evidence. Aside from the likelihood of numerical exaggeration, such reports reveal precious little about the reactions of such audiences to what they heard or saw or why they were there in the first place. Much the same can be said about the number of workers who showed up for work on religious holidays.

The question of the religiosity of peasants in particular stimulated a good deal of research and controversy in the middle 1920s. Surveys of various kinds were conducted. One, based on budget studies, determined that in the course of a year, approximately half of all households had no expenditures related to "religious needs." Another, carried out by Strumilin, found that 37.4 percent of peasants below the age of 24 did not engage in religious customs, while still another found that of 368 Red Army recruits (most of whom were peasants), 56 percent said they attended church and believed in God. Other than confirming that women and the elderly tended to be more religious than men and youths – something that anti-religious propagandists knew very well and may account for the element of misogyny in their literature – the research and arguments it generated were inconclusive.[59]

The problem was that while on the philosophical level, the two world views of religious idealism and atheistic materialism obviously clashed, on the level of daily life (*byt*) their rituals, imagery and even language were compatible or at least space and time could be found to accommodate both. "Peasants," writes Stites,

had a fantastic ability to absorb new "faiths" and rituals when necessary and combine them with their own ways. Peasants who accepted atheism and its forms may have done so as accommodation, just as the Christianized peasants of ancient Russia had retained the old pagan thought forms and modes of worship alongside the new in a culture known as *dvoeverie* – dual faith. There was not only much *dvoeverie* in rural Russia in the 1920s, but *tvoeverie* and perhaps even *mnogoverie* (multiple faith).[60]

In short, they wanted to have it both – or many – ways. The same peasants who placated house-spirits residing in the stove and crossed themselves before the icon (or "red") corner, hung newspaper photographs of Lenin, Kalinin, and other Bolshevik "saints" on their walls, or in some cases, replaced the icons of Orthodox saints with Lenin. "As far as God is concerned," one peasant was reported to have declared, "from my own experience I have come to the conclusion that there is no God . . . but as for the devil, I don't know." Another who identified himself as godless explained that he attended church because "If there is no God, I'm not risking anything. But if God exists, I will have a small guarantee of passing into the heavenly realm." These statements are interpreted by the Soviet historian from whom I have taken them as evidence of peasants' "wavering" faith, but there was probably more stability to such "wavering" than might appear at first glance.[61]

Anthropologists have observed such practices and listened to such explanations the world over. But it would be wrong to assume that only the relatively "primitive" engaged in them. "A worker will not trouble to buy new icons, but has not sufficient will to discard the old ones . . . " He "does not go to church – and reads *Bezbozhnik*, but sends for a priest to christen his child – just in case." Trotsky, who made these observations in 1923, argued that such ties to religion were vestigial, for "[r]eligiousness among the Russian working classes practically does not exist." But probably closer to the mark was Tomskii who, five years later, told a trade union congress that "If we dismissed all believers from our ranks, who would be left in the unions? The core of our unions would not be much larger than that of the party."[62]

Matters were not made any easier for the bestowers of enlightenment by the adaptability of the bestowers of darkness. "The gospel rewritten in atheist script," was the way that Vvedenskii characterized Marxism in his debate with Lunacharskii. *Trud* reported cases of "Red" priests establishing good relations with local soviets, Church elders attending anti-religious lectures to provide the lecturer with "information," and other instances of "priests . . . putting old wine in new bottles." Both priests and mullahs were active among women, organizing study circles, choirs, and meetings to insulate them from the Zhenotdel.[63]

But the most chameleon-like – or syncretic – were the religious sectarians. Communities of Dukhobors, Molokans, New Israelites, Evangelists, and Baptists interpreted the revolution as a godsend and freely took to socialist economic forms (communes and cooperatives with names like "Red Banner," "Sickle and Hammer" and "Labor and Peace") and Bolshevik methods of mass mobilization (the Baptomol, Christomol, and Trezvomol – Union of Teetotaller Youth – instead of the Komsomol). Anti-religious leaders were very much divided about how to respond to the sectarians. Iaroslavskii argued against differentiating them from other believers or otherwise favoring them. The Thirteenth Party Congress nevertheless passed a resolution drafted by Kalinin which pointed out that sectarians had been subjected to "the harshest persecution under tsarism" and urged that the "significant numbers of economically-cultured" people among them be directed into soviet work. By the late 1920s, however, this policy was reversed, and sectarians of all tendencies tended to be lumped together with kulaks as "the most dangerous enemy."[64]

The adaptability of old cultures to new circumstances was paralleled by the reverse kind of syncretism. This was the development of what Stites calls "rituals of a counterfaith" or in the larger sense, "Godless religion." As one-time constituents of the Second International, the Bolsheviks inherited its traditions of May Day parades, International

Women's Day commemorations, revolutionary workers' songs, and red symbolism. From 1918 onward, the national components of these foreign-derived traditions became increasingly evident. May Day, for example, was harnessed to immediate concerns and national themes – victory over the Whites, the inculcation of a communist labor ethic (Subbotnik), military preparedness – which also featured in the Anniversary of the October Revolution celebrations. The fact that redness in Russian is linguistically related to "beauty" made the square outside the Kremlin walls and the icon corners of the peasants' huts ripe for revolutionary appropriation.

At the same time, other traditions were invented – by whom it is not clear – with a more personal focus. These life-cycle rituals included Octobering (the dedication of newborns who were given names from the Pantheon of revolutionary heroes, heroines, and ideals as well as technological wonders), "Red Weddings," and revolutionary funerals, preferably accompanied by cremation. In each case, and in all socialist *rites de passage*, the timing and structural features were patterned after the Christian (as opposed to other religions') ceremonies that, it was hoped, would be supplanted. They never did become mass phenomena, though they evidently did strike responsive chords among many intellectuals and urban workers.[65]

Clearly, though, the most self-conscious syncretic blending of Christian and communist imagery was the cult of Lenin. Notwithstanding Lenin's well-known abhorrence of such adulation and idolization, there was no more powerful image in all of Bolshevik mythology. The cult pre-dated Lenin's death, being inculcated by high-ranking party officials, sympathetic artists and writers, and journalists writing for a mass peasant audience. Thus, shortly after the assassination attempt on Lenin in August 1918, Zinoviev referred to him as the "apostle of world communism," and "leader by the grace of God." This speech was published in 200,000 copies. Others described Lenin in Christlike terms, as a martyr and savior, "Welding together peasants, workers, and soldiers / In the flame of crucifixions."[66]

Lenin's long illness and then untimely death (he was only 54) produced a vast outpouring of genuine apprehension and grief. It also produced a Funeral Commission (later renamed the Commission for the Immortalization of the Memory of V. I. Ulianov (Lenin)) which charged V. D. Bonch-Bruevich, a student of religions and an anti-religious propagandist, with organizing the construction of Lenin's crypt. The funeral and associated events – Trotsky's politically disastrous absence, Stalin's catechistic "oath speech," the thousands upon thousands who lined up in the bitter cold to view Lenin lying in state, the Funeral Commission's decision to preserve the body indefinitely, and the construction of a mausoleum, first in wood and later in gleaming stone – had great symbolic significance, as much religious as political.[67]

It remains to state what already should be obvious. This is that in the war of maneuver between tradition and modernity, two processes can be observed. One was the modernization of tradition – the Living Church instead of the supposedly moribund variety, "red" priests, "Moslem clergymen and village and clan notables launch[ing] . . . the first conscious organizational effort in local cultural history . . . to 'win back' women and youth."[68] The other was the traditionalization of modernity of which the Lenin cult was the quintessential example. These two processes occasionally intersected, as in the state's fleeting support for the Living Church, but for the most part competed and coexisted in the space provided by NEP.

One could go further by pointing to the ambiguities inherent in these processes. Like most reformist movements, the Living Church claimed to be restoring eastern Christianity to its original, true identity. By the same token, it has been noted that the Lenin cult "was not an undiluted traditional religious affair. Elements of science, technology and modernism insinuated themselves at many points and at many levels." The cult's reception also can be variously interpreted. Did the evident grief displayed by large numbers of people at Lenin's death signify identification with his political philosophy, vestiges of peasant monarchism – or both?[69]

To conclude on a less diffident note, we may say that Soviet political culture of the 1920s was very much a composite affair. There was a strong element of "militarized socialism" – the interweaving of socialist and military values derived from the civil war experience.[70] But there were others as well: elements of nationalism – both Russian and non-Russian – of religion which have been discussed here, and of technological utopianism. Each could be asserted in the name of building socialism, touching responsive chords with some constituencies while offending others. It is to the last of these cultures that we now turn.

Industrialization debates

The condition of Soviet industry by all accounts took a marked turn for the better in 1924. For the next two years, steady progress was made in the expansion of output, employment, productivity, and profitability. Consumer goods industries continued to lead the way, financing their operations mainly from the quick turnover of sales to an expanding peasant market. But in the economic year 1924/5, the production of iron and steel rose dramatically thanks to a more liberal long-term credit policy and the revival of coal production in the Donbass. Still, the extractive and capital goods industries had a long way to go to reach the volume of production attained before the war. Whereas the production of cigarettes had reached 102 percent of the 1913 total and textiles were at 66 percent, steel output amounted to only 43.8 percent and iron ore was no more than 23.8 percent.[71]

The question of whether and how to redress this persistent imbalance was the point of departure for what has become known as the Soviet industrialization debate. This debate, which was inextricably linked with party policy toward the peasantry, was *the* test case for living with NEP. On it would depend not only the viability of that policy, but a good deal else of what distinguished Soviet society in the 1920s from succeeding decades. It "extended much further than . . . an extension of the productive capacity and technological level of an arbitrarily defined sector of the economy; the debate coalesced 'growth theory' . . . with, *inter alia*, conceptions of political relationships and economic organis-ation, of international relations and defence policy, of the articulation of educational development and scientific/technological research with the economy."[72]

Indeed, as at least some of the participants were aware, the indus-trialization debate was a critical moment in the history of socialism. For better or for worse – the collapse of the Soviet economy in the late 1980s and early 1990s having done much to cloud memory of more favorable judgments – the strategy that emerged from this debate would define for the rest of the world what a socialist economy meant. It would be the Soviet Union's answer to the question of how to overcome backward-ness in the modern era, serving as the only "real" alternative to a capitalist framework of development for much of the rest of the world.

With so much at stake, it is understandable why scholars have paid so much attention to the industrialization debate. For some, the aim has been to rescue discarded alternatives and their authors from the oblivion and obloquy to which they were consigned by the Stalinist "victors." To others, it was to demonstrate the supposed verities of neo-classical economic thinking, and still others, the advantages of planning on the basis of material balances. More recently, Soviet academics have returned to the debate, this time to try to understand what went wrong, with at least one prominent historian claiming that "[t]he turning point of 1929, in the forms in which it occurred, had its origin in serious oversights committed in 1925 with respect to assessing the socio-economic situation . . . "[73] In briefly recapitulating the debate here, scant attention will be paid to the technical details which have been admirably if not exhaustively covered by Carr and Davies. Rather, I will focus on the discursive contours of the debate, the institutional frameworks in which the debate occurred, and the shifting political power blocs up to the point when several simultaneously occuring crises overdetermined its outcome.

From the previous discussion of the agrarian debates, it is clear that a broad spectrum of opinion existed within the party – as well as among "non-party specialists" – about the proper roles of agriculture and industry, the market and planning, and consumption and accumulation in Soviet economic life. While all participants looked forward to the industrialization of agriculture via electrification and tractorization and the eventual obliteration of the contradictions between town and country, the timetable for achieving such epochal changes and the means for doing so remained uncertain. In addition to these broad conceptual parameters and the already-mentioned increases in industrial output, the industrialization debate was prefigured by several decisions taken by the party in 1924. Among these were the appointment of the deputy chairman of Sovnarkom, A. D. Tsuriupa, as president of Gosplan; the instruction of the party's Central Control Commission and Workers' and Peasants' Inspectorate to Gosplan to establish a "general perspective plan of economic activity of the USSR for a number of years (five or ten)"; and the upgrading of the metal industry to a matter of high priority.[74]

The latter two decisions may well have been sops to the Left Opposition, since both greater attention to planning and an emphasis on the development of capital goods industries were prominent in its programmatic statements. But throughout 1924 and into the following year the thrust of the party's economic policy was actually in the opposite direction, toward financial restraint and the conciliation of the peasantry. This was encapsulated in Zinoviev's slogan of "Face to the countryside." Facing the countryside worked so long as industrial expansion could continue on the basis of regaining lost ground, that is, bringing back into production unutilized plant. By 1925, however, the upward limits of industrial recovery were in sight. According to official estimates, existing factories were being utilized up to 85 percent of capacity. "The next requirement, if industry was to expand further, or even to maintain its existing level of production, was the accumulation of capital resources . . . to transform and modernize obsolescent factories, plant and equipment."[75]

Such was the thinking within Vesenkha and Gosplan, each of which set up commissions to investigate fixed capital requirements. However, there was strong resistance to stepped-up investment in "heavy" industry, most notable from Narkomfin. As Commissar of Finance, G. Ia. Sokolnikov had long advocated a cautious approach toward industrial reconstruction, arguing on the grounds of financial responsibility and worrying that excessive haste would strain the smychka with the peasants. He proposed instead a policy that favored export-oriented mineral, timber and agricultural production and primary processing industries over more complex and costly industries whose products could be more cheaply imported. Another Narkomfin official, Lev Shanin, was an even more zealous advocate of agriculturally led development. He argued that investment in capital goods industries was already excessive resulting in an excess of demand for consumer goods over supply. Even after the Fourteenth Congress had rejected such an approach, Shanin insisted that "preference should be given to agriculture," because "it throws goods on the market much faster than industry" and because "the scope for achieving an economic upsurge via agricultural exports – i.e., the cheapest way possible – is our economy's greatest asset."[76]

The chief audience for such arguments was the Politburo and the Central Committee. But with the break up of the ruling triumvirate, these organs were in turmoil. The struggle between Zinoviev and Kamenev on the one side and Stalin on the other was thinly clothed in doctrinal garb. The former claimed that Lenin's characterization of the Soviet economy as "state capitalist" still held while the latter, supported by Bukharin, opined that the threshhold between state capitalism and socialism had been crossed. The division also assumed the dimension of rivalry between the two "capitals" – Leningrad, the crucible of revolution and Zinoviev's satrapy versus Moscow. The chief effect of the struggle was to put off confronting the issue of industrialization and indeed the party congress, which originally had been scheduled to be held in Leningrad in the spring of 1925. In the meantime, Sokolnikov gravitated to Zinoviev's camp, which in view of Zinoviev's new-found enthusiasm for industrial investment, must have surprised many party stalwarts. But Sokolnikov was far more comfortable with the notion of state capitalism than with the autarchic implications of the Stalin–Bukharin watchword of "socialism in one country." The cancellation of grain exports for the second successive year may well have convinced him of the "kulak danger," a standard bugaboo of the Left which Zinoviev had appropriated for his own (demagogic) purposes. Thus, a "New Opposition" emerged in the autumn of 1925.

The Left Opposition meanwhile took advantage of the indecisiveness and division among its political adversaries to press its case. Interpreting the reluctance of the peasants to market their surplus after the 1925 harvest as the inevitable consequence of a shortage of industrial goods, Preobrazhenskii continued to hammer away at the necessity for comprehensive dirigiste planning, priority for heavy industry incorporating large-scale capital intensive methods, and access to foreign technology via state monopolized trade. Although tarred with the brush of Trotskyism, Preobrazhenskii's views differed in significant ways from those of Trotsky. Whereas Preobrazhenskii placed greatest emphasis on sources of internal accumulation to be obtained from the systematic squeezing of peasant surpluses and private capitalist profit, Trotsky stressed accumulation through rationalization, specialization and standardization. While both saw the state's monopoly of foreign trade as an important lever for technological development, Trotsky made the USSR's integration into the international division of labor a central theme of his program. Indeed, Trotsky was (privately) critical of Preobrazhenskii's failure to take into account the "world law of value" in the "duel" which the latter posited between socialist accumulation and the market within the USSR.[77]

For Bukharin, as we saw in an earlier chapter, there was no "duel" except in the minds of "super-industrializers" like Preobrazhenskii. Exuding optimism about the possibility of balanced, mutually reinforcing development of agriculture and industry, Bukharin sought to give the notion of "socialism in one country" economic respectability. "We are growing on the basis of our ties with the outside world," he told a party meeting in Moscow shortly before the Fourteenth Congress, "[B]ut on the other hand . . . we are becoming to a certain degree more vulnerable. How can we avoid this danger? We can avoid it by ensuring that our economy and our country do not become in any manner or degree too dependent economically on the foreign market so long as it is controlled by the bourgeoisie and capitalism."[78] Whatever benefits would be derived from obtaining western technology were thus outweighed by the dangers of dependency.

Bukharin was thus closer to Preobrazhenskii than was Trotsky in assuming that industrialization would have to rely mainly on internal resources, that is, a transfer of resources from the agrarian to the state sector. "The real disagreement," notes Cohen, "was over methods and limits," or as Bukharin explained, "Comrades of the opposition stand for pumping over excessively, for such intense pressure on the peasantry which . . . is economically irrational and politically impermissible. Our position in no way renounces this pumping over; but we calculate much more soberly." It was a calculation based on the formula "from circulation (money, prices, trade) to production," of "growing into socialism through exchange." This meant, as he told the Fourteenth Congress, a slower but surer course of "build[ing] socialism even on this wretched technological level" – "at a snail's pace."[79]

Nowhere was the technological level of industry more "wretched" than in the small-scale industrial sector. Based primarily in the countryside and overwhelmingly single-family artisanal in character, small-scale industrial production almost defied statistical or analytical precision. Was it proto-capitalist, semi-capitalist or proto-socialist? In a sense it was all three. Even the distinction between those enrolled in industrial cooperatives or artels – analogous to the agricultural cooperatives – and artisans who worked on a putting out basis for nepmen was somewhat artificial, as private capitalists frequently formed bogus cooperatives to evade restrictions on the hiring of labor and the terms of employment mandated by the 1922 Labor Code. It was, in any case, no easy matter to integrate these small-scale operations into the large-scale schemes of the planning agencies. Despite their obvious and officially acknowledged function as safety-valves in times of goods shortages and the indulgence that Bukharin in particular urged toward them, the kustari were a source of constant irritation to central planners. However, their wish to see them eliminated would have to wait for a few more years.[80]

A key moment in the industrialization debate was the release in August 1925 of Gosplan's *Control Figures of the National Economy for the Year 1925–1926*. This was the first exercise in comprehensive economic planning, and by all accounts, it was an impressive document. Ironically, in view of the identification of state planning with communist economics, "communists were very weakly represented . . . among the planners." Of Gosplan's 527 employees, a mere 49 were party members of whom nearly half performed menial tasks.[81] Among the chief planners working in Gosplan were V. G. Groman and V. A. Bazarov, "non-party specialists" who, like Bukharin, were influenced by the dynamic equilibrium or "systems thinking" of A. Bogdanov. The control figures they produced represented a synthesis of two approaches. One was known as "genetic" planning according to which certain objective "regularities" of the pre-war economy were extrapolated to forecast future feasibilities. This approach bore the stamp of Groman's contribution. The other, the "teleological" approach, was most closely identified with S. G. Strumilin, one of the few communists in Gosplan. It was used to alter proportions in the economy in the interests of maximum growth, in effect making the market adapt to state aims rather than the reverse. In this sense, the document reflected the balance that Bazarov had recommended in his own work between directive planning and market forces, state industry and peasant agriculture, and desired ends and empirical investigation of existing capacities.[82]

Throughout the autumn of 1925, the control figures were subjected to close scrutiny and criticism by leading governmental and party personnel. Although the figures lacked binding authority, a good deal else was at stake – not only the political struggle, but the principle of "operational" or prescriptive planning and the institutional prestige of Gosplan. The most trenchant criticisms came, predictably, from Narkomfin and to a lesser extent from Vesenkha. A common theme of their complaints was that Gosplan's plan did not anticipate the peasants' "plan" of withholding grain from the market and otherwise bore little relation to real life. Kamenev, who presided over the Council of Labor and Defense's deliberations, considered the figures "a formula for inflation"; others expressed skepticism about projections of industrial output, and still others questioned the usefulness of the whole enterprise. Among the party elite, only Trotsky unequivocally praised the Gosplan statisticians, and as Carr noted, "[p]raise from this quarter did nothing to commend the innovation of the control figures to the party leadership."[83]

In the final analysis, it was the party's judgment that counted most. But, embroiled in the political power struggle, the Central Committee ducked the issue of planning at its plenary session in October and the party congress' resolutions virtually ignored the control figures. Nevertheless, the Fourteenth Congress, convened in Moscow in late December, was a watershed in the industrialization debate and overall party policy. Delivering for the first time the Central Committee's political report, Stalin proclaimed the party's intention "to make our country an economically independent unit." This was, of course, one of Bukharin's favorite themes. But the General Secretary went on: "This line demands the maximum expansion of our industry . . . We ourselves will produce machines and other means of production," a point that was reiterated in the congress' resolutions. According to Stalin, then, the Soviet people could have their industrialization and eat too. One can do no better than Carr in putting this doctrine into historical perspective: "Hitherto the economic development of Russia and the westernization of Russia had been integral parts of the same process. After 1925 they were separated. Industrialization would be pursued independently of the west and, if necessary, against the west. It was this self-reliance which distinguished industrialization under Stalin from industrialization under Witte."[84]

The Fourteenth Congress was significant in yet another respect. It was the last occasion on which a prominent party member, in this case Kamenev, publicly denounced Stalin's aggrandizement of power. In a lengthy speech recounting his numerous differences with the "school of Bukharin," Kamenev wound up by boldly declaring himself against "the theory of the 'leader'" (in Russian, *vozhd*, roughly equivalent to *Duce* or *Führer*) and asserting that "Comrade Stalin cannot perform the function of uniting the Bolshevik general staff." To this challenge, Stalin's supporters replied with paens of praise for the General Secretary and taunts about Kamenev's and Zinoviev's "factionalism" and pretentions to leadership. In his concluding speech, Stalin adopted a characteristically modest posture. He claimed "it is impossible to lead the party except by a collegium . . . without Rykov, without Kalinin, without Tomskii, without Molotov, without Bukharin. It is impossible to lead the party without the comrades I have mentioned." And he underlined his support for the last of these "comrades" in terms which, because of the fate that met Bukharin twelve years later, are nothing if not ironic: "What in fact do they want of Bukharin? They demand the blood of comrade Bukharin. That is what comrade Zinoviev demands when in his concluding speech he sharpens the issue of Bukharin. You demand the blood of Bukharin? We shall not give you that blood, be sure of that."[85]

Despite such (rare) moments of high drama and the resolution to proceed with industrialization, the Fourteenth Congress did not in itself change very much. The message enunciated by Stalin that the period of recovery had ended and that of "reconstruction" based on internal accumulation had begun was repeated many times in succeeding months but with no visible effect. Like the Left Opposition before them, the Zinovievists were rooted out of key administrative positions. But their standard-bearers remained within the Politburo and, like Trotsky, took an active part in the Central Committee's plenary session in April 1926. Here again the principle of industrialization was affirmed. It now was linked to the "planning principle," the two being defined as "the current tasks of the coming period of economic development." But whereas the planning agencies had been hard at work in the intervening months, the economic directives issued by the plenum were noteworthy for their cautiousness. There was some discussion of the project to construct a dam across the Dnepr (Dneprostroi, as it became known), but according to Trotsky who strongly supported the idea, Stalin regarded it as so much wasteful expenditure, like "a *muzhik* who had saved up a few kopecks and, instead of repairing his plough or renewing his stock, bought a gramophone and ruined himself." The project was held up for nearly a year.[86]

Planning activity resulted in two five-year plan drafts, one drawn up by Osvok, the Special Commission on the Restoration of Fixed Capital appointed by Vesenkha, and the other the product of Gosplan's labors. Both plans were restricted to the state sector. Of the two, Gosplan's was the more modest, calling for capital investment of 900 million rubles rather than Osvok's 1,549 million in 1926–7, and 1,000 million compared to 1,450 million for the following economic year. Seeking to reconcile the two drafts, Vesenkha appointed another commission, under A. Shtern, a former Menshevik who had been transferred from Narkomfin. The Shtern commission recommended as part of the control figures for 1926–7 a level of capital investment of 916 million rubles. At this level, the production of capital goods (Group A) industry was expected to rise by 24 percent, that of consumer goods (Group B) industry by only half as much.[87]

These recommendations were strongly endorsed by G.L. Piatakov, deputy president of Vesenkha in charge of the commission to draft the 1926/7 control figures, but vehemently attacked as excessive by Dzerzhinskii, Vesenkha's president. But Dzerzhinskii, a powerful figure within party circles, seemed to be out of step with the prevailing sentiment in Vesenkha's presidium. When he died suddenly of a heart attack, virtually within hours of having denounced Piatakov, the major obstacle to approving Shtern's figures was removed. From July 1926 onward, the trend was toward the upward revision of Vesenkha's recommendations based on the teleological approach to planning. Resistance from Narkomfin and Gosplan was futile. Actual gross capital investment in "Vesenkha-planned" industry in 1926/7 was reported as 1,068 million rubles. This represented an increase of 31 percent over the previous year and a doubling of the amount invested in new construction.[88]

What, other than Dzerzhinskii's death, can account for this trend? One can piece together a number of ideological and situational factors.

First, it was in the summer of 1926 that Zinoviev and Trotsky forged an alliance, known as the "Joint" or "United Opposition." The Opposition had many complaints – not the least of which was its own persecution – but the failure of state industry to keep pace with economic development, thus perpetuating the goods shortage, was a prominent theme. Well into 1927 Opposition spokesmen had access to the party press and meetings to level their indictment of party policy or the lack thereof, criticise "restorationist ideology" and demand that the party unleash the forces of industrialization. They thus compelled the party majority to defend itself in terms of its own version of Leninist orthodoxy and the party's historic mission to build socialism. However, one should not overemphasize the role of the Opposition in this respect. As Carr and Davies note, "[t]he defeat of the united opposition did not result in any slackening of the pressure for industrialization."[89]

Whence this other pressure? In part, it came from the planning agencies and their specialists – not all specialists, to be sure, but those who were much taken with models of teleological planning, who in effect were telling the party that it was possible to step up capital investments still within the existing framework of the economy (but, critically, without reference to actual stresses and strains in the marketplace). By remaining aloof from intra-party squabbles, these specialists could articulate the Opposition's position without its political liabilities. Strumilin and his Gosplan colleagues, Feldman and Vaisberg, are cited frequently in this connection, though even Groman eventually was willing to concede that "in the plan the genetical and teleological points of view represent a dialectical unity."[90] For them, the plan had acquired thaumaturgical powers, analogous to what (electrical) "power," "metal," and bigness represented to party leaders.

Pressure also came from within Vesenkha's already vast administrative bureaucracy. After its restructuring in April 1926, Vesenkha consisted of a presidium of eleven top officials, a larger plenum, a separate industrial planning agency (Promplan), and eight glavki reporting directly to the presidium. Each glavk presided over a variety of institutes and, most importantly, industrial trusts. Competing with each other for investment funds, the trusts invariably exaggerated their needs in their industrial and financial plans (*promfinplany*), which, more often than not, were passed on by the glavki to Vesenkha's plenary sessions. Whereas Dzerzhinskii was a strong advocate of financial discipline and had been able to blunt such pressures, this was less the case with his successor, V. Kuibyshev.[91]

As many trusts were delimited by geography as well as function, competition among them assumed a regional-political dimension, with respective republic and oblast party organizations lobbying intensely on their behalf. The best-known example involved the Urals and Ukrainian party organizations. The latter was particularly keen to expand the metallurgical industry whence it recruited the most proletarian of its cadres and where it had the strongest presence. The Ukrainian party's interest in expanding and modernizing industry thus closely coincided with the republic's Vesenkha which frequently expressed its displeasure with the union body's lack of support for additional credits.

Countervailing pressure from the center did exist. It took the form of periodic campaigns to reduce costs via rationalization (of which more below) and investigations by the dual organ of state and party control, the Commissariat of Workers' and Peasants' Inspection (RKI) and the Central Control Commission (TsKK). Whipped into shape by G. K. Ordzhonikidze, who replaced Kuibyshev as commissar in 1926, RKI-TsKK went after Vesenkha, charging it with sloppy administration and financial profligacy. The confrontation over Vesenkha's failure to curb the appetite of the Southern Steel trust (Iugostal') and its boisterous chairman, Stepan Birman, was to become a particularly heated and drawn out affair, lasting until the end of 1929.[92]

Finally, and somewhat paradoxically, pressure for abandoning balanced growth in favor of capital goods expansion came as a result of the very success of the former. For the second successive year the peasants brought in a bumper harvest. At 76.8 million tons of grain it was a record for the post-revolutionary period. More importantly, thanks to an increase in the agricultural tax and the rationalization of collection procedures, collections increased from 8.4 million to 10.6 million tons and the average price that the state paid for grain declined by some 20 percent. The "socialized" cooperative sector also was expanding, mainly at the expense of the nepmen. While in 1925–6 the former accounted for 41 percent of total trade turnover and private trade comprised 26.5 percent, in 1926–7 the proportions were 48 and 20 percent respectively.[93]

Although these figures would not be available until later, the trends they document were already apparent in the autumn of 1926. Thus, Carr and Davies refer to "this happy progress," "the resulting atmosphere of unclouded optimism," and "[t]he buoyant mood induced by the favourable economic situation in the first quarter of 1926–7" as "propitious to further advance." Such was the script of the Party's Fifteenth Conference, which met in October 1926. In between denunciations of the United Opposition's negativism, the conference resolved "to catch up and surpass" the "levels of industrial development of the leading capitalist countries in a relatively minimal historical period."[94]

To recapitulate, several factors combined to put the party and the entire country on the path of industrialization based on forcing the pace of producing the means of production. Among these the most salient were the recovery of industry to the point where it was approaching pre-war capacity; attacks by the Left, Zinovievite and then United Oppositions on the party's "pro-kulak" policies; the supercession of equilibrated models of planning by those transcending the difficulties and contradictions posited by equilibrium theorists and Preobrazhenskii alike; the inflation of requirements for the reconstruction of industry stemming from regional rivalries and bureaucratic gamesmanship; and finally, the fortuitous improvement of major economic indices in what was to prove to be the last year of "High NEP."

By 1927, industrialization was no longer merely a theoretical issue but an emerging reality. The question now was how fast to proceed, or, to switch to a musical metaphor much in vogue in the following years, tempo. In the spring a new note of urgency entered discussions as a result of the deterioration of relations with Great Britain. Whether manufactured for the purpose of arousing popular opinion or genuinely felt – there seems to be no consensus among historians – the "war scare" that followed the raid on the Soviet trade mission in London and the subsequent severing of diplomatic relations served to highlight the necessity of building up the Soviet Union's military preparedness. This, it was now broadly recognized, required not just a trained fighting force imbued with revolutionary spirit, but the construction of an armaments industry based on iron, steel and chemicals. In August, Vesenkha's presidium rejected the relatively modest control figures for 1927–8 that its commission had drafted in favor of higher investments in the iron and steel industries. Already by this time, STO had granted approval for the start of the Dnepr power station project and resolved to proceed with a number of other *stroiki* that were to "form the backbone of new construction in industry during the first five-year plan."[95]

We are now in a position to ask whether the path that was being pursued necessarily led away from NEP and, more precisely, the market relations that were at its core. That is, was industrialization incompatible with NEP even if the planning and party apparatuses

claimed otherwise? Most economic historians argue that it was,
stressing that beyond a certain point the market simply could not bear
the strain created by the rate of accumulation built into perspective
planning. Alec Nove has contested this view, arguing that it was not the
turn toward industrialization as such (or the amount of capital tied up
in investment), but pricing policy that doomed NEP. He points out that
ever since the "scissors crisis" of 1923 the state had endeavored to
reduce industrial costs and prices. But, as both urban and rural incomes
rose faster than the volume of output in succeeding years, massive
evidence of a "goods famine" accumulated – that is, a situation exactly
the reverse of the scissors crisis. Rather than allowing prices to reflect
this excess of demand over supply, "the government obstinately
persisted with its policy of price cuts, and in order to make them
effective extended price control over an ever wider portion of state
industry and state and cooperative trade." Hence, the STO could issue
a decree on 2 July 1926 under the revealing title of "The reduction in
retail prices of goods in short supply made by state industry." Another
reduction of 10 percent was ordered in February 1927.[96]

Claiming that such policies were "totally out of line with the principles of NEP," Nove suggests three reasons why they were pursued.
First, there was a certain amount of inertia stemming from measures to
close the price scissors. Second, the party center wanted to distinguish
itself from the Left which advocated higher prices for manufactured
goods as a means of increasing revenue for investment. Third, the deep-
seated ideological antipathy toward commerce and the growing faith in
the planning principle made the party leadership all but deaf to the
pleadings of several Narkomfin officials to let the market determine
prices. "If we succeed in this maneuvre," Kuibyshev told the Vesenkha
plenum in August 1927, "the future historian will evaluate it as one of
our most brilliant victories. To reduce prices when there is a goods
shortage is indeed a direct contradiction of the normal laws of development of capitalist society." But, it also would be "a very great
achievement of the planning principle."[97]

There were other considerations as well. Since the state sector was the
main consumer of capital goods, mandating lower prices for them
made sense from a budgetary point of view. Then there was the
relationship between industrial and agricultural prices, an ever-
present concern since the scissors crisis. Although lower than effective
demand would warrant, the former were still sufficiently high in the
middle of 1926 to arouse fears of a new price scissors. Yet to allow the
latter to rise was deemed unacceptable in view of the depressive effect

such an increase would have on real wages and the longer term aim of accumulation for investment.

Pricing policy was thus intricately bound up with the emerging strategy for industrialization. Each guided – or misguided – the other. In this sense, I cannot agree that pricing policy caused the death of NEP, "without additional help," as Nove contends. Still, Nove is right to point out that the more a price policy deemed appropriate for industrialization deviated from market conditions, the more the suppression of the market and those acting in accordance with its laws was interpreted as part of the solution.

It was the nepmen who first and most obviously bore the brunt of this "solution." In 1926, the government increased surcharges on the transportation of privately owned goods, raised income tax rates on employers of labor and "excess profits," and amended article 107 of the Criminal Code to broaden its definition of speculation. Assessing the results of these measures in February 1927, the Central Committee noted with satisfaction the drop in the proportion of turnover controlled by private capital. To be sure, it cautioned against "leaping ahead" and assuming it was "now possible to *completely* drive private capital from the market and concentrate all 100 percent of commerce in the hands of cooperatives and state stores." But the intention was clear.[98]

Taking into account that both the volume of trade and the proportion handled by the cooperatives were rising, the party pressed ahead with further price reductions for manufactured goods. The result was that the ratio of industrial to agricultural prices continued to fall throughout 1927. But this was a macro-statistical illusion. In many parts of the country the only available sources of manufactured goods were private traders who, having obtained them from the state or via cooperatives, resold them at higher prices. The curtailment in the number and activity of private firms, therefore, "was accompanied by now chronic shortages of these goods in both town and country."[99]

By this time, the autumn of 1927, there was no question of turning back. The nepmen were in retreat and it was now the kulaks' turn to feel the heat. None other than Bukharin, apparently having become aware "that some of his economic assumptions had been flawed or were becoming obsolete," announced in October a "forced offensive against the kulak." Bukharin was careful to characterize the offensive as a "continuation of our political line," but his biographer is more accurate in interpreting it as "a partial abrogation of the 1925 agrarian reforms" and an end to the possibility of a "kulak solution" to Soviet Russia's agricultural problems. In addition to prohibitions on land transferences and a strict application of the Labor Code, it was to involve the disenfranchisement of kulaks from the "land society," the Soviet juridical term for the village commune.[100]

Still, as if aware it had reached a precipice, the party elite hesitated before taking the leap. In preparation for the Fifteenth Congress, the Central Committee met on 21 October 1927, and approved theses drafted by Molotov on agriculture and Krzhizhnovskii and Rykov on the Five-Year Plan. These spoke respectively of "a more decisive offensive against the kulak" and "the possibility of a transition to a further, more systematic and persistent limitation of the kulak and private trader," but not their elimination.[101]

A similar hesitancy has been detected in the speeches of party leaders at, and the resolutions approved by, the Fifteenth Congress. The campaign to exclude the private trader from the market by cooperatives and state commercial outlets was to continue, even intensify, but not to the point where it could cause "a breach in the trading network and interruptions in supplies to the market." Much was made of the growth of the producer cooperatives and the need to transform "individual peasant holdings into large-scale farming enterprises" (i.e., collective farms) but this was to be done, as Stalin put it, "slowly but surely, not as a result of pressure, but of example and conviction." Heavy industry was to become the "center of gravity" of industrialization, but the rapid development of light industry and an increase in wage levels and peasant living standards were also foreseen. Rykov admitted that "for some time to come, we will have to make sacrifices" for the sake of industrialization, but also spoke of the need for preserving "market equilibrium," the watchword of the incipient moderate or "Rightist" faction.[102]

Much of this ambiguity can be attributed to the reluctance of party leaders to reveal the extent to which they were now appropriating the platform of the recently silenced Opposition. But, so it has been argued, there also was genuine fear on the part of at least some leading party members (i.e., the future "Right") of provoking a serious crisis by pushing too hard, too fast. Indeed, the country was already on the verge of such a crisis. While Vesenkha and Gosplan kept returning to the drawing board to come up with a five-year plan acceptable to party leaders, and the party itself was working out strategies that stopped just short of dismantling the foundations on which NEP had been built, both urban and rural inhabitants were adopting their own strategies based on their own calculations. With so much talk of the prospect of war, townspeople began to stock up on goods, exacerbating shortages and creating a ubiquity of queues on the streets. Peasants also had been debating strategies among themselves. Should they, in the light of three successive good harvests, depressed grain prices and a dearth of manufactured goods, withhold food stocks from the market and switch to cultivating more remunerative industrial crops? Many decided to do just that. The grain procurements crisis and the adoption of "extra-ordinary measures" to combat it were just around the corner.

Making workers productive

The debate over industrialization and the intra-party factional struggles that intersected with it were largely confined to the upper echelons of political society. Rank-and-file party and trade union members did not participate in generating teleological and genetic planning models, working out price indices, or determining financial and investment strategies. Yet, just as industrial policy profoundly affected what was happening on the industrial shop floor, so the behavior of workers and their immediate supervisors influenced the calculations of central planners and party leaders. The social relations of industry were thus a vital component of the industrialization debate and a critical factor in the viability of NEP.

Those relations revolved around the central issues of wages and productivity. Since 1921, official policy had been to link the former with the latter. But, as already indicated, the circumstances prevailing in industry made it extremely difficult to establish this link in reality. According to one estimate, while average nominal wages increased by 90 percent between October 1922 and January 1924, productivity rose by only 23 percent.[103] It was not until the scissors crisis, which threatened to break the fragile smychka with the countryside, that a fresh start was made. The imperatives of lowering industrial prices and maintaining khozraschet dictated a reduction of production costs which to a significant degree meant intensifying labor.

The strategy for intensifying labor was outlined in a Central Committee resolution of August 1924. This was to extend the application of piece rates and to mandate the periodical revision of output norms. Already by this time, some 60 percent of industrial workers were paid by the piece (as compared to 40 percent a year earlier) and in succeeding months, collective agreements stipulated norm increases of 20 to 30 percent. Subsequently, the party launched a massive economization drive (*rezhim ekonomii*) and another aimed at rationalizing production.

Initiated at a time when strike activity and other forms of worker discontent were rife, this was a dangerous strategy indeed. That it succeeded at all can be attributed in large part to the party's revised definition of worker activism, what amounted to its terms for renegotiating the party's historic alliance with the working class. Three types of worker mobilization or cooptation were involved: mass enrollment of workers into the party, the organization of production conferences, and the promotion of workers into administrative positions.[104]

The mass enrollment campaign began in December 1923 with a decision of the Politburo and the Presidium of the Central Control Commission (subsequently approved by the Thirteenth Party Conference) to admit 100,000 workers into the party. In 1924 and 1925, two recruitment drives were conducted under the banner of the Lenin Levy (in honor of the dead leader). As a result, 638,070 people entered the party, of whom 439,715 were workers by "social situation." Total membership in the party, which had stood at 446,089 on 1 January 1924, reached slightly over 1 million by 1 January 1926. Some 400,000 were enrolled in the Komsomol as well. A third campaign, initiated in October 1927, brought in an additional 108,000 recruits, 80 percent of whom were production workers.[105]

Western historians have offered several plausible explanations for this "re-proletarianization" of the party. Traditionally, it was viewed as a card played by the ruling triumvirate in its attempt to counter the Left's charges of bureaucratism and/or part of Stalin's grand scheme to swamp the party with members who would be obedient to the secretariat. Alternatively, it has been seen as a reflection of the leadership's genuine alarm at the deproletarianization of the party, and its determination to restore the party's proletarian identity. A less Machiavellian or ideologically inspired motive may have been to increase the weight of the party in the factories at a time when the necessity of raising productivity had become paramount. This is the argument of John Hatch, who has detailed the procedures by which Moscow workers were recruited, and it is persuasive.[106]

What kind of proletarians entered the party? In Moscow, an overwhelming majority were male workers under the age of 34, and most were classified as skilled. About half of the workers who joined the party in 1924–5 – the so-called *lenintsy* – had served in the Red Army and most had had some experience in factory committee or trade union work. After the 1924 Lenin Levy, two-thirds of the Moscow party organization's members were workers by social origin and 48 percent were employed in manual labor. The proportion of party members among Moscow's industrial work force rose from 4 to 13 percent, being considerably higher in the metal industry but "often . . . under 5 percent" in the large textile mills where the majority of workers were women.[107]

A second kind of mobilization consisted of production meetings and conferences at which managerial and technical personnel and worker delegates could exchange ideas about improving the performance of their enterprises. The call for establishing such forums under the auspices of the trade unions' factory committees came in a circular issued by Vesenkha, VTsSPS, and STO in November 1923. Like the Japanese-invented quality circles of more recent times, production conferences were organized according to formal procedures outlined by supervening bodies. Judging from reports in the press and party and union resolutions, they were slow to catch on. Worker delegates – many of them, lenintsy – complained that administrators' reports were too technical and otherwise intimidating; administrators claimed that workers were only interested in narrow shop questions. Periodic investigations by party and union officials found that attendance was poor and that many suggestions were not followed up. Behind these failures of communication and execution one can discern the residue of class hostility and skepticism. The party eventually did manage to breathe life into these forums but with certain unexpected consequences to be discussed shortly.[108]

Finally, the promotion of workers "from the bench" into administrative positions and to a lesser extent, higher education, began to assume considerable importance in the mid-1920s. Such promotions – the very term belies the egalitarian pretentions of the revolution – were common in the civil war years as the party sought to staff the burgeoning bureaucracies (civil, military, party, trade union) with reliable cadres. But, it was "[i]n 1924 [that] the Bolshevik leadership unanimously reaffirmed its commitment to the working class as the primary source of elite recruitment, at the same time emphasizing its continued hostility to the 'bourgeois' class enemy." Such a commitment overlapped with the party recruitment. As the party census of January 1927 revealed, slightly over 300,000 communists who had joined the party as workers subsequently changed their occupation, for the most part moving into white-collar or administrative positions. The commitment also dovetailed with factional politics, for in 1924 purge commissions were established to root out "social aliens" from higher educational institutions whose party cells had been a major source of the Left's support. This provoked some students to invent proletarian parents, one of many strategies to which non-proletarian urban residents resorted to survive juridical and administrative discrimination.[109]

Taken together, these policies indicate that at the height of NEP a momentous change was occurring within the party and in its relation to the industrial working class. Seeking to overcome the breach between the party and its putative social base, the party elite coopted what it identified as influential and potentially reliable strata of industrial workers. Constituting a re-proletarianization of the party, this strategy might just as well be termed the "Bolshevization" of the working class in the sense that "advanced" workers were intended to represent the class to the party and the party to the class. They thus could be defined as "agents" in two senses of the word: social activists whose infusion of proletarian blood could revivify the party, and faithful instruments who could structure the aspirations of their fellow but more "backward" workers into officially sanctioned channels.[110]

This was the authentic origin of the historic bloc that consisted of the Stalinist secretarial leadership of the party and primarily young, male and ethnically Russian industrial workers. Without the prior consolidation of power in the hands of regional secretaries linked to the party center, the influx of so many worker-communists might have overwhelmed the party's capacity to exercise control over the socioeconomic system; without such an influx, the party's program of "socialist industrialization" and the sacrifices it would entail might have encountered even more resistance than proved to be the case. The centralizing and mobilizing initiatives thus had far-reaching implications. Mutually reinforcing, they also reinforced certain tendencies within Bolshevik political culture that had always been present but had not necessarily been dominant. Among these were a subordination of individual and sectional interests to hegemonically defined proletarian class and national interests, Great Russian nationalism, anti-intellectualism, anti-bureaucratism, an impatience with if not hostility towards the untidiness of peasant society, a near obsession with class categorization, and an identification of socialist construction with national power and both with the development of heavy industry. When, on more than one occasion, Stalin admitted to being "blunt and rude," – the very qualities that had so alarmed the bed-ridden Lenin – he was, in effect, declaring the legitimacy of such an outlook.[111]

Cementing this bloc was not, however, automatic. New party members had to be willing to be schooled in communist resoluteness and discipline while at the same time retaining the trust of non-party workers. Historians with a state-centered perspective have tended to minimize the difficulties associated with this balancing act. Carr, for example, writes of "the availability of a ladder of promotion and the opening of the party ranks to a relatively large number of workers suffic[ing] to create a nucleus of approval for the regime among the more advanced and articulate sectors of the proletariat" and of "the mass of workers [being] docile, if not actively sympathetic to the regime." More recently, it has been argued that "the regime succeeded in structuring basic-level leadership positions that carried sufficient advantage and legitimacy to attract a substantial segment of young, ambitious, literate urbanized workers."[112]

Labor historians tell another story. It is one based on digging into trade union archives and the bulletins of regional trade union and party committees, disaggregating – if not deconstructing – the categories of "advanced" and "mass" workers, and paying attention to the varieties of technologies and divisions of labor within different branches of industry. It involves clashes that were at once economic, centering on wage-rates, quotas and productivity, and political, with the party's investment of its own legitimacy at stake. It also contains a cultural dimension, embodied in the concept of work culture. The subjects of the story are not only workers and the party and trade union hierarchies, but line supervisors (primarily foremen) and middle-level managers, as well as Taylorist-inspired NOTists, labor hygienists, and psycho-technicians. If the denouement prescribed by the party – increased productivity in the context of wage discipline – was partially realized, there was a good deal more in the way of negotiation, compromise and the shifting of alliances than was called for in the party's script.

Some of the complexities of the productivity drive can be illustrated by the struggles over norm or quota determination and the challenge it posed to the pre-revolutionary shop floor culture. This culture placed much emphasis on seniority, on the acquisition of skills through on-the-job training and the prerogatives of foremen. Typically, foremen enjoyed wide discretionary power in classifying workers according to skill grades, assigning them to particular jobs and setting output norms on the basis of observation (*glazomer*, literally, eye-measure). Adjustments were made in favor of those who had propitiated them with money, drink, or in the case of female workers, sexual favors. These powers were limited from below by artels (or in textiles, komplekty), village- or kinship-based work groups that collectively assigned tasks and pooled wages, and from above by the technical-norm bureaus (TNBs) and party intervention. This "system" obviously had its tensions but from the productionist point of view was reprehensible for another reason, namely its tendency to reproduce existing levels of output.[113]

Flushed from their success at the second conference on NOT and encouraged by the Central Committee resolution of August 1924, Gastev and his allies in the institutes of labor weighed in against glazomer and other "artisan" practices. Their panacea was the application of technically based norms determined via time-and-motion study (*khronometrazh*). Here was "science" harnessed to the purpose of increasing the intensity of labor and hence productivity. Kuibyshev, the future chairman of RKI, left no doubt about this aim when at the NOT conference he argued,

It would be a mistake to deny the possibility of intensifying labor in those sectors of industry where the current level of intensity is behind that of capitalist countries. Raising intensity in conditions of the dictatorship of the proletariat does not mean the exploitation of the working class, but strengthening the working class in catching up to the bourgeoisie's economic position.[114]

Nowhere was the drive to intensify labor more intensely pursued than in the textile industry, an industry whose products were critical to the success of the smychka. "Science" showed that it was possible to intensify production by increasing the number of spindle banks and looms tended by each spinner and weaver. To make this intensification (*uplotnenie*) more appealing among workers, wage rates were adjusted in favor of the multi-machine operatives.[115]

But the whole business ran into difficulties from the start. Science met its match in the unpredictability of thicknesses of thread, poorly trained normers, and worker and overseer sabotage of time-and-motion study. Labor hygienists recorded increased fatigue and rates of accidents among operatives. Some workers, eager to increase their wages, volunteered for multi-machine work. But many others, particularly in the Central Industrial Region, resisted. By the summer of 1925, virtually all factories where uplotnenie had been introduced were affected by strikes. This, the last major strike action in the Soviet Union until 1989, resulted in a partial victory for the workers. The party and the textile union responded by emphasizing the voluntary nature of uplotnenie and permitting elections to factory committees without prepared lists of delegates.[116]

Party officials must have been alarmed at the behavior of many new recruits, the lenintsy, who threw in their lot with other workers in resisting rationalization measures. "Because I am a Communist," one leninets reportedly told a more responsible comrade, "vanguard of the working class, I therefore went to the head of the strike movement." The most reliable elements within the proletariat had proved to be less than completely reliable. New measures were devised to win them over: more intensive political education, promotion of candidates to full membership, the distribution of specific party assignments to the lenintsy, and undoubtedly other tactics that were neither advocated nor recorded in party literature – but were probably all the more effective for that.[117]

However, lenintsy still found it possible to articulate the grievances of their fellow workers by taking an active part in production conferences. Beginning in late 1926, these forums "entered a new phase," in which "workers . . . expressed their anger and frustration with their bosses and *spetsy* with increasing frequency and virulence." As much as workers resented foremen's arbitrariness, they evidently did not care for the more modern and "scientific" alternative. Much of the tension focused on how to effectuate the economization drive that was launched with great fanfare in April 1926. Coupled with a price reduction campaign, the economization drive put enormous pressure on managers and workers as each group sought to make the other pay.[118]

High politics both mirrored and intensified these tensions. While the Left advocated wage relief and otherwise reducing pressure on workers at the expense of the kulaks, Bukharin revived the theme of intensifying labor. "This is completely inevitable," he argued in 1927, and "it would be stupid to turn one's back on it." Finally, the emerging Stalin line sounded yet another theme, that of anti-bureaucratism. There was more than just demagogy here. Throughout 1927, RKI-TsKK carried out investigations of swollen staffs, mismanagement, token efforts to cut costs and cost-cutting at the expense of workers' safety and livelihoods, all of which resonated with workers' own antipathies. Ordzhonikidze, the new Peoples' Commissar of RKI, called for a heightening of local activism, "show trials" to mobilize public/worker opinion, and "revolutionary zeal" to accomplish a *"perestroika* of the apparatus." We are only a short step from the Shakhty affair of early 1928 and the crisis of the intelligentsia it inaugurated.[119]

Anti-bureaucratism was the ideological cement binding the party *aktiv* to the secretarial apparatus. Whether broader sections of the working class – including the substantial sector of white-collar workers who could be mistaken for bureaucrats at least of the "petty" kind – adhered as well is not clear. Anti-bureaucratism was in any case only one aspect of the workerist strategy pursued by the party. Another was the introduction of the seven-hour work day, the announcement of which was timed to coincide with the tenth anniversary of the October Revolution. Historians have adduced several motives here. One was to outbid the Left which was involved in a last ditch and ultimately fatal effort to garner working-class support. There were economic motives, for it soon became clear that the reduction of the working day was to be tied to the introduction of a third shift and a more intense pace of production. The haste with which the system was introduced and the fact that the Central Industrial Region's textile industry was chosen to pioneer the change-over suggests another factor: difficulties with grain procurements and the hope of attracting peasants to market by providing increased quantities of cotton goods.[120]

The implementation of the three-shift system was a foretaste of what was to occur on a grander scale during the First Five-Year Plan. To staff the extra shift it was necessary to recruit thousands of peasants, for the most part new to industrial production. Experienced operatives feared that machines which they had learned to tame would be shared with newcomers. The Labor Code's prohibition against night-work for women and youths was ignored on a massive scale, and eventually the article in the Code was revised. The three hours' interval between shifts proved inadequate for cleaning the machines and ventilating the shop floor, and several enterprises experienced a shortage of raw material. Absenteeism, unpunctuality, power failures, accidents, and stoppages increased. Productivity fell.[121]

The experience was illustrative of what Moshe Lewin has called "the contamination effect" – a hasty state initiative contaminated by traditional social behavior. It also exemplified two other developments that were already occurring in other industries but would become much more prevalent in the coming years: the influx of new workers into the factories, and the introduction of new technology and corresponding efforts to reconfigure the division of labor. These developments would have a destabilizing effect on the industrial work force and the factory order. They were, in fact, constitutive of a crisis of the working class that coincided with the larger crisis of NEP and the abandonment of that policy before the end of the decade.[122]

5   Dangers and opportunities

Stalin had the knack of turning crises into catastrophes. (Yuri Afanasev, November 1989)

"weiji" [in Chinese "crisis"] = danger + timing/juncture/opportunity

If only they had left it alone. If only the communists had allowed NEP to continue "seriously and for a long time." Such has been the retrospective plaint of western scholars and more recently, their Soviet counterparts. It is evident that Stalin was increasingly unwilling to remain within the bounds of NEP, that at some point he saw the limits on state action imposed by NEP as part of the problem rather than the solution. Historians are in general agreement that the point was reached in late 1927, early 1928. In 1925 when there was an unexpected shortfall in grain procurements, official agencies increased the price of grain at the expense of industrial crop production and the timetable for industrialization. At the end of 1927, when a similar situation arose, the price of grain was kept stable and the authorities pressed ahead with industrialization. "This was," writes R. W. Davies, "the beginning of the end of NEP."[1]

Why the party acted as it did, why at this juncture it resorted to "extraordinary measures" which set in motion the Stalin revolution, requires both long-term and situational explanations. The retrospective explanation stresses the deep-seated mutual suspicion and antipathy between the party and the peasantry, the commitment of the communists to industrialization which derived from both ideological and national security considerations, the growing consumption needs of an expanding urban population, and the social and political tensions arising out of the NEP system itself. The way these factors exerted themselves or were played out in the years preceding the grain procurement crisis largely determined how the party responded to that crisis.

In the shorter term, the grain procurements crisis came hard on the heels of the decisive showdown between the majority faction in the party and the combined forces of the Left (Trotskyist) and Leningrad (Zinovievist) oppositions. That showdown was itself prefigured by several foreign policy disasters – notably, the break in diplomatic relations with Britain, and the crushing defeat of the communists in China at the hands of the Kuomintang – which roused the opposition to action. In May 1927, eighty-three leading oppositionists signed a declaration and forwarded it to the Politburo. A swingeing denunciation of both foreign and domestic policies, the declaration held the leadership responsible for the rise of rightist forces within the party, the strengthening of capitalist elements throughout the country, and the emboldening of the imperialists abroad. The Democratic Centralists followed suit with their own protest, which was sent to the Central Committee. The ruling group responded by assigning oppositionists to remote posts at home and abroad, orchestrating a vituperative press campaign against the opposition, and recommending the expulsion of Trotsky and Zinoviev from the Central Committee. Even this did not quell the oppositionist surge. In early September, the opposition produced its Platform of the United Opposition, an elaboration of the earlier declaration. All the while, rumors of conspiratorial activity, of secret strike funds and plans to stage a coup with the assistance of army officers, circulated within ruling circles. The discovery by the OGPU of a printing press used to duplicate the opposition platform resulted in several arrests and further reprimands.[2]

Things got nastier thereafter. At a joint session of the TsKK and Central Committee in late October, Trotsky and Zinoviev were shouted down as they tried in vain to defend their records. Several objects – a glass and books – were hurled at Trotsky. Both were expelled from the Central Committee after Stalin had introduced a motion to that effect. The final showdown came during the tenth anniversary celebrations of the October Revolution. Oppositionist demonstrators in Moscow and Leningrad were surrounded by police and party activists who tore up their banners, beating and arresting many. By the time the Fifteenth Congress opened in early December, the opposition had split wide open, with Zinoviev and Kamenev advocating capitulation and Trotsky urging negotiation. As previously mentioned, the congress was less than forthright in dealing with the substantive issues on its agenda. But there was no hesitation or lack of unanimity when it came to villifying the opposition. During his brief speech, Khristian Rakovsky, a prominent ally of Trotsky, was interrupted fifty-seven times by

Bukharin, Kaganovich, Riutin, and others; Kamenev, who opened his speech with an appeal for reconciliation, was given the same treatment, being interrupted twenty-four times.[3]

These clashes reveal a curious mixture of outward conformity to established party procedures – declarations submitted to the Politburo, theses and counter-theses, a special investigatory commission, formal resolutions voted by open ballot – and some ominous departures from them. In the latter category, the intervention of the OGPU was perhaps the most salient. As revealed in documents unearthed by Michal Reiman in the Political Archive of the German Foreign Ministry, a close working relationship had been established between Stalin and V. R. Menzhinskii, president of the OGPU. This and the narrowing of the parameters of political debate within the party were the main consequences of the opposition's defeat. Henceforward, as the party lurched from one crisis to the next, its reliance on the secret police as monitor and enforcer would increase.[4]

The crises analyzed below were all interrelated. The crisis over grain procurements "was the catalyst, accelerating and sharpening all economic and political processes in the country." It not only seriously jeopardized the industrialization program and the fragile unity achieved within the party, but worsened conditions in the cities and particularly among the industrial working class. The social tensions arising therefrom were channeled by the party apparatus into attacks on kulaks, technical specialists, the state bureaucracy, and eventually the scientific and cultural intelligentsia and their "Rightist" patrons within the party. Simultaneously, there was an expansion of rank-and-file upward mobility. The dangers associated with the crises of the late 1920s were thus also opportunities. The disorganization of social classes created "a free field for the state and its institutions . . . to act and grow." By the end of the decade, the Stalin revolution was well underway.[5]

The countryside in crisis

The general consensus among historians is that the shortfall in grain procurements came as a major shock to party authorities. A "deceptive air of success," "official complacency," and "a dangerous complacency" are the terms used to characterize official reactions to the initial phase of the collection campaign. This is what is called the advantage of hindsight. At the outset, success was not deceptive and there were grounds for satisfaction if not complacency. In August 1927, the cereal harvest was officially estimated as 2.5 percent less than the previous year's bumper crop. This was later adjusted downward to 6 percent less. But because sizeable stocks had been built up by the peasantry over the previous two years, it was assumed that collections would rise by as much as 11 percent over the course of the year. Again, this did not appear to be an overly optimistic assessment. Collections by state agencies and consumer cooperatives of the principal bread grains (wheat and rye) ran ahead of the previous year's figures for July, August, and September and were 45 percent greater than in the equivalent quarter of 1925. This was despite the fact that planned procurement prices for these items were set well below those of 1925 and only slightly higher than in 1926.[6]

It was in the succeeding quarter, from October through December, that collections ran into difficulties. The following figures[7] tell the story:

	Procurement of grain (in millions of tons)	
	1926	1927
July–September	2.41	2.62
October–December	4.58	2.40

What had caused the problem? Aside from the slightly lower grain harvest, not in itself a major factor, historians have stressed five factors: (1) the price offered by official agencies for grain was low relative to those of industrial crops and livestock and dairy products, thus making it advantageous for peasants to acquire cash by selling these other products and either consuming more of or storing their grain; (2) industrial goods – clothing and footwear, agricultural implements – were in short supply; (3) peasant cash reserves were relatively high partly because increased industrial activity had expanded opportunities for off-farm income, partly because of favorable terms of trade in previous years, and also because of tax concessions granted in connection with the tenth anniversary celebration; (4) rumors of impending war, compounded by apprehensiveness over recent party decisions (particularly, the "reinforced offensive" against the kulaks and the Fifteenth Congress' resolutions on collectivization), induced peasants to hoard their grain in anticipation of calamity; (5) collection agencies, particularly the cooperatives, did not vigorously press the campaign.[8]

Two caveats are in order. One refers to regional variations, always important in considering agriculture. The real deficit areas in terms of collections were Siberia, the Urals, the Volga regions, and the North Caucasus. Ukraine did better, and in the Central Black-Soil region, grain collections for the last six months of 1927 were ahead of the corresponding period in 1926. The other qualification has to do with differences among peasants. It would appear that the bulk of grain collected in July–September consisted of "carry over" from the previous year's harvest, most of which came from the more well-to-do peasants. The grain coming onto the market in October–December evidently was derived from those who could not afford not to sell, that is, the poorer elements.[9] Did this mean, as Stalin and subsequent generations of Soviet historians argued, that the kulaks were holding the state to ransom, that the "kulaks" were engaged in a "grain strike"?

Western historians have answered in the negative. To them, peasants withholding grain from the market were acting rationally on the basis of experience as recent as 1925. This raises the question of the state's own rationality. Couldn't it have been predicted that higher prices offered for non-cereal crops would lead to a shift toward the marketing of those products? Perhaps, but this concern seems to have been outweighed by a determination not to repeat the mistake of the previous year when prices of technical crops (cotton, sugar beets, tobacco) were beaten down by the trusts with resulting shortages. In general one can say that the regime acted irrationally only in terms of the market principles it was increasingly anxious to overcome, and that especially for Stalin, political rationality had become paramount.

The procurement crisis in this sense was almost serendipitous. It enabled Stalin to rally both party stalwarts and Komsomol youth behind the anti-kulak campaign and to exert urban Russia's hegemony over the countryside. From January through March, Stalin's closest comrades, officials from the USSR and RSFSR Commissariats of Trade, and thousands of provincial and regional party workers fanned out across the grain producing areas of the country. Stalin himself toured Siberia – apparently the first time since 1918 that he had ventured into the countryside on a political expedition. The methods used to extract grain were none too subtle. They included the dispatch of trainloads of manufactured goods to the most critical areas; the formation of police and party emissaries (*troiki*) to assign grain quotas to districts, villages and individual households; searches of barns and warehouses; the banning of local private trade; the application of article 107 of the RSFSR Criminal Code under which concealment, hoarding or holding back of commodities with the intention of causing their price to rise was a punishable offense; the distribution of 25 percent of confiscated grain among poor peasants at low prices or long-term credit; a stepping up of tax collections to soak up peasants' liquid cash reserves; and even in some isolated instances, attempts at forced collectivization. By these measures, large quantities of grain were obtained:[10]

	Procurement of grain (in millions of tons)	
	1927	1928
January–March	2.53	4.21
April–June	1.02	0.87

That the campaign required this hands-on approach organized from the center reflects not only the breakdown of market mechanisms, but the weakness and unreliability of rural party organizations. By 1927, there were 307,000 rural-based communists comprising 26.8 percent of total party membership. This works out to about 1 communist for every 100 peasant households compared to 1 in 10 urban workers. Most had received an elementary education and had been recruited into the party since 1924. The overwhelming majority (86 percent) were attached to the party's 17,456 rural-based cells. An occupational breakdown of cell members shows that 42.3 percent were peasants, 39.8 percent were in white-collar positions, 9.1 percent were workers, and 3.5 percent were listed as unemployed. Of the peasants, 76 percent worked their individual holdings while another 17.7 percent combined agricultural labor with paid non-manual work. This left only 6.3 percent who belonged to collective farms. Finally, investigations conducted in 1926 revealed that rural party peasants were more prosperous, had more recourse to hired labor and rented out more means of production for longer periods than non-party peasants. Those who could be identified as *batraks* (landless peasants) comprised no more than 10 percent of rural party members.[11]

The conclusion to be drawn from this data is that the party had been sucked into the vortex of rural society at least as much as the rural masses had been drawn into the party. The more enterprising and independent peasants, if not the rural intelligentsia, who together numerically dominated the rural party organizations had a strong stake in maintaining NEP's pro-peasant orientation. This was precisely what had alarmed the Leningrad Opposition in 1925 when the party had opened up its ranks to large numbers of peasants and expanded its modest network of rural cells. At that time, Stalin had defended the policy as a necessary means of strengthening the alliance of workers and peasants. But the defeat of the Left, the procurements crisis, and resistance to the application of the extraordinary measures radically altered the situation and, evidently, Stalin's views. The need for party renovation was one of the lessons Stalin learned from his foray into Siberia. Before addressing some of the others that directly affected the countryside, let us see how this lesson played itself out.

A week after Stalin returned from his expedition, the Central Committee called for the "checking and decisive purging of alien elements and hangers-on from party, soviet and cooperative organizations." The selective "screenings" of party members and the self-criticism campaign against bureaucratism and party degeneracy that followed were clearly part of the fallout from the procurement campaign. In Daniel Brower's analysis of the "Smolensk Scandal," the "NEP faction" that had dominated the provincial party apparatus bore the brunt of the purge. Rejecting the General Secretary's methods, it sought grain for the largely flax-growing province by insisting that the market be allowed to operate freely. For this it was accused by OGPU officers and TsKK investigators of colluding with kulaks and was removed. Later in the year, Stalin mentioned that "a number of communists in the volosts and villages [had] . . . pursued a policy forming a bond with kulak elements," and "were cleaned out of the party last spring." At a slightly higher level, some 13 percent of the membership of seven provincial and oblast' organizations was expelled.[12]

But just as clearly, the initiative to renovate the party rural organizations intensified other tensions both within and outside the party. In Siberia, inter-regional rivalries between the *kraikom* and the Irkutsk party committee as well as personal differences between their respective leaders complicated the purge process. In contrast to the Smolensk affair, the pro-NEP faction under kraikom secretary Syrtsov took the offensive against the Irkutsk party leader, N. N. Zimin, and proved victorious. This was despite the fact that "Zimin's political views on the offensive against the kulak and the need for a more rapid tempo of industrialisation were much closer to Stalin's position in early 1928 than the moderate-Rightist approach of Syrtsov."[13]

A closer inspection of the Smolensk affair reveals several plot lines in addition to the anti-kulak campaign scripted by central authorities. As would be the case with the more lethal purges of 1936–8, officials' denunciations of wayward provincial bosses were seized upon by rank-and-file members and non-party workers and peasants to express their own grievances – against the three-shift system and higher output norms introduced at the Iarstevo and other textile mills; against the perquisites of high provincial office; and against communists and Jews in general. Gender issues also surfaced, for example in the (published) characterization of the provincial party secretary's wife as a "slut" whose taste for luxury had brought her husband down, and in revelations about sexual favors extracted by foremen and drunken orgies in which party officials participated along with local landowning notables.[14]

Cleaning out pro-kulak and degenerate elements from rural-based institutions was part of Stalin's larger project to establish strong points in the countryside. This larger project apparently began to take shape even while Stalin toured Siberia. If Bukharin and other moderate Rightists tended to blame grain shortages on the state's unpreparedness, ill-conceived pricing policies and local lethargy, Stalin had become convinced that NEP itself was to blame and that the state's reliance on market exchanges with peasants was incompatible with industrialization. Casting about for an alternative agrarian policy, he discovered the kolkhozy and sovkhozy and their considerable marketing potential.[15]

Up to this point, the history of kolkhozy and sovkhozy had been one of disappointment. Set up on former estates and state lands during the civil war years, these various forms of collective cultivation attracted mostly landless peasants and unemployed workers. With the introduction of NEP, they fell on hard times, becoming in Moshe Lewin's piquant phrase, "the Cinderellas of the regime." Until 1927, official policy was to support agricultural cooperatives rather than collective farms as the high road to socialism in the countryside. The latter were correspondingly subordinated to cooperative organs which were stingy with agronomic assistance. No more than 2 percent of the land was said to be in collective and state farm hands as of 1925, and much of that was leased to individual peasant families. The state farms, run along industrial lines with wages paid on both hourly and piece-work bases, were especially penurious and their numbers steadily dwindled. Among kolkhozy, there was a marked shift towards the looser forms of collectivism. The *kommuny*, in which members worked, lived and distributed what they produced on a communal basis, almost disappeared. Artels, which collectivized land and at least a proportion of working animals and implements, remained largely restricted to producers of technical crops. It was the TOZy (Associations for Common Cultivation), representing "the minimum element of collective enterprise of limited scope and for limited purposes," that made some headway at this time.[16]

The revival of the official interest in collectivized agriculture can be dated from 1927. In March of that year, a joint Sovnarkom–TsIK resolution promised tax relief, assistance with reallocating strips (*zemleustroistvo*), and a liberal credit policy to kolkhozy – modest measures that do not appear to have been carried out. A simultaneously issued decree on sovkhozy condemned past neglect of these institutions and called for the establishment of contractual links between them and surrounding peasant households. In April, the foundations were laid for a "Kolkhoz center" (Kolkhoztsentr) of the RSFSR to coordinate administrative and technical assistance. The Central Committee began urging local committees to become involved in organizing kolkhozy and supervising elections of their chairmen. And in December, the Fifteenth Congress put "the gradual transformation of individual peasant holdings into large-scale farming" on its (long-term) agenda.

The winter and spring of 1928 saw a significant increase in the number and membership of kolkhozy. However, this upsurge was far from constituting an adequate basis for large-scale farming. Most of the new kolkhozy were small, roughly half the size of those already in existence; approximately three-quarters were of the loose TOZ variety, limited in scope and purpose; and many were alleged to be covers for kulaks to hire laborers and rent out land. Exhorted by local party organizations and regional branches of Kolkhoztsentr but otherwise left to their own devices, the mostly poor peasants who formed kolkhozy lacked the necessary infrastructural support to make collective farming attractive to the mass of peasants or satisfy the ambitions of party leaders.[17]

In comparing the two classic accounts on which much of this section has relied, one is struck by their divergent interpretations, as much implied as explicit, of state activity. Lewin frames his analysis around three tropes – Stalin's groping for a solution to the crisis, or crises, of his own making; the barely concealed divisions within the party's upper echelons; and the complete failure of soviet and party institutions to cope with the tasks thrust upon them. Reconstructing Stalin's "new thinking" on the basis of texts which in many cases were not made public at the time, Lewin carefully avoids the impression that the General Secretary had a well-developed plan for full-scale collectivization or was even striving toward one. Stalin's aims were short term, primarily, how to assure the cities, the key industrial sectors and army of adequate grain supplies. For this, he envisioned the development of large-scale sovkhozy and kolkhozy capable of marketing as much as half of what they produced. The trick was finding a device to persuade the producers to hand over the requisite amounts at prices unfavorable to them. Stalin thought he found this in the threat to withhold state subsidies and credits. In general, he had come around to Preobrazhenskii's conclusion that pumping out agricultural surpluses through unequal exchange, what Stalin now privately referred to as "tribute," was necessary to maintain high rates of accumulation for investment in heavy industry. Whatever resistance such a policy would provoke had to be met head on.

Stalin did encounter resistance within the Politburo, primarily from Bukharin and Rykov. In a secret meeting with Kamenev, Bukharin now referred to his former ally as "a Genghis Khan" bent on "military-feudal exploitation" which would lead to civil war. But for nearly a year, unsure of their own strength and mesmerized by the doctrine of party unity, both sides shied away from open confrontation. The resolutions issued by successive Central Committee plenums in April and July were compromise documents that gave off mixed signals. The extraordinary measures had been necessary and would continue until the "kulak offensive" had been overcome, but excesses were to be avoided, the middle peasants were not to be alienated, and a more flexible price policy was to be adopted. New sovkhozy, capable of providing 100 million puds of marketable grain in three to four years, were to be established, and there was to be a general socialist trans-formation of the countryside coincidental with a "radical increase in productivity and marketability." But individual small and medium-sized farming was recognized as "still the basis of the grain economy for a significant period," and would be assisted by provision of machines, fertilizers, pre-harvest contracts, land consolidations, and other measures.[18]

Thus 1928 was a "year of drift," a "rudderless year" in which "the leadership was feverishly searching for programs, methods, or devices which would bring about the desired transformation" and "the agri-cultural sector in particular . . . drifted from one expedient to the next." As state intervention in agriculture increased, state agencies from Sovnarkom down to selsovety were simply overwhelmed. Projects had to be pigeon-holed for lack of funds, contracts signed with peasants were "ill-coordinated," credits "arrived too late" and "were then distributed haphazardly." Preconceived theories about the objective interests of different social strata were "translated into vague and impractical instructions which were then 'wrongly' carried out." All of this took place in the absence of a comprehensive five-year plan, although the Sixteenth Party Conference's approval of the plan in April 1929 hardly would lead to a reduction of the chaos.[19]

Within the master trope of the "foundations of a planned economy," Carr's and Davies' analysis is considerably more up-beat than Lewin's. Resolutions, produced in an atmosphere of "profound anxiety," are credited with bringing results. For example, following a governmental appeal to all peasants to increase their sowings, "[t]he supply of seeds was improved both in quantity and quality." To be sure, the anxiety did not dissipate. Utterances of Stalin and Molotov throughout 1928 were reflective of "men hesitant and bewildered in face of an intractable problem, and still hoping somehow to muddle through." But muddle through they did. After the Fifteenth Congress had resolved to "strengthen the Sovkhozy by converting them in practice into model large-scale farms of a socialist type," "[d]evelopments . . . moved quickly." Sovnarkom issued instructions to Gosplan to study the organization of such sovkhozy; the Politburo appointed a "strong commission" to hasten the deliberations; and in May 1928, the commission "laid down plans for immediate action." Despite the skepticism of Narkomzem experts and Bukharin, there were "some real achievements." "The year 1928," the authors inform us, "was marked by a sharp increase in services of all kinds rendered by Sovkhozy to surrounding peasant households."

Essentially the same story is told with respect to the mechanization, and more particularly, the "tractorization" of agriculture. At first, it was the well-to-do peasants that took advantage of the availability of tractors, but "Sovkhoz and tractor increasingly proved to be instruments of the same policy, and supported each other." The Shevchenko Sovkhoz's example of organizing tractor columns to plough surrounding farms "was catching." By the summer of 1928, "[p]rogress was now more rapid." The machine and tractor station (MTS), also pioneered by Shevchenko Sovkhoz, proved to be an even "more effective and permanent institution." Resented by the cooperatives as an unwarranted intrusion of the state principle, the MTS soon overcame "[t]hese petty jealousies." "Substantial progress" was registered in the supply of implements, machinery and tractors. "Through all these channels the principles of large-scale, collectively organized, up-to-date and efficient agriculture were seeping into the backward Russian village."[20]

But how did peasants react to these innovations, breathtaking in their implications? Both Lewin and Carr-Davies cite instances of a distinct lack of enthusiasm, fearfulness, and even overt resistance. Yet, each gives these responses a different twist. The latter account tends to take at face value the categories employed in party literature. Thus, in discussing the reduction of sowing in the spring of 1928, Carr and Davies refer to "the kulak" who "refused to rent land from the poor peasant, or to work the poor peasant's land, or grant him advances of seed . . . or, in return for help rendered . . . would exact an assurance that the recipient would not take sides against his 'benefactor.'" They do recognize that "not all the tales told against *kulaks* were probably true, and by no means all who resisted government measures could plausibly be called *kulaks*." But they are only willing to include the "well-to-do" category in their discussion of "increased hostility to the regime and increased lawlessness." Otherwise, they fall back on "[t]he traditional prejudice of the peasant against state intervention in his affairs, however efficient and however beneficent."[21]

Lewin sees peasant resistance as more broadly based, if not universal: "In his deep distress and uncertainty, the peasant was turning his back on the Soviet regime, and this was happening irrespective of any consideration of class stratification." This was partly because "[a]ll of the measures which were officially devised as 'anti-kulak' instruments were potentially 'anti-serednyak' in their side-effects." The tightening up of the agrarian code with respect to leasing and the early 1929 campaign for the "renewal of the soviets," which amounted to bringing the village assembly (*skhod*) under the control of the selsovet, are cases in point. Yet, at this stage, resistance was mostly passive, turning one's back rather than taking up torches or pitchforks. There were instances, hundreds of them, of violent acts committed against grain procurers and representatives of MTSs. But it should be remembered that fire and violence were endemic to the tens of thousands of villages that dotted the landscape.

As for poor peasants, the supposed beneficiaries of the regime's new agrarian policy, Lewin acknowledges the existence of "a deeply pro-Soviet attitude." However, this attitude was likely to be expressed in the form of complaints that the regime had ignored the bedniaki except during a soviet election or procurements campaign. Irrespective of their attitudes, poor peasants were compelled to rely on more well-to-do peasants or nepmen-turned-speculators for supplies which the state was incapable of providing. As (unidentified) peasants were heard to say, it was 1919 and 1920 all over again. There was, in short, little in the way of a revolution from below in the countryside.[22]

Lewin's analysis is to be preferred for two reasons. One is that it is relatively free of the teleological implications that Carr and Davies build into their narrative of the foundations of a planned economy. The latter do detail the tentativeness and confusion among state and party personnel as they confronted the truly awesome tasks. But they do not sufficiently integrate such details into their analytical framework which, as noted above, stresses growing efficiency and modernity. Lewin's *leitmotif* is struggle, not necessarily or even mainly among classes, but rather between peasant society and the increasingly étatist party representing itself as the instrument of social construction. The hastiness with which the party implemented its "left turn" is seen as a function of political circumstances (e.g., the defeat of the Left) and Stalin's assessment of them, but also of socio-economic breakdown which itself was caused by the lack of market equilibrium.

The second reason concerns their respective interpretations of peasant attitudes and behavior. Both Lewin and Carr and Davies cite numerous instances of party officials acknowledging that the class struggle was not turning out as expected. "The serednyak is sometimes influenced by the kulak and expressed his dissatisfaction," Lewin quotes Kaganovich as saying. Both cite an official report complaining that "the attitude of the peasants remains negative: [t]here is no particular enthusiasm for the sovkhozes, nor interest in their economic development." But whereas the latter attribute such an attitude to "traditional peasant prejudice against state intervention" and leave it at that, Lewin goes further:

The only way of convincing the peasants would have been to offer them tangible proof of the superiority of collective farming. Without this proof, the regime was, in effect, demanding of a group of people who were traditionally conservative and cautious in their outlook that they should abandon their way of life, and make a great leap of faith into the unknown. It would be irrelevant, in any case, to speak of conservatism in this particular instance. Is there any social class or stratum, no matter what its level of education or adaptability, which will give up its way of life and its institutions . . . without fierce internal conflicts and a bigger struggle?

This failure of peasants to give up a way of life impelled the party to denounce "henchmen of the kulaks" (*podkulachniki*) and other groups "devoid of sociological significance."[23]

The outlook for Soviet agriculture and particularly grain procurements in 1928–9 was bleak indeed. Already in September, a report to the Central Committee spoke of "serious difficulties on the grain market." Peasants eager to replenish stocks extracted earlier in the year, speculators buying up grain at inflated prices and "a wave of bagmen from the consuming regions" competed with state and cooperative agencies for what was actually a smaller harvest of wheat and rye than the previous year. Meanwhile demand in the cities and the army grew.[24]

The ominousness of the situation prompted Bukharin to publish in *Pravda* his "Notes of an Economist." A reprise of positions for which Bukharin was well known, the article was to be his swan song and, in a sense, NEP's as well. Its critique of Vesenkha's revised Five-Year Plan (trying "to build 'present-day' factories with 'future bricks,'") was prophetic, though dismissed at the time as "neo-Slavophile." Indeed, the article and a resolution of the Moscow party committee in the same vein precipitated a concerted campaign against the "Right deviation." By the end of the year, Uglanov had been dismissed as secretary of the Moscow committee and Tomskii, who had sided with Bukharin and Rykov in the Politburo, had resigned as chairman of VTsSPS.[25]

After some improvement in grain collections in September and October, the situation rapidly deteriorated. Compulsory deliveries – razverstka in effect – made their reappearance in the form of self-taxation voted by local soviets at the instigation of local officials. Peasants who refused to pay or did not turn over the assigned amounts were subjected to fines, expulsion from cooperatives and confiscations of property. Stalin endorsed these measures as "the Urals-Siberian method of grain collection." But the amount of grain collected continued to fall off. By the end of the agricultural year (30 June 1929), official agencies had obtained 8.3 million tons of grain as against 10.3 million in 1927–8. This represented only 14.2 percent of the total harvest compared to 17.6 percent the previous year. As Carr and Davies laconically put it, "[t]he system of voluntary deliveries had broken down." Panic buying in the cities compelled the authorities to introduce rationing. This marked the first (but as we know from recent years, not the last) time that such a measure was taken in the absence of war or its aftermath. It was to last for six years.[26]

Food policy had come full circle. Having imposed razverstka in the desperate circumstances of the civil war, the regime had abandoned it in 1921 under pressure from a thriving black market, peasant uprisings, workers' strikes and rebellion among soldiers and sailors. Now, after an eight-year interlude in which the market had played the decisive role in exchange, administrative measures were again coming to the fore. At the Sixteenth Party Conference in April 1929, Rykov and Bukharin made a last-ditch effort to bring the country back from the brink of internal war. They proposed purchasing grain from abroad with scarce foreign currency reserves earmarked for industrial equipment, refraining from extraordinary measures, and utilizing the tax and price levers to stimulate agricultural production. But for Stalin and his supporters it was already too late. The industrialization program could not be sacrificed; the rural and urban petty-bourgeoisie was pointing a dagger at the heart of socialist construction; concessions would only encourage them while demoralizing the proletariat. The limitations of backward agriculture had to be overcome once and for all.[27]

The climax of the processes set in motion by the procurements crisis, what amounted to the abolition of NEP in the countryside, came in the latter half of 1929. The approval of the Five-Year Plan by the Sixteenth Conference and the accompanying visions of an industrialized society were in stark contrast to the apprehensions about the forthcoming harvest and a repetition of the difficulties of the previous two collections. Since the beginning of the year, the trade unions had been organizing workers' brigades to assist with the grain collection and anti-kulak campaigns. Reminiscent of the food detachments of the civil war period, these brigades were also forerunners of the 25,000ers who played such a critical role in the collectivization drive. Unlike the latter cohort, little is known about who these workers were or even how they fared. But for them, as for Stalin, the crisis presented opportunities as well as dangers.[28]

All the while, plans were proceeding for the collectivization of agriculture. In July 1928, Narkomzem presented a draft, according to which 1.2 million peasant households (approximately 5 percent of the total), accounting for 10 percent of total agricultural production and 21 percent of marketable grain, would be collectivized by the end of 1932. Gosplan's upwardly revised plan, approved by the Sixteenth Conference, called for 4.5 million collectivized households (approximately 18 percent of the total) and the sovkhoz sector providing 43 percent of marketable grain. Most of the collectives were to be of the TOZ type, with about half the livestock remaining as private property of kolkhoz households. This was a tall order, presupposing a significant expansion of the contract system, the MTS network of tractor columns, and agricultural cooperatives. Yet, as Lewin argues, it was not inconsistent with what the Right envisioned or with real possibilities.[29]

It was inconsistent with the increasingly dichotomistic thinking of Stalin and, it must be said, many others inside and outside the party. For them, it had come to a showdown between kulak and kolkhoz. Either peasants were for the one or the other. Either activists brought in collections ahead of time or they objectively were helping the kulaks. Reading the newspapers from the summer and autumn of 1929, one is struck by the militant, near-hysterical tone of the articles devoted to agriculture. Headlines screamed "Communists and Non-Party Proletarians – Face to Unfolding Collectivization!" "Uninterrupted Fire on the Right Deviation!" "Let Us Break Kulak Resistance!" One cannot help but wonder to what extent the editors and still more the Central Committee had become prisoners of their own rhetoric, of their fantasies and nightmares, their ambitiousness and their short-sightedness, their revolutionary faith in marching in step with history and their vanguardist skepticism concerning the spontaneity of the masses. Of course, militant, hyperbolic language was endemic to Bolshevik discourse. Many undoubtedly had become inured to its mobilizational intent. But towards the end of 1929, as material conditions in both the cities and villages worsened, as ordinary civility no less anything resembling a civil society seemed to have vanished, and as world capitalism appeared to be on a course towards self-destruction, the hyperbole suddenly seemed to correspond to reality. The country had indeed entered upon another revolution.

The crisis of the working class

Throughout the 1920s, the party's propaganda apparatus worked hard to distinguish the situation of the Soviet working class from its counterparts elsewhere. By virtue of the nationalization of industry, Soviet workers, it was claimed, were masters (*khoziaine*) of their factories. Through the increasingly "proletarianized" party and state, they exercised collective political power. Through their unions they were assured of an array of cultural opportunities, benefits and protection from managerial violations of the Labor Code. To be disciplined and productive workers in these circumstances – to learn how to work – was not to increase the profits of owners, but to help industrialize the country. Output norms, skill-based differentials, and NOT were designed to help them learn to work better.

Comparing the lot of workers under tsarism with their situation by 1927, party propagandists did not have to invent accomplishments. Wage levels were estimated to be about 11 percent above the 1913 average – a good deal higher in textiles, about the same in metallurgy, and lower in mining. Like the peasantry, industrial workers were eating better than before the revolution. While the per capita consumption of bread was dropping, consumption of meat, dairy products and sugar was rising. Workers and their children were also better educated thanks to the expansion of primary and general secondary schools as well as the factory apprentice schools, rabfaks and technicums. Social insurance, which covered some 9 million trade union members (3.4 million of whom were industrial workers), included disability pensions, maternity, death and unemployment benefits, and medical care. Its provision without cost to the individual worker was thus more extensive than anywhere else in the world.[30]

Then there was the exalted status accorded to workers in official ideology and practice. This was manifested in several ways: the party's recruitment drives which targeted workers, privileged access to educational institutions for workers and their children, the opening up to workers of museums, theaters, and other sanctuaries of the formerly privileged classes, the deprivation of voting and other civil rights to the latter, and the glorification of the proletariat in the arts and propagandistic literature. It may be that the psychological impact of these policies diminished as the decade wore on, but they cannot be discounted entirely.[31]

On the other side of the ledger, the level of unemployment was high and rising. In 1927 the number of unemployed reached 1.5 million or twice the level of three years earlier. The rate of industrial accidents rose as well. It was highest in mining, where fatalities jumped from 214 in 1923–4 to 452 in 1926–7, and lowest in textiles. Overall, in 1926 accidents claimed victims at the rate of 169.2 per 1,000 insured workers. A year later, the rate stood at 175.7. Housing space remained tight. Official statistics for 1927–8 put the average living space for the urban population at 5.9 square meters, down from 7.0 square meters in 1913. For workers it was only 4.9 and for miners lower still (3.7 square meters). Drunkenness and hooliganism, far from having been eradicated, were widespread and, particularly among youth, rampant. These banes of working-class existence generally were attributed to the vestiges of the old order and the new influx of peasants. But clearly other factors were involved, not the least of which were the state's economization and rationalization campaigns and the diversion of construction activity to the *novostroiki* (new factory, railway, and river dam construction projects).[32]

There is abundant evidence that material conditions for workers and other urban residents started to deteriorate in the autumn of 1927, and got much worse thereafter. Eyewitness accounts speak of long queues for bread and the scarcity or complete absence of other foodstuffs in Moscow and other major cities. Failing to obtain goods at state stores or cooperatives, consumers turned to private traders, if they could afford their prices. What they did not do, at least not in significant numbers, was abandon the cities for the countryside as had been the case ten years earlier. On the contrary, the flow was in the other direction. Whereas roughly 1 million peasants settled in towns between 1923–4 and 1925–6, the number of permanent migrants recorded for 1926 alone was 945,000. This rose to 1,062,000 in 1928 and 1,392,000 in 1929. The number of seasonal migrants (otkhodniki) also increased, from slightly over 3 million in 1926–7 to 3.9 million in 1927–8 and 4.3 million in 1928–9. Not all sought employment in the cities; between a third and a half were engaged in agriculture and forestry. But those who did – day laborers (chernorabochie), construction workers, and other cast-offs from the emerging agrarian revolution – pressed upon already inadequate urban resources.[33]

Demographers explain rural to urban migration in terms of "push" and "pull" factors. Rural dwellers typically are pushed off the land by a combination of population growth, limited resources, low or falling prices for agricultural goods and other internal and external pressures. They are pulled into the cities by employment opportunities associated with expanding industry, networks established by their predecessors which ease the transition to urban ways, and the promise of a better life. But rarely if ever in a predominantly market economy have push and pull been coordinated or of equal force. The disjuncture between the two has contributed to the phenomenon dubbed by Marx as the "reserve army of labor."[34]

Push and pull factors operated in pre-revolutionary Russia but were vitiated by the commune's control over the social and geographical mobility of its members, the rural location of much industry, and the near absence in the towns of social security for the unemployed, the disabled and the elderly. The maintenance of allotments and family ties in the village, seasonal migration, and when all else failed, begging were the strategies to which millions of peasants without secure employment resorted. Notwithstanding all the revolutionary upheavals, these patterns persisted, or rather, were recreated under NEP.

Why, though, did the number of unemployed continue to grow throughout the decade. The rural push, intensified by the anti-kulak, procurement, and early collectivization campaigns, provides only a partial explanation. Pending further research, it would appear that three urban-based groups swelled the ranks of the unemployed in the late 1920s: non-industrial workers, many of whom were the victims of the rationalization campaign and the anti-bureaucratic purge of state institutions; youths who had reached working age but could not be accommodated in the factory-apprentice schools or the ironclad minimum scheme according to which industrial enterprises were required to employ a fixed percentage of juveniles (but often failed to do so); and women who previously had not been engaged in wage labor but were now actively seeking jobs. Thus, between 1926 and 1929 the proportion of women and youths in large-scale industry remained nearly constant (28–29 percent for the former, and 25–26 percent for the latter). But between 1928 and 1929, their relative weight among the registered unemployed rose from 50 to 64 percent.[35]

At the same time, employment opportunities continued to expand, with roughly 600,000 new workers being added to the industrial work force in the years 1926–9. This was a natural concomitant of the industrialization drive as was the need for white-collar workers and administrative personnel. The party sought to meet this need and at the same time strengthen the proletarian component among "leading personnel" via its massive program for promotion (*vydvizhenie*) of workers. This involved both direct promotion from the shop floor and the recruitment of workers for full-time study. In what Sheila Fitzpatrick has called "the making of a proletarian intelligentsia," the key educational institutions were the rabfaks and technicums and at the higher level, the VUZy and VTUZy. While the increase in the number of such schools and their student bodies was small relative to the early 1930s, there was a significant rise in the proportion of students of working-class background.[36]

In the meantime, the foundations for new factories – and much else – were being laid by a burgeoning army of construction workers. The labor force in construction rose dramatically in these years, from an average of 547,000 in 1926 to 918,000 in 1929. For male peasant youths, construction work and/or army service historically had served as way stations on the road from field to factory. The army continued to perform this function, but as the battle lines shifted toward the industrialization front, the role of construction in tempering "raw" peasant youth expanded. The Dneprostroi project alone employed between 7,000 and 11,000 workers in 1928, rising to 17,000 by November 1929. Included among them were former industrial workers, many with electrical, carpentry and masonry skills; German Mennonites from the Volga region, hard-working but religious and therefore politically suspect; and seasonal workers from the central Russian provinces and Ukraine who organized themselves into artels and provided most of the unskilled labor.[37]

What, in short, was happening to the job market in the late 1920s was an acceleration of processes characteristic of the NEP period. The term "crisis" is apposite here, for the quickening of the pace of industrial development – industrialization – entailed both strain, even danger, as well as opportunity. The thoroughgoing transformation of the labor market, involving the entry of millions of peasants (and in certain regions, large numbers of forced laborers) but also the effective elimination of unemployment, still lay in the future. But the increasing mobility of workers, or to put it another way, their deracination, was portentous.

The cultural dimensions of these developments, how they were processed or understood by those experiencing them, only recently has become part of historians' agenda. In analyzing what he terms "the crisis of proletarian identity," Hiroaki Kuromiya has discerned "two distinct groups of workers often called 'new' and 'old.'" Both displayed "a consciousness characteristic of their social backgrounds." The older group consisted of workers with pre-revolutionary industrial experience who were generally categorized as skilled. According to a trade union census of the spring of 1929, they comprised just over half of all workers surveyed. Having enjoyed high status on the shop floor and "good credentials within the party leadership," these workers began to feel besieged and betrayed in the late 1920s. Their "universalist" skills and indeed the entire work culture of the shop floor appeared threatened under the impact of increasing mechanization and the NOT-inspired campaigns to install a functional organization of labor and replace artisan-like apprenticeship traditions with more rapid, narrow training. A wage scale reform, adopted in 1927 but applied gradually over the next two years, significantly narrowed differentials between the most and least skilled workers, further undermining the former's prestige. Yet, far from giving a sympathetic ear to skilled workers' concerns, party organs condemned them as reflective of "labor aristocratic" reaction, "shoppist interests," and "trade union opportunism."

The older generation of skilled workers was also upset at the effects new workers had on shop floor solidarities. In Kuromiya's rendition of their views, older workers regarded the newcomers as "uncultured, unskilled, and politically illiterate [knowing] little about the history and discipline of factories." Clearly more than generational tension was involved here. Distinguished by the recentness of their peasant backgrounds, new workers were referred to as "country bumpkins," "dark people," and undeserving of the honorable title of "worker." They were said to curry favor with the bosses, to willingly work overtime thereby giving management a pretext to "beat down" piece rates, and to frequently damage machinery and equipment. Party and union officials (and undoubtedly management as well) had their own complaints. These reflected their overriding concern with productivity and control of the labor force. The undisciplined nature of new workers thus was given a different twist. It was claimed that, true to their "petty bourgeois" origins, new workers shirked responsibility, slept on the job, flitted from one place of work to another in search of better conditions and otherwise behaved in an "anarchic fashion." Concerted efforts, inspired by the rationalization campaign, to disband artels in the mining industry, only intensified new workers' disorientation and, quite possibly, their hostility.[38]

To what extent such attitudes and behavior were typical of new workers, or even whether they were more common in the late 1920s than earlier are questions not easily answered. These were, after all, the least articulate of workers, the least likely to have access to the trade union and party press. While there is some statistical evidence that a disproportionate share of penalties were assessed against the unskilled (presumably new workers), the historian cannot be too careful in suspecting scapegoating by both management and skilled workers. It seems clear, though, that as the rules of the game began to change in the late 1920s, the breaking in of new workers became increasingly problematic and correspondingly, the centripetal forces binding workers together became increasingly tenuous. In the rough and tumble of industrial life, many recent recruits fell by the wayside, but others adapted successfully. From their midst were to emerge some of the most celebrated Stakhanovites of the Second Five-Year Plan period, including Aleksei Stakhanov himself.[39]

Both old workers and those recently recruited from the countryside were the bearers of traditional work cultures – pre-revolutionary industrial in the case of the former, peasant in the latter. In connection with industrialization, a third group emerged, embodying a new culture of work that challenged the other two. It consisted of young (23 to 29-year old), primarily male workers of urban origin with industrial skills. Since the definition of skill was itself changing in the context of increased mechanization and wage-tariff reform, it needs to be emphasized that this last characteristic was very much a social construction, and a contentious one at that. At least as critical as their industrial skills, though, was the fact that "this cohort contained the largest contingent of . . . communists" and, one should add, Komsomol members.[40]

Almost as soon as they appeared in reality, such workers found their role model in fiction. He was Volodia Makarov, the adopted son of a sausage trust director, in Yuri Olesha's novella, *Envy*. A Soviet Evgenii Bazarov (Turgenev's [anti-]heroic "son" in *Fathers and Sons*), Makarov is envied by all who come in contact with him. But he too envies. As he writes to his foster father,

I have become a human machine. And if I am not really one yet, it is what I want to be. The machines in the workshops here are pedigreed! They are terrific, so proud, so dispassionate, nothing like the ones in your sausage factories. Yours are just artisans . . . I want to be proud of my work, to be indifferent to everything outside it. So I have become envious of the machine; why am I not just as good? We invented, designed and constructed it. It turns out to be much harder than we are. Switch it on and it starts working. It won't make a single wiggle. That's the way I would like to be: not a single unnecessary wiggle.[41]

Kuromiya points out that it was these "core workers" whom "the leadership deliberately removed . . . from the shop floor, and sent . . . to engineering schools for technical education and to the countryside for the collectivization drive." But before they departed, their youthful enthusiasms found application in industry. In 1926–7, partly in connection with the economization campaign and partly inspired by the NOT movement, youth and shock brigades began to appear in various industries and regions. Soviet historians generally give pride of place to the Red Triangle Rubber Factory in Leningrad, where in September 1926 a brigade applied a new method of producing galoshes and thereby overfulfilled its norm. By this date, however, members of the Komsomol in the Ukrainian metallurgical industry were already declaring themselves to be "shock" (*udarnye*) brigades, imposing strict labor discipline, organizing technical training and achieving production successes.[42]

The transformation of what had been isolated and not well-publicized initiatives into a sustained movement occurred in the autumn of 1928. A turning point in this process was the success of Komsomol-organized shock brigades at the Ravenstvo (Equality) Spinning Mill in Leningrad. The origins of these brigades and the controversy they aroused have been told many times, most recently by Chris Ward. In his view, there was nothing technologically or organizationally innovative about the work of the brigades: "[W]hat was under threat was due process. Deference to age and experience and slow rise through the *komplekt* were being challenged, but not the *komplekt* itself." In the face of opposition from managers, engineers, and older operatives, intervention by the party committee was required to select the forty-nine shock workers and secure for them the best machines and the highest grade Egyptian cotton. This pattern was soon to be repeated at other mills in Leningrad and throughout the Central Industrial Region.[43]

Simultaneously, other Komsomol initiatives appeared and were soon linked with the emerging shock brigades. Public calls (*pereklichki*) were issued by workers from one enterprise to those in other, usually suppliers of unfinished materials, to deliver goods promptly and to improve the quality of goods delivered. Calls sometimes were followed up by inter-factory conferences and inspections and reviews by groups of workers. Within factories and eventually within entire industries, contests (*konkursy*) were held to determine "the best young producer-activist" or the enterprise that had the best record for reducing production costs and introducing rationalization measures.[44]

All these initiatives were constitutive of socialist competition, a term that gained wide currency after 20 January 1929 when *Pravda* printed a hitherto unpublished article by Lenin on "How to Organize Competition." The harsh, anti-intelligentsia tone of Lenin's article (written in December 1917) and its call to unleash the creative energy of workers and toiling peasants well suited the militantly workerist line adopted by the Stalinist leadership. It also suited the ambitions of younger workers who resented their elders' output-restrictive behavior and condescension as well as trade union and managerial indifference. Their pledges or "revolutionary vows" to reduce production costs and raise productivity by not sleeping on the job, leaving the shop floor to attend to personal business, or appearing at work in a drunken state may well have been self-seeking, but they also contained an unmistakable moral component.

Socialist competition and shock work shook up Soviet industry in 1929. Even as the enrollment of workers in shock brigades, the forms of competition in which they engaged, and the computation of results became increasingly standardized, resistance – often vocal and sometimes violent – persisted. On one side were ranged the older skilled workers and the unskilled; on the other, younger workers who had recently acquired their skills. Contemporary accounts spoke of struggles between "fathers and sons," or more frequently, kulaks and shock workers. From the perspective of older workers, the initiators of competition were "aliens" or "shock worker-idiots" (*chudaki-udarniki*); from that of peasant recruits, they were "detachments of Antichrist."[45]

The demands of shock brigades for ready supplies of materials and timely technical assistance irritated not only other workers, but management and trade union officials. For them, such demands, linked to the fulfillment of competition agreements, were a major test of their own competence and political reliability. As Stalin emphasized in May 1929, competition was not "the latest Bolshevik fashion . . . bound to die out when the 'season' passes." It was "a manifestation of a practical revolutionary *self-criticism* by the masses." And, he warned, "all who, wittingly or unwittingly, restrict this self-criticism and creative initiative of the masses must be brushed aside as an impediment to our great cause."[46]

What was management to do? How was it to distinguish "self-criticism" from "spets-baiting," "creative initiative" from indiscipline? The safest thing to do was to shift responsibility to party cells and trade union committees, both of which had become intricately involved in managerial decision-making. But "[w]eak, inefficient management was the last thing the party leadership wanted." This lack of a clear-cut command structure was addressed in a series of decrees culminating in the Central Committee resolution of 5 September 1929, "On Measures to Regularize the Administration of Production and Establish One-Man Management." Management by a single person (*edinonachalie*) was a Leninist principle to which the Left Communists had taken objection in 1918. Its reassertion has been interpreted as vesting in the factory director despotic power over workers. The party's definition of management's proper role suggests otherwise. It stressed not so much the authoritativeness of managers and still less their authoritarian power, but rather their accountability – to the party, but also to various forms of control from below (temporary worker control commissions, production conferences, socialist competition).[47]

As for the unions, they were neither to interfere in management (the "managerial deviation") nor fight against it ("trade unionism"). In the new circumstances of the planned economy, they were to fight for labor discipline and productivity, assisting both workers and management in uncovering hidden resources. This redefinition of the unions' role, articulated in April 1929 at a joint plenum of the Central Committee and Central Control Commission, did not sit well with Tomskii and his associates in VTsSPS. Their time of reckoning had come. Having failed to prevent the inclusion of Stalin's ally, Kaganovich, on the council's presidium, Tomskii resigned his post as chairman and was replaced in June 1929. Subsequently, almost the entire trade union apparatus was purged by RKI, apparently under the supervision of Kaganovich.[48]

Shaken up by the Stalinist leadership and shadowed by party activists, the unions and management took over the organization of socialist competition. What had been confined mainly to young workers was thus transformed into a much broader-based but also less militant movement. To entice older workers and the unskilled, Sovnarkom issued a decree in September 1929 which linked bonuses to the amount of savings achieved from competition and shock work. Provisions for other rewards and honors soon followed. By the end of the year, some 63 percent of industrial workers were said to be involved in one or another form of socialist competition and one-quarter of all workers belonged to shock brigades. Clearly, though, quantity had overwhelmed quality. Artels of construction workers renamed themselves shock brigades merely by their members promising to stay on the job for another six months. Articles in the press and leading party officials condemned "false shock work" (*lzheudarnichestvo*), the conclusion of agreements to compete between factories whose workers were completely ignorant of the terms of competition, and the statistical inflation of results. These contaminations occurred on yet a wider scale after the "Leninist enrolment" of an additional 1.5 million workers in shock brigades during the first weeks of 1930.[49]

The extent to which shock work and socialist competition actually reoriented older workers, socialized recent recruits or disciplined managerial personnel is therefore questionable. But the shock movement was not the only *démarche* of the late 1920s. As already indicated, the introduction of the three-shift system was accompanied by an intensification of the pace of work as well as a deterioration of working conditions. In the textile industry, where the system was first and most extensively applied, the results were mixed indeed. By mid-1929, daily output per worker in 24 enterprises surveyed rose by 10 to 15 percent in 8, but fell by an average of 9–10 percent in the remaining 16. The number of hours that spinning and weaving machines were in use increased substantially as did the volume of their output. But hourly output of machinery was still below what it had been before the change-over to the new system.

It was at this point that the idea of a continuous workweek (*nepreryvnaia nedelia*, often abbreviated to *nepreryvka*) surfaced. Its basic premise was that while workers required days off, machines did not. As Kuibyshev, the chairman of Vesenkha, put it: "One fifth of the time in the course of a year, machines – that is, our mechanical slaves – stand idle and do no work. It is completely natural that man rest, but why must these mechanical slaves rest?" The solution was to arrange work schedules so that on any given day, only a small fraction of an enterprise's work force would not be on the job. Continuous production for all 365 days of the year, minus 5 days for general observation of revolutionary holidays, could thus be assured. A variety of work schedules were possible (by December 1929 some fifty were in operation), but the most common arrangement was the so-called five-day week, that is, four days on followed by one day off.[50]

To visionaries within the party and the planning organs, nepreryvka seemed to hold the key to a revolution in time, unlocking vast new potentials of productivity. It also had ancillary benefits for the anti-religious movement, for Sundays and religious holidays were now to be regular working days. Indeed, this change affected not only the religious. Over the decades, workers had developed a number of traditions associated with such holidays that had little to do with religious observance but were nonetheless rooted in the religious calendar. These included holiday-eve drinking bouts, festive family dinners, and visits to native villages. All this was to be disrupted. Not surprisingly, then, many workers chose to disrupt the new schedules, staying away from work, or instituting go-slows on Sundays. As for those with greater religious commitment, particularly the sectarian communities, it has been suggested that nepreryvka "may have been the catalyst which galvanized some into action," that is, protest action.[51]

Meanwhile, it was reported that institutions servicing workers – baths, day-care facilities, shops, cafeterias, laundries, cultural establishments, and clubs – were slow to adjust their schedules, creating "chaos" and "confusion" in many provincial centers. Within the factories, it was discovered that while plants could be in continuous operation, machines could not. Three production shifts left little time for maintenance causing an alarmingly high rate of breakdowns. Subsequently, many enterprises reverted to the *status quo ante*, while formally adhering to the nepreryvka. The experiment did not survive the First Five-Year Plan.[52]

By 1930, then, the market mechanisms that had mediated if not guided economic decisions throughout NEP had been sundered, driven underground or in the case of the labor market, radically transformed. At the same time, the alternative mechanisms of what would become the administrative-command system of economic management (a.k.a., the planned economy) had not yet taken hold. It was just these circumstances of an "economy in turmoil" that produced such wildly disparate and/or fluctuating reactions among workers – exhilaration and disorientation; revolutionary eschatology and Christian pre-millennialism; worship of machines and barbaric treatment of them – and made plausible Stalin's pernicious assertion that as the era of socialism approached, the class struggle would intensify.

The crisis of the working class, like that of the peasantry, was not created by NEP but by its deliberate sabotage. Apprehensive about its ability to overcome the forces of petty bourgeois capitalism and the still older and more deeply rooted forces of "Russian" or "semi-Asiatic" backwardness, the Stalinist leadership hastily constructed ideological edifices to represent and extend its revolutionary actions. That it did not do so alone, that it required a new intelligentsia whose function was to represent (or re-present) Bolshevism, was very much a part of the intelligentsia's own crisis.

The crisis of the intelligentsia

The very same issue of *Pravda* that published Lenin's article on "How to Organize Competition," also contained one by Bukharin under the title, "Lenin and the Tasks of Science in Socialist Construction." Couched in commemorative terms – this was the fifth anniversary of Lenin's death – the article invoked a Lenin very different from the one who had heaped scorn on "bourgeois intellectuals" and their "haughtiness and contempt" for the common people. Bukharin's Lenin was not a populist demagogue but a far-sighted chief executive who appreciated the necessity of applying science to production as had the Germans. Bukharin wrote:

The slogans "Learn from the Germans!" "Learn from the American!" have become the order of the day and an iron task which must be realized no matter what . . . We will triumph with scientific economic leadership or we shall not triumph at all. This might seem an exaggeration of even, God help us, an "academic deviation." But it is nevertheless the historical truth of the reconstruction period . . . The objectivity of statistics, their application to reality and not subjective wishes is, as Il'ich said, the elementary precondition of a correct policy . . . Our youth must pass through the serious school of science and must *prove* its knowledge rather than relying on Communist one-hundred percentness . . . [53]

To say that Bukharin was swimming against the tide is something of an understatement. Precisely at this time "Communist one-hundred percentness" was sweeping all before it, and young communist intellectuals, non-communist visionaries, and those whose career paths had been blocked were denouncing the "bourgeois specialists." They denounced them for their lack of enthusiasm for the revolution, for their caste-like mentality, their fawning before western-derived theories and theorists, and their insistence on professional autonomy. Bukharin's article could only have confirmed suspicions among these circles that the intelligentsia had protectors in high places.

The tide began to turn against the old intelligentsia and its patrons nine months earlier with the so-called Shakhty Affair. This involved the arrest and trial of fifty-three mining engineers, three of them German nationals, employed in the Shakhty district of the North Caucasus. The engineers were accused of having engaged in wrecking and sabotage of mining installations at the instigation of the mines' former owners and foreign interests. The case against the Shakhty engineers crystallized many of the trends we have already observed, and it is not surprising that historians have devoted a good deal of attention to it.

By 1928, the Donbass region, of which Shakhty was the eastern-most extension, was in a state of high tension. High and growing rates of accidents and fatalities, outworn equipment, the relatively privileged position and high salaries of specialists, and the lack of amenities for workers were only part of the problem. The impending introduction of a new collective wage agreement calling for increased output norms and cuts in the piece rate contributed to the unrest. The concern of local authorities is evident in a letter dated 22 February 1928 and marked "secret" by the head of the OGPU's secret division (*sekretnaia chast'*) in the Stalin Metallurgical Works in Stalino. The letter asks trade union committee chairmen to report "any change in the attitudes [of workers] in relation to increases in norms." A further undated letter alerts them to the likelihood that "some groups will express discontent and raise unclear questions" and that they must be ready to react accordingly.[54]

The OGPU, "ready to seize any opportunity to offer the workers a scapegoat," was already by this time conducting investigations of engineers and technicians in Shakhty. After being rebuffed by Menzhinskii, E. G. Evdokimov, the OGPU chief of the North Caucasus District, turned to Stalin who happened to be (!) the Central Committee's representative on the governing board of the OGPU. Several days later, the engineers were arrested. On 10 March 1928 *Pravda* published a front-page editorial and the indictment drawn up by the prosecutor-general of the USSR. What had started as a local affair now took on broader national and even international implications.[55]

Public statements by party leaders reveal considerable differences over the lessons to be learned from the case. On the one side were ranged those whose chief concern was to minimize possible damage to the economy. They included Rykov (chairman of Sovnarkom), Kuibyshev (chairman of Vesenkha), and Ordzhonikidze (commissar of RKI-TsKK). Seeking to reassure specialists, they emphasized the atypicality of the Shakhty engineers and warned rank-and-file party members against indiscriminate specialist-baiting. Stalin drew very different conclusions. To him the conspiracy pointed up the danger of collusion between internal and external enemies of Soviet power, the dependence of "Red directors" on more technically competent specialists, the lack of political vigilance on the part of trade union and party organizations, and the need for more rapid and practical training of "our own" technical intelligentsia. Bukharin, who "may not have been aware . . . of the use to which the Shakhty case would soon be put by Stalin," did not seek to intervene on behalf of the specialists.[56]

All this was occurring in the midst of a flurry of organizational activity within the engineering profession. As will be recalled, engineers had been represented by two organizations: the All-Russian Association of Engineers (VAI), a professional association consisting of the most highly qualified graduates of polytechnics and engineering institutes, and the Inter-Bureau of Engineering Sections (VMBIT), a *de facto* union open to both engineers and technicians. In 1927 the VAI spawned a Circle on General Questions of Technology which "expressed a clear technocratic tendency." Although explicitly non-political, its aim of "work[ing] out a whole new world view, fully adapted to contemporary technical culture," could not but be interpreted by party ideologues as a denial of the hegemony of Marxism. In the meantime, the small minority of party members and sympathizers within the scientific-technical community formed a new organization to rally support for the party and its program of industrialization. This was the All-Union Association of Scientific and Technical Workers to Assist Socialist Construction of the USSR (VARNITSO).

In responding to the Shakhty trial and its aftermath, engineers were thus divided. Generally, those who occupied senior positions in the research institutes and planning agencies continued to believe that the need for their expertise made them invulnerable. Indeed, in the context of the emerging centralized planning system, they appeared ideally suited to make the key decisions about standardization, rationalization, and the application of science to industry. This at least seems to have been the expectation of Vesenkha's Scientific-Technical Administration which boldly proclaimed in October 1929 that "the future belongs to managing-engineers and engineering-managers." VMBIT and VARNITSO were more defensive, decrying indiscriminate attacks on the technical intelligentsia and the general decline in labor discipline which they attributed to production engineers' fears of antagonizing workers. At the same time, they worked to wean their constituents away from their guild mentality, to overcome the barriers that divided them from workers, and to recruit them into the Communist Party.[57]

Neither response worked, at least not in the short term. Leading engineers found themselves in the dock during the Industrial Party trial of 1930, while those involved directly in production continued to suffer from specialist-baiting and the mania for social purging. The persecution of engineers and other non-party specialists at a time when the Soviet Union remained desperately short of their skills was clearly irrational in economic terms. However, it did follow logically from the militantly workerist strategy being pursued by the Stalinist leadership. Whether Stalin was aware of the broader implications of his move against the specialists, including its impact on the struggle against the moderate faction within the party, is difficult to prove. But that it was popular with – indeed, was spurred on by – certain elements of the working class, lower-level party members and intellectuals who spoke in the name of the proletariat soon became evident. As one historian recently noted:

The intersection between the Stalinist elite and a vocal part of the factory workforce was brief. It relied on their mutual failure to specify the full implications of their thinking . . . But it was fruitful.

Historians may conclude that proletarian support was not "necessary" at this point, that the leadership was powerful enough to act alone, but at that time an explicitly proletarian mandate was valued by all who planned to take risky and unprecedented steps forward.[58]

Bukharin's invocation of the "objectivity of statistics" and his prophesy of disaster should it be violated, have vindicated him in the eyes of historians. But at that time such publicly expressed dissent merely sealed his fate as a Right deviationist.

The events outlined here parallel what happened to the scientific and cultural elites within the USSR between 1928 and 1931. To better understand what did happen, it might be useful to recapitulate the circumstances in which these elites found themselves and how they responded in the years before the "Great Break." "An anxious sense of mutual dependence and hostility" is the way David Joravsky has characterized the ambiguity of the intelligentsia's relations with the state. The Bolsheviks had extracted from the intelligentsia its recognition (*priznanie*) of the October Revolution's legitimacy in return for a large measure of professional autonomy. But the terms of that exchange were not iron-clad. On the one hand, the scientific and cultural elites had their supporters within the regime, most notably Lunacharskii, who fought hard – if not very successfully – for funds to support their research and other creative activities. On the other, there was strong sentiment within the party's lower echelons to be done with the intelligentsia, the only surviving component of the old privileged society. The official policy of steering a middle course between these extremes was not easily maintained.[59]

For their own part, the scientific and cultural elites jealously guarded their professional and creative autonomy, regarding themselves as the embodiment of transcendant wisdom and values. This sense of its own importance, of being needed and of being useful, of sharing the commanding heights of Soviet society and taking part in a great creative enterprise the final shape of which it could help determine, sustained the intelligentsia's belief in a bright future. At the very least, such sentiments assuaged the intelligentsia's residual antipathy toward the political regime and its uneasiness about the precariousness or provisionality of its privileges.

The intelligentsia was not exactly left to its own devices. But within certain (or rather, uncertain) limits, it did experience considerable freedom of inquiry and expression. Scientific and cultural life in the 1920s was vibrant, cosmopolitan, and filled with epistemological controversy that often cut across political lines. It was an extension of the modernist impulse that coursed through western culture in the last decades of the nineteenth and the first decades of the twentieth centuries. This impulse, as Stephen Kern has argued, had its material foundations in certain pre-war technological innovations (telephone, wireless telegraphy, x-ray, cinema, automobile, airplane) and scientific-cultural developments (psychoanalysis, Cubism, theory of relativity) both of which exploded conventional certainties about time and space. The unsettling effects of this explosion were strengthened by the Great War, which "released . . . powerful and dislocating forces that broke up the old dividers and forged new unities."[60]

We already have observed the impact of the explosion in the arts, where visionary avant-gardism jostled uncomfortably with the "new unity" of proletarian culture. Within the sciences, broadly conceived, there were three currents, none of which was peculiar to Russia but which were strongly exhibited there. One was the breakdown of disciplinary boundaries and the profusion of multi-disciplinary theories. One can point to numerous examples of this, from A. N. Bakh's biological physics to V. M. Bekhterev's reflexology, V. I. Vernadsky's geochemical concept of the "biosphere," and even perhaps Mikhail Bakhtin's philosophy of dialogism. Mark Adams, who notes that "In the 1920s no traditional disciplinary boundary was sacred," attributes this development to turn of the century attempts to establish the scientific basis and legitimacy of anthropology, psychology, and other social sciences. But the more temporally immediate environment was the uncertainties of war, revolution, and civil war and the intimacy of the circles established by intellectuals, often in out-of-the-way provincial towns to which they repaired for material sustenance and safety. In the case of the circles to which Bakhtin belonged, first in Nevel then in Vitebsk, avant-garde artists rubbed shoulders with philologists, musicologists, philosophers, and literary critics. Debates, often held in auditoriums before the public, focused on love, art, religion, and culture.[61]

A second current involved competing claims among different professional groups to expertise in the practical application of scientific methods. Evident in pedagogy and criminology, the conflicts were also sharply delineated in the area of public health. These conflicts had their origins in the medicalization of social problems, a trend well advanced in Germany from where Russian practitioners derived much of their terminology and status. Thus, in the treatment of alcoholism, social hygienists squared off against psychiatrists; in combatting labor fatigue and industrial accidents, labor hygienists competed with psychotechnical specialists. Each group had its own journals, research methodologies, links with an international professional community and patrons within the Soviet bureaucracy.[62]

The third development consisted of paradigmatic or philosophical reformulations within pre-existing scientific fields – Einsteinian relativistic cosmology in physics, genetic evolutionary theories in biology, various behavioralist schools (of which I. P. Pavlov's neurophysiological was only one) in psychology, and mechanistic and dialectical approaches to the philosophy of natural science. With the exception of the philosophy of science which was dominated by Marxists, Marxism played a supportive but largely subordinate role in such reformulations. A. K. Timiriazev, a mature physicist who entered the Communist Party in 1921, lashed out at the theory of relativity, but "from the start . . . was virtually isolated in his crusade . . . " Marxist biologists were "eclectically broadminded," embracing both Mendelian (and other forms of) genetics and Lamarckian "epigeneticism." And, notwithstanding official adulation for Pavlov – who himself was explicitly anti-Marxist – Freudianism, *Gestalt*, cognitive psychology, and alternative approaches to behavioral psychology all had their Soviet Marxist proponents.[63]

There was, however, what Joravsky refers to as an "ominous portent," namely the "striving for synthesis" under the banner of Marxism. In and of itself, such striving was no different from non-Marxian attempts to achieve closure in debates that raged in the sciences and arts. But linked with growing official impatience at the fragmentation of high culture and Marxism's own transformation into a catechism of certitudes appropriate to an emerging state church, the officially sanctioned Marxist world-view began to crowd out others. Between 1928 and 1931, the years of "cultural revolution," virtually every branch of the sciences and arts was politicized and the old authorities were ousted.[64]

This, at least, is one reading of what happened. But, like the question of whether NEP was politically sabotaged or succumbed to its own contradictions, the onset of cultural revolution has lent itself to two different interpretations. The "revisionist" view has been advanced most forthrightly by Sheila Fitzpatrick who argued that "cultural revolution directed and manipulated from above . . . is only one part of the picture. Cultural revolution also involved a response on the part of the leadership to pressures within the Communist movement and the society as a whole." Indeed, tensions within the professions were so great, that once the party abandoned its position of neutrality, "class war" erupted. Fitzpatrick points out that class war had both "pseudo-proletarian and genuinely proletarian aspects." Within the professions, "'class war' . . . was conducted by and on behalf of groups that only *claimed* to be proletarian, but in fact consisted of Communist intellectuals of overwhelmingly white-collar or intelligentsia background." The substantive proletarian dimension of the cultural revolution was the promotion of workers into responsible positions and their recruitment to higher education. In both cases, there was a strong element of generational friction, reflected in the heightened militance of the Komsomol, of students within higher education, and of junior members of the professions.[65]

Empirical investigations of specific scientific disciplines and professions allow us to draw some general conclusions about these interpretive models. The first is that neither adequately covers all cases. The explosiveness of tensions and contradictions within the professions between Marxists and non-Marxists as well as among Marxists varied in intensity. It was perhaps greatest in the literary field, less so in the case of rural studies and other social sciences, and still less in some of the natural sciences. As Susan Solomon has pointed out:

the transformation of Soviet culture at the end of the twenties did not take place according to any single pattern. In some fields, young Communist intellectuals chafed at the norms of their profession and therefore, at the first opportunity, converted their disagreements with their non-Marxist (or sometimes Marxist) senior colleagues into all-out war. In other fields, the in-fighting among intellectuals, however bitter, was contained because of the existence of intellectual and social cohesion within the profession; in these cases it was intervention by the Party and its deputies that set the revolution in motion.[66]

Why, though, was there greater "intellectual and social cohesion" in rural studies – and, by implication, even more so in the natural sciences – than in, say, literature or the historical profession? Robert Lewis believes that the answer lies in the relatively "monoparadigmatic nature" of the natural sciences and the inaccessibility of their discourses to the lay public. In these cases, "cultural revolution was likely to occur only through action from without." By contrast, in history, legal theory, pedagogy, and literature – fields where there were weak or multiple paradigms – Marxist cultural revolutionaries succeeded in overthrowing or isolating their "bourgeois" rivals only to be denounced later by the party's highest organs (if not Stalin himself) for one or another deviation from the true teachings of Marxism-Leninism.[67]

The great irony here is that where outside intervention was initially decisive, professional autonomy seems to have survived to a greater degree than in those cases where revolution from below or within occurred. Joravsky explains this irony in terms of political authorities claiming the same privileged understanding as scholarly professionals in the learned disciplines that study human beings. It was easier in these cases to predetermine and alter research agendas and conclusions to the inevitable zig-zags of political policy than it was in the more recondite natural sciences. Within the latter, biology was an exception, explicable by the agricultural crisis attending collectivization and the disappointment of "the leaders' great expectations of immense practical benefit."[68]

A second conclusion is that the revisionist challenge to the traditional interpretation of cultural revolution has lacked conceptual rigor, particularly in distinguishing between "revolution from above" and "revolution from below." Sometimes these two categories appear to be identical to state and society; sometimes to those without and those within the professions; and sometimes to different echelons within the party. Even in Solomon's judgment cited above, it is unclear who the "deputies" of the party were, and whether they were part of the "revolution from above." Fitzpatrick appears to be sensitive to some of the ambiguities of these categories, as in her discussion of whether the "Stalinist 'revolution from above' not only permitted but actually *required* lower-level officials to respond to urgent but imprecise 'signals' by improvising and taking initiatives . . . "[69]

Finally, it seems appropriate to suggest some future lines of research. Women are hardly mentioned in accounts of the cultural revolution and the reverse is true as well. Is this because cultural revolution was an almost entirely male affair? The campaign to unveil Central Asian women suggests otherwise. But the launching of that campaign pre-dated the cultural revolution in Russia by some eighteen months and its at best ambiguous results led to a strategy for the mobilization and training of women that was more accommodating to local (male) sensitivities. Nor should it be overlooked that the Zhenotdel was a casualty of this period, being eliminated in a reorganization of the Central Committee's secretariat in 1930. Whatever else it was, the cultural revolution does not appear to have been about women's emancipation. Its gendered language, replete with such military terms as "light cavalry charges," "shock troops," "cultural staffs" and "cultural campaigns," undoubtedly resonated with male youth far more than their female counterparts. But this question requires further research.

More attention also needs to be paid to the cultural revolution in the non-Russian republics. Since the non-Russian intelligentsia was in many cases both bourgeois in social background and culturally nationalist, it was doubly suspect. This is particularly evident in Ukraine where the party's vigorous pursuit of korenizatsiia contributed to the flowering of a national cultural identity. In 1929–30 the republic's Academy of Sciences and the Autocephalous Orthodox Church, both bastions of cultural Ukrainianization, were subjected to massive repression and in the latter case, annihilation. But who did the repressing? Was it primarily Stalin, the "Muscovites" and their agents/deputies, or local Russian or Russianized communists anxious to lay the specter of Ukrainian separatism? To what extent did the "proletarianization of the intelligentsia" mean its Russianization in the non-Russian republics?[70]

Without pre-judging research that still needs to be done, we can say that the cultural revolution both intensified and suppressed struggles within the intelligentsia, resulting in a crisis. For many within the old scientific and cultural elites, the crisis was a catastrophe. They were harassed, stripped of their titles and authority within their respective professions and in not a few instances, temporarily imprisoned. Such was the fate by 1931 of half of the mining engineers who had been working in the Donbass before the Shakhty trial. The Academy of Sciences, the olympus of scientific stature, was effectively captured by the party in 1929 and thoroughly renovated. By the end of the year, 520 members of the Academy's staff had been dismissed and another 128 were under arrest. By 1933, the Academy numbered among its full and corresponding members "almost" 350 communists compared to a "lonely pair of Party comrades" in 1928.[71]

For others, the crisis was a storm that had to be weathered and they trimmed their sails accordingly. Enduring bouts of "self-criticism" and attacks from neophytes within the professions, they emerged, chastened, to celebrate advances all along the front of socialist construction. As Bukharin, now a member of the Academy of Sciences but in political disgrace, told a session of the All-Union Conference for the Planning of Scientific Research in April 1931: "All technicians, engineers and scientists must understand that history has posed again a basic question about two camps, in all its sharpness: for there is no third, and one must definitely choose, and choose boldly, directly, decisively, irrevocably."[72]

Finally, for those whom Moshe Lewin uncharitably refers to as the "less intelligent," the vydvizhentsy trained via short courses, the *praktiki* and the mass of lower officials with little education and a low level of professional skills, the crisis provided a tremendous opportunity for career advancement. They were the cadres of the new Soviet intelligentsia, a term that now embraced all "mental workers." History has judged them quite harshly and indeed many found themselves overwhelmed by the tasks to which they were assigned. But as the Soviet Union entered the 1920s, their trajectory was in an upward direction.[73]

Epilogue and conclusion

The changes that swept the Soviet Union during the First Five-Year Plan (1928–32) were sufficiently radical and far-reaching in their consequences to warrant the term "revolution." The fact that this revolution was made in the name of principles that were consistent with Bolshevism and had been invoked at every opportunity since 1917 should not obscure its specific character. It was more than an acceleration of processes and tendencies underway in previous years – though it was that too. It was a Promethean leap into the unknown which left the Soviet state and society deeply marked – scarred we might say – for many decades to come.

Actually, it was several simultaneous revolutions: an agrarian revolution that obliterated communal land tenure, dispossessed millions of households of their livestock and tools and created some 250,000 collective farms; an industrial revolution that transformed the USSR into an industrial power and several millions of its citizens into industrial workers; and a cultural revolution that replaced the pre-revolutionary scientific, technical and cultural elites with a much larger and more plebeian class of mental workers, circumscribed their permissible intellectual discourse, and reduced cultural traffic with other nations to a trickle. Whether it was a political revolution as well is less certain. While there were significant changes in the social composition of governmental and party organizations and a phenomenal expansion in the number of tasks assumed by these bodies, the institutional framework within which they functioned remained pretty much intact.

To speak of this composite revolution as Stalinist is not to imply that it was manufactured or engineered by Stalin alone. Rather, it is to acknowledge that the official meanings attached to it were based on Stalin's own understanding of the relationship of the Soviet state to society. Socialist in rhetoric and total(itarian) in aim, the revolution might most accurately be characterized as étatist, that is, involving the

224

vast expansion of the party–state's administrative apparatus over previously autonomous areas of social life. Did this mean, as used to be argued by so many political scientists and historians, that a Leviathan/ totalitarian state had strangled society? Not quite.

Civil society ceased to exist, but social forces continued to make themselves felt, as much within the state as without. Rather than enabling the state to refashion society as the state saw fit, "statization" meant absorbing traditions, habits and people into the state, rendering it cumbersome, internally divided and maddeningly inefficient – in short, more backward in some respects than it had been before 1929. "Rural backwardness," that catch-all phrase denoting everything about peasant life that was recalcitrant to urban-based solutions, continued to impact upon the urban sector – more so than previously – in the form of peasant migration, the shirking of kolkhoz responsibilities, and shortages of food everywhere. Precisely because the planned economy was imposed in such a hasty and clumsy manner, elements of spontaneity kept on reappearing – in the collusion between management and workers that made a mockery of the centralized determination of wage rates and production methods not to mention the laws against lateness and absenteeism, in the form of "expediters" (*tolkachi*) who in many cases were former nepmen, in the peasant markets, among regional party "barons," and so forth. The contradictions endemic to NEP were not so much resolved as transformed into new contradictions that were sutured over with ideological strands, some borrowed from the distant past and others manufactured, as it were, on the run.

This conceptualization is by no means universally shared. Many would reject outright the association of Stalin with revolution or at most are willing to concede that the events of 1928–32 constituted a "revolution from above." While there is much to be said in favor of such views, their implicit denial of agency to social groups "down below" renders them incomplete and problematic. Still another approach is to regard the Stalin revolution as in some sense a fulfillment or at least the capstone to a process begun in 1917. This "revisionist" view, developed most fully by Sheila Fitzpatrick, stresses the extraordinary upward mobility of the vydvizhentsy and the idea that for this cohort, "industrialization was an heroic achievement – their own, Stalin's and that of Soviet power – and their promotion, linked with the industrialization drive, was a fulfillment of the promises of the revolution." Fitzpatrick acknowledges that the 1917 revolution contained other promises or premises – egalitarian, libertarian and utopian. But these emancipatory ideals fit awkwardly into the Bolsheviks' short-term objective of "modernization" via the proletarian dictatorship and, as the history of other revolutions has shown (here, Fitzpatrick cites Crane Brinton's schema), were unrealizable in any case.[1]

Such hard-headed realism is a welcome antidote to Stalin-centered explanations and moralistic judgments that long pervaded western scholarship and more recently have gained a significant following in the Soviet Union. But, as one reviewer of Fitzpatrick's book noted, her employment of "the Russian Revolution" ultimately derives from a reading back of its Stalinist outcome.[2] History becomes destiny. What the revolution meant is what Stalin and the forces he mobilized and unleashed made of it. The denouement drives the narrative. The period corresponding to NEP is relegated to an "interval" of retreat that was bound to pass. Of course, we know that NEP did pass. The point is not so much that there were other possible outcomes, but that NEP became more – and in some ways, less – than what it was intended to be. The identification of this interval with retreat limits one's appreciation of a whole range of experiences.

To appreciate what the Bolshevik Revolution meant before the Stalin revolution, to examine the ways that the promise of a new society, indeed a new chapter in world history, infused the thinking and actions of people who had experienced the old order has been one of the primary concerns of the present book. Much attention has been devoted to what was made of the bequeathals of the revolution, how the legacies of the old order delimited new possibilities and how difficult it was to know what to retain, borrow or transform. It has been demonstrated that the Communist Party leaders were not alone in confronting these questions or devising answers to them, that the revolution had meaning for artists and writers, technocratically minded engineers, religious communities, non-Russians seeking to define their national identity, peasants in cooperatives and workers within their work collectives and shops. It has been argued that how these groups understood the revolution and tried to make it work for them varied, and in many ways were mutually contradictory. Indeed, what is so striking about this "interval" between revolutions, what sets it apart from subsequent decades of Soviet history – up to but not including the present moment – was its tremendous indeterminacy. It makes sense, therefore, to treat the period in social historical terms, that is, to regard the constituent groups of Soviet society not merely as objects of official policy but as collective subjects.

The state itself was founded on the premise that a new form of government, the soviets, could obliterate social distinctions based on property and direct, indeed, transform the creative energies of its citizens. However, the main task of the state during its first years of existence was in arresting the socio-economic breakdown that had brought it into existence in the first place, and in beating back military resistance from a variety of White armies. That it eventually succeeded is testimony to both the inspired determination and ruthlessness of the Communist Party leadership, its plenipotentiaries and others who identified with Soviet power, and the spiritual and physical exhaustion of their widely dispersed enemies. It also, of course, had a great deal to do with the appropriation of available resources by institutions created for that purpose.

Four distinct but overlapping apparatuses – military, civilian, political and economic – carried out the appropriation of resources. The party, which dominated and eventually monopolized political life, tried to mediate among and determine priorities for the army, the commissariats, the soviet executive committees, and the central and regional economic councils and trade unions. It did so by "saturating" them with its cadres. The cadres took instructions from the central organs which in turn spawned new departments to handle their expanded functions including keeping track of the cadres. In this manner, state-building proceeded apace.

All the while, the industrial base of the country was withering and with it, the industrial working class. The idea(l) of the proletarian dictatorship lived on, however, reinforced by a reconceptualization of the proletariat itself. No longer exploited by capitalists yet deprived of basic sustenance, the proletariat had to exhibit its firmness, its "iron discipline" at the front and, as the military threat of counterrevolution receded but material conditions worsened, at the workplace as well. Consciousness and unconsciousness, previously defined in terms of identification with or participation in the Bolshevik Party, now turned on one's punctuality, willingness to carry out work assignments, and participation in union functions. The apotheosis of this discursive tyranny was reached in 1920–1 when the Bolshevized trade unions deprived repeated violators of labor discipline of their ration cards, assigned them to forced labor or sent them to concentration camps.

But the task-masters of labor discipline were not alone in defining proletarianness. Groups on the margins of the industrial working class such as state employees, watchmen, and Red Army soldiers claimed the status of proletarians; Maiakovskii assumed the role of a "producer of poetical labor" in a dispute with Gosizdat (the State Publishing House) over a "proletarian play" for which he demanded payment; Proletkult sought to redefine not only the theater but other art forms in proletarian terms; and the Bolshevik Tatar, Sultan Galiev, tried to do the same for the peoples of the East.

The peasantry, whose social weight increased as the urban population shrank, was less idealized but more definitionally unstable than the proletariat. Peasants were at one and the same time the (junior) partners of the proletariat in the Republic and "petty bourgeois" incubators of capitalism. Some peasants, namely the poor, were deemed worthy political allies, but as early as 1919, the small-holding "middle" peasantry was acknowledged as the mainstay of food production. The process of leveling down during the civil war years thinned the ranks of the "well-to-do," but even so, "kulak" influence was said to be responsible for peasant rebellions that punctuated rural life.

The language of discipline, so critical to the party's self-conception as an educative institution, continued even while the party reversed itself on the issue that had been at the heart of much indiscipline and indeed rebellion, namely food procurement. The retreat was engineered by Lenin under the (redefined) concept of state capitalism and with some retrospective apologies for "War Communist" excesses. The already complex machinery for overseeing requisitions, labor conscription, rationing, and violations of labor discipline was dismantled; the Red Army was demobilized; and, under the watchword of cost accounting (khozraschet), other state institutions vastly reduced their staffs. Within the space vacated by the state emerged cooperative institutions and previously proscribed private enterprises. Both were to play a substantial role in the economic life of the country, particularly during the early years of NEP.

The idea of going back to capitalism in order to move ahead to socialism was tricky. Lenin was able to master the dialectic, but then Lenin had set the terms for understanding it in the first place. As for his would-be successors, all but Stalin eventually foundered on the shoals of deviations, either Left or Right. Why this was so, why the rude Georgian who had so annoyed the bed-ridden Lenin was able to maneuvre between the Scylla of leftist impatience and the Charybdis of excessive cautiousness has been one of that decade's most perplexing questions. In fact, the terms Left and Right were political constructions that tended to obscure similarities between those so labelled and indeed between both and the center. But this very fact made them all the more useful to Stalin in isolating his would-be challengers. To say that Stalin had found the golden mean is not quite accurate. Having assiduously built up the party machine through his power of appointment, he was in an impregnable position. What Trotsky assailed as the bureaucratiz-ation of the party, Stalin and his lieutenants proclaimed as party construction. When the party line swung precipitously toward forced pace industrialization, its detractors became the Right.

Inner-party struggles were reflected in frequent shifts of party line or emphasis. The periodic squeezes on nepmen, the recruitment of industrial workers into the party, cultural policy and, of course, foreign policy can be correlated with party politics. But one should not over-estimate the ability of the party to effectuate changes in social and economic life. Almost everywhere, even within the "commanding heights," the grip of the party was vitiated by its lack of experienced cadres, reliance on the expertise of non-party specialists, and regional and branch loyalties. It periodically launched campaigns – to raise out-put norms and rationalize industrial production, to combat illiteracy in the countryside, to liberate women in Central Asia. Each involved mobilizations, the establishment of targets, the convening of con-ferences, and claims of spectacular successes. But each also led to circumvention and resistance, the diversion of attention and funds elsewhere and the eventual abandonment of the campaigns.

That there was more to the period between revolutions than party struggles and campaigns, that identities constructed on the basis of profession, confession, gender and ethnicity profoundly affected what was made of the revolution is something that historians are only beginning to appreciate and study. With the advent of glasnost and the hitherto unimaginable access that scholars have received to archives – albeit state and party archives – it has become possible to broaden the scope and increase the depth of historical inquiry. One may now examine court records, unpublished letters to the editors of news-papers, petitions to high state officials, the deliberations of local bodies concerning road maintenance and housing construction – in short, the stuff of public life.

It would be unwise to try to make this period of Soviet history – or any other – resemble what went on in other societies. The socialist experiment and the conditions in which it was conducted were too special to accommodate such a project. But if what is found is bound to be different, the techniques for looking and at least some of the ques-tions informing the search need not be reinvented. At last, the prospect of normalizing the writing of Soviet history is becoming a reality. If this book moves us a little closer to that goal, it will have served the purpose for which it was intended.

Notes

Introduction

1 Richard Stites, "The 1920s as a Period of History," *Russian History/Histoire russe*, vol. 9, pts. 2–3 (1982), pp. i–ii.
2 V. P. Danilov in "The Soviet Union in the 1920s, A Roundtable," *Soviet Studies in History*, vol. 28 (1989), p. 8, originally published as "Kruglyi stol': Sovetskii Soiuz v 20-e gody," *Voprosy istorii* (1988), pp. 3–58.
3 John Keane, "Introduction," in John Keane, ed., *Civil Society and the State* (London, 1988), p. 20.

1 Bequeathals of the revolution, 1918–1920

1 Isaac Deutscher, *The Prophet Armed: Trotsky, 1879–1921* (New York, 1965), pp. 485–513.
2 Neil Harding, *Lenin's Political Thought* (2 vols., Atlantic Highlands, NJ, 1983), vol. 1, p. 85.
3 Engels quoted in *ibid.*, p. 91.
4 V. I. Lenin, *Polnoe sobranie sochinenii* (hereafter *PSS*), 55 vols., 5th ed. (Moscow, 1958–62), vol. 33, pp. 86–95.
5 Harding, *Lenin's Political Thought*, pp. 91–2. Cf. Alfred B. Evans, "Rereading Lenin's *State and Revolution*," *Slavic Review*, vol. 46 (1987), pp. 1–19.
6 Nicolai I. Bukharin, *Economics of the Transformation Period* (New York, 1971), p. 79.
7 Leon Trotsky, *Terrorism and Communism* (Ann Arbor, MI, 1961), p. 170.
8 Richard Stites, *Revolutionary Dreams. Utopian Vision and Experimental Life in the Russian Revolution* (New York and Oxford, 1989), pp. 23–4.
9 Lenin, *PSS*, vol. 39, pp. 261–2.
10 The heterogeneous origins of Soviet governmental institutions are discussed in Don K. Rowney, *Transition to Technocracy. The Structural Origins of the Soviet Administrative State* (Ithaca and London, 1989), esp. pp. 65–93; Richard Sakwa, *Soviet Communists in Power, A Study of Moscow during the Civil War, 1918–1921* (New York, 1988), p. 165. Sakwa includes the "workers' state" of direct management as a residual category.

11 S. I. Gusev, *Uroki grazhdanskoi voiny* (Moscow, 1921), p. 18, quoted in Mark von Hagen, *Soldiers in the Proletarian Dictatorship. The Red Army and the Soviet Socialist State, 1917–1930* (Ithaca and London, 1990), pp. 137–8.

12 V. M. Selunskaia, *Sotsial'naia struktura sovetskogo obshchestva, istoriia i sovremennost'* (Moscow, 1987), p. 48; P. S. Kabytov, V. A. Kozlov, and B. G. Litvak, *Russkoe krest'ianstvo, etapy dukhovnogo osvobozhdeniia* (Moscow, 1988), p. 137. On the army as a "school of the revolution," see Mark von Hagen, "School of the Revolution: Bolsheviks and Peasants in the Red Army, 1918–1928" (Ph.D. dissertation, Stanford University, 1985).

13 E. H. Carr, *The Bolshevik Revolution, 1917–1923* (3 vols., Harmondsworth, 1966), vol. 1, p. 176; George Leggett, *The Cheka, Lenin's Political Police* (Oxford, 1981), pp. 232–3, 346, 359; and Sheila Fitzpatrick, *The Russian Revolution, 1917–1932* (Oxford, 1982), p. 82.

14 Peter H. Juviler, *Revolutionary Law and Order. Politics and Social Change in the USSR* (New York, 1976), pp. 20, 26; also, Eugene Huskey, *Russian Lawyers and the Soviet State: The Origins and Development of the Soviet Bar, 1917–1939* (Princeton, 1986), pp. 39–79.

15 *Vserossiiskaia Kochegarka*, 15 August 1920. In the Donbass, 385 of the 469 cases resolved by the union of mineworkers' disciplinary courts in September 1921 resulted in sentences that included warnings, fines, compulsory overtime, deprivation of rations, dismissal from the union, and forced labor. Gosudarstvennyi Arkhiv Donetskoi Oblasti, f. R-2607, op. 1, d. 88, l. 15.

16 On those deprived of civil rights (*lishentsy*), see Elise Kimmerling, "Civil Rights and Social Policy in Soviet Russia, 1918–1936," *Russian Review*, vol. 41 (1982), pp. 24–46.

17 E. G. Gimpel'son, *Rabochii klass v upravlenii sovetskim gosudarstvom: noiabr' 1917–1920 gg.* (Moscow, 1982), p. 47; von Hagen, *Soldiers in the Proletarian Dictatorship*, pp. 84, 91–2.

18 T. H. Rigby, *Lenin's Government: Sovnarkom 1917–1922* (Cambridge, 1979), p. 223, emphasis mine. On the personal backgrounds of commissars, see pp. 142–59.

19 For an elaboration of this point, see *ibid.*, pp. 65–83.

20 Carr, *Bolshevik Revolution*, vol. 1, pp. 224–5.

21 P. N. Trigub, "Deiatel'nost' sovetov Ukrainy po sozdaniiu voenno-politicheskogo soiuza sovetskikh respublik," in A. A. Druzhul, ed., *Sovety natsional'nykh raionov Rossii 1917–1922* (Riga, 1985), pp. 199–206; Stephen Blank, "Bolshevik Organizational Development in Early Soviet Trans-caucasia: Autonomy vs. Centralization, 1918–1924," in Ronald Grigor Suny, ed., *Transcaucasia, Nationalism and Social Change* (Ann Arbor, 1983), pp. 305–38.

22 This term used by an official of Narkomnats, quoted in Carr, *Bolshevik Revolution*, vol. 1, pp. 287–8.

23 Neil Harding, "The Organic Labor State," in Neil Harding, ed., *The State in Socialist Society* (Albany, 1984), pp. 15–21.

24 Trotsky, *Terrorism and Communism*, p. 47.

25 To speak of orthodoxy is not to imply unanimity. For a recent discussion of dissident "democratic" strains within Bolshevism, see Samuel Farber, *Before Stalinism. The Rise and Fall of Soviet Democracy* (London, 1990). On Vesenkha's infrastructure, see list and diagram in Silvana Malle, *The Economic Organization of War Communism, 1918–1921* (Cambridge, 1985), pp. 214–17.

26 Malle, *Economic Organization*, p. 232; also Maurice Dobb, *Soviet Economic Development since 1917* (London, 1978), pp. 108–16; Carr, *Bolshevik Revolution*, vol. 2, pp. 367–9.

27 Thomas Remington, *Building Socialism in Bolshevik Russia. Ideology and Industrial Organization, 1917–1921* (Pittsburgh, 1984), pp. 92–101.

28 N. Bukharin and E. Preobrazhensky, *The ABC of Communism* (Harmondsworth, 1969), p. 447.

29 Bukharin and Preobrazhensky, *The ABC of Communism*, pp. 333, 335–6; William Rosenberg, "The Social Background to Tsektran," in Diane Koenker, William Rosenberg, and Ronald Grigor Suny, eds., *Party, State and Society in the Russian Civil War* (Bloomington, 1989), pp. 349–73.

30 Carr, *Bolshevik Revolution*, vol. 1, p. 227.

31 Robert Service, *The Bolshevik Party in Revolution. A Study in Organisational Change, 1917–1923* (London, 1979), pp. 89–92, 115.

32 TsK VKP (b), Statisticheskii otdel, *Sotsial'nyi i natsional'nyi sostav VKP (b), itogi vsesoiuznoi partiinoi perepisi 1927 goda* (Moscow-Leningrad, 1928), p. 15; Carr, *Bolshevik Revolution*, vol. 1, p. 211; Service, *Bolshevik Party in Revolution*, pp. 116, 148; E. G. Gimpel'son, *Sovetskii rabochii klass, 1918–1920 gg.* (Moscow, 1974), p. 206. For a critical discussion of statistics on party membership, see Daniel Orlovsky, "Gimpel'son on the Hegemony of the Working Class," *Slavic Review*, vol. 48 (1989), pp. 104–6.

33 Moshe Lewin, "The Civil War, Dynamics and Legacy," in Koenker et al., *Party, State, and Society in the Russian Civil War*, pp. 412–13.

34 Service, *Bolshevik Party in Revolution*, pp. 100–4.

35 *Ibid.*, pp. 106, 96; *KPSS v rezoliutsiiakh i resheniiakh s'ezdov, konferentsii i plenumov TsK*, 9th ed. (15 vols., Moscow, 1983–9), vol. 2, p. 105.

36 Carr, *Bolshevik Revolution*, vol. 1, pp. 201–12; Leonard Schapiro, *The Origin of Communist Autocracy, Political Opposition in the Soviet State*, 2nd ed. (London, 1977), pp. 261–6. A Politburo had been formed on the eve of the October Revolution but met only twice before disbanding. See V. I. Startsev, "Vopros o vlasti v Oktiabr'skie dni 1917 goda," *Istoriia SSSR*, no. 5 (1987), p. 41.

37 A. I. Mikoian, *V nachale dvadtsatykh* (Moscow, 1975), p. 24.

38 Diane Koenker, "Labor Relations in Socialist Russia: Printers, Their Union, and the Origins of Soviet Socialism, 1917–1921," final report to National Council for Soviet and East European Research (unpublished, 1990), pp. 50–5.

39 Sawka, *Soviet Communists in Power*, pp. 108, 109.

40 Lenin, *PSS*, vol. 39, pp. 17–18.

41 L. S. Gaponenko, *Rabochii klass Rossii v 1917 godu* (Moscow, 1970), p. 72;

Gimpel'son, *Sovetskii rabochii klass*, p. 80. For Lenin's use of "semi-proletarians," see Carr, *Bolshevik Revolution*, vol. 2, p. 57.

42 Cf. Gimpel'son, *Sovetskii rabochii klass*, p. 80; D. A. Baevskii, *Rabochii klass v pervye gody sovetskoi vlasti (1917–1921 gg.)* (Moscow, 1974), p. 238; Iu. A. Poliakov, *Sovetskaia strana posle okonchaniia grazhdanskoi voiny: territoriia i naselenie* (Moscow, 1986), pp. 214–19. For the number of kustari, see Roger Pethybridge, *The Social Prelude to Stalinism* (London, 1974), p. 231.

43 Baevskii, *Rabochii klass*, pp. 246–7, 254; Gimpel'son, *Sovetskii rabochii klass*, pp. 90–1; V. B. Zhiromskaia, *Sovetskii gorod v 1921–1925 gg.* (Moscow, 1988), pp. 22–3; Diane Koenker, "Urbanization and Deurbanization in the Russian Revolution and Civil War," in Koenker et al., *Party, State and Society in the Russian Civil War*, pp. 81–8.

44 Koenker, "Urbanization and Deurbanization," pp. 78–9. For an analysis of the "double breakdown" (economic and political) amounting to a "time of troubles," see Lars Lih, *Bread and Authority in Russia, 1914–1921* (Berkeley and Los Angeles, 1990).

45 Isaac Deutscher, *The Prophet Unarmed: Trotsky, 1921–1929* (New York, 1965), p. 7; William Chase, *Workers, Society and the Soviet State. Labor and Life in Moscow, 1918–1929* (Urbana and Chicago, 1987), p. 308; Stephen Wheatcroft, "Public Health in Russia during the War, Revolution and Famines, 1914–1923: Moscow, Petrograd and Saratov," paper presented at the International Conference on the History of Russian and Soviet Public Health, Toronto, May 1986.

46 Moshe Lewin, *The Making of the Soviet System. Essays in the Social History of Interwar Russia* (New York, 1985), p. 212; von Hagen, "School of the Revolution," p. 29.

47 See for example Baevskii, *Rabochii klass*, p. 259; Poliakov, *Sovetskaia strana*, p. 218.

48 Chase, *Workers, Society and the Soviet State*, pp. 16, 35.

49 Koenker, "Urbanization and Deurbanization"; Baevskii, *Rabochii klass*, p. 258.

50 Koenker, "Urbanization and Deurbanization," pp. 97–8. Emphases mine.

51 Sheila Fitzpatrick, "The Bolsheviks' Dilemma: Class, Culture, and Politics in Early Soviet Years," *Slavic Review*, vol. 47 (1988), pp. 599–613.

52 Anthony Giddens, *A Contemporary Critique of Historical Materialism* (Berkeley and Los Angeles, 1981), pp. 19–29.

53 Malle, *Economic Organization*, pp. 125–7.

54 Chase, *Workers, Society and the Soviet State*, p. 35.

55 For such claims, see Lenin, *PSS*, vol. 41, pp. 27–34; Gimpel'son, *Sovetskii rabochii klass*, pp. 124–7.

56 Carr, *Bolshevik Revolution*, vol. 2, p. 234.

57 Lev Kritsman, *Geroicheskii period veliloi russkoi revoliutsii* (Moscow, n.d. [1926]), pp. 133–4; Chase, *Workers, Society and the Soviet State*, p. 37.

58 Rosenberg, "The Social Background to Tsektran," pp. 358–9.

59 S. G. Strumilin, "Rabochee vremia v promyshlennosti SSSR (1897–1935 gg.)," in *Izbrannye proizvedeniia v piati tomakh* (Moscow, 1964), vol. 3, p. 367.

Interestingly, according to a Moscow-based survey of late 1919, rates were lowest in food processing, presumably because workers were paid with the food they processed. See Rosenberg, "The Social Background to Tsektran," p. 349.

60 Kritsman, *Geroicheskii period*, p. 186.

61 James Bunyan, ed., *The Origins of Forced Labor in the Soviet State, 1917–1921: Documents and Materials* (Baltimore, 1967), pp. 135–6.

62 *Ibid.*, p. 121.

63 *Ibid.*, pp. 163–4.

64 *KPSS v rezoliutsiiakh*, vol. 2, p. 249.

65 Lenin, *PSS*, vol. 40, pp. 254–5; vol. 42, p. 210.

66 Gimpel'son, *Sovetskii rabochii klass*, p. 67.

67 Robert Tucker, *Political Culture and Leadership in Soviet Russia, from Lenin to Gorbachev* (New York, 1987), pp. 51–87.

68 Bunyan, *Origins of Forced Labor*, p. 171; Gimpel'son, *Sovetskii rabochii klass*, p. 131.

69 Remington, *Building Socialism*, pp. 155–62.

70 William Chase, "Voluntarism, Mobilization and Coercion: *Subbotniki* 1919–1921," *Soviet Studies*, vol. 41 (1989), pp. 111–28.

71 Teodor Shanin, *The Awkward Class. Political Sociology of Peasantry in a Developing Society* (Oxford, 1972), pp. 145–7.

72 Cf. Dorothy Atkinson, *The End of the Russian Land Commune, 1905–1930* (Stanford, 1983), pp. 165–85 and Esther Kingston-Mann, *Lenin and the Problem of Marxist Peasant Revolution* (Oxford, 1983), pp. 108–65.

73 M. A. Waters, ed., *Rosa Luxemburg Speaks* (New York, 1970), pp. 374–5.

74 John Channon, "The Bolsheviks and the Peasantry: the Land Question During the First Eight Months of Soviet Rule," *Slavonic and East European Review*, vol. 66 (1988), pp. 603–4.

75 Shanin, *The Awkward Class*, pp. 153–7.

76 Lewin, *Making of the Soviet System*, pp. 43, 13.

77 On Lenin's views, see Channon, "Bolsheviks and the Peasantry," pp. 614–15. Maxim Gorky, "On the Russian Peasantry," in R. E. F. Smith, ed., *The Russian Peasant in 1920 and 1984* (London, 1977), p. 23; on cottage industry, Pethybridge, *Social Prelude*, pp. 231, 249.

78 Carr, *Bolshevik Revolution*, vol. 2, pp. 57–9 (Lenin quoted on p. 59); Tsiurupa quoted in Lars Lih, "Bolshevik *Razverstka* and War Communism," *Slavic Review*, vol. 45 (1986), p. 674; see also Bertrand Mark Patenaude, "Bolshevism in Retreat: The Transition to the NEP, 1920–1922," (Ph.D. dissertation, Stanford University, 1987), pp. 18–20.

79 Lih, "Bolshevik *Razverstka*," pp. 673–4.

80 Malle, *Economic Organization*, p. 368.

81 See Lenin, *PSS*, vol. 38, pp. 193–8. Lenin related the dilemma of an agitator surrounded by peasants "and every one of them asked: Tell me, am I a middle peasant or not? I have two horses and one cow . . . I have two cows and one horse." Trotsky also admitted to this difficulty. See his *Kak vooruzhalas' revoliutsiia* (2 vols., Moscow, 1923–5), vol. 2, pt. 1, p. 51.

82 Lih, *Bread and Authority*, pp. 48–56, 167–98.

83 Lenin, *PSS*, vol. 38, pp. 194–200.

84 Carr, *Bolshevik Revolution*, vol. 2, pp. 165–6; Tucker, *Political Culture*, pp. 83–5, 205.

85 Malle, *Economic Organization*, pp. 401–2, 427–8; Kritsman, *Geroicheskii period*, pp. 131–3; Dobb, *Soviet Economic Development*, pp. 116–17; Patenaude, "Bolshevism in Retreat," p. 56; A. M. Bol'shakov, "The Soviet Countryside 1917–1924," in Smith, *The Russian Peasant in 1920 and 1984*, p. 57; Orlando Figes, *Peasant Russia, Civil War: The Volga Countryside in Revolution (1917–1921)* (Oxford, 1989), p. 272.

86 Deutscher, *Prophet Armed*, pp. 490–8; Patenaude, "Bolshevism in Retreat," pp. 59–71.

87 Kalinin quoted in Patenaude, "Bolshevism in Retreat," p. 72; see also Figes, *Peasant Russia*, p. 244.

88 See V. A. Sidorov, *Klassovaia bor'ba v dokolkhoznoi derevne, 1921–1929 gg.* (Moscow, 1978), pp. 27–8.

89 Seth Singleton, "The Tambov Revolt (1920–1921)," *Slavic Review*, vol. 25 (1966), pp. 497–512; Oliver Radkey, *The Unknown Civil War in Soviet Russia: A Study of the Green Movement in the Tambov Region, 1920–21* (Stanford, 1976); Jan M. Meijer, "Town and Country in the Civil War," in Richard Pipes, ed., *Revolutionary Russia: A Symposium* (New York, 1969), pp. 331–60.

90 Shanin, *Awkward Class*, p. 198.

91 von Hagen, *Soldiers in the Proletarian Dictatorship*, p. 69; Frunze quoted in von Hagen, "School of the Revolution," p. 285. See also statement by Gusev in 1924 that unlike the proletarian, the peasant soldier "sees no need to fight for anything more," quoted in *ibid.*, pp. 433–4.

92 Orlando Figes, "The Village and *Volost* Soviet Elections of 1919," *Soviet Studies*, vol. 40 (1988), pp. 35, 37, 41.

93 Radkey, *Unknown Civil War*, p. 31; Lenin, *PSS*, vol. 43, pp. 16–17. See also Lenin's earlier condemnation of the "careerists and adventurers . . . whose only aim is to make a career [and who] resort in the localities to coercion, and imagine they are doing a good thing." *PSS*, vol. 36, p. 199.

94 V. A. Kozlov, *Kul'turnaia revoliutsiia i krest'ianstvo, 1921–1927* (Moscow, 1983), pp. 50, 66–7; Peter Kenez, *The Birth of the Propaganda State: Soviet Methods of Mass Mobilization, 1917–1929* (Cambridge, 1985), pp. 121–38. See also the soon to be completed dissertation by Charles Clark of the University of Illinois, " 'Doloi negramotnost'!': The Literacy Campaign in the RSFSR, 1923–1927."

95 Beatrice Farnsworth, "Village Women Experience the Revolution," in Abbott Gleason, Peter Kenez, and Richard Stites, eds., *Bolshevik Culture: Experiment and Order in the Russian Revolution* (Bloomington, 1985), pp. 241, 244; Atkinson, *End of the Russian Land Commune*, p. 220; Barbara Taylor, *Eve and the New Jerusalem. Socialism and Feminism in the Nineteenth Century* (New York, 1983).

96 Kenez, *Birth of the Propaganda State*, pp. 65–9; Stites, *Revolutionary Dreams,*

pp. 121–3; Moshe Lewin, "Popular Religion in Twentieth Century Russia," in *Making of the Soviet System*, pp. 57–71.

97 A. I. Klibanov, *Religioznoe sektantstvo i sovremennost'* (Moscow, 1969), pp. 219–42.

98 Antonio Gramsci, *Selections from the Prison Notebooks*, trans. and ed. Quintin Hoare and Geoffrey Nowell Smith (New York, 1971), pp. 5–14. Among the rich literature on the Russian intelligentsia, see Nicholas Riasanovsky, *A Parting of Ways: Government and the Educated Public in Russia, 1801–1855* (Oxford, 1976) and Daniel Brower, *Training the Nihilists: Education and Radicalism in Tsarist Russia* (Ithaca, 1975).

99 William Rosenberg, *Liberals in the Russian Revolution: The Constitutional Democratic Party, 1917–1921* (Princeton, 1974); Jane Burbank, *Intelligentsia and Revolution* (Oxford, 1986), pp. 113–69; Robert H. Johnston, *New Mecca, New Babylon: Paris and the Russian Exiles, 1920–1945* (Kingston and Montreal, 1988). Quotation from p. 27.

100 Schapiro, *Origin of Communist Autocracy*, pp. 156–62.

101 Burbank, *Intelligentsia and Revolution*, pp. 13–65; Vladimir Brovkin, *The Mensheviks after October: Socialist Opposition and the Rise of the Bolshevik Dictatorship* (Ithaca and London, 1987); Leopold Haimson, "The Mensheviks After the October Revolution," *Russian Review*, vol. 38 (1979), pp. 456–73; and vol. 39 (1980), pp. 181–207.

102 Vladimir Brovkin, "The Failed Legalization of Mensheviks and SRs in 1919," unpublished paper presented at AAASS Conference, Chicago, November 1989.

103 Robert Darnton, "What Was Revolutionary about the French Revolution?" *The New York Review of Books*, vol. 35, nos. 21–2 (1989), p. 10.

104 Lenin, *PSS*, vol. 39, pp. 127–8.

105 *Ibid.*, p. 416.

106 Carr, *Bolshevik Revolution*, vol. 1, p. 184.

107 *Ibid.*, p. 185.

108 Lenin, *PSS*, vol. 30, p. 224.

109 For a useful guide to Futurism's many variants, see the Introduction in Anna Lawton, ed., *Russian Futurism through its Manifestoes, 1912–1928* (Ithaca, 1988), pp. 1–48.

110 Stites, *Revolutionary Dreams*, p. 70; Lynn Mally, "Intellectuals in the Proletkult: Problems of Authority and Expertise," in Koenker et al., *Party, State and Society in the Russian Civil War*, pp. 289–90.

111 Maurice Meisner, "Iconoclasm and Cultural Revolution in China and Russia," in Gleason et al., *Bolshevik Culture*, pp. 286–92; Zenovia A. Sochor, *Revolution and Culture. The Bogdanov–Lenin Controversy* (Ithaca, 1988), pp. 99–124.

112 Sheila Fitzpatrick, *The Commissariat of the Enlightenment: Soviet Organization of Education and the Arts under Lunacharsky, October 1917–1921* (Cambridge, 1970), chs. 7–9.

113 Jeffrey Brooks, "The Breakdown in Production and Distribution of Printed Material," in Gleason et al., *Bolshevik Culture*, pp. 168–9; Marc Slonim,

Soviet Russian Literature. Writers and Problems 1917–1967 (Oxford, 1967), p. 5; Kenez, *Birth of the Propaganda State*, pp. 104–10, 197–204.

114 Stites, *Revolutionary Dreams*, p. 92.

115 Kenez, *Birth of the Propaganda State*, pp. 111–18, 124.

116 James McClelland, "The Professoriate in the Russian Civil War," in Koenker et al., *Party, State, and Society in the Russian Civil War*, pp. 243–66; also, Iurii V. Got'e, *Time of Troubles. The Diary of Iurii Vladimirovich Got'e, Moscow, July 8, 1917–July 23, 1922*, trans. and ed., Terrence Emmons (Princeton, 1988). Got'e was Professor of History at Moscow University.

117 Fitzpatrick, *Commissariat*, pp. 78–83, 101–3; James McClelland, "The Utopian and the Heroic: Divergent Paths to the Communist Educational Ideal," in Gleason et al., *Bolshevik Culture*, pp. 114–30.

118 Fitzpatrick, *Commissariat*, p. 83.

119 Kendall E. Bailes, "Natural Scientists and the Soviet System," in Koenker et al., *Party, State, and Society in the Russian Civil War*, p. 281.

120 Oldenberg quoted in Fitzpatrick, *Commissariat*, p. 82; letter from Gorky to Lunacharskii, 23 July 1921, published in *Izvestiia TsK KPSS*, no. 5 (292) (1989), pp. 215–17; McClelland, "The Professoriate," p. 260. See also the vivid description of how the pioneering sociologist, Pitrim Sorokin, survived in Petrograd in Pitrim A. Sorokin, *Hunger as a Factor in Human Affairs*, trans. and with a Prologue by Elena P. Sorokin (Gainesville, FL, 1975), pp. xxix–xxxvi; Got'e, *Time of Troubles*, and Donald J. Raleigh, ed., *A Russian Civil War Diary: Alexis Babine in Saratov, 1917–1922* (Durham, NC, 1988).

121 Kendall E. Bailes, *Technology and Society under Lenin and Stalin* (Princeton, 1978), pp. 23–5.

122 *Ibid.*, p. 48; see also Lenin, *PSS*, vol. 44, pp. 350–1: "If all our leading institutions, that is, the Communist Party, the Soviet Government and the trade unions do not cherish, like the apple of their eye, each specialist who is working conscientiously with a knowledge of his work and love for it, even if completely foreign to communism ideologically, then there can be no talk about any serious successes in building socialism."

123 GADO, f. R-2607, op. 1, d. 72, ll. 1–28; Tsentral'nyi Gosudarstvennyi Arkhiv Oktiabr'skoi Revoliutsii (TsGAOR), f. 5469; op. 4, d. 166, ll. 3, 10, 19; Bailes, *Technology and Society*, p. 61.

124 S. A. Fediukin, "Oktiabr'skaia revoliutsiia i intelligentsiia," *Istoriia SSSR*, no. 5 (1977), p. 70; L. V. Ivanova, "Bol'shevistskaia partiinaia intelligentsiia i velikii oktiabr'," in K. V. Gusev, ed., *Intelligentsiia i revoliutsiia XX vek* (Moscow, 1985), pp. 138–45; also Fitzpatrick, "The Bolsheviks' Dilemma."

125 Malle, *Economic Organization*, p. 127; Remington, *Building Socialism*, p. 68.

126 Robert V. Daniels, *The Conscience of the Revolution: Communist Opposition in Soviet Russia* (Cambridge, MA, 1961), p. 136.

127 Orlovsky, "Gimpel'son and the Hegemony of the Working Class," p. 104; Antonov quoted in Orlovsky, "State Building in the Civil War Era: The Role of the Lower-Middle Strata," in Koenker et al., *Party, State, and Society in the Russian Civil War*, p. 180.

128 Orlovsky, "State Building," pp. 180–95.

129 Fitzpatrick, *Commissariat*, pp. 34–43; T. P. Korzhikhina, *Obshchestvennye organizatsii v SSSR, 1917–1936 gg. (profsoiuzy intelligentsii)* (Moscow, 1984), pp. 6–18, 50–64.

130 V. M. Selunskaia, ed., *Izmenenie sotsial'noi struktury sovetskogo obshchestva, 1921-sredina 30-kh godov* (Moscow, 1979), p. 56. For 1919 figures, see E. G. Gimpel'son, "Rabochii klass i privilechenie intelligentsii k upravleniiu sovetskim gosudarstvom (noiabr' 1917–1920 gg.)," in *Intelligentsiia i revoliutsiia XX vek*, p. 161.

131 The term actually was employed earlier, in 1917, by Lenin's one-time rival and chief philosophical nemesis, Alexander Bogdanov, but used in quite a different sense. So far as I know, Bogdanov did not apply it to the Soviet regime during the civil war. See John Biggart, "Alexander Bogdanov and the Theory of a 'New Class,'" *Russian Review*, vol. 49 (1990), pp. 270–4; V. I. Buldakov and V. V. Kabanov, "'Voennyi kommunism': ideologiia i obshchestvennoe razvitie," *Voprosy istorii*, no. 3 (1990), p. 41.

132 Donald Treadgold, *Twentieth Century Russia* (Chicago, 1981), p. 165; also Paul Craig Roberts, "'War Communism': A Reexamination," *Slavic Review*, vol. 29 (1970), pp. 238–61.

133 M. K. Dziewanowski, *A History of Soviet Russia*, 2nd ed. (Englewood Cliffs, NJ, 1985), p. 133.

134 Dobb, *Soviet Economic Development*, pp. 120–4; Stephen F. Cohen, *Rethinking the Soviet Experience. Politics and History since 1917* (Oxford, 1985), p. 57.

135 Lenin, *PSS*, vol. 43, p. 220; vol. 44, pp. 157, 162–5.

136 Lih, "Bolshevik *Razverstka*," pp. 684–5.

137 Quoted in Carr, *Bolshevik Revolution*, vol. 2, pp. 261–2.

138 Malle, *Economic Organization*, p. 175 (emphasis mine).

139 Patenaude, "Bolshevism in Retreat," pp. 108–12.

140 Stephen F. Cohen, *Bukharin and the Bolshevik Revolution: A Political Biography, 1888–1938* (New York, 1974), p. 78.

141 Carr, *Bolshevik Revolution*, vol. 3, pp. 166–8.

142 Lars Lih, "The Bolshevik Sowing Committees of 1920, Apotheosis of War Communism?" *Carl Beck Papers in Russian and East European Studies*, no. 803 (1990), pp. 36–7.

143 This is essentially the argument presented by Lih, "Bolshevik *Razverstka*," pp. 684–8. For another argument in favor of burying the concept, see the contribution of V. P. Dmitrenko to a roundtable among Soviet historians held in May 1988, in "The Soviet Union in the 1920s, A Roundtable," *Soviet Studies in History*, vol. 28 (1989), p. 75.

144 Hence, the Soviet sociologist, Lev Karpinsky, could state that "War Communism was a negation of many universal achievements of human civilization. At least it negated the market as a mechanism of distribution." See "The Fate of Lenin's NEP," *Moscow News*, no. 6, 1989, p. 10.

2 The crisis of 1920–1921

1 Patenaude, "Bolshevism in Retreat," p. 119; Figes, *Peasant Russia, Civil War*, pp. 264–71 for the Volga region.

2 Quoted in Figes, *Peasant Russia, Civil War*, p. 272.

3 *Ibid.*; Lenin, *PSS*, vol. 41, pp. 363–4.

4 Figes, *Peasant Russia, Civil War*, pp. 271-2.

5 Lenin, *PSS*, vol. 41, p. 359.

6 Lenin, *PSS*, vol. 37, p. 481; Bukharin and Preobrazhensky, *The ABC of Communism*, p. 452 and p. 377 where trade is characterized as "the capitalist method of distribution" which the Soviet Republic "was compelled to undertake its abolition by degrees"; officials quoted in Patenaude, "Bolshevism in Retreat," pp. 64, 70–1.

7 Lenin, *PSS*, vol. 41, pp. 359–64. In November, Lenin was counting on 250–300 million puds (*PSS*, vol. 42, p. 26); for the Baku congress, Carr, *Bolshevik Revolution*, vol. 3, pp. 262–5.

8 Lenin, *PSS*, vol. 42, pp. 91–117, 135.

9 *Ibid.*, pp. 158–9.

10 Pethybridge, *The Social Prelude to Stalinism*, ch. 5; Stites, *Revolutionary Dreams*, p. 48; Lenin, *PSS*, vol. 42, pp. 30, 156–61.

11 Lenin, *PSS*, vol. 42, pp. 343–5.

12 Michael Farbman, *Bolshevism in Retreat* (London, 1923), p. 247; Alec Nove, *An Economic History of the USSR* (London, 1969), p. 77; Paul Avrich, *Kronstadt 1921* (Princeton, 1970), p. 17; Lewin, *Making of the Soviet System*, pp. 260–1; Carr, *Bolshevik Revolution*, vol. 2, pp. 175–6. See also Malle, *Economic Organization*, pp. 445–50.

13 Lih, "The Bolshevik Sowing Committees of 1920"; Lenin, *PSS*, vol. 42, pp. 178–89. See also Baevskii, *Rabochii klass*, p. 327: "Individual bonuses to industrious peasants in a socially variegated peasant midst was a step from the policy of 'war communism' toward NEP."

14 See Avrich, *Kronstadt 1921*, pp. 18–19 for some relevant quotations; on Menshevik pressure to end requisitions, see David Dallin, "Between the World War and NEP," in Leopold Haimson, ed., *The Mensheviks from the Revolution of 1917 to the Second World War* (Chicago, 1974), pp. 234–9.

15 Teodorovich quoted in Carr, *Bolshevik Revolution*, vol. 2, pp. 174–5; Malle, *Economic Organization*, p. 451.

16 Strumilin quoted in Patenaude, "Bolshevism in Retreat," p. 90.

17 Lenin, *PSS*, vol. 42, pp. 51, 387; Gimpel'son, *Sovetskii rabochii klass*, pp. 64–5; E. B. Genkina, *Perekhod sovetskogo gosudarstva k novoi ekonomicheskoi politike, 1921–1922* (Moscow, 1954), pp. 88–100; V. P. Dmitrenko, "Nekotorye voprosy NEPa v sovetskoi istoriografii 60-kh godov," *Voprosy istorii*, no. 3 (1972), pp. 18–31; Patenaude, "Bolshevism in Retreat," pp. 107–10; Nove, *An Economic History*, p. 77.

18 Cf. Lenin, *PSS*, vol. 42, p. 333 and *Collected Works* (Moscow, 1965), vol. 32, p. 133.

19 Avrich, *Kronstadt 1921*, pp. 21–7, 35.

20 Patenaude, "Bolshevism in Retreat," pp. 133–8; Farbman, *Bolshevism in Retreat*, p. 275. Vyshinskii quoted in Patenaude, p. 138; see also Chase, *Workers, Society and the Soviet State*, p. 50.

21 *Dekrety sovetskoi vlasti* (Moscow, 1989), vol. 13, pp. 50–2, 137–8, 160–2, 164.

22 Avrich, *Kronstadt 1921*, pp. 35–87, 193–217; Israel Getzler, *Kronstadt 1917–1921* (Cambridge, 1983), pp. 205–45.

23 Deutscher, *The Prophet Armed*, p. 510; William Chamberlin, *The Russian Revolution* (2 vols., New York, 1965), vol. 2, pp. 439–40; Avrich, *Kronstadt 1921*, pp. 64–5.

24 Lenin, *PSS*, vol. 42, pp. 234–44.

25 For details, see E. B. Genkina, "V. I. Lenin i perekhod k novoi ekonomicheskoi politike," *Voprosy istorii* (1964), pp. 15–16; Isaac Deutscher, *Soviet Trade Unions. Their Place in Soviet Labour Policy* (London, 1950), pp. 42–51; Carr, *Bolshevik Revolution*, vol. 2, 220–9; Daniels, *Conscience*, pp. 119–36.

26 Deutscher, *The Prophet Armed*, p. 510; Daniels, *Conscience*, p. 134; Schapiro, *Origin of Communist Autocracy*, pp. 295, 287; Cohen, *Bukharin*, p. 102.

27 Daniels, *Conscience*, pp. 135, 128; Schapiro, *Origin of Communist Autocracy*, pp. 294–5. See also Larry Holmes, "For the Revolution Redeemed: The Workers' Opposition in the Bolshevik Party 1919–1921," *Carl Beck Papers in Russian and East European Studies*, no. 802 (1990), p. 12. Holmes considers that the Opposition's "comprehensive program of guarantees for working-class control of unions, union control of industrial administration, and freedom of criticism within the Party . . . snapped any bonds with Leninism, past or present."

28 Carr, *Bolshevik Revolution*, vol. 1, p. 203; Daniels, *Conscience*, p. 134; Deutscher, *The Prophet Armed*, p. 508; Carmen Sirianni, *Workers Control and Socialist Democracy: The Soviet Experience* (London, 1982), p. 235.

29 Schapiro, *Origin of Communist Autocracy*, p. 291, emphasis mine. One should also note the convention of referring to her as "Madame Kollontai."

30 Barbara Evans Clements, *Bolshevik Feminist: The Life of Aleksandra Kollontai* (Bloomington, 1979), esp. pp. 178–201; Beatrice Farnsworth, *Aleksandra Kollontai: Socialism, Feminism and the Bolshevik Revolution* (Stanford, 1980), pp. 212–48. Service, *Bolshevik Party in Revolution*, p. 210. Essentially the same point has been made more recently by Larry E. Holmes, "For the Revolution Redeemed," p. 3.

31 Alexandra Kollontai, *The Workers Opposition*, Solidarity Pamphlet No. 7 (London, n.d.), p. 39; Shliapnikov quoted in Sakwa, *Soviet Communists in Power*, p. 256.

32 Sakwa, *Soviet Communists in Power*, pp. 233–9, 255-6.

33 See, for example, William Rosenberg's discussion of the controversy over Tsektran in Rosenberg and Drobizhev, "Sotsial'no-ekonomicheskoe polozhenie i politika sovetskogo gosudarstva pri perekhode k NEPu," *Istorii SSSR*, no. 4 (1989), pp. 109–10. Sheila Fitzpatrick, "The Bolsheviks' Dilemma," pp. 599–613, quotation on p. 605.

34 Daniel Orlovsky, "Social History and its Categories," *Slavic Review*, vol. 47 (1988), pp. 621–2; Erik Olin Wright, *Classes* (London, 1985), pp. 78–86.

35 For relevant quotations, see *Desiatyi s"ezd RKP (b) (mart 1921 goda)*. *Stenograficheskii otchet* (Moscow, 1963), pp. 543–4; and *Odinnadtsatyi s"ezd RKP (b)*. *Stenograficeshii otchet* (Moscow, 1961), p. 24; Service, *Bolshevik Party in Revolution*, p. 152.
36 Holmes, "For the Revolution Redeemed," p. 17.
37 *Ibid.*, p. 23.
38 Lenin, *PSS*, vol. 43, pp. 24, 61, 69–70.
39 *Ibid.*, pp. 371, 92.

3 The perils of retreat and recovery

1 On Lenin's revision of "state capitalism," cf. A. I. Kossoi, "Razrabotka V. I. Leninym problem goskapitalizma v usloviiakh sotsialisticheskogo stroitel'stva," in Akademiia nauk SSSR, Institut istorii SSSR, *Novaia ekonomicheskaia politika, voprosy teorii i istorii* (Moscow, 1974), pp. 36–48; Charles Bettelheim, *Class Struggles in the USSR. First Period: 1917–1923*, trans. Brian Pearce (New York and London, 1976), pp. 464–76; and V. E. Manevich, *Ekonomicheskie diskussii 20-kh godov* (Moscow, 1989), pp. 10-22.
2 Lewin, *Making of the Soviet System*, p. 263.
3 Lenin, *PSS*, vol. 43, p. 62; *Pravda*, 23 March 1921, quoted in Chamberlin, *Russian Revolution*, vol. 2, pp. 502–3.
4 For an exception, see V. P. Danilov, "Sovetskaia nalogovaia politika v dokolkhoznoi derevne," in Akademiia nauk SSSR, Institut istorii SSSR, *Oktiabr' i sovetskoe krest'ianstvo* (Moscow, 1977), pp. 164–91.
5 Lenin, *PSS*, vol. 43, pp. 269, 313, also 334–5, 355–6. By the autumn of 1921, however, Lenin felt compelled to condemn overly zealous collectors. See *PSS*, vol. 53, pp. 286, 317; vol. 54, p. 200.
6 Danilov, "Sovetskaia nalogovaia politika," pp. 167–9, 173.
7 von Hagen, "School of the Revolution," p. 129; James E. Mace, *Communism and the Dilemmas of National Liberation: National Communism in Soviet Ukraine, 1918–1933* (Cambridge, MA, 1983), p. 65. The figure of 10,000 does not include some 10–15,000 associated with Makhno's anarchist army. See also R. D. Liakh, "Osobennosti osushchestvleniia agrarnykh preobrazovanii v Donbasse (1917–1923 gg.)," in Akademiia nauk SSSR, Institut istorii SSSR (ed.), *Problemy agrarnoi istorii sovetskogo obshchestva, materialy nauchnoi konferentsii 9–12 iiunia 1969 g.* (Moscow, 1971), pp. 33–4. Oliver Radkey, *The Unknown Civil War*, pp. 366–7; cf. Singleton, "The Tambov Revolt," p. 510: "Most villages could not meet the single tax in kind."
8 A. M. Bol'shakov, "The Soviet Countryside 1917–1924," in Smith, ed., *The Russian Peasant 1920 and 1984*, pp. 40, 48 (this is a translation of *Sovetskaia derevnia, 1917–1924 gg.* (Leningrad, 1924)).
9 Lenin, *PSS*, vol. 43, pp. 350–1 and Frumkin as cited in Lenin, *PSS*, vol. 44, p. 63; Iu. P. Bokarev, *Sotsialisticheskaia promyshlennost' i melkoe krest'ianskoe khoziaistvo v SSSR v 20–30 gody* (Moscow, 1989), p. 170; for slightly different figures, see Danilov, "Sovetskaia nalogovaia politika," p. 175.

10 John Maynard, *The Russian Peasant and Other Studies* (New York, 1962), p. 186; on the confiscation of church valuables, cf. Mikhail Heller and Aleksandr M. Nekrich, *Utopia in Power*, trans. Phyllis B. Carlos (New York, 1982), pp. 136–9 and I. Ia. Trifonov, *Ocherki istorii klassovoi bor'by v SSSR v gody NEPa, 1921–1937* (Moscow, 1960), pp. 31–5. For ARA, see Frank Alfred Golder and Lincoln Hutchinson, *On the Trail of the Russian Famine* (Stanford, 1927), p. 138. See also Charles M. Edmondson, "The Politics of Hunger: The Soviet Response to Famine, 1921," *Soviet Studies*, vol. 29 (1977), pp. 506–18.

11 Richard G. Robbins Jr., *Famine in Russia 1891–1892* (New York, 1975); S. G. Wheatcroft, "Famine and Factors Affecting Mortality in the USSR: The Demographic Crises of 1914–1922 and 1930–1933," CREES (University of Birmingham) Discussion Paper, SIPS nos. 20–21 (1981).

12 GADO, f. R-1, op. 1, d. 16, l. 124. Only a week earlier, the fuel industry was placed on a commercial footing which meant, among other things, that state organs were no longer responsible for providing food to miners and other fuel workers. Carr, *Bolshevik Revolution*, vol. 2, p. 307.

13 This is all the more remarkable in that the number of livestock continued to fall into 1923. See figures in V. P. Danilov, *Rural Russia under the New Regime*, trans. Orlando Figes (Bloomington, 1988), pp. 276, 289; and Atkinson, *End of the Russian Land Commune*, pp. 225, 259.

14 Danilov, "Sovetskaia nalogovaia politika," pp. 175, 179. See the suggestive remarks in E. H. Carr, *Socialism in One Country, 1924–1926* (3 vols., Harmondsworth, 1970), vol. 1, pp. 269–71.

15 Atkinson, *End of the Russian Land Commune*, pp. 260-2.

16 Lenin, *PSS*, vol. 45, pp. 285–6; Carr, *Bolshevik Revolution*, vol. 2, p. 294.

17 William Shinn, "The Law of the Russian Peasant Household," *Slavic Review*, vol. 20 (1961), p. 602; and Shanin, *The Awkward Class*, p. 226.

18 Lewin, *Making of the Soviet System*, p. 86; Lewin, *Russian Peasants and Soviet Power*, p. 86.

19 Atkinson, *End of the Russian Land Commune*, p. 235.

20 Danilov, *Rural Russia*, pp. 207, 231.

21 von Hagen, "School of the Revolution," p. 167.

22 Kozlov, *Kul'turnaia revoliutsiia i krest'ianstvo 1921–1927*, pp. 55, 56, 58. On the financial constraints imposed on Narkompros, see Fitzpatrick, *Commissariat*, pp. 256–90; for a tendentious argument absolving NEP of responsibility, see V. L. Soskin, "O nekotorykh chertakh kul'turnogo stroitel'stva v period perekhoda k NEPu," in *Novaia ekonomicheskaia politika, voprosy teorii i istorii*, pp. 238–42.

23 Samuel C. Ramer, "Feldshers and Rural Health Care in the Early Soviet Period," in Susan Gross Solomon and John F. Hutchinson, eds., *Health and Society in Revolutionary Russia* (Bloomington and Indianapolis, 1990), pp. 129, 132; see also Christopher Davis, "Economic Problems of the Soviet Health Service: 1917–1930," *Soviet Studies*, vol. 35 (1983), pp. 343–61.

24 Lewin, *Russian Peasants*, p. 82 quoting Zdanovich, "Selsovety i zemobshchestva," *Bol'shevik*, no. 6, 1928, p. 46; see also Shanin, *Awkward*

Class, pp. 183–5; Yuzuru Taniuchi, *The Village Gathering in Russia in the Mid-1920s* (Birmingham, 1968), p. 47.

25 Shanin, *Awkward Class*, pp. 187–8; see also Lewin, *Russian Peasants*, pp. 119–20. As of September 1924, there were 13,558 village party cells with 152,993 members.

26 Sula Benet, ed. and trans., *The Village of Viriatino* (New York, 1970), pp. 277–8; Shanin, *Awkward Class*, p. 188.

27 Shanin, *Awkward Class*, p. 192.

28 Danilov, *Rural Russia*, p. 103. For Lenin's views, see L. E. Fain, *Isotriia razrabotki V. I. Leninym kooperativnogo plana* (Moscow, 1970); "Leninskii kooperativnyi plan i ego osushchestvlenie v SSSR," contributions by participants in Akademiia nauk SSSR, Institut istorii SSSR, *Problemy agrarnoi istorii*, pp. 93–211; E. B. Genkina, "V. I. Lenin i nekotorye voprosy rukovodstva sel'skim khoziaistvom posle perekhoda k nepu," *Istoriia SSSR*, no. 3 (1969), pp. 5–27; on *Sel'skosoiuz*, see L. F. Morozov, *Ot kooperatsii burzhuaznoi k kooperatsii sotsialisticheskoi, iz istorii stanovleniia sovetskoi kooperatsii* (Moscow, 1969), pp. 194–215. See also V. P. Danilov, ed., *Kooperativno-kolkhoznoe stroitel'stvo v SSSR, 1917–1922* (Moscow, 1990), a useful collection of documents. The same process already had occurred within Tsentrosoiuz and the intermediate organs of the consumers' cooperative structure.

29 Lewin, *Making of the Soviet System*, p. 101; Danilov, *Rural Russia*, pp. 155–6.

30 Lenin, *PSS*, vol. 43, pp. 225–6.

31 Lenin, *PSS*, vol. 45, pp. 369, 376.

32 V. P. Dmitrenko, "Bor'ba sovetskogo gosudarstva za ovladenie derevenskim rynkom v pervye gody nepa," *Voprosy istorii*, no. 9 (1964), p. 63; Lenin, *PSS*, vol. 45, p. 376; Lewin, *Russian Peasants*, p. 94. For a revisionist argument that "the themes and concerns of the final writings [including "On Cooperation" – L.S.] faithfully reflect Lenin's long-term outlook," see Lars Lih, "Political Testament: Lenin, Bukharin and the Meaning of NEP," *Slavic Review*, vol. 59 (1991), pp. 141–52.

33 For a discussion of Lenin's "On Cooperation" and its subsequent invocations/distortions, cf. E. H. Carr and R. W. Davies, *Foundations of a Planned Economy 1926–1929* (2 vols., Harmondsworth, 1971–4), vol. 1, pp. 973–8; Cohen, *Bukharin and the Bolshevik Revolution*, pp. 134–8; Moshe Lewin, *Lenin's Last Struggle* (London, 1975), pp. 113–16; Michal Mirski, *The Mixed Economy: NEP and its Lot* (Copenhagen, 1984), pp. 34–47; Lih, "Political Testament." Having faithfully followed the Stalinist interpretation that collectivization was the fulfillment of Lenin's plan, Soviet historians more recently have tried to extricate Lenin from collectivization and mobilize him to legitimate the proliferation of cooperatives. See V. Sirotkin, "Uroki NEPa," *Izvestiia*, 9, 10 March 1989; V. Bashmachnikov and K. Kozhevnikova, "Zemlia, arenda, chelovek," *Literaturnaia gazeta*, no. 7, 1989.

34 *KPSS v rezoliutsiiakh i resheniiakh*, vol. 2, p. 585; Morozov, *Ot kooperatsii burzhuaznoi*, p. 202.

35 Lenin, *PSS*, vol. 45, pp. 46, 133. Interestingly, there is no mention of either better-off peasants or kulaks in "On Cooperation."

36 Lenin, *PSS*, vol. 43, pp. 233, 254; vol. 45, pp. 82, 98. See Lenin's response to the remark of one "comrade Semkov" that "They didn't teach us to trade in prison," in *PSS*, vol. 44, pp. 216–19.

37 Alan M. Ball, *Russia's Last Capitalists. The Nepmen, 1921–1929* (Berkeley and Los Angeles, 1987), p. 17; also Carr, *Bolshevik Revolution*, vol. 2, pp. 330–4; N. G. Sokolov, "Ispol'zovanie tovaroobmena pri perekhode k NEPu," in *Novaia ekonomicheskaia politika, voprosy teorii i istorii*, pp. 121–6.

38 Nove, *An Economic History*, p. 103; Selunskaia, *Izmeneniia sotsial'noi struktury sovetskogo obshchestva, 1921–seredina 30-kh godov*, p. 113; Ball, *Russia's Last Capitalists*, pp. 99, 104, 191. Ball (pp. 111–12), citing several Soviet sources, claims that industrial trusts and syndicates sold roughly 50 percent of their goods to private traders in 1922. Though the proportion fell to only 15 percent by 1923/4 and 8 percent two years thereafter, the ruble value of such trade continued to grow.

39 For a useful disaggregation of these categories, see Sheila Fitzpatrick, "After NEP: The Fate of NEP Entrepreneurs, Small Traders and Artisans in the 'Socialist Russia' of the 1930s," *Russian History/Histoire russe*, vol. 13 (1986), pp. 187–234. See also Ball, *Russia's Last Capitalists*, pp. 127–40; A. A. Matiugin, *Rabochii klass SSSR v gody vosstanovleniia narodnogo khoziaistva (1921–1925)* (Moscow, 1962), pp. 113–14.

40 Ball, *Russia's Last Capitalists*, p. 144.

41 *Ibid.*, pp. 99–100; Nora Levin, *The Jews in the Soviet Union since 1917. Paradox of Survival* (2 vols., New York, 1988), vol. 1, pp. 165–7.

42 Among private traders surveyed in Petrograd in 1922, 28.4 percent gave their previous occupation as housewives. *Izmeneniia sotsial'noi struktury*, p. 117; on female *samogonshchiki*, see Louise Shelley, "Female Criminality in the 1920s: A Consequence of Inadvertent and Deliberate Change," *Russian History/Histoire russe*, vol. 9, pts. 2–3 (1982), pp. 269–70. Shelley, relying on a 1922 study in Moscow, describes them as consisting primarily of "impoverished urban women of peasant background, aged thirty to forty-nine who had minimal education, knew no trade and had been house-wives. Many . . . became heads of households as a result of the casualties of the war years."

43 For some choice descriptions of Moscow's cafe and casino nightlife, see Chase, *Workers, Society, and the Soviet State*, pp. 200–3; for a fascinating discussion of attempts to find "acceptable gender roles within Bolshevik ideology during the civil war and early NEP years," see Elizabeth Wood, "The Three Faces of Masha: The *Baba*, the Mother, and the Prostitute in Postrevolutionary Bolshevik Ideology," paper for American Historical Association, San Francisco, December 1989.

44 E. Kviring, "Zheny i byt," *Vserossiiskaia kochegarka*, 20 July 1923; 5 September 1923. Already in 1920, the phenomenon of "soviet ladies . . . put[ting] on a whole shop-window of gold," and party members who "can't even talk their own wives around," was noted. See speech by Kotliar

in *Deviataia konferentsiia RKP (b). Protokoly* (Moscow, 1972), pp. 168–9, quoted in T. H. Rigby, "Early Provincial Cliques and the Rise of Stalin," *Soviet Studies*, vol. 33 (1981), pp. 11–12. Even (or especially?) Kollontai was disturbed by this type whom she dubbed "doll-parasites." See Clements, "Effects of the Civil War on Women and Family Relations," in Koenker et al., *Party, State and Society in the Russian Civil War*, p. 113.

45 Carr, *Bolshevik Revolution*, vol. 2, p. 303; Nove, *An Economic History*, p. 87.

46 A. V. Venediktov, *Organizatsiia gosudarstvennoi promyshlennosti v SSSR* (2 vols., Leningrad, 1957–61), vol. 2, pp. 55–6.

47 Carr, *Bolshevik Revolution*, vol. 2, p. 313; Bokarev, *Sotsialisticheskaia promyshlennost'*, pp. 180–1 points out that the fall in grain prices was exacerbated by the need of administrative and economic organs to convert grain received as tax into money.

48 Carr, *Bolshevik Revolution*, vol. 2, p. 306; Dobb, *Soviet Economic Development*, p. 153; *Izvestiia TsK RKP(b)*, no. 9–10 (1923), p. 12, quoted in Matiugin, *Rabochii klass SSSR*, p. 105.

49 Dobb, *Soviet Economic Development*, p. 152; Akademiia nauk Ukrainskoi SSR, Institut istorii, *Istoriia rabochikh donbassa* (2 vols., Kiev, 1981), vol. 1, pp. 207–16.

50 Chris Ward, *Russia's Cotton Workers and the New Economic Policy* (Cambridge, 1990), pp. 26–7; Carr, *Bolshevik Revolution*, vol. 2, p. 315.

51 Carr, *Bolshevik Revolution*, vol. 2, pp. 317–19; Paul Ashin, "Wage Policy in the Transition to NEP," *Russian Review*, vol. 47 (1988), pp. 293–307. On the origins of penal labor camps (known as "concentration camps"), see Carr, *Bolshevik Revolution*, vol. 2, pp. 212–13; and, more tendentiously, Richard Pipes, *The Russian Revolution* (New York, 1990), pp. 832–7.

52 L. S. Rogachevskaia, *Likvidatsiia bezrabotitsy v SSSR 1917–1930 gg.* (Moscow, 1973), pp. 76–7; for a different set of figures which nonetheless shows the same upward trend, see Bokarev, *Sotsialisticheskaia promyshlennost'*, p. 196.

53 The army's manpower dropped from 4.1 million in January 1921 to 600,000 in February 1923. von Hagen, "School of the Revolution," p. 129.

54 A. Rashin, "Perspektivy bezrabotitsy v Rossii," *Vestnik truda* (1922), p. 78; Rogachevskaia, *Likvidatsiia*, p. 91; Chase, *Workers, Society, and the Soviet State*, pp. 149–51; Bokarev, *Sotsialisticheskaia promyshlennost'*, pp. 197–8.

55 Rogachevskaia, *Likvidatsiia*, pp. 88–9.

56 *Ibid.*, p. 88; Bokarev, *Sotsialisticheskaia promyshlennost'*, p. 196.

57 Bokarev, *Sotsialisticheskaia promyshlennost'*, pp. 197–8; Chase, *Workers, Society, and the Soviet State*, pp. 157–64.

58 Ward, *Russia's Cotton Workers*, pp. 138–40.

59 For example, see Jacquelyn Dowd Hall et al., *Like a Family. The Making of a Southern Cotton Mill World* (Chapel Hill, NC, 1987).

60 Ashin, "Wage Policy in the Transition to NEP," pp. 297–300; Ashin, "Workers' Wages and the NEP in Moscow, 1921-28," paper presented at IV World Congress on the Soviet Union and Eastern Europe, Harrogate, July 1990.

61 Quoted in E. H. Carr, *The Interregnum, 1923–1924* (Harmondsworth, 1969), pp. 80–1; also, p. 84.

62 Ward, *Russia's Cotton Workers*, p. 163; Chase, *Workers, Society, and the Soviet State*, p. 230; John Hatch, "Bringing Economics Back In: Industrial Arbitration and Collective Bargaining during NEP," unpublished paper for Conference on "The Making of the Soviet Working Class," Michigan State University, 9–11 November 1990.

63 Chase, *Workers, Society, and the Soviet State*, pp. 231–2.

64 The leader was I. I. Kutuzov, president of the Textile Workers Union, quoted in Ward, *Russia's Cotton Workers*, p. 176.

65 Diane Koenker, "Labor Relations in Socialist Russia: Printers, Their Union and the Origins of Soviet Socialism, 1917–1921," final report to the National Council for Soviet and East European Research (unpublished 1989), pp. 72–6. Cf. J. B. Sorenson, *The Life and Death of Soviet Trade Unions* (New York, 1969). The notion of unions as social mediators is discussed in Daniel Orlovsky, "Class Boundaries: White Collar Workers, 1918–24," unpublished paper for Conference on "The Making of the Soviet Working Class," Michigan State University, 9–11 November 1990, pp. 26–7.

66 Samuel Lieberstein, "Technology, Work, and Sociology in the USSR: The NOT Movement," *Technology and Culture*, vol. 16 (1975), pp. 48–66; Kendall E. Bailes, "Alexei Gastev and the Soviet Controversy over Taylorism, 1918–1924," *Soviet Studies*, vol. 29 (1977), pp. 373–94; Zenovia A. Sochor, "Soviet Taylorism Revisited," *Soviet Studies*, vol. 33 (1981), pp. 246–64; Richard Huw Jones, "Taylorism in Russia, 1910–1925," unpublished University of Birmingham Ph.D. thesis, 1988.

67 Sheila Fitzpatrick, "NEP Society and Culture: Introductory Remarks," SSRC Conference on NEP Society, Bloomington, 2–4 October 1986, p. 11. Selected papers from this conference have been published as Sheila Fitzpatrick, Alexander Rabinowitch, and Richard Stites, eds., *Russia in the Era of NEP: Explorations in Soviet Society and Culture* (Bloomington, 1991). See also Fitzpatrick, *Education and Social Mobility in the Soviet Union, 1921–1934* (Cambridge, 1979) and her "The 'Soft' Line on Culture and its Enemies: Soviet Cultural Policy 1922–27," *Slavic Review*, vol. 33 (1974), pp. 267–87; and John Hatch, "The Politics of Mass Culture: Workers, Communists, and Proletkul't in the Development of Workers' Clubs, 1921–1925," *Russian History/Histoire russe*, vol. 13 (1986), pp. 119–48.

68 Fitzpatrick, "NEP Society and Culture," p. 14.

69 Peter Juviler, "Contradictions of Revolution: Juvenile Crime and Rehabilitation," in Gleason, *Bolshevik Culture*, p. 265. See also Jennie A. Stevens, "Children of the Revolution: Soviet Russia's Homeless Children (Besprizorniki) in the 1920s," *Russian History/Histoire russe*, vol. 9, pts. 2–3 (1982), pp. 262–64.

70 The most famous – and controversial – commune leader was A. S. Makarenko. For two English language studies of his work, see Frederic Lilge, *Anton Semyonovich Makarenko: An Analysis of His Educational Ideas in the Context of Soviet Society* (Berkeley, 1958) and James Bowen,

Soviet Education: Anton Makarenko and the Years of Experiment (Madison, 1962).

71 *Architectural Drawings of the Russian Avant-Garde* (New York, 1990).

72 *Kazimir Malevich, 1878–1935* (Washington, DC, 1990); Stites, *Revolutionary Dreams*, p. 169.

73 Christina Lodder, *Russian Constructivism* (New Haven and London, 1983), pp. 127–44; Natalia Adaskina, "Constructivist Fabrics and Dress Design," *The Journal of Decorative and Propaganda Arts* (1987), pp. 144–59.

74 Stites, *Revolutionary Dreams*, pp. 133, 135–40. For Lenin's analogy, see his "Immediate Tasks of the Soviet Government, in *PSS*, vol. 36, p. 200. Stites reports that by 1928 there were eleven conductorless orchestras in the Soviet Union and some imitators in Europe and the United States. That such a phenomenon can exist in very different circumstances has been demonstrated by the recent success of the Orpheus Chamber Orchestra, a New York-based ensemble. None of its members with whom I talked in March 1989 had heard of Persimfans.

75 *LEF*, no. 3 (1923), p. 3; S. A. Kozlov, "Problemy kul'turnoi revoliutsii v SSSR v noveishei nemarksistskoi istoriografii (1917-nachalo 1930-kh gg.)," *Istoriia SSSR*, no. 4 (1989), pp. 89–90; V. V. Gulev, "Deiatel'nost' sovetskogo gosudarstva v oblasti kinematografii (1918–1921 gg.)," *Istoricheskie zapiski*, no. 116 (1988), pp. 80–102.

76 Bailes, *Technology and Society*, pp. 60–2; Viacheslav Kostikov, "Izgnanie iz raia," *Ogonek*, no. 24 (1990), pp. 14–16.

77 Fitzpatrick, "The Soft Line on Culture"; Robert A. Maguire, *Red Virgin Soil* (Princeton, 1968), pp. 101–47; S. A. Fediukin, *Velikii Oktiabr' i intelligentsiia* (Moscow, 1972), pp. 348–75.

78 Quotations from Carr, *Socialism in One Country*, vol. 1, pp. 66, 71. See also Fediukin, *Velikii Oktiabr'*, pp. 267–77; Mikhail Agursky, *Ideologiia national-bol'shevizma* (Paris, 1980), pp. 103–6, 159–61; and Boris Kagarlitsky, *The Thinking Reed. Intellectuals and the Soviet State from 1917 to the Present*, trans. Brian Pearce (London–New York, 1988), pp. 60–3.

79 Nikolai Valentinov, "Non-Party Specialists and the Coming of the NEP," *Russian Review*, vol. 30 (1971), pp. 161, 163. Valentinov's informants were A. A. Fedotov, I. A. Kalinnikov, and N. K. von Meck, all of whom were arrested in 1929–30 and sentenced to death or ten-year prison terms in connection with alleged "wrecking" activities.

80 Fediukin, *Velikii Oktiabr'*, pp. 276–7; Nicholas Lampert, *The Technical Intelligentsia and the Soviet State* (London, 1979), pp. 25–8.

81 Tomskii quoted in Lampert, *Technical Intelligentsia*, p. 34.

82 Lampert, *Technical Intelligentsia*, pp. 22–3. On Uchraspred see below.

83 Carr, *Bolshevik Revolution*, vol. 1, pp. 392–3.

84 *Ibid.*, pp. 281–91, 387–8; Stephen Blank, "Bolshevik Organizational Development in Early Soviet Transcaucasia: Autonomy vs. Centralization, 1918–1924," in Ronald Grigor Suny, ed., *Transcaucasia, Nationalism and Social Change* (Ann Arbor, 1983), pp. 334–6.

85 Lenin, *PSS*, vol. 27, p. 255.

86 V. I. Startsev, "Political Leaders of the Soviet State in 1922 and Early 1923," *Soviet Studies in History*, vol. 28, no. 3 (1989–90), p. 14. For perceptive analyses of these differences, see Gregory Massell, *The Surrogate Proletariat: Moslem Women and Revolutionary Strategies in Soviet Central Asia, 1919–1929* (Princeton, 1974), pp. 38–55; Richard Pipes, *The Formation of the Soviet Union: Communism and Nationalism, 1917–1923*, rev. ed. (New York, 1968), pp. 242–93.

87 For details of the affair see, among others, Lewin, *Lenin's Last Struggle*, pp. 43–62; Pipes, *Formation of the Soviet Union*, pp. 266–93; and Ronald Grigor Suny, *The Making of the Georgian Nation* (Bloomington, IN, 1988), pp. 209–19.

88 For Lenin's "Testament," *PSS*, vol. 54, pp. 355–6; for his notes, vol. 45, pp. 356–62; Deutscher, *The Prophet Unarmed. Trotsky: 1921–1929*, p. 71.

89 See, for example, Daniels, *The Conscience of the Revolution*, pp. 172–208; Startsev, "Political Leaders of the Soviet State." Daniels holds Trotsky primarily responsible for failing to make more of opportunities and particularly his silence on the national question at the Twelfth Congress. Startsev is inclined to place primary responsibility on Zinoviev and Kamenev.

90 Stalin, *Sochineniia*, vol. 5, pp. 236–75, quotations on pp. 238, 268. According to Deutscher, Stalin's characterization of Russian chauvinism as the "main danger" was the result of a deal struck with Trotsky. See *The Prophet Unarmed*, pp. 90–3. On the "national communists," see Mace, *Communism and the Dilemmas of National Liberation*; A. Bennigsen and S. Enders Wimbush, *Muslim National Communism in the Soviet Union* (Chicago, 1979). Cf. Stalin's theses in *Sochineniia*, vol. 5, pp. 181–94 and the congress' resolutions in *KPSS v rezoliutsiiakh i resheniiakh*, vol. 4, pp. 79–88.

91 On Sultan Galiev, see Bennigsen and Wimbush, *Muslim National Communism* and A. Bennigsen and Chantal Lemercier-Quelquejay, *Les Mouvements Nationaux chez les Musulmans de Russie: 1. Le "Sultangalievisme" au Tatarstan* (Paris, 1960). Stalin's speech at the conference is reproduced as an appendix in Bennigsen and Wimbush, pp. 158–65; Stalin, *Sochineniia*, vol. 5, pp. 292–339; Carr, *Bolshevik Revolution*, vol. 1, p. 406.

92 Pipes, *Formation of the Soviet Union*, pp. 293, 296.

93 Bohdan Nahaylo and Victor Swoboda, *Soviet Disunion. A History of the Nationalities Problem in the USSR* (New York, 1990), p. 59.

94 Martha B. Olcott, "The Basmachi or Freemen's Revolt in Turkestan 1918–1924," *Soviet Studies*, vol. 33 (1981), pp. 352–69; Nahaylo and Swoboda, *Soviet Disunion*, pp. 61–6.

95 Carr, *Socialism in One Country*, vol. 2, pp. 258–69 (Enukidze quoted, p. 258).

96 Massell, *The Surrogate Proletariat*, p. 36. Massell is referring to Central Asia, but his observations apply for the most part to other non-Russian areas.

97 For figures which refer to a 1922 party census covering 375,948 of a total membership of 410,000, see Tsk VPK(b), Statisticheskii otdel, *Sotsial'nyi i natsional'nyi sostav VPK(b), itogi vsesoiuznoi partiinoi perepisi 1927 goda* (Moscow–Leningrad, 1928), pp. 118–19. Richard Pipes blithely asserts that

"In a democratic state such a one-sided ethnic composition of a party would not necessarily have had great practical consequences; it was different in a totalitarian country" (p. 279). On ethnic composition of state employees, see Pipes, *Formation of the Soviet Union*, pp. 278–80; Carr, *Bolshevik Revolution*, vol. 1, pp. 379–81.

98 *KPSS v rezoliutsiiakh i resheniakh*, vol. 3, p. 86; Geoffrey Hosking, *The Awakening of the Soviet Union* (London, 1990), p. 79.

99 *Sotsial'nyi i natsional'nyi sostav VKP(b)*, p. 118.

100 Belorussia is an obvious case. See Mace, *Communism and the Dilemmas of National Liberation*; A. P. Nenarokov, "Iz opyta natsional'no-iazykovoi politiki pervykh let sovetskoi vlasti," *Istoriia SSSR*, no. 2 (1990), pp. 3–14; Zvi Gitelman, *Jewish Nationality and Soviet Politics: The Jewish Sections of the CPSU, 1917–1930* (Princeton, 1972); Stephen Jones, "The Establishment of Soviet Power in Transcaucasia: The Case of Georgia, 1921–1928," *Soviet Studies*, vol. 40 (1988), pp. 616–39; Nicholas Vakar, *Belorussia: The Making of a Nation* (Cambridge, MA, 1956).

101 On Trotsky's critique, see Robert H. McNeal, "Trotskyist Interpretations of Stalinism," in Robert Tucker, ed., *Stalinism. Essays in Historical Interpretation* (New York, 1977), pp. 30–52; Perry Anderson, "Trotsky's Interpretation of Stalinism," *New Left Review*, no. 139 (1983), pp. 49–58; Paul Bellis, *Marxism and the U.S.S.R., The Theory of Proletarian Dictatorship and the Marxist Analysis of Soviet Society* (Atlantic Highlands, NJ, 1979), pp. 56–92.

102 See, for example, the official Institut marksizma-leninizma pri TsK KPSS, *Istoriia kommunisticheskoi partii sovetskogo soiuza* (Moscow, 1970), vol. 4, bk. 1, pp. 109–12, 296–309, 349–57. For the recent recasting of party history, see Haruki Wada, "Perestroika and the Rethinking of History in the Soviet Union, 1986–88," in Takayuki Ito, ed., *Facing Up to the Past. Soviet Historiography under Perestroika* (Sapporo, 1989), pp. 35–80.

103 A. F. Ilin-Zhenevsky, "Nakanune oktiabria," *Krasnaia letopis'* (1926), pp. 15–16, cited (with emendations) in Alexander Rabinowitch, *The Bolsheviks Come to Power. The Revolution of 1917 in Petrograd* (New York, 1976), pp. 57–9. There is also, of course, a feminist reading of the passage.

104 T. H. Rigby, "Early Provincial Cliques and the Rise of Stalin," *Soviet Studies*, vol. 33 (1981), pp. 3–28. The center's appointee in Nizhni-Novgorod was Anastas Mikoian. See his *V nachale dvadsatykh* (Moscow, 1975), pp. 24–161.

105 Merle Fainsod, *How Russia is Ruled* (Cambridge, MA, 1965), p. 181; Leonard Schapiro, *The Communist Party of the Soviet Union*, 2nd rev. ed. (London, 1970), p. 261.

106 Service, *Bolshevik Party in Revolution*, pp. 181-2.

107 Quotation from Organization-Instruction Section report to Twelfth Congress, cited in Robert V. Daniels, "The Secretariat and the Local Organizations in the Russian Communist Party, 1921–1923," *American Slavic and East European Review*, vol. 16 (1957), pp. 37–8. T. H. Rigby, "Staffing USSR Incorporated: The Origins of the Nomenklatura System,"

Soviet Studies, vol. 40 (1988), pp. 529–30. See also Michael Voslensky, *Nomenklatura. The Soviet Ruling Class*, trans. Eric Mosbacher (Garden City, NY, 1984), pp. 43–50; Carr, *Bolshevik Revolution*, vol. 1, pp. 209-10.

108 T. H. Rigby, *Communist Party Membership in the U.S.S.R., 1917–1967* (Princeton, 1968), pp. 96–7.

109 Diane Koenker, "Introduction: Social and Demographic Change in the Civil War," in Koenker et al., *Party, State, and Society in the Russian Civil War*, p. 51. See also Rigby, *Communist Party Membership*, pp. 102–5; Sakwa, *Soviet Communists in Power*, pp. 152–64.

110 Rigby, *Communist Party Membership*, p. 109.

111 Carr, *Interregnum*, pp. 88–93, 276–8, 300–2; Daniels, *Conscience of the Revolution*, pp. 159–61, 204, 210.

112 Quoted in Daniels, *Conscience of the Revolution*, p. 219. For the text of the Platform, see Carr, *Interregnum*, pp. 374–80. For Michels' "law," first published in 1911, see his *Political Parties. A Sociological Study of the Oligarchical Tendencies of Modern Democracy* (New York, 1962), and especially the Introduction by Seymour Martin Lipset.

113 Quoted in Daniels, *Conscience of the Revolution*, p. 228. Trotsky's past hostility toward the Workers' Opposition was repaid in kind by Shliapnikov and others.

114 The two relevant articles, "How We Should Reorganize the Workers' and Peasants' Inspection," and "Better Fewer, But Better," and the drafts of the first are in Lenin, *PSS*, vol. 45, pp. 383–406, 442–50. My interpretation follows Lih, "Political Testament: Lenin, Bukharin and the Meaning of NEP." See also Harding, *Lenin's Political Thought*, vol. 2, pp. 294–308.

4 Living with NEP

1 Carr, *Socialism in One Country*, vol. 1, p. 438.

2 For an exemplary but neglected study of one such organization, the Society of Friends of Defense and Aviation-Chemical Construction, see William E. Odom, *The Soviet Volunteers: Modernization and Bureaucracy in a Public Mass Organization* (Princeton, 1973).

3 Terry Cox, *Peasants, Class, and Capitalism: The Rural Research of L. N. Kritsman and his School* (Oxford, 1986), pp. 33–48; Shanin, *Awkward Class*, pp. 45–51.

4 Shanin, *Awkward Class*, p. 57; Nove, *Economic History of the USSR*, p. 106.

5 Quoted in Carr, *Socialism in One Country*, vol. 1, p. 241.

6 E. A. Preobrazhenskii, *Novaia ekonomika* (1926), published in English as *The New Economics* (Oxford, 1965); Mark Harrison, "Soviet Primary Accumulation Processes: Some Unresolved Problems," *Science and Society*, vol. 45 (1981–2), pp. 387–408.

7 Cohen, *Bukharin and the Bolshevik Revolution*, p. 163; N. Bukharin, *Kritika ekonomicheskoi platformy Oppozitsii* (Moscow, 1926). This is a reprint of articles originally appearing in 1924 and 1925. See also his

"Novoe otkrivenie o sovetskoi ekonomike ili kak mozhno pogubit' raboche-krest'ianskii blok" (1925), reprinted in *Izbrannye proizvedeniia* (Moscow, 1988), pp. 86–115. For the other dimensions, see especially his *Put' k sotsializmu i raboche-krest'ianskii soiuz* (1925) reprinted in *Izbrannye proizvedeniia*, pp. 146–230. For assessments of both the Left's and Bukharin's positions, cf. Alexander Erlich, *The Soviet Industrialization Debate, 1924–1928* (Cambridge, MA, 1960), Moshe Lewin, *Political Undercurrents in Soviet Economic Debates* (Princeton, 1974), pp. 33–96; and Michal Mirski, *The Mixed Economy. NEP and its Lot* (Copenhagen, 1984). For Bukharin's conception of the "road to socialism," see Cohen, *Bukharin and the Bolshevik Revolution*, ch. 6, and for recent Soviet assessments, see the collection of articles in the special issue on "The Bukharin Alternative," *Soviet Studies in History*, vol. 29 (1990).

8 Quoted in Harrison, "Soviet Primary Accumulation," p. 401; Bukharin, "Doklad na XXIII chrezvychainoi leningradskoi gubernskoi konferentsii VKP(b), 10–11 fevralia 1926 g." in *Izbrannye proizvedeniia*, p. 249.

9 Bukharin, *Izbrannye proizvedeniia*, p. 196, emphasis in original.

10 Carr, *Socialism in One Country*, vol. 1, pp. 274–95, 303; and the resolutions of the Central Committee plenum of 23–30 April 1925 in *KPSS v rezoliutsiiakh i resheniiakh*, vol. 3, pp. 340–9.

11 Bukharin, *Izbrannye proizvedeniia*, pp. 203-4.

12 It is indicative that the chapter on "Agriculture" in the relevant volume of Carr's *Socialism in One Country* is two and a half times longer than any other.

13 Kamenev quoted in Carr, *Socialism in One Country*, vol. 1, p. 319 and Danilov in "The Soviet Union in the 1920s, A Roundtable," *Soviet Studies in History*, vol. 28, no. 2 (1989), p. 18.

14 Carr, *Socialism in One Country*, vol. 1, p. 321; for a critique of these figures, see Sigrid Grosskopf, *L'Alliance ouvrière et paysanne en U.R.S.S. (1921–1928). Le Problème du blé* (Paris, 1976), pp. 138–42.

15 Carr, *Socialism in One Country*, vol. 1, pp. 317, 209. See, though, R. W. Davies' account of his exchanges with Carr in 1956–8 in which Davies adumbrated some of Lewin's points. R. W. Davies, "'Drop the Glass Industry': Collaborating with E. H. Carr," *New Left Review*, no. 145 (1984), pp. 60–4.

16 Lynne Viola, "Rehabilitating the Soviet Kulak in Western Historiography," unpublished paper presented to AAASS conference, Washington, DC, October 1990.

17 See the epigraph to this chapter, and *Derevnia pri NEP'e. Kogo schitat' kulakom, kto – truzhenikom. Chto govoriat ob etom krest'iane?* (Moscow, 1924), cited in Sheila Fitzpatrick, "The Bolshevik Invention of Class: Marxist Theory and the Making of 'Class Consciousness' in Soviet Society," p. 6, published as "L'Usage bolchevique de la 'Class': Marxisme et construction de l'identité individuelle," *Acte de la Recherche en Sciences sociales*, no. 85 (1990). See Lih, *Bread and Authority*, pp. 142–9 for the argument that the Bolsheviks derived the latter meaning from the SRs.

18 Lewin, *Russian Peasants*, p. 69. See, for example, Stalin's speech to the Fourteenth Party Congress, in *Sochineniia*, vol. 7, pp. 337–8.

19 Stalin, *Sochineniia*, vol. 7, p. 337.

20 Grosskopf, *L'Alliance ouvrière*, p. 310; Lewin, *Russian Peasants*, p. 75.

21 Danilov, *Rural Russia under the New Regime*, pp. 66, 72. It is unclear why women householders could not be kulaks. Danilov presumably is referring to widows, divorcees and others lacking adult male partners.

22 G. T. Robinson, *Rural Russia under the Old Regime* (Berkeley and Los Angeles, 1969 reprint of 1932 edition), pp. 240, 242. Kritsman cited in Lewin, *Russian Peasants*, p. 75.

23 Cox, *Peasants, Class and Capitalism*, pp. 105, 143–4, 172–97; J. R. Hughes, "The Irkutsk Affair: Stalin, Siberian Politics and the End of NEP," *Soviet Studies*, vol. 41 (1989), pp. 235–8; Lewin, *Russian Peasants*, p. 72.

24 See Susan Gross Solomon, *The Soviet Agrarian Debate: A Controversy in Social Science, 1923–1929* (Boulder, CO, 1977), pp. 3–36, 113–83; Solomon, "Rural Scholars and the Cultural Revolution," in *Cultural Revolution in Russia, 1928–1931*, pp. 145–53. Chaianov was one of many who had to wait for the advent of glasnost to have their names cleared of the absurd but politically important charge of having formed an oppositional Working Peasants Party. For translations of Chaianov's work, see D. Thorner, B. Kerblay, and R. E. F. Smith, eds., *Chayanov: The Theory of Peasant Economy* (Homewood, IL, 1966; reprinted by University of Wisconsin Press, 1987) and his 1920 novel set in 1984, "The Journey of My Brother Alexei to the Land of the Peasant Utopia," in *The Russian Peasant in 1920 and 1984*, pp. 63–107. The list of works comprising this latter debate is too long to cite here. For the most bibliographically comprehensive contribution, see Cox, *Peasants, Class, and Capitalism*.

25 Herbert J. Ellison, "Russian Agrarian Theory in the 1920s: Climax of a Great Tradition," in G. L. Ulmen, ed., *Society and History. Essays in Honor of Karl August Wittfogel* (The Hague, 1978), pp. 480–1.

26 Cox, *Peasants, Class, and Capitalism*, pp. 106–13.

27 See contributions by Robert Sharlet, David Joravsky, and George M. Enteen in Fitzpatrick, ed., *Cultural Revolution in Russia, 1928–1931*; Louise Shelley, "The 1929 Dispute on Soviet Criminology," *Soviet Union/Union soviétique*, vol. 6, pt. 2 (1979), pp. 175–85; and Fitzpatrick, *Education and Social Mobility in the Soviet Union, 1921–1934*, pp. 82–6.

28 In this respect, Teodor Shanin's *The Awkward Class* was immensely influential. See, however, Mark Harrison, "Resource Allocation and Agrarian Class Formation: The Problem of Social Mobility among Russian Peasant Households, 1880–1930," *Journal of Peasant Studies*, vol. 4 (1977), pp. 127–61; and Terry Cox and Gary Littlejohn, eds., *Kritsman and the Agrarian Marxists* (London, 1984).

29 Cox, *Peasants, Class and Capitalism*, pp. 205–6. For the observation, Claudia Koonz, *Mothers in the Fatherland: Women, the Family and Nazi Politics* (New York, 1987), p. 21. For an imaginative reconstruction of the nineteenth-century peasant household, see Mary Matossian, "The Peasant Way of

Life," in Wayne S. Vucinich, ed., *The Peasant in Nineteenth Century Russia* (Stanford, 1968), pp. 1-40. Also, Christine E. Worobec, *Peasant Russia, Family and Community in the Post-Emancipation Period* (Princeton, 1991).

30 Vladimir Gsovski, *Soviet Civil Law* (2 vols., Ann Arbor, 1948), vol. 1, p. 126; John Hazard, Isaac Shapiro and Peter B. Maggs, *The Soviet Legal System* (Dobbs Ferry, NY, 1969), p. 491; John Quigley, "The 1926 Soviet Family Code: Retreat from Free Love," *Soviet Union/Union soviétique*, vol. 6, pt. 2 (1979), pp. 166, 174.

31 Beatrice Brodsky Farnsworth, "Bolshevik Alternatives and the Soviet Family: The 1926 Marriage Law Debate," in D. Atkinson, A. Dallin, and G. Lapidus, eds., *Women in Russia* (Sussex, 1978), pp. 140–1; Wendy Goldman, "Freedom and its Consequences: The Debate on the Soviet Family Code of 1926," *Russian History/Histoire russe*, vol. 11 (1984), pp. 364–6. Significantly, Kollontai's assessment dated from 1926 and was not therefore contemporary. Farnsworth argues that although "Kollontai participated in framing the Family Code . . . her influence was held in check and the Code did not reflect her radicalism." Farnsworth, *Aleksandra Kollontai*, p. 159).

32 For an English translation of the 1918 Code, see Rudolf Schlesinger, ed., *Changing Attitudes in Soviet Russia: The Family in the U.S.S.R., Documents and Readings* (London, 1949), pp. 33-40.

33 Barbara Evans Clements, "The Effects of the Civil War on Women and Family Relations," in Koenker et al., *Party, State, and Society in the Russian Civil War*, pp. 107–9; for marriage rates, see Wesley Fisher, *The Soviet Marriage Market. Mate Selection in Russia and the USSR* (New York, 1980), pp. 64–5.

34 Clements, "The Effects of the Civil War," pp. 110–13; see also her "Working Class and Peasant Women in the Russian Revolution, 1917–1923," *Signs*, vol. 8 (1982), pp. 215–35.

35 Carr, *Socialism in One Country*, vol. 1, p. 42; Leon Trotsky, *Problems of Everyday Life* (New York, 1973), pp. 36–47. See also Trotsky's "Address to the Third All-Union Conference on Protection of Mothers and Children" (December 1925), translated in L. D. Trotskii, *Women and the Family* (New York, 1970), pp. 34–6.

36 Carr, *Socialism in One Country*, vol. 1, pp. 43–4.

37 Schlesinger, ed., *Changing Attitudes*, p. 120.

38 On rural soviet elections, see Carr, *Socialism in One Country*, vol. 2, pp. 370–4; Schlesinger, ed., *Changing Attitudes*, p. 107.

39 Wendy Goldman, "Working-Class Women and the 'Withering Away' of the Family: Popular Responses to Family Policy," in Fitzpatrick, Rabinowitch, and Stites, eds., *Russia in the Era of NEP*, pp. 138–9.

40 Schlesinger, ed., *Changing Attitudes*, p. 143.

41 Farnsworth, "Bolshevik Alternatives," in Atkinson, et al., eds., *Women in Russia*, pp. 149–52.

42 Quoted in Fanina Halle, *Women in Soviet Russia* (London, 1934), pp. 123–4; Farnsworth, "Bolshevik Alternatives," pp. 153–60; for an English

translation of parts one and two of the Code, see Schlesinger, ed., *Changing Attitudes*, pp. 154–68.

43 Carr, *Socialism in One Country*, vol. 1, pp. 45–6; Stevens, "Children of the Revolution," pp. 259-60.

44 Gail Lapidus, *Women in Soviet Society* (Berkeley and Los Angeles, 1978), pp. 82–94; Farnsworth, *Aleksandra Kollontai*, pp. 336–67.

45 On the *Eseninshchina*, see Boris Thomson, *The Premature Revolution: Russian Literature and Society, 1917–1946* (London, 1972), pp. 134–5, and Constantin Ponomaroff, *Sergey Esenin* (Boston, 1978), pp. 154–61. On the rape case, which occurred in September 1926, and its wider significance, see Eric Naiman, "The Case of Chubarov Alley: Collective Rape, Utopian Desire and the Mentality of NEP," *Russian History/Histoire russe*, vol. 17 (1990), pp. 1–30, quotations from p. 17.

46 Carr, *Socialism in One Country*, vol. 1, pp. 47–8.

47 Massell, *The Surrogate Proletariat*, pp. 226–45.

48 *Ibid.*, pp. 93-125, 213–321; quotation on p. 355.

49 Quotations are from documents in Boleslaw Szczesniak, ed., *The Russian Revolution and Religion* (Notre Dame, IN, 1959), pp. 34–7, 49; see also John Shelton Curtiss, *The Russian Church and the Soviet State, 1917–1950* (Boston, 1953), chs. 1-4.

50 Robert Conquest, *Religion in the USSR* (New York, 1968), pp. 13-16; Nicholas S. Timasheff, *Religion in Soviet Russia, 1917–1942* (New York, 1942), pp. 15–30; Curtiss, *The Russian Church*, ch. 5.

51 Szczesniak, ed., *The Russian Revolution and Religion*, pp. 67–8. On the confiscation as "pretext for persecution," see Dimitry V. Pospielovsky, *A History of Marxist–Leninist Atheism and Soviet Anti-Religious Practices* (2 vols., New York, 1987–8), vol. 1, pp. 47–56 and his *The Russian Church under the Soviet Regime 1917–1982* (2 vols., Crestwood, NY, 1984), vol. 1, 93–9; for a more balanced appraisal, see Curtiss, *The Russian Church*, ch. 6.

52 Gregory L. Freeze, *The Parish Clergy in Nineteenth Century Russia* (Princeton, 1983). Freeze defines the liberal reformist agenda as follows: "to ease their lot, to revitalize the Church, and to shift power from bishops to priests and laymen" (p. 470), and the Living Church as the "apotheosis of clerical liberalism" (p. 472). For the smena vekh analogy, see Carr, *Socialism in One Country*, vol. 1, p. 52; for background to the "Ukrainian schisms," see Bohdan R. Bociurkiw, "The Church and the Ukrainian Revolution: The Central Rada Period," in Taras Hunczak, ed., *The Ukraine, 1917–1921: A Study in Revolution* (Cambridge, MA, 1977), pp. 220–46; also, Pospielovsky, *The Russian Church*, pp. 73–9.

53 Pospielovsky, *The Russian Church*, p. 61. See also Timasheff, *Religion in Soviet Russia*, p. 32: "a bold government may prevent people from going to church, but no government can compel them to attend a church which they dislike." On the *modus vivendi*, see Curtiss, *The Russian Church*, pp. 174, 190 and Carr, *Socialism in One Country*, vol. 1, pp. 54-5. On the divisions among the Renovationists, A. A. Shishkin, *Sushchnost' i kriticheskaia otsenka*

'*Obnovlencheskogo*' *raskola russkoi pravoslavnoi tserkvi* (Kazan, 1970) and Anatolii Levitin and Vadim Shavrov, *Ocherki po istorii russkoi tserkovnoi smuty* (3 vols., Kusnacht, Switzerland, 1977). Tikhon died in 1925 and was eventually succeeded as *locum tenens* by Sergei, the Metropolitan of Nizhni Novgorod.

54 Curtiss, *The Russian Church*, pp. 85–7, 196–200; on God-building, which sought to create a "proletarian deity," and had strong affinities to Proletkult, see Jutta Scherrer, "Culture prolétarienne et religion socialiste entre deux revolutions: les Bolscheviks de gauche," *Europa*, vol. 2 (1979), pp. 67–90 and Christopher Read, *Religion, Revolution and the Russian Intelligentsia, 1900–1912* (London, 1979), pp. 77–92; on the Red Army, G. Struchkov, "Antireligioznaia rabota v Krasnoi armii," in *Voinstvuiushchee bezbozhie v SSSR za 15 let. Sbornik* (Moscow, 1932), pp. 412–26.

55 *KPSS v rezoliutsiiakh i resheniiakh*, vol. 3, pp. 114–16; on the importance of the resolution see N. A. Krylov, "Iz istorii propagandy ateizma v SSSR (1923–1925 gg.), *Voprosy istorii religii i ateizma*, no. 8 (1960), pp. 166–80.

56 Krylov, "Iz istorii propagandy," pp. 183–4; A. I. Mazaev, *Prazdnik kak sotsial'no-khudozhestvennoe iavlenie* (Moscow, 1978), pp. 356–69; Stites, *Revolutionary Dreams*, p. 109. Stites claims that 417 cities witnessed such scenes. On the Evsektsiia's activities, see Zvi Gitelman, "The Communist Party and Soviet Jewry: The Early Years," in Richard Marshall, Jr., ed., *Aspects of Religion in the Soviet Union, 1917–1967* (Chicago, 1971), pp. 321–40; Levin, *Jews in the Soviet Union*, vol. 1, pp. 68ff.

57 Kenez, *Birth of the Propaganda State*, pp. 184–5; Stites, *Revolutionary Dreams*, pp. 107–8; Krylov, "Iz istorii propagandy," pp. 181-2.

58 *Bezbozhnik u stanka*, no. 7 (1923), no. 9–10 (1923). For other examples which "were known to have sent peasants into a frenzy of rage," see Stites, *Revolutionary Dreams*, p. 106. On the dispute between the two approaches see Joan Delaney, "The Origins of Soviet Antireligious Organizations," in Marshall Jr., ed., *Aspects of Religion in the Soviet Union*, pp. 103–30. The association of godlessness with health and religion with disease was a prominent feature of anti-religious propaganda. See the editorial in *Trud*, 18 September 1927 by Iaroslavskii referring to an icon on Barricade Street in Moscow which is kissed by "thousands" of passers-by – "the sick, syphilitic, consumptive and healthy."

59 For summaries, see V. A. Kozlov, *Kul'turnaia revoliutsiia i krest'ianstvo, 1921–1927* (Moscow, 1983), pp. 138–42. "Backward women" was a standard trope in the discourse of anti-religious activists.

60 Stites, *Revolutionary Dreams*, p. 122.

61 Kozlov, *Kul'turnaia revoliutsiia*, p. 142.

62 Leon Trotsky, *Problems of Everyday Life* (New York, 1973), pp. 33–5; *Pravda*, 22 December 1928.

63 *Trud*, 18 April 1928; Krylov, *Kul'turnaia revoliutsiia*, p. 187; Massell, *The Surrogate Proletariat*, pp. 270–3. Massell lists twelve different "components" of such a strategy.

64 A. I. Klibanov, *Religioznoe sektantstvo i sovremennost'* (Moscow, 1969), pp. 238–46; *KPSS v rezoliutsiiakh*, vol. 3, p. 249; *Trud*, 4, 5 March and 8, 14 April 1928.

65 Stites, *Revolutionary Dreams*, pp. 109–14; Christel Lane, *The Rites of Rulers, Ritual in Industrial Society – the Soviet Case* (Cambridge, 1981), esp. pp. 153–73, 200–1, 232.

66 Nina Tumarkin, *Lenin Lives! The Lenin Cult in Soviet Russia* (Cambridge, MA, and London, 1983), pp. 82–5. She notes the "syncretism of ideology and mysticism that came to characterize the later cult of Lenin."

67 *Ibid.*, pp. 134–206; Isaac Deutscher, *Stalin, a Political Biography*, rev. ed. (Harmondsworth, 1966), pp. 267–73.

68 Massell, *The Surrogate Proletariat*, p. 270.

69 Stites, *Revolutionary Dreams*, p. 120.

70 von Hagen, *Soldiers in the Proletarian Dictatorship*, pp. 331–8.

71 Carr, *Socialism in One Country*, vol. 1, p. 373.

72 Keith Smith, "The Closure of the Soviet Industrialisation Debate," in Keith Smith, ed., *Soviet Industrialisation and Soviet Maturity* (London and New York, 1986), p. 24.

73 V. A. Kozlov, in "The Soviet Union in the 1920s, A Roundtable," p. 37.

74 Carr, *Socialism in One Country*, vol. 1, p. 521.

75 *Ibid.*, p. 363.

76 Quoted in Robert Bideleux, *Communism and Development* (London and New York, 1985), p. 100; on Sokolnikov, see V. L. Genis, "Grigorii Iakovlevich Sokol'nikov," *Voprosy istorii*, no. 12 (1988), pp. 59–86; and Samuel A. Oppenheim, "Between Right and Left: G. Ia. Sokolnikov and the Development of the Soviet State," *Slavic Review*, vol. 48 (1989), pp. 593–613.

77 E. A. Preobrazhenskii, *The Crisis of Soviet Industrialization. Selected Essays*, Donald Filtzer, trans. and ed. (White Plains, NY, 1979), pt. 2; Bideleux, *Communism and Development*, pp. 83–5, 102–15; Richard Day, *Leon Trotsky and the Politics of Economic Isolation* (Cambridge, 1973), pp. 122–47; Erlich, *The Soviet Industrialization Debate*, pp. 31–59; Alec Nove, "New Light on Trotskii's Economic Views," *Slavic Review*, vol. 40 (1981), pp. 84–97.

78 Quoted in Day, *Leon Trotsky and the Politics*, p. 119.

79 Quotations from Cohen, *Bukharin and the Bolshevik Revolution*, pp. 174, 177. Alec Nove argues that Trotsky anticipated this position already in 1923. See Nove, "O sud'bakh NEPa," *Voprosy istorii*, no. 8 (1989), p. 173.

80 The number of people employed in small-scale (*melkaia*) industry was reported to be 2.7 million in 1925 and 4.5 million (3.6 million living in the countryside) in 1928–9. See Carr and Davies, *Foundations*, vol. 1, pp. 416–27; Pethybridge, *The Social Prelude to Stalinism*, pp. 229–35.

81 Nove, *An Economic History of the USSR*, p. 134.

82 Ilmari Susiluoto, *The Origins and Development of Systems Thinking in the Soviet Union* (Helsinki, 1982), esp. pt. 1; A. A. Belykh, "A. A. Bogdanov's Theory of Equilibrium and the Economic Discussions of the 1920s," *Soviet*

Studies, vol. 42 (1990), pp. 572–82; V. A. Bazarov, "On the Methodology of Perspective Plan Formation," originally published in *Planovoe khoziaistvo* (1926) and translated and republished in Nicholas Spulber, ed., *Foundations of Soviet Strategy for Economic Growth: Selected Soviet Essays, 1924–30* (Bloomington, 1964), pp. 365–77.

83 Carr, *Socialism in One Country*, vol. 1, pp. 533–9.

84 *XIV S"ezd Vsesoiuznoi Kommunisticheskoi Partii (B)* (Moscow–Leningrad, 1926), pp. 27–33, 958–9; Carr, *Socialism in One Country*, vol. 2, p. 59.

85 *XIV S"ezd*, pp. 274–5 (Kamenev), 344 (Rudzutak), 628 (Kuibyshev), 504–8 (Stalin). Later editions of Stalin's speech eliminate mention of Rykov, Tomskii and Bukharin as well as the entire passage about the latter's "blood." Sokolnikov also considered it a conflict of interest to have the General Secretary sit in the Politburo. See his speech on pp. 332–6.

86 Carr, *Socialism in One Country*, vol. 1, p. 544; on Dneprostroi, see Anne Rassweiler, *The Generation of Power. The History of Dneprostroi* (Oxford, 1988), pp. 40–50; quotation on p. 50.

87 Figures from Carr and Davies, *Foundations*, vol. 1, pp. 298–300, 318. Gosplan's revised planned expenditure was reduced to 800 million.

88 Carr and Davies, *Foundations*, vol. 1, p. 298; Alec Nove, *An Economic History of the USSR*, p. 144.

89 Carr and Davies, *Foundations*, vol. 1, p. 309.

90 Quoted in *ibid.*, p. 841.

91 *Ibid.*, pp. 376–86.

92 For details, see Sheila Fitzpatrick, "Ordzhonikidze's Takeover of Vesenkha: A Case Study in Soviet Bureaucratic Politics," *Soviet Studies*, vol. 37 (1985), esp. pp. 155–60; E. A. Rees, *State Control in Soviet Russia* (New York, 1987), pp. 149–54, 175–80.

93 Carr and Davies, *Foundations*, vol. 1, pp. 997, 1000, 1023, 1016.

94 *Ibid.*, pp. 308–11; *KPSS v rezoliutsiiakh*, vol. 4, p. 72.

95 On the war scare, see Reiman, *The Birth of Stalinism*, pp. 11–18; Carr and Davies, *Foundations*, vol. 1, pp. 317–24, quotation from p. 317.

96 Cf. R. W. Davies, *The Industrialisation of Soviet Russia 3: The Soviet Economy in Turmoil, 1929–1930* (London, 1989), pp. 47–70; Mark Harrison, "Why Did NEP Fail?," in Keith Smith, ed., *Soviet Industrialisation and Soviet Maturity*, pp. 14–21; Nove, *An Economic History of the USSR*, pp. 139–41. On pricing policy, see also Stephan Merl, *Der Agrarmarkt und die Neue Okonomische Politik* (Munich, 1981), pp. 86–122.

97 Nove, "O Sud'bakh NEPa," pp. 173–4. Nove modestly attributes the explanation to the Soviet economist, A. L. Vainshtein. Quotation from Carr and Davies, *Foundations*, vol. 1, p. 670.

98 On the measures see R. W. Davies, *The Soviet Budgetary System* (London, 1958), pp. 111-13; Carr and Davies, *Foundations*, vol. 1, pp. 794–7; Nove, *An Economic History of the USSR*, pp. 137–8; and Ball, *Russia's Last Capitalists*, pp. 56–8. For the Central Committee's resolution, *KPSS v rezoliutsiiakh*, vol. 4, p. 147. Emphasis in original.

99 Carr and Davies, *Foundations*, vol. 1, p. 730.

100 Speech to Leningrad party activists, 26 October 1927, in Bukharin, *Izbrannye proizvedeniia*, pp. 339–40; Cohen, *Bukharin and the Bolshevic Revolution*, pp. 247, 251.

101 Carr and Davies, *Foundations*, vol. 1, p. 36; for the entire resolutions, see *KPSS v rezoliutsiiakh*, vol. 4, pp. 210–49.

102 Lewin, *Russian Peasants*, pp. 198–204; *KPSS v rezoliutsiiakh*, vol. 4, pp. 278–88, 295-302, 305–8.

103 Carr, *Socialism in One Country*, vol. 1, p. 413.

104 Chase, *Workers, Society, and the Soviet State*, pp. 219–20, 239; for slightly lower figures based on the "per cent of hours worked in large-scale industry . . . paid at piece-rates," see Carr, *Socialism in One Country*, vol. 1, pp. 418–19. See also Lewis H. Siegelbaum, "Soviet Norm Determination in Theory and Practice, 1917–1941," *Soviet Studies*, vol. 36 (1984), p. 48; and John Hatch, "The 'Lenin Levy' and the Social Origins of Stalinism: Workers and the Communist Party in Moscow, 1921–1928," *Slavic Review*, vol. 48 (1989), p. 565.

105 TsK VPK(b), *Sotsial'nyi i natsional'nyi sostav VKP(b)*, pp. 22, 31; Rigby, *Communist Party Membership in the USSR*, pp. 121–5, 166–7. The discrepancy between the two sets of figures is due to those who left the party or were expelled.

106 Hatch, "The 'Lenin Levy,'" pp. 558–65; cf. Linda Cook, "Political Mobilization Strategies in the Stalinist Revolution from Above" (Columbia University Ph.D. dissertation, 1985), pp. 35–62.

107 Hatch, "The 'Lenin Levy,'" pp. 565–6; Chase, *Workers, Society, and the Soviet State*, p. 263.

108 Chase, *Workers, Society, and the Soviet State*, pp. 264–71; E. B. Genkina, "Vozniknovenie proizvodstvennykh soveshchanii v gody vosstanovitel'nogo perioda (1921–1926 gg.)," *Istoriia SSSR*, no. 3 (1958), pp. 63–88; N. B. Lebedeva and O. I. Shkaratan, *Ocherki istorii sotsialisticheskogo sorevnovaniia* (Leningrad, 1966), pp. 55-65; I. P. Ostapenko, *Uchastie rabochego klassa SSSR v upravlenii proizvodstvom* (Moscow, 1964), pp. 9–55.

109 Sheila Fitzpatrick, "Social Origins of the 'New Class,'" paper presented to AAASS Conference, Monterey, September 1981, p. 10; *Sotsial'nyi sostav*, p. 45; Fitzpatrick, *Education and Social Mobility in the Soviet Union, 1921–1934*, pp. 97–102.

110 Hatch, "The 'Lenin Levy,'" pp. 574–5; Cook, "Political Mobilization Strategies," pp. 65–72.

111 Stalin, *Sochineniia*, vol. 10, p. 175; *XIV s"ezd vsesoiuznoi kommunisticheskoi partii (B)*, p. 499.

112 Carr, *Socialism in One Country*, vol. 1, p. 124; Cook, "Political Mobilization Strategies," pp. 66–7.

113 Siegelbaum, "Soviet Norm Determination," p. 48, and "Masters of the Shopfloor: The Role of Foremen in Soviet Industrialization," paper for National Seminar on Russian Social History in the Twentieth Century: Industrialization and Change in Soviet Society, 1928–1941, at University of Michigan, Ann Arbor, April 1988; in the textile industry, the propitiation of

overseers was known as *magarych*. See Ward, *Russia's Cotton Workers*, pp. 93–100.

114 Quoted in A. V. Smetanin, "Metodologicheskie i organizatsionnye osnovy v rabote TsITa," in *TsIT i ego metody NOT* (Moscow, 1970), p. 25.

115 Ward, *Russia's Cotton Workers*, pp. 141–75; John Hatch, "Labor and Politics in NEP Russia: Workers, Trade Unions and the Communist Party in Moscow, 1921–1926," (Ph.D. dissertation, University of California, Irvine, 1985), ch. 2.

116 Ward, *Russia's Cotton Workers*, pp. 176–98; Siegelbaum, "Soviet Norm Determination," p. 50. On accidents, see Siegelbaum, "Industrial Accidents and Their Prevention in the Interwar Period," in William McCagg and Lewis Siegelbaum, eds., *The Disabled in the Soviet Union: Past and Present, Theory and Practice* (Pittsburgh, 1989), pp. 85–117.

117 Quotation from Hatch, "The 'Lenin Levy,'" p. 567.

118 Chase, *Workers, Society, and the Soviet State*, pp. 274–8; John Hatch, "The Politics of Industrial Efficiency During NEP: the 1926 'Rezhim ekonomii' Campaign in Moscow," paper presented at IV World Congress for Soviet and East European Studies, Harrogate, England, 21–26 July 1990; for a more humorous and fictional rendition of the economization drive, see Mikhail Zoshchenko, "The Economy Campaign," in *Scenes from the Bathhouse and Other Stories of Communist Russia* (Ann Arbor, 1961), pp. 35–6.

119 Bukharin quoted in A. K. Gastev, *Normirovanie i organizatsiia truda* (Leningrad, 1929), p. 113; also N. Bukharin, "O starinnykh traditsiiakh i sovremennom kul'turnom stroitel'stve," *Revoliutsiia i Kul'tura*, no. 1 (1927), pp. 17–22; Daniel Orlovsky, "Anti-Bureaucratic Campaigns of the 1920s," unpublished paper, pp. 17–24; Rees, *State Control in Soviet Russia*, pp. 144–55.

120 Carr and Davies, *Foundations*, vol. 1, pp. 528–34; Ward, *Russia's Cotton Workers*, pp. 204–9.

121 Ward, *Russia's Cotton Workers*, pp. 214–29.

122 Lewin, *The Making of the Soviet System*, p. 126.

5 Dangers and opportunities

1 R. W. Davies, *The Industrialisation of Soviet Russia 1: The Socialist Offensive. The Collectivisation of Soviet Agriculture, 1929–1930* (Cambridge, MA, 1980), p. 41.

2 Carr, *Foundations of a Planned Economy*, vol. 2, pp. 26–42; Reiman, *The Birth of Stalinism*, pp. 19–32.

3 Isaac Deutscher, *The Prophet Unarmed: Trotsky, 1921–1929* (New York, 1963), pp. 356–89; *Piatnadtsatyi s"ezd VKP (b), dekabr' 1927 goda, stenograficheskii otchet* (2 vols., Moscow, 1961), vol. 1, pp. 207–14, 279–85.

4 Reiman, *The Birth of Stalinism*, pp. 35–6, 46–50, 124–8, 133–4; also Robert H. McNeal, *Stalin. Man and Ruler* (New York, 1988), pp. 105–6.

5 V. Bogushevskii, "Kanun piatiletki," in M. Gor'kii, L. Averbakh et al., eds., *God XVIII. Al'manakh vosmoi* (Moscow, 1935), p. 461; Moshe Lewin, "State,

Society and Ideology during the First Five-Year Plan," in *Cultural Revolution in Russia*, p. 41; also Cook, "Political Mobilization Strategies," pp. 278–80.

6 Grosskopf, *L'Alliance ouvrière*, pp. 327–35; Jerzy F. Karcz, *The Economics of Communist Agriculture. Selected Papers* (Bloomington, 1979), p. 45.

7 Karcz, *Economics of Communist Agriculture*, p. 51.

8 Carr and Davies, *Foundations*, vol. 1, pp. 47–9; Davies, *Industrialisation of Soviet Russia 1*, pp. 39–40. Alec Nove boldly states that "The grain crisis of the winter of 1927–28 was due much more to price relationships . . . than to any other single cause in the short run." See Alec Nove, "Was Stalin Really Necessary? A Debate on Collectivisation," *Problems of Communism*, vol. 25 (1976), p. 55.

9 Carr and Davies, *Foundations*, vol. 1, pp. 47–8; Karcz, *Economics of Communist Agriculture*, p. 49.

10 Karcz, *Economics of Communist Agriculture*, p. 51.

11 TsK VKP(b), *Sotsial'nyi i natsional'nyi sostav VKP(b)*, pp. 18, 80, 87; Daniel Thorniley, *The Rise and Fall of the Soviet Rural Communist Party, 1927–39* (New York, 1988), pp. 11-20.

12 Stalin, *Sochineniia*, vol. 11, p. 19; Daniel Brower, "The Smolensk Scandal at the End of NEP," *Slavic Review*, vol. 45 (1986), pp. 689–706; Stalin quoted in Rigby, *Communist Party Membership*, p. 177.

13 J. R. Hughes, "The Irkutsk Affair: Stalin, Siberian Politics and the End of NEP," *Soviet Studies*, vol. 41 (1989), pp. 228–53, quotation on p. 247.

14 Merle Fainsod, *Smolensk under Soviet Rule* (New York, 1958), pp. 48–52; Carr, *Foundations*, vol. 2, pp. 144–8; Brower, "The Smolensk Scandal," pp. 695–8.

15 Cohen, *Bukharin and the Bolshevik Revolution*, p. 283; Stalin, *Sochineniia*, vol. 11, p. 81; Lewin, *The Making of the Soviet System*, pp. 98–9, 320.

16 Lewin, *The Making of the Soviet System*, p. 98; and *Russian Peasants and Soviet Power*, pp. 107–16; Carr, *Socialism in One Country*, vol. 1, pp. 234–6; Carr and Davies, *Foundations*, vol. 1, pp. 158–66, 174.

17 Lewin, *Russian Peasants and Soviet Power*, pp. 117–19, 205–6; Carr and Davies, *Foundations*, vol. 1, pp. 160, 172–7, and for figures on the three main types of kolkhozy, p. 1002.

18 Lewin, *Russian Peasants and Soviet Power*, pp. 296–302; *Ot XV s"ezda do XVI konferentsii VKP(b). Sbornik rezoliutsii i postanovlenii* (Moscow–Leningrad, 1929), pp. 111–24, 146–52.

19 Lewin, *Russian Peasants and Soviet Power*, pp. 267–93, 391; and *The Making of the Soviet System*, pp. 100–7.

20 Carr and Davies, *Foundations*, vol. 1, pp. 67, 85, 193, 208, 211, 214, 217, 269.

21 *Ibid.*, pp. 73, 103, 209.

22 Lewin, *Russian Peasants and Soviet Power*, pp. 241, 284, 59–60. For the reference to 1919 and 1920, see Carr and Davies, *Foundations*, vol. 1, p. 77.

23 Lewin, *Russian Peasants and Soviet Power*, pp. 420–1, 285, 391, 491-2.

24 Carr and Davies, *Foundations*, vol. 1, pp. 90–3; also, Dorothy Atkinson, *The*

End of the Russian Land Commune, 1905–1930, pp. 323–6; Davies, *Industrial-isation of Soviet Russia*, 1, pp. 56–60.

25 For the article, see N. I. Bukharin, *Izbrannye proizvedeniia*, pp. 391–418; for summary and analysis, Cohen, *Bukharin and the Bolshevik Revolution*, pp. 295–6.

26 Lewin, *Russian Peasants and Soviet Power*, pp. 385–95; Carr and Davies, *Foundations*, vol. 1, pp. 106-11.

27 For a recent reprise of these arguments by two Soviet historians, see G. A. Bordiugov and V. A. Kozlov, "Povorot 1929 goda i al'ternativa Bukharina," *Voprosy istorii KPSS*, no. 8 (1988), pp. 22–8.

28 GADO, f. 1, op. 1, d. 710, ll. 1–5; d. 773, ll. 56–71; *Politicheskii i trudovoi pod"em rabochego klassa SSSR* (Moscow, 1960), pp. 416–20, 423–37. On the 25,000ers, see Lynne Viola, *The Best Sons of the Fatherland. Workers in the Vanguard of Soviet Collectivization* (New York, 1987). Strangely, Viola has nothing to say about this early 1929 mobilization.

29 Carr and Davies, *Foundations*, vol. 1, p. 285; Lewin, *Russian Peasants and Soviet Power*, pp. 352-8; also V. P. Danilov, "Ispol'zovanie perekhodnykh form khoziaistva v protsesse sotsialisticheskogo preobrazovaniia ekonomiki," in *Ekonomicheskaia politika Sovetskogo gosudarstva v perekhodnyi period ot kapitalizma k sotsializmu* (Moscow, 1986), pp. 143–7.

30 See *Vlast' sovetov za desiat' let, 1917–1927* (Leningrad, 1927); Solomon M. Schwarz, *Labor in the Soviet Union* (New York, 1952), pp. 130–2; Carr and Davies, *Foundations*, vol. 1, pp. 545, 605–10.

31 Cohen, *Bukharin and the Bolshevik Revolution*, p. 275.

32 Carr and Davies, *Foundations*, vol. 1, pp. 457, 612–14; Rogachevskaia, *Likvidatsiia bezrabotitsy v SSSR*, pp. 92, 147; Siegelbaum, "Industrial Accidents and Their Prevention in the Interwar Period," in *The Disabled in the Soviet Union*, p. 94. Statistics on unemployment and accidents vary widely depending on the source.

33 Carr and Davies, *Foundations*, vol. 1, p. 454; V. P. Danilov, "Krest'ianskii otkhod na promysly v 1920-kh godakh," *Istoricheskie zapiski*, no. 94 (1974), pp. 80, 109; A. I. Vdovin and V. Z. Drobizhev, *Rost rabochego klassa SSSR, 1917–1940 gg.* (Moscow, 1976), pp. 119-21.

34 See Michael J. Piore, *Birds of Passage, Migrant Labor and Industrial Societies* (Cambridge, 1979).

35 Vdovin and Drobizhev, *Rost rabochego klassa*, pp. 130–3; Carr and Davies, *Foundations*, I, pp. 500–13. Statistics on the number of employees in state institutions mask a high rate of turnover resulting from the purge of 1929. See Daniel Orlovsky, "Anti-Bureaucratic Campaigns of the 1920's," unpublished paper, pp. 24–7.

36 *Trud v SSSR* (Moscow, 1932), p. 61; Fitzpatrick, *Education and Social Mobility*, pp. 181–205.

37 Davies, *The Industrialisation of Soviet Russia*, 3, p. 524; Rassweiler, *The Generation of Power*, pp. 96–7, 140–1; Carr and Davies, *Foundations*, vol. 1, p. 496.

38 Hiroaki Kuromiya, *Stalin's Industrial Revolution: Politics and Workers, 1928–*

1932 (Cambridge, 1988), pp. 88–100 and his "The Crisis of Proletarian Identity in the Soviet Factory, 1928–1929," *Slavic Review*, vol. 44 (1985), pp. 280–97. Quotations from pp. 282, 285, 286. Kuromiya conflates these two discourses.

39 Kuromiya, "The Crisis of Proletarian Identity," p. 286; on Stakhanov and the movement named after him, see Lewis Siegelbaum, *Stakhanovism and the Politics of Productivity in the USSR, 1935–1941* (Cambridge, 1988).

40 Kuromiya, "The Crisis of Proletarian Identity," p. 295.

41 Yuri Olesha, *Envy and Other Works*, trans. A. MacAndrew (New York, 1967), p. 49. The novel first appeared in 1927.

42 See, for example, A. L. Oprishchenko, *Istoriografiia sotsialisticheskogo sorevnovaniia rabochego klassa SSSR* (Khar'kov, 1975), pp. 62–7; I. N. Mikhailovskii, *Komsomol' ukrainy v bor'be za postroenie sotsializma v SSSR (1925–1937 gg.)* (L'vov, 1966), p. 82.

43 Ward, *Russia's Cotton Workers*, pp. 244–8. Cf. N. B. Lebedeva and O. I. Shkaratan, *Ocherki istorii sotsialisticheskogo sorevnovaniia* (Leningrad, 1966), pp. 79–81; and the memoir accounts of E. G. Kozhevnikova in *Neizvedannymi putiami. Vospominaniia uchastnikov sotsialisticheskogo stroitel'stva* (Leningrad, 1967), pp. 127–35, and M. Dubrov, *Pervaia udarnaia* (Leningrad, 1960).

44 I. E. Vorozheikin, *Letopis' trudovogo geroizma* (Moscow, 1979), pp. 50-3; L. S. Rogachevskaia, *Sotsialisticheskoe sorevnovanie v SSSR, istoricheskie ocherki 1917–1970 gg.* (Moscow, 1977), pp. 78–82, 92–4.

45 *Ratsionalizatsiia proizvodstva*, no. 12 (1929), pp. 1, 12; *Proizvodstvennyi zhurnal*, no. 14 (1929), p. 8; Lewis Siegelbaum, "Socialist Competition and Socialist Construction in the USSR – The Experience of the First Five-Year Plan," *Thesis Eleven*, no. 4 (1982), pp. 48–67; Davies, *The Industrialisation of Soviet Russia*, 3, p. 261; and Kuromiya, *Stalin's Industrial Revolution*, pp. 128–35 (for "Antichrist" reference, see p. 129).

46 Stalin, *Sochineniia*, vol. 12, pp. 115–16.

47 Kuromiya, *Stalin's Industrial Revolution*, p. 123; and "Edinonachalie and the Soviet Industrial Manager, 1928–1937," *Soviet Studies*, vol. 36 (1984), pp. 185-204; Davies, *The Industrialisation of Soviet Russia*, 3, pp. 272–4.

48 Kuromiya, *Stalin's Industrial Revolution*, pp. 40–7; Cohen, *Bukharin and the Bolshevik Revolution*, pp. 300–1; I. S. Kulikova and B. Ia. Khazanov, "Mikhail Pavlovich Tomskii," *Voprosy istorii*, no. 8 (1988), pp. 80–2.

49 Siegelbaum, "Socialist Competition and Socialist Construction," pp. 54–7; *Trud v SSSR* (1932), pp. 89–92.

50 William Chase and Lewis Siegelbaum, "Worktime and Industrialization in the U.S.S.R., 1917–1941," in Gary Cross, ed., *Worktime and Industrialization. An International History* (Philadelphia, 1988), pp. 200-3.

51 Ward, *Russia's Cotton Workers*, pp. 256–9.

52 Chase and Siegelbaum, "Worktime and Industrialization," pp. 204-5.

53 *Pravda*, 20 January 1929.

54 GADO, f. 1, op, 1, d. 590-e, ll. 6, 13.

55 Quotation from Reiman, *The Birth of Stalinism*, p. 58; Bailes, *Technology and Society*, pp. 74-5.

56 Bailes, *Technology and Society*, pp. 75–94; Carr, *Foundations*, vol. 2, pp. 579–88.

57 Bailes, *Technology and Society*, pp. 95-140; Lampert, *The Technical Intelligentsia and the Soviet State*, pp. 46-55.

58 Catherine Merridale, "Moscow Politics and the Rise of Stalin: The Communist Party in the Capital, 1925–1932," unpublished manuscript, pp. 388–9.

59 David Joravsky, "The Construction of the Stalinist Psyche," in *Cultural Revolution in Russia, 1928–1931*, p. 110.

60 Stephen Kern, *The Culture of Time and Space, 1880–1918* (Cambridge, MA, 1983), p. 307.

61 Mark Adams, "The Soviet Nature-Nurture Debate," in Loren Graham, ed., *Science and the Soviet Social Order* (Cambridge, MA, 1990), p. 97. On Vernadsky, see Kendal E. Bailes, *Science and Russian Culture in the Age of Revolutions: V. I. Vernadsky and His Scientific School, 1863–1945* (Bloomington, 1990); on Bakhtin, see Michael Holquist and Katerina Clark, *Mikhail Bakhtin* (Cambridge, MA, 1984).

62 Susan Gross Solomon, "David and Goliath in Soviet Public Health: The Rivalry of Social Hygienists and Psychiatrists for Authority over the *Bytovoi* Alcoholic," *Soviet Studies*, vol. 41 (1989), pp. 254–75; Lewis H. Siegelbaum, "'Okhrana Truda': Industrial Hygiene, Psychotechnics and Industrialization in the USSR, 1917–41," in Susan G. Solomon and John F. Hutchinson, eds., *Health and Society in Revolutionary Russia* (Bloomington, 1990), pp. 224–45.

63 David Joravsky, *Soviet Marxism and Natural Science, 1917–1932* (New York, 1961), pp. 279–80, 299; Joravsky, "Cultural Revolution and the Fortress Mentality," in Gleason et al., *Bolshevik Culture*, p. 108. For an alternative perspective which gives more weight to Marxism, see Loren Graham, *Science and Philosophy in the Soviet Union* (New York, 1972).

64 Joravsky, "Cultural Revolution and the Fortress Mentality," pp. 101, 109.

65 Sheila Fitzpatrick, "Cultural Revolution as Class War," in *Cultural Revolution in Russia, 1928–1931*, pp. 8–40. Fitzpatrick subsequently modified her position in her "New Perspectives on Stalinism," *Russian Review*, vol. 45 (1986), pp. 357–74.

66 Susan Solomon, "Rural Scholars and the Cultural Revolution," in *Cultural Revolution in Russia*, p. 153.

67 Robert Lewis, "Science, Nonscience, and the Cultural Revolution," *Slavic Review*, vol. 45 (1986), pp. 286–92; essays by George Enteen, Robert Sharlet and Gail Lapidus in *Cultural Revolution in Russia*.

68 David Joravsky, "The Stalinist Mentality and the Higher Learning," *Slavic Review*, vol. 42 (1983), pp. 586–7.

69 Fitzpatrick, "New Perspectives on Stalinism," p. 369.

70 Mace, *Communism and the Dilemmas of National Liberation*, pp. 267–75; Yaroslav Bilinsky, "Mykola Skypnyk and Petro Shelest: An Essay on the

Persistence and Limits of Ukrainian National Communism," in Jeremy R. Azrael, ed., *Soviet Nationality Policies and Practices* (New York, 1978), pp. 105–43.
71 Bailes, *Technology and Society*, p. 150; Loren Graham, *The Soviet Academy of Sciences and the Communist Party, 1927–1932* (Princeton, 1967), pp. 80–153.
72 Quoted in Graham, *The Soviet Academy*, p. 186.
73 Moshe Lewin, "Society, State, and Ideology during the First Five-Year Plan," in *Cultural Revolution in Russia*, pp. 70–3.

Epilogue and conclusion

1 Fitzpatrick, *Education and Social Mobility in the Soviet Union*, p. 254; and *The Russian Revolution, 1917–1932*, pp. 1–9, 135–61.
2 Allan Wildman in *Slavic Review*, vol. 42 (1984), pp. 309–11.

Select bibliography

Archives

Gosudarstvennyi Arkhiv Donetskoi Oblasti (GADO)
    f. R-1 – All-Russian Union of Metalworkers, Donetsk Province
    f. R-2607 – All-Russian Union of Mineworkers, Donetsk Province
Tsentral'nyi Gosudarstvennyi Arkhiv Oktiabr'skoi Revoliutsii (TsGAOR)
    f. 5469 – All-Russian Central Committee of Union of Mineworkers

Unpublished works

Ashin, Paul, "Workers' Wages and the NEP in Moscow, 1921-28," IV World Congress on the Soviet Union and Eastern Europe, Harrogate, July 1990.

Brovkin, Vladimir, "The Failed Legalization of Mensheviks and SRs in 1919," AAASS Conference, Chicago, November 1989.

Cook, Linda, "Political Mobilization Strategies in the Stalinist Revolution from Above," Ph.D. dissertation, Columbia University, 1985.

Fitzpatrick, Sheila, "The Bolshevik Invention of Class: Marxist Theory and the Making of 'Class Consciousness' in Soviet Society," manuscript.

"NEP Society and Culture: Introductory Remarks," NEP Society Conference, Bloomington, October 1986. Published as Sheila Fitzpatrick, Alexander Rabinowitch, and Richard Stites, eds., *Russia in the Era of NEP: Explorations in Soviet Society and Culture*, Bloomington, 1991.

"Social Origins of the 'New Class,'" AAASS Conference, Monterey, September 1981.

Hatch, John, "Bringing Economics Back In: Industrial Arbitration and Collective Bargaining During NEP," unpublished paper for Conference on "The Making of the Soviet Working Class," Michigan State University, 9–11 November 1990.

"Labor and Politics in NEP Russia: Workers, Trade Unions and the Communist Party in Moscow, 1921–1926," Ph.D. dissertation, University of California at Irvine, 1985.

"The Politics of Industrial Efficiency During NEP: The 1926 '*Rezhim ekonomii*' Campaign in Moscow," IV World Congress on the Soviet Union and Eastern Europe, Harrogate, July 1990.

Jones, Richard Huw, "Taylorism in Russia, 1910–1925," Ph.D. thesis, University of Birmingham, 1988.

Koenker, Diane, "Labor Relations in Socialist Russia: Printers, Their Union, and the Origins of Soviet Socialism, 1917–1921," Final Report to National Council for Soviet and East European Research, 1990.

Merridale, Catherine, "Moscow Politics and the Rise of Stalin: The Communist Party in the Capital, 1925–1932," manuscript.

Orlovsky, Daniel, "Anti-Bureaucratic Campaigns of the 1920s," manuscript.
"Class Boundaries: White Collar Workers, 1918–1924," Conference on "The Making of the Soviet Working Class," Michigan State University, 9–11, November 1990.

Patenaude, Bertrand Mark, "Bolshevism in Retreat: The Transition to the NEP, 1920-1922," Ph.D. dissertation, Stanford University, 1987.

Siegelbaum, Lewis, "Masters of the Shopfloor: The Role of Foremen in Soviet Industrialization," National Seminar on Russian Social History in the Twentieth Century: Industrialization and Change in Soviet Society 1928–1941," Ann Arbor, April 1988.

Viola, Lynne, "Rehabilitating the Soviet Kulak in Western Historiography," AAASS Conference, Washington, DC, October 1990.

von Hagen, Mark, "School of the Revolution: Bolsheviks and Peasants in the Red Army, 1918–1928," Ph.D. dissertation, Stanford University, 1985.

Wheatcroft, Stephen G., "Public Health in Russia during the War, Revolution and Famines, 1914–1923: Moscow, Petrograd and Saratov," International Conference on the History of Russian and Soviet Public Health, Toronto, May 1986.
"Famine and Factors Affecting Mortality in the USSR: The Demographic Crises of 1914–1922 and 1930–1933," CREES (University of Birmingham) Discussion Paper, SIPS nos. 20–1 (1981).

Wood, Elizabeth, "The Three Faces of Masha: The *Baba*, the Mother, and the Prostitute in Postrevolutionary Bolshevik Ideology," American Historical Association Conference, San Francisco, December 1989.

Contemporary newspapers and journals

Bezbozhnik u stanka
LEF
Pravda
Ratsionalizatsiia proizvodstva
Trud
Vserossiiskaia Kochegarka

Communist Party Congresses and Central Committee decisions

Desiatyi s"ezd RKP (b) (mart 1921 goda). Stenograficheskii otchet, Moscow, 1963.
Odinnadtsatyi s"ezd RKP (b). Stenograficheskii otchet, Moscow, 1961.
XIV S"ezd Vsesoiuznoi Kommunisticheskoi Partii (B), Moscow–Leningrad, 1926.

Piatnadtsatyi s"ezd VKP (b), dekabr' 1927 goda, stenograficheskii otchet, 2 vols., Moscow, 1961.

KPSS v rezoliutsiiakh i resheniiakh s"ezdov, konferentsii i plenumov TsK, 9th ed., 15 vols., Moscow, 1983–89.

Ot XV s"ezda do XVI konferentsii VKP (b). Sbornik rezoliutsii i postanovlenii, Moscow–Leningrad, 1929.

Books and articles

Adaskina, Natalia, "Constructivist Fabrics and Dress Design," *The Journal of Decorative and Propaganda Arts* (1987): 144–59.

Agursky, Mikhail, *Ideologiia natsional-bol'shevizma*, Paris, 1980.

Akademiia nauk SSSR, Institut istorii SSSR, *Problemy agrarnoi istorii sovetskogo obshchestva, materialy nauchnoi konferentsii 9–12 iiunia 1969 g*, Moscow, 1971.

Akademiia nauk Ukrainskoi SSR, Institut istorii, *Istoriia rabochikh donbassa*, 2 vols., Kiev, 1981.

Anderson, Perry, "Trotsky's Interpretation of Stalinism," *New Left Review* (1983), no. 139: 49–58.

Architectural Drawings of the Russian Avant-Garde, New York, 1990.

Ashin, Paul, "Wage Policy in the Transition to NEP," *Russian Review*, vol. 47 (1988): 292-307.

Atkinson, Dorothy, *The End of the Russian Land Commune, 1905–1930*, Stanford, 1983.

Atkinson, D., Dallin, A. and Lapidus, G., eds., *Women in Russia*, Sussex, 1978.

Avrich, Paul, *Kronstadt 1921*, Princeton, 1970.

Azrael, Jeremy R., ed., *Soviet Nationality Policies and Practices*, New York, 1978.

Baevskii, D. A., *Rabochii klass v pervye gody sovetskoi vlasti (1917–1921 gg.)*, Moscow, 1974.

Bailes, Kendall E., "Alexei Gastev and the Soviet Controversy over Taylorism, 1918–1924," *Soviet Studies*, vol. 29 (1977): 373–94.

Science and Russian Culture in the Age of Revolutions: V. I. Vernadsky and His Scientific School, 1863–1945, Bloomington, IN, 1990.

Technology and Society under Lenin and Stalin, Princeton, 1978.

Ball, Alan M., *Russia's Last Capitalists. The Nepmen, 1921–1929*, Berkeley and Los Angeles, 1987.

Bellis, Paul, *Marxism and the U.S.S.R., The Theory of Proletarian Dictatorship and the Marxist Analysis of Soviet Society*, Atlantic Highlands, NJ, 1979.

Belykh, A. A., "A. A. Bogdanov's Theory of Equilibrium and the Economic Discussions of the 1920s," *Soviet Studies*, vol. 42 (1990): 571–82.

Benet, Sula, ed. and trans., *The Village of Viriatino*, New York, 1970.

Bennigsen, A. and Lemercier-Quelquejay, Chantal, *Les Mouvements nationaux chez les Musulmans de Russie: 1. Le "Sultangalievisme" au Tatarstan*, Paris, 1960.

Bennigsen, A. and Wimbush, S. Enders, *Muslim National Communism in the Soviet Union*, Chicago, 1979.

Bettelheim, Charles, *Class Struggles in the USSR. First Period: 1917–1923*, trans. Robert Pearce, New York and London, 1976.

Bideleux, Robert, *Communism and Development*, London and New York, 1985.

Biggart, John, "Alexander Bogdanov and the Theory of a 'New Class,'" *Russian Review*, vol. 49 (1990): 265–82.

Bokarev, Iu. P., *Sotsialisticheskaia promyshlennost'i melkoe krest'ianskoe khoziaistvo v SSSR v 20–30 gody*, Moscow, 1989.

Bol'shakov, A. N., "The Soviet Countryside, 1917–1924," in R. E. F. Smith, ed., *The Russian Peasant in 1920 and 1984*, London, 1977.

Bordiugov, G. A. and Kozlov, V. A., "Povorot 1929 goda i al'ternativa Bukharina," *Voprosy istorii KPSS* (1988), no. 8: 22–8.

Bowen, James, *Soviet Education: Anton Makarenko and the Years of Experiment*, Madison, 1962.

Brovkin, Vladimir, *The Mensheviks after October: Socialist Opposition and the Rise of the Bolshevik Dictatorship*, Ithaca and London, 1987.

Brower, Daniel, "The Smolensk Scandal at the End of NEP," *Slavic Review*, vol. 45 (1986): 689–706.

Bukharin, N. I., *Economics of the Transformation Period*, New York, 1971.
  Izbrannye proizvodeniia, Moscow, 1988.
  Kritika ekonomicheskoi platformy oppozitsii, Moscow, 1926.

Bukharin, N. and Preobrazhensky, E., *The ABC of Communism*, Harmondsworth, 1969.

Buldakov, V. I. and Kabanov, V. V., "'Voennyi kommunism': ideologiia i obshchestvennoe razvitie," *Voprosy istorii* (1990), no. 3: 40-58.

Bunyan, James, ed., *The Origins of Forced Labor in the Soviet State, 1917–1921: Documents and Materials*, Baltimore, 1967.

Burbank, Jane, *Intelligentsia and Revolution*, Oxford, 1986.

Carr, E. H., *The Bolshevik Revolution, 1917–1923*, 3 vols., Harmondsworth, 1966.
  The Interregnum, 1923–1924, Harmondsworth, 1969.
  Socialism in One Country, 1924–1926, 3 vols., Harmondsworth, 1970.

Carr, E. H. and Davies, R. W., *Foundations of a Planned Economy, 1926–1929*, 2 vols., Harmondsworth, 1971-4.

Chamberlin, William H., *The Russian Revolution*, 2 vols., New York, 1965.

Channon, John, "The Bolsheviks and the Peasantry: The Land Question During the First Eight Months of Soviet Rule," *Slavonic and East European Review*, vol. 66 (1988): 593–624.

Chase, William, "Voluntarism, Mobilisation and Coercion: *Subbotniki* 1919–1921," *Soviet Studies*, vol. 41 (1989): 111–28.
  Workers, Society and the Soviet State: Labor and Life in Moscow, 1918–1929, Urbana and Chicago, 1987.

Clements, Barbara Evans, *Bolshevik Feminist: The Life of Aleksandra Kollontai*, Bloomington, 1979.
  "Working Class and Peasant Women in the Russian Revolution, 1917–1923," *Signs*, vol. 8 (1982): 215–35.

Cohen, Stephen F., *Bukharin and the Bolshevik Revolution: A Political Biography, 1888–1938*, New York, 1974.

Rethinking the Soviet Experience. Politics and History since 1917, Oxford, 1985.

Conquest, Robert, *Religion in the USSR*, New York, 1968.

Cox, Terry, *Peasants, Class, and Capitalism: The Rural Research of L. N. Kritsman and his School*, Oxford, 1986.

Cox, Terry and Littlejohn, Gary, eds., *Kritsman and the Agrarian Marxists*, London, 1984.

Cross, Gary, ed., *Worktime and Industrialization. An International History*, Philadelphia, 1988.

Curtiss, John Shelton, *The Russian Church and the Soviet State, 1917–1950*, Boston, 1953.

Daniels, Robert V., *The Conscience of the Revolution: Communist Opposition in Soviet Russia*, Cambridge, MA, 1961.

"The Secretariat and the Local Organizations in the Russian Communist Party, 1921–1923," *American Slavic and East European Review*, vol. 16 (1957): 32–49.

Danilov, V. P., "Krest'ianskii otkhod na promysly v 1920-kh godakh," *Istoricheskie zapiski* (1974), no. 94: 55–122.

Rural Russia under the New Regime, trans. Orlando Figes, Bloomington, 1988.

"Sovetskaia nalogovaia politika v dokolkhoznoi derevne," in Akademiia nauk SSSR, Institut istorii SSSR, *Oktiabr' i sovetskoe Krest'ianstvo*, Moscow, 1977, pp. 164–91.

Danilov, V. P., ed., *Kooperativno-kolkhoznoe stroitel'stvo v SSSR, 1917–1922*, Moscow, 1990.

Darnton, Robert, "What Was Revolutionary about the French Revolution?" *The New York Review of Books*, vol. 35 (1989), nos. 21–22: 3–10.

Davies, R. W., "'Drop the Glass Industry': Collaborating with E. H. Carr," *New Left Review* (1984), no. 145: 56–70.

The Industrialisation of Soviet Russia 1: The Socialist Offensive. The Collectivization of Soviet Agriculture, 1929-1930, Cambridge, MA, 1980.

The Industrialisation of Soviet Russia 3: The Soviet Economy in Turmoil, 1929–1930, London, 1989.

The Soviet Budgetary System, London, 1958.

Davis, Christopher, "Economic Problems of the Soviet Health Service: 1917–1930," *Soviet Studies*, vol. 35 (1983): 343–61.

Day, Richard, *Leon Trotsky and the Politics of Economic Isolation*, Cambridge, 1973.

Dekrety sovetskoi vlasti, vol. 13, Moscow, 1989.

Deutscher, Isaac, *The Prophet Armed: Trotsky, 1879–1921*, New York, 1965.

The Prophet Unarmed: Trotsky, 1921–1929, New York, 1963.

Soviet Trade Unions. Their Place in Soviet Labour Policy, London, 1950.

Stalin, a Political Biography, rev. ed., Harmondsworth, 1966.

Dmitrenko, V. P., "Bor'ba sovetskogo gosudarstva za ovladenie derevenskim rynkom v pervye gody nepa," *Voprosy istorii* (1964), no. 9: 57–71.

"Nekotorye voprosy NEPa v sovetskoi istoriografii 60-kh godov," *Voprosy istorii* (1972), no. 3: 18–31.

Dobb, Maurice, *Soviet Economic Development Since 1917*, London, 1966.

Druzhul, A. A., ed., *Sovety national'nykh raionov Rossii, 1917–1922*, Riga, 1985.

Dziewanowski, M. K., *A History of Soviet Russia*, 2nd ed., Englewood Cliffs, NJ, 1985.

Edmondson, Charles M., "The Politics of Hunger: The Soviet Response to Famine, 1921," *Soviet Studies*, vol. 29 (1977): 506–18.

Erlich, Alexander, *The Soviet Industrialization Debate, 1924–1928*, Cambridge, MA, 1960.

Evans, Alfred B., "Rereading Lenin's *State and Revolution*," *Slavic Review*, vol. 46 (1987): 1–19.

Fain, L. E., *Istoriia razrabotki V. I. Leninym kooperativnogo plana*, Moscow, 1970.

Fainsod, Merle, *How Russia is Ruled*, Cambridge, MA, 1965.
  Smolensk under Soviet Rule, New York, 1958.

Farber, Samuel, *Before Stalinism. The Rise and Fall of Soviet Democracy*, London, 1990.

Farbman, Michael, *Bolshevism in Retreat*, London, 1923.

Farnsworth, Beatrice, *Aleksandra Kollontai: Socialism, Feminism and the Bolshevik Revolution*, Stanford, 1980.

Fediukin, S. A., "Oktiabr'skaia revoliutsiia i intelligentsiia," *Istoriia SSSR* (1977), no. 5.
  Velikii Oktiabr' i intelligentsiia, Moscow, 1972.

Figes, Orlando, *Peasant Russia, Civil War: The Volga Countryside in Revolution (1917–1921)*, Oxford, 1989.
  "The Village and *Volost* Soviet Elections of 1919," *Soviet Studies*, vol. 40 (1988): 21–45.

Fisher, Wesley, *The Soviet Marriage Market. Mate Selection in Russia and the USSR*, New York, 1980.

Fitzpatrick, Sheila, "After NEP: The Fate of NEP Entrepreneurs, Small Traders and Artisans in the 'Socialist Russia' of the 1930s," *Russian History/Histoire russe*, vol. 13 (1986): 187–234.
  "The Bolsheviks' Dilemma: Class, Culture and Politics in Early Soviet Years," *Slavic Review*, vol. 47 (1988): 599–613.
  The Commissariat of Enlightenment: Soviet Organization of Education and the Arts under Lunacharsky, October 1917–1921, Cambridge, 1970.
  Education and Social Mobility in the Soviet Union, 1921–1934, Cambridge, 1979.
  "New Perspectives on Stalinism," *Russian Review*, vol. 45 (1986): 357–74.
  "Ordzhonikidze's Takeover of Vesenkha: A Case Study in Soviet Bureaucratic Politics," *Soviet Studies*, vol. 37(1985): 153–72.
  The Russian Revolution, 1917–1932, Oxford, 1982.
  "The 'Soft' Line on Culture and its Enemies: Soviet Cultural Policy 1922–1927,' *Slavic Review*, vol. 33 (1974): 267–87.

Fitzpatrick, Sheila, ed., *Cultural Revolution in Russia, 1928–1931*, Bloomington, 1978.

Fitzpatrick, Sheila, Alexander Rabinowitch, and Richard Stites, eds., *Russia in the Era of NEP: Explorations in Soviet Society and Culture*, Bloomington, 1991.

Freeze, Gregory L., *The Parish Clergy in Nineteenth Century Russia*, Princeton, 1983.

Gaponenko, L. S., *Rabochii klass Rossii v 1917 godu*, Moscow, 1970.

Gastev, A. K., *Normirovanie i organizatsiia truda*, Leningrad, 1929.

Genis, V. L., "Grigorii Iakovlevich Sokol'nikov," *Voprosy istorii* (1989), no. 12: 59–86.

Genkina, E. B., *Perekhod sovetskogo gosudarstva k novoi ekonomicheskoi politike, 1921–1922*, Moscow, 1954.

"V. I. Lenin i nekotorye voprosy rukovodstva sel'skim khoziaistvom posle perekhoda k nepu," *Istoriia SSSR* (1969), no. 3: 5–27.

"V. I. Lenin i perekhod k novoi ekonomicheskoi politike," *Voprosy istorii* (1964), no. 5: 3–27.

"Vosniknovenie proizvodstvennykh soveshchanii v gody vosstanovitel'nogo perioda (1921–1926 gg.)," *Istoriia SSSR* (1958), no. 3: 63–88.

Getzler, Israel, *Kronstadt 1917–1921*, Cambridge, 1983.

Giddens, Anthony, *A Contemporary Critique of Historical Materialism*, Berkeley and Los Angeles, 1981.

Gimpel'son, E. G., "Rabochii klass i privlechenie intelligentsii k upravleniiu sovetskim gosudarstvom (noiabr' 1917–1920 gg.)," in K. V. Gusev, ed., *Intelligentsiia i revoliutsiia XX vek*, Moscow, 1985.

Rabochii klass v upravlenii sovetskim gosudarstvom: noiabr' 1917–1920 gg., Moscow, 1982.

Sovetskii rabochii klass, 1918–1920 gg., Moscow, 1974.

Gitelman, Zvi, *Jewish Nationality and Soviet Politics: The Jewish Sections of the CPSU, 1917–1930*, Princeton, 1972.

Gleason, Abbott, Kenez, Peter, and Stites, Richard, eds., *Bolshevik Culture: Experiment and Order in the Russian Revolution*, Bloomington, 1985.

Golder, Frank Alfred, and Hutchinson, Lincoln, *On the Trail of the Russian Famine*, Stanford, 1927.

Goldman, Wendy, "Freedom and its Consequences: The Debate on the Soviet Family Code of 1926," *Russian History/Histoire russe*, vol. 11 (1984): 362–88.

"Working-Class Women and the 'Withering Away' of the Family: Popular Responses to Family Policy," in Fitzpatrick, Rabinowitch and Stites, eds., *Russia in the Era of NEP*.

Got'e, Iurii V., *Time of Troubles. The Diary of Iurii Vladimirovich Got'e, Moscow, July 8, 1917–July 23, 1922*, trans. and ed. Terrence Emmons, Princeton, 1988.

Graham, Loren, *Science and Philosophy in the Soviet Union*, New York, 1972.

The Soviet Academy of Sciences and the Communist Party, 1927–1932, Princeton, 1967.

Graham, Loren, ed., *Science and the Soviet Social Order*, Cambridge, MA, 1990.

Gramsci, Antonio, *Selections from the Prison Notebooks*, trans. and eds., Quintin Hoare and Geoffrey Nowell Smith, New York, 1971.

Grosskopf, Sigrid, *L'Alliance ouvrière et paysanne en U.R.S.S. (1921–1928). Le problème du blé*, Paris, 1976.

Gsovski, Vladimir, *Soviet Civil Law*, 2 vols., Ann Arbor, 1948.

Gulev, V. V., "Deiatel'nost' sovetskogo gosudarstva v oblasti kinematografii (1918–1921 gg.)," *Istoricheskie zapiski* (1988), no. 116: 80–102.

Haimson, Leopold, "The Mensheviks After the October Revolution," *Russian Review*, vol. 38 (1979): 456–73; vol. 39 (1980): 181-207.

Haimson, Leopold, ed., *The Mensheviks from the Revolution of 1917 to the Second World War*, Chicago, 1974.

Halle, Fanina, *Women in Soviet Russia*, London, 1934.

Harding, Neil, *Lenin's Political Thought*, 2 vols., Atlantic Highlands, NJ, 1983.

Harding, Neil, ed., *The State in Socialist Society*, Albany, 1984.

Harrison, Mark, "Resource Allocation and Agrarian Class Formation: The Problem of Social Mobility among Russian Peasant Households, 1880–1930," *Journal of Peasant Studies*, vol. 4 (1977): 127–61.

"Soviet Primary Accumulation Processes: Some Unresolved Problems," *Science and Society*, vol. 45 (1981–82): 387–408.

Hatch, John, "The 'Lenin Levy' and the Social Origins of Stalinism: Workers and the Communist Party in Moscow, 1921–1928," *Slavic Review*, vol. 48 (1989): 558–77.

"The Politics of Mass Culture: Workers, Communists, and Proletkul't in the Development of Workers' Clubs, 1921–1925," *Russian History/Histoire russe*, vol. 13 (1986): 119–48.

Hazard, John, Shapiro, Isaac, and Maggs, Peter B., *The Soviet Legal System*, Dobbs Ferry, NY, 1969.

Heller, Mikhail and Nekrich, Aleksandr M., *Utopia in Power*, trans. Phyllis B. Carlos, New York, 1982.

Holmes, Larry, "For the Revolution Redeemed: The Workers' Opposition in the Bolshevik Party, 1919–1921," *Carl Beck Papers in Russian and East European Studies*, no. 802 (1990).

Holquist, Michael and Clark, Katerina, *Mikhail Bakhtin*, Cambridge, MA, 1984.

Hosking, Geoffrey, *The Awakening of the Soviet Union*, London, 1990.

Hughes, J. R., "The Irkutsk Affair: Stalin, Siberian Politics and the End of NEP," *Soviet Studies*, vol. 41 (1989): 228–53.

Hunczak, Taras, ed., *The Ukraine, 1917–1921: A Study in Revolution*, Cambridge, MA, 1977.

Huskey, Eugene, *Russian Lawyers and the Soviet State: The Origins and Development of the Soviet Bar, 1917–1939*, Princeton, 1986.

Institut markzisma–leninizma pri TsK KPSS, *Istoriia kommunisticheskoi partii sovetskogo soiuza*, 6 vols., Moscow, 1967–71.

Isvestiia Tsk KPSS, no. 5 (292) (1989).

Ito, Takayuki, ed., *Facing Up to the Past. Soviet Historiography under Perestroika*, Sapporo, 1989.

Johnston, Robert H., *New Mecca, New Babylon: Paris and the Russian Exiles, 1920–1945*, Kingston and Montreal, 1988.

Jones, Stephen, "The Establishment of Soviet Power in Transcaucasia: The Case of Georgia, 1921–1928," *Soviet Studies*, vol. 40 (1988): 616–39.

Joravsky, David, *Soviet Marxism and Natural Science, 1917–1932*, New York, 1961.

"The Stalinist Mentality and the Higher Learning," *Slavic Review*, vol. 42 (1983): 575–600.

Juviler, Peter H., *Revolutionary Law and Order. Politics and Social Change in the USSR*, New York, 1976.

Kabytov, P. S., Kozlov, V. A. and Litvak, B. G., *Russkoe krest'ianstvo, etapy dukhovnogo osvobozhdeniia*, Moscow, 1988.

Kagarlitsky, Boris, *The Thinking Reed. Intellectuals and the Soviet State from 1917 to the Present*, trans. Brian Pearce, London and New York, 1988.

Karcz, Jerzy F., *The Economics of Communist Agriculture. Selected Papers*, Bloomington, 1979.

Karpinsky, Lev, "The Fate of Lenin's NEP," *Moscow News* (1989), no. 6: *Kazimir Malevich, 1878–1935*, Washington, DC, 1990.

Keane, John, ed., *Civil Society and the State*, London, 1988.

Kenez, Peter, *The Birth of the Propaganda State: Soviet Methods of Mass Mobilization, 1919–1929*, Cambridge, 1985.

Kern, Stephen, *The Culture of Time and Space, 1880–1918*, Cambridge, MA, 1983.

Kimmerling, Elise, "Civil Rights and Social Policy in Soviet Russia, 1918–1936," *Russian Review*, vol. 41 (1982): 24–46.

Kingston-Mann, Esther, *Lenin and the Problem of Marxist Peasant Revolution*, Oxford, 1983.

Klibanov, A. I., *Religioznoe sektantstvo i sovremennost'*, Moscow, 1969.

Koenker, Diane, Rosenberg, William, and Suny, Ronald G., eds., *Party, State and Society in the Russian Civil War*, Bloomington, 1989.

Kollontai, Alexandra, *The Workers' Opposition* (Solidarity Pamphlet No. 7), London, n.d.

Koonz, Claudia, *Mothers in the Fatherland: Women, the Family and Nazi Politics*, New York, 1987.

Korzhikhina, T. P., *Obshchestvennye organizatsii v SSSR, 1917–1936 gg. (profsoiuzy intelligentsii)*, Moscow, 1984.

Kozlov, S. A., "Problemy kul'turnoi revoliutsii v SSSR v noveishei nemarksistskoi istoriografii (1917-nachalo 1930-kh gg.)," *Istoriia SSSR* (1989), no. 4: 186–99.

Kozlov, V. A., *Kul'turnaia revoliutsiia i krest'ianstvo, 1921–1927*, Moscow, 1983.

Kritsman, Lev, *Geroicheskii period velikoi russkoi revoliutsii*, Moscow, n.d. [1926].

Krylov, N. A., "Iz istorii propagandy ateizma v SSSR (1923–1925 gg.)," *Voprosy istorii religii i ateizma* (1960), no. 8: 166–80.

Kulikova, I. S. and Khazanov, B. Ia, "Mikhail Pavlovich Tomskii," *Voprosy istorii* (1988), no. 8: 64–83.

Kuromiya, Hiroaki, "The Crisis of Proletarian Identity in the Soviet Factory, 1928–1929," *Slavic Review*, vol. 44 (1985): 280–97.

"Edinonachalie and the Soviet Industrial Manager, 1928–1937," *Soviet Studies*, vol. 36 (1984): 185–204.

Stalin's Industrial Revolution: Politics and Workers, 1928–1932, Cambridge, 1988.

Lampert, Nicholas, *The Technical Intelligentsia and the Soviet State*, London, 1979.

Lane, Christel, *The Rites of Rulers. Ritual in Industrial Society – The Soviet Case*, Cambridge, 1981.

Lapidus, Gail, *Women in Soviet Society*, Berkeley and Los Angeles, 1978.

Lawton, Anna, ed., *Russian Futurism through its Manifestoes, 1912–1928*, Ithaca, 1988.

Lebedeva, N. B. and Shkaratan, O. I., *Ocherki istorii sotsialisticheskogo sorevnovaniia*, Leningrad, 1966.

Leggett, George, *The Cheka. Lenin's Political Police*, Oxford, 1981.

Lenin, V. I., *Polnoe sobranie sochinenii*, 5th ed., 55 vols., Moscow, 1958–62.

Levin, Nora, *The Jews in the Soviet Union since 1917. Paradox of Survival*, 2 vols., New York, 1988.

Lewin, Moshe, *Lenin's Last Struggle*, London, 1975.

    The Making of the Soviet System. Essays in the Social History of Interwar Russia, New York, 1985.

    Political Undercurrents in Soviet Economic Debates, Princeton, 1974.

Lewis, Robert, "Science, Nonscience, and the Cultural Revolution," *Slavic Review*, vol. 45 (1986): 286–92.

Liakh, R. D., "Osobennosti osushchestvleniia agrarnykh preobrazovanii v Donbasse (1917–1923 gg.)," in Akademiia nauk SSSR, Institut istorii SSSR (ed.), *Problemy agrarnoi istorii sovetskogo obshchestva, materialy nauchnoi konferentsii 9–12 iiunia 1969 g.*, Moscow, 1971, pp. 33-4.

Lieberstein, Samuel, "Technology, Work, and Sociology in the USSR: The NOT Movement," *Technology and Culture*, vol. 16 (1975): 48–66.

Lih, Lars, "Bolshevik *Razverstka* and War Communism," *Slavic Review*, vol. 45 (1986): 673–88.

    "The Bolshevik Sowing Committees of 1920, Apotheosis of War Communism?," *Carl Beck Papers in Russian and East European Studies*, no. 803 (1990).

    Bread and Authority in Russia, 1914–1921, Berkeley and Los Angeles, 1990.

    "Political Testament: Lenin, Bukharin and the Meaning of NEP," *Slavic Review*, vol. 59 (1991): 241–52.

Lilge, Frederic, *Anton Semyonovich Makarenko: An Analysis of His Educational Ideas in the Context of Soviet Policy*, Berkeley, 1958.

Lodder, Christina, *Russian Constructivism*, New Haven and London, 1983.

Mace, James E., *Communism and the Dilemmas of National Liberation: National Communism in Soviet Ukraine, 1918–1933*, Cambridge, MA, 1983.

Maguire, Robert A., *Red Virgin Soil. Soviet Literature in the 1920s*, Princeton, 1968.

Malle, Silvana, *The Economic Organization of War Communism, 1918–1921*, Cambridge, 1985.

Manevich, V. E., *Ekonomicheskie diskussii 20-kh godov*, Moscow, 1989.

Marshall, Richard, Jr., ed., *Aspects of Religion in the Soviet Union, 1917–1967*, Chicago, 1971.

Massell, Gregory, *The Surrogate Proletariat: Moslem Women and Revolutionary Strategies in Soviet Central Asia, 1919–1929*, Princeton, 1974.

Matiugin, A. A., *Rabochii klass SSSR v gody vosstanovleniia narodnogo khoziaistva (1921–1925)*, Moscow, 1962.

Maynard, John, *The Russian Peasant and Other Studies*, New York, 1962.

Mazaev, A. I., *Prazdnik kak sotsial'no-khudozhestvennoe iavlenie*, Moscow, 1978.

McCagg, William and Siegelbaum, Lewis, eds., *The Disabled in the Soviet Union: Past and Present, Theory and Practice*, Pittsburgh, 1989.

McNeal, Robert H., *Stalin. Man and Ruler*, New York, 1988.

Merl, Stephan, *Der Agrarmarkt und die Neue Okonomische Politik*, Munich, 1981.

Michels, Robert, *Political Parties. A Sociological Study of the Oligarchical Tendencies of Modern Democracy*, New York, 1962.

Mikhailovskii, I. N., *Komsomol' ukrainy v bor'be za postroenie sotsializma v SSSR (1925–1937 gg.)*, L'vov, 1966.

Mikoian, A. I., *V nachale dvadsatykh*, Moscow, 1975.

Mirski, Michal, *The Mixed Economy: NEP and its Lot*, Copenhagen, 1984.

Morozov, L. R., *Ot kooperatsii burzhuaznoi k kooperatsii sotsialisticheskoi, iz istorii stanovleniia sovetskoi kooperatsii*, Moscow, 1969.

Nahalyo, Bohdan and Swoboda, Victor, *Soviet Disunion. A History of the Nationalities Problem in the USSR*, New York, 1990.

Naiman, Eric, "The Case of Chubarov Alley: Collective Rape, Utopian Desire and the Mentality of NEP," *Russian History/Histoire russe*, vol. 17 (1990): 1–30.

Nenarokov, A. P., "Iz opyta natsional'no-iazykovoi politiki pervykh let sovetskoi vlasti," *Istoriia SSSR* (1990), no. 2: 3–14.

Nove, Alec, *An Economic History of the USSR*, London, 1969.

"New Light on Trotskii's Economic Views," *Slavic Review*, vol. 40 (1981): 84–97.

"O sud'bakh NEPa," *Voprosy istorii* (1989), no. 8: 172–6.

"Was Stalin Really Necessary? A Debate on Collectivization," *Problems of Communism*, vol. 25 (1976): 49–62.

Odom, William E., *The Soviet Volunteers: Modernization and Bureaucracy in a Public Mass Organization*, Princeton, 1973.

Olcott, Martha B., "The Basmachi or Freemen's Revolt in Turkestan, 1918–1924," *Soviet Studies*, vol. 33 (1981): 352–69.

Olesha, Yuri, *Envy and Other Works*, trans. A. MacAndrew, New York, 1967.

Oppenheim, Samuel A., "Between Right and Left: G. Ia. Sokolnikov and the Development of the Soviet State," *Slavic Review*, vol. 48 (1989): 593–613.

Oprishchenko, A. L., *Istoriografiia sotsialisticheskogo sorevnovaniia rabochego klassa SSSR*, Khar'kov, 1975.

Orlovsky, Daniel, "Gimpel'son on the Hegemony of the Working Class," *Slavic Review*, vol. 48 (1989): 104–6.

"Social History and its Categories," *Slavic Review*, vol. 47 (1988): 620–3.

Ostapenko, I. P., *Uchastie rabochego klassa SSSR v upravlenii proizvodstvom*, Moscow, 1964.

Pethybridge, Roger, *The Social Prelude to Stalinism*, London, 1974.

Piore, Michael J., *Birds of Passage. Migrant Labor and Industrial Societies*, Cambridge, 1979.

Pipes, Richard, *The Formation of the Soviet Union: Communism and Nationalism, 1917–1923*, rev. ed., New York, 1968.

The Russian Revolution, New York, 1990.

Pipes, Richard, ed., *Revolutionary Russia: A Symposium*, New York, 1969.

Poliakov, Iu. A., *Sovetskaia strana posle okonchaniia grazhdanskoi voiny: territoriia i naselenie*, Moscow, 1986.

Pospielovsky, Dimitry V., *A History of Marxist–Leninist Atheism and Soviet Anti-Religious Policies*, 2 vols., New York, 1987–8.

The Russian Church under the Soviet Regime, 1917–1982, 2 vols., Crestwood, NY, 1984.

Preobrazhenskii, E. A., *The Crisis of Soviet Industrialization. Selected Essays*, trans. and ed. Donald Filtzer, White Plains, NY, 1979.

The New Economics, Oxford, 1965.

Quigley, John, "The 1926 Soviet Family Code: Retreat from Free Love," *Soviet Union/Union soviétique*, vol. 6, pt. 2 (1979): 166–74.

Rabinowitch, Alexander, *The Bolsheviks Come to Power. The Revolution of 1917 in Petrograd*, New York, 1976.

Radkey, Oliver, *The Unknown Civil War in Soviet Russia: A Study of the Green Movement in the Tambov Region, 1920-21*, Stanford, 1976.

Rashin, A., "Perspektivy bezrabotitsy v Rossii," *Vestnik truda* (1922).

Rassweiler, Anne, *The Generation of Power: The History of Dneprostroi*, Oxford, 1988.

Rees, E. A., *State Control in Soviet Russia*, New York, 1987.

Remington, Thomas, *Building Socialism in Bolshevik Russia. Ideology and Industrial Organization, 1917–1921*, Pittsburgh, 1984.

Rigby, T. H., *Communist Party Membership in the U.S.S.R., 1917–1967*, Princeton, 1968.

"Early Provincial Cliques and the Rise of Stalin," *Soviet Studies*, vol. 33 (1981): 3–28.

Lenin's Government: Sovnarkom 1917-1922, Cambridge, 1979.

"Staffing USSR Incorporated: The Origins of the Nomenklatura System," *Soviet Studies*, vol. 40 (1988): 523–37.

Robbins, Richard G., *Famine in Russia 1891–1892*, New York, 1975.

Roberts, Paul Craig, "'War Communism': A Reexamination," *Slavic Review*, vol. 29 (1970): 238–61.

Robinson, G. T., *Rural Russia under the Old Regime*, Berkeley and Los Angeles, 1969 reprint of 1932 edition.

Rogachevskaia, L. S., *Likvidatsiia bezrabotitsy v SSSR, 1917–1930 gg.*, Moscow, 1973.

Sotsialisticheskoe sorevnovanie v SSSR, istoricheskie ocherki 1917–1970 gg., Moscow, 1977.

Rosenberg, William, *Liberals in the Russian Revolution: The Constitutional Democratic Party, 1917–1921*, Princeton, 1974.

Rosenberg, William and Drobizhev, V. Z., "Sotsial'no-ekonomicheskoe polozhenie i politika sovetskogo gosudarstva pri perekhode k NEPu," *Istoriia SSSR* (1989), no. 4: 109–22.

Rowney, Don K., *Transition to Technocracy. The Structural Origins of the Soviet Administrative State*, Ithaca and London, 1989.

Sakwa, Richard, *Soviet Communists in Power. A Study of Moscow during the Civil War, 1918–1921*, New York, 1988.

Schapiro, Leonard, *The Communist Party of the Soviet Union*, 2nd rev. ed., London, 1970.

Origin of Communist Autocracy. Political Opposition in the Soviet State, 2nd ed., London, 1977.

Schlesinger, Rudolf, ed., *Changing Attitudes in Soviet Russia: The Family in the U.S.S.R., Documents and Readings*, London, 1949.

Schwarz, Solomon, M., *Labor in the Soviet Union*, New York, 1952.

Selunskaia, V. M., *Sotsial'naia struktura sovetskogo obshchestva, istoriia i sovremennost'*, Moscow, 1987.

Selunskaia, V. M., ed., *Izmenenia sotsial'noi struktury sovetskogo obshchestva, 1921-seredina 30-kh godov*, Moscow, 1979.

Service, Robert, *The Bolshevik Party in Revolution. A Study in Organisational Change, 1917–1923*, London, 1979.

Shanin, Teodor, *The Awkward Class. Political Sociology of Peasantry in a Developing Society*, Oxford, 1972.

Shelley, Louise, "Female Criminality in the 1920s: A Consequence of Inadvertent and Deliberate Change," *Russian History/Histoire russe*, vol. 9, pts. 2–3 (1982): 265–84.

"The 1929 Dispute on Soviet Criminology," *Soviet Union/Union soviétique*, vol. 6, pt. 2 (1979): 175–85.

Shinn, William, "The Law of the Russian Peasant Household," *Slavic Review*, vol. 20 (1961): 601-21.

Shishkin, A. A., *Sushchnost' i kriticheskaia otsenka 'Obnovlencheskogo' raskola russkoi pravoslavnoi tserkvi*, Kazan', 1970.

Sidorov, V. A., *Klassovaia bor'ba v dokolkhoznoi derevne, 1921–1929 gg.*, Moscow, 1978.

Siegelbaum, Lewis H., "Socialist Competition and Socialist Construction in the USSR – The Experience of the First Five-Year Plan," *Thesis Eleven* (1982), no. 4: 48–67.

"Soviet Norm Determination in Theory and Practice, 1917–1941," *Soviet Studies*, vol. 36 (1984): 45–68.

Singleton, Seth, "The Tambov Revolt (1920–1921)," *Slavic Review*, vol. 25 (1966): 497–512.

Sirianni, Carmen, *Workers' Control and Socialist Democracy: The Soviet Experience*, London, 1982.

Slonim, Marc, *Soviet Russian Literature. Writers and Problems 1917–1967*, Oxford, 1967.

Smith, Keith, ed., *Soviet Industrialisation and Soviet Maturity*, London and New York, 1986.

Sochor, Zenovia, A., *Revolution and Culture. The Bogdanov–Lenin Controversy*, Ithaca, 1988.

"Soviet Taylorism Revisited," *Soviet Studies*, vol. 33 (1981): 246–64.

Sokolov, N. G., "Ispol'zovania tovaroobmena pri perekhode k NEPu," in Akademiia nauk SSSR, Institut istorii SSSR, *Novaia ekonomicheskaia politika, voprosy teorii i istorii*, Moscow, 1974.

Solomon, Susan Gross, "David and Goliath in Soviet Public Health: The Rivalry of Social Hygienists and Psychiatrists for Authority over the *Bytovoi* Alcoholic," *Soviet Studies*, vol. 41 (1989): 254-75.

The Soviet Agrarian Debate: A Controversy in Social Science, 1923–1929, Boulder, 1977.

Solomon, Susan Gross and Hutchinson, John F., eds., *Health and Society in Revolutionary Russia*, Bloomington and Indianapolis, 1990.

Sorenson, J. B., *The Life and Death of Soviet Trade Unions*, New York, 1969.

Sorokin, Pitrim A., *Hunger as a Factor in Human Affairs*, trans. and with Prologue by Elena P. Sorokin, Gainsville, FL, 1975.

Soskin, V. L., "O nekotorykh chertakh kul'turnogo stroitel'stvo v period perekhoda k NEPu," in Akademiia nauk SSSR, Institut istorii SSSR, *Novaia ekonomicheskaia politika, voprosy teorii i istorii.*

"The Soviet Union in the 1920s, A Roundtable," *Soviet Studies in History*, vol. 28 (1989), no. 2.

Spulber, Nicholas, ed., *Foundations of Soviet Strategy for Economic Growth: Selected Essays, 1924-30*, Bloomington, 1964.

Stalin, I. V., *Sochineniia*, 13 vols., Moscow, 1946–51.

Startsev, V. I., "Political Leaders of the Soviet State in 1922 and Early 1923," *Soviet Studies in History*, vol. 28 (Winter, 1989–90), no. 3: 5–40.

"Vopros o vlasti v Oktiabr'skie dni 1917 goda," *Istoriia SSSR* (1987), no. 5: 36–54.

Stevens, Jennie A., "Children of the Revolution: Soviet Russia's Homeless Children (Besprizorniki) in the 1920s," *Russian History/Histoire russe*, vol. 9, pts. 2–3 (1982): 242–64.

Stites, Richard, *Revolutionary Dreams. Utopian Vision and Experimental Life in the Russian Revolution*, New York and Oxford, 1989.

Suny, Ronald G., *The Making of the Georgian Nation*, Bloomington, 1988.

Suny, Ronald G., ed., *Transcaucasia. Nationalism and Social Change*, Ann Arbor, 1983.

Susiluoto, Ilmari, *The Origins and Development of Systems Thinking in the Soviet Union*, Helsinki, 1982.

Szczesniak, Boleslaw, ed., *The Russian Revolution and Religion*, Notre Dame, 1959.

Taniuchi, Yuzuru, *The Village Gathering in Russia in the Mid-1920s*, Birmingham, 1968.

Taylor, Barbara, *Eve and the New Jerusalem. Socialism and Feminism in the Nineteenth Century*, New York, 1983.

Thomson, Boris, *The Premature Revolution: Russian Literature and Society, 1917–1946*, London, 1972.

Thorner, Daniel, Kerblay, B. and Smith, R. E. F., eds., *Chayanov: The Theory of Peasant Economy*, Homewood, IL, 1966.

Thorniley, Daniel, *The Rise and Fall of the Soviet Rural Communist Party, 1927–39*, New York, 1988.

Timasheff, Nicholas S., *Religion in Soviet Russia, 1917–1942*, New York, 1942.

Treadgold, Donald, *Twentieth Century Russia*, Chicago, 1981.

Trifonov, I. Ia., *Ocherki istorii klassovoi bor'by v SSSR v gody NEPa, 1921–1937*, Moscow, 1960.

Trotsky, L. D., *Kak vooruzhalas' revoliutsiia*, 2 vols., Moscow, 1923–5.

Trotsky, Leon, *Problems of Everyday Life*, New York, 1973.
   Terrorism and Communism, Ann Arbor, 1961.
   Women and the Family, New York, 1970.
Trud v SSSR , Moscow, 1932.
TsK VKP (b), Statisticheskii otdel, *Sotsial'nyi i natsional'nyi sostav VKP (b). Itogi vsesoiuznoi partiinoi perepisi 1927 goda.*, Moscow–Leningrad, 1928.
Tucker, Robert, *Political Culture and Leadership in Soviet Russia, from Lenin to Gorbachev*, New York, 1987.
Tucker, Robert, ed., *Stalinism. Essays in Historical Interpretation*, New York, 1977.
Tumarkin, Nina, *Lenin Lives! The Lenin Cult in Soviet Russia*, Cambridge, MA, and London, 1983.
Vakar, Nicholas, *Belorussia: The Making of a Nation*, Cambridge, MA, 1956.
Valentinov, Nikolai, "Non-Party Specialists and the Coming of the NEP," *Russian Review*, vol. 30 (1971): 154–63.
Vdovin, A. I. and Drobizhev, V. Z., *Rost rabochego klassa SSSR, 1917–1940 gg.*, Moscow, 1976.
Venediktov, A. V., *Organizatsiia gosudarstvennoi promyshlennosti v SSSR*, 2 vols., Leningrad, 1957–61.
Viola, Lynne, *The Best Sons of the Fatherland. Workers in the Vanguard of Soviet Collectivization*, New York, 1987.
Vlast' sovetov za desiat' let, 1917–1927, Leningrad, 1927.
Voinstvuiushchee bezbozhie v SSSR za 15 let. Sbornik, Moscow, 1932.
von Hagen, Mark, *Soldiers in the Proletarian Dictatorship. The Red Army and the Soviet Socialist State, 1917–1930*, Ithaca and London, 1990.
Voslensky, Michael, *Nomenklatura. The Soviet Ruling Class*, trans. Eric Mosbacher, Garden City, NY, 1984.
Ward, Chris, *Russia's Cotton Workers and the New Economic Policy*, Cambridge, 1990.
Waters, M. A., ed., *Rosa Luxemburg Speaks*, New York, 1970.
Wright, Erik Olin, *Classes*, London, 1985.
Zhiromskaia, V. B., *Sovetskii gorod v 1921–1925 gg.*, Moscow, 1988.
Zoshchenko, Mikhail, *Scenes from the Bathhouse and Other Stories of Communist Russia*, Ann Arbor, 1961.

Index

Trotsky, L. D. (*cont.*)
  party struggle, 6–7, 127, 131, 132–3,
    189; and Left Opposition, 86, 127, 169;
    and militarization of labor, 21–2,
    35–6, 65; and Stalin, 121, 173, 248; as
    theorist, 11, 12, 18–19, 39; and United
    Opposition, 174, 189
trusts, 101–2
Tsentrosoiuz, 66, 142
Tsiurupa, A. D., 43, 167
TsSU, 138, 145
Tucker, Robert, 37, 44

Ukraine, 17, 18, 88, 118, 125, 175, 222
unemployment, 104–6, 204
Union of Soviet Socialist Republics,
    formation of, 121–4
United Opposition, 174, 189
Ustrialov, N. V., 115–16

VAI, 60, 216
Valentinov, N., 116
VARNITSO, 216
Vesenkha, 19–20, 21, 32, 58, 60, 71, 116,
    171, 173, 174, 175, 176, 179
village commune, 40–1, 92–1; *see also*
    peasants
Volga region, 47, 68–9, 89
VSI, 59, 60
VTsIK, 16, 17–18, 19, 87
VTsSPS, 20, 110, 121
Vvedenskii, A. I., 161, 163
Vyshinskii, A. Ia., 76

wages, 107–8, 203; naturalized, 33–4, 37,

65, 107; and piece-rates, 37, 180; and
    productivity, 180
War Communism, 19, 26, 34, 36, 63–6, 73,
    238
Ward, Chris, 196, 209
White armies, 52, 68
women, 99–100, 206; Central Asian, 150,
    222; and cultural revolution, 222; and
    marriage law debate, 149–54; and
    NEP, 99–100, 151, 244; peasants, 49,
    92; workers, 105, 151, 206
workers, 26–8, 136, 203–4; in Bolshevik
    discourse, 25–6, 30, 103, 131, 184, 227;
    clerical, 32, 33; and Communist Party,
    7, 22, 26, 29–30, 76–7, 131, 181–3;
    culture(s) of, 30–1, 184–5, 208;
    identity of, 7, 31, 107, 110, 207;
    juvenile, 105; *lenintsy*, 181, 185–6;
    metal, 82, 182; and NEP, 103–9;
    "new," 207–8; "old," 207; in
    production conferences, 182, 186;
    promotion of, 182, 206; and
    specialists, 116–17, 186, 215; textile,
    106, 182, 185; white collar, 61–2, 105,
    186
Workers' Opposition, 6, 21, 24, 79–83, 129,
    132, 240
Wright, Eric Olin, 82

youths, 112, 155, 205

zemstvos, 39, 62
Zhenotdel, 49, 125, 155–6, 222
Zinoviev, G. E., 56, 77, 121, 130, 135, 164,
    167, 168, 172, 174, 189